HEALTH AND HEALTH CARE IN THE NATION'S PRISONS

HEALTH AND HEALTH CARE IN THE NATION'S PRISONS

Issues, Challenges, and Policies

Melvin Delgado and
Denise Humm-Delgado

ROWMAN & LITTLEFIELD PUBLISHERS, INC.
Lanham • Boulder • New York • Toronto • Plymouth, UK

ROWMAN & LITTLEFIELD PUBLISHERS, INC.

Published in the United States of America
by Rowman & Littlefield Publishers, Inc.
A wholly owned subsidary of The Rowman & Littlefield Publishing Group, Inc.
4501 Forbes Boulevard, Suite 200, Lanham, Maryland 20706
www.rowmanlittlefield.com

Estover Road
Plymouth PL6 7PY
United Kingdom

British Library Cataloguing in Publication Information Available

Library of Congress Cataloging-in-Publication Data:

Delgado, Melvin.
  Health and health care in the nation's prisons : issues, challenges, and policies /
Melvin Delgado and Denise Humm-Delgado.
      p. ; cm.
  Includes bibliographical references and indexes.
  ISBN-13: 978-0-7425-6300-1 (cloth : alk. paper)
  ISBN-10: 0-7425-6300-6 (cloth : alk. paper)
  ISBN-13: 978-0-7425-6346-9 (electronic)
  ISBN-10: 0-7425-6346-4 (electronic)
  1. Prisoners—Medical care—United States. 2. Prisoners—Health and
hygiene—United States. I. Humm-Delgado, Denise. II. Title.
  [DNLM: 1. Delivery of Health Care—organization & administration—United
States. 2. Prisoners—United States. 3. Health Policy—United States. 4. Health
Services Needs and Demand—United States. 5. Prisons—organization &
administration—United States. WA 300 D352h 2008]
  HV8843.D448 2009
  365'.6670973—dc22   2008008097
Printed in the United States of America

♾™ The paper used in this publication meets the minimum requirements of
American National Standard for Information Sciences—Permanence of Paper for
Printed Library Materials, ANSI/NISO Z39.48-1992.

To our beloved daughters, Laura and Barbara

CONTENTS

ACKNOWLEDGMENTS

Alison Conway, Sara Bruno, Laura Cantrell, Rebehka Gowler, and Kristine Orazem.

I

CONTEXT

1

INTRODUCTION

There is probably no period in United States history in which incarceration has not posed challenges for society and raised ethical dilemmas that strike at the heart of democracy (Clear, 2008). Prisons in the twenty-first century certainly are not proving to be an exception to this because there are various sociopolitical perspectives on incarceration, and, therefore, it has its share of controversy (Butterfield, 2002b). Nevertheless, regardless of one's point of view, the health of the nation's inmates, and the racial composition of prisons, cannot be overlooked or ignored by prison administrators, elected officials, and those who ultimately elect officials and pay the costs, the taxpayer (Walker, Spohn, & DeLone, 2000; Wimsatt, 2000). There is little disputing that the nature and quality of, and extent of access to, health care prior to incarceration have significant effects on health care needs within prisons. The social and economic costs to society cannot be measured easily or overlooked (Caulkins et al., 1997). There is no question that this area of corrections is one of the most important topics facing this country in the early part of this century and millennium (Murphy, 2001).

Incarceration affects more lives than just those of the inmates, and it seems as if no aspect of society escapes its grasp or influence. There are far-reaching consequences for those who are imprisoned, and no correctional outcome is as severe, except for capital punishment. Imprisonment affects taxpayers as well as the lives of the families and the communities in which the inmates lived before imprisonment, and in the case of those fortunate enough to experience freedom, communities to which they return (Butterfield, 2004b; Lee, 1994a,b,c). If the released prisoner is of ill health, then the challenges to society are immense (Haberman, 2001; Restum, 2005). Until inmates officially are released back into their communities, they are the responsibility of the correctional system housing them, with all its responsibilities and challenges.

Jacobi (2005) discusses public-health rationales for improving health care in prisons. He makes some particularly compelling points about communicable diseases. Not only does effective treatment reduce transmission to the larger community when inmates are released from prison, but ineffective treatment in prison can have disastrous public health results. He states (p. 475) that, "One of the most frightening consequences of inconsistent, discontinuous treatment of prisoners with communicable diseases is that mistreatment can lead to mutation of the infectious agent, rendering it resistant to some or all available treatments."

In 2001, approximately $57 billion was spent nationally on incarceration in jails and prisons, an increase from $9.6 billion in 1982, and criminal justice accounted for 7% of all state and local government spending, equal to the funding of health and hospitals (Butterfield, 2004a). A 2008 Pew Center study, which notes that there is no national data source that counts costs in prisons alone, found that total state spending on corrections, including bonds and federal contributions, was over $49 billion in 2007, a dramatic increase from $12 billion in 1987. It is estimated that these costs will increase by another $25 billion by the year 2011. The growth rate outpaced the rate of increases in education and Medicaid. The same study found corrections to be the fifth-largest average state budget category, with health, elementary and secondary education, higher education, and transportation being higher.

The social, economic, and health costs of imprisonment also touch upon the lives of countless service workers in virtually every health and social service arena (Firestone, 2001b; Tuhus, 2001). Potter (2002) observes that over twenty-five years ago the terms "health care" and "corrections" were rarely covered in conversations and the professional literature. Now it is impossible to talk about corrections without also including health care.

For most of us in the human service field, it can be compared to a "black hole" in that what "goes on" in prisons is a subject we generally see when we go to the movies. Illnesses, diseases, sexual assaults, gangs, death, and for that matter, gerontology, are all subjects that occur outside and inside of prisons. The discussion of these topics, however, invariably takes on an "outside" of prison perspective. The term "aging in place," with notable exceptions, generally is talked about as if this only can occur in the general population. However, it also can apply to an aging prison population. More accurately, aging in place can just as easily be replaced with "dying in place," for many inmates.

Like the rest of the population, prisons are "graying." Historically there has been an absence of research from a gerontological perspective with a specific focus on elder involvement in crime and the criminal justice system (Rothman & Dunlop, 2000). The topic of graying of America's prisons is certainly not new (Black, 1989). However, the graying of the prison population now is receiving considerably more attention from scholars and policymakers alike (Greco, 2002; Jones, Connelly & Wagner, 2001; Krane, 1999f; Yates & Gillespie, 2000). The challenges of incarcerating, treating, and classifying older inmates are not new discoveries in the twenty-first century, since they were identified in the early 1980s and reidentified in the early 1990s (Black, 1989; Clark, 1991; Potter, 1991; Sluder & Sapp, 1994).

Older prisoners present correctional systems with unprecedented challenges (Flynn, 2000), and not just in the realm of costs. Wheeler, Connelly, and Wheeler (1994, p. 1) pose questions that, although pertaining to elder inmates, strike at the heart of the correctional system in the United States and whose answers will have profound implications for services within prisons:

> The imperative question for the future, then, is: How will state correctional systems handle this increase of their aged and aging inmate populations? That is, how will they handle the two different offender cultures that arise—younger short-termers with little interest in long-term prison environments and older long-termers with great interest in establishing the best possible quality of life under the circumstances? How will state correctional institutions handle the treatment of older offenders by those younger, who will likely see many of their "elders" as prey? How will they handle the different needs for recreation, security, food, vocation, health care, and other concerns of the offender 50 years old and up?

Those who face long-term imprisonment face dramatically different needs and challenges from those who are short-termers (Flanagan, 1996). These differences translate into the need for policy changes pertaining to the structure of prisons, delivery of health and social services, availability of educational and recreational resources, and sentencing requirements. The longer sentences and the incarceration of older inmates necessitate the rethinking of traditional premises regarding punishment. In addition, the idea of "special status" can have a very broad meaning when applied to prisoners because the number of prisoners who are terminally ill, or will be within the confines of their prison sentence, only can be expected to increase in the early part of the twenty-first century.

Further, prisons are breeding grounds for some of this nation's most deadly diseases (Weed, 2001; McKinley, 2007). A *New York Times* editorial (2005b, p. A20) summed up the prevailing consensus on diseases in prisons: "The emerging consensus is that prison has become the perfect environment for the transmission of dangerous diseases like tuberculosis, hepatitis C and AIDS because of crowding, unprotected sex among inmates and widespread needle-sharing for intravenous drug use." Increased presence of deadly diseases, an ever-aging population with concomitant illnesses, and longer prison sentences, all combine to bring hospice-related care to the forefront in correctional systems across the country (*Hospice Management Advisor* Archives, 2000; Ratcliff & Cohn, 2000; U.S. Department of Justice, 1998).

United States prisons (federal and state) have been established to incarcerate young men (Aday, 1994; Sizemore, 2000). However, as a result of dramatic shifts in the sociodemographic profile of prisoners, prisons find themselves housing an increasing number of women and an increasing number of inmates who are older or who have disabilities or chronic illnesses. Young prisoners were expected to leave prison while they still were relatively young. Nevertheless, this has changed, resulting in prisons housing and caring for inmates who are serving lengthy prison sentences. The consequences of "get tough" sentencing policies were increased numbers of prisoners (male and female) and the lengthening of their prison time (T. J. Flanagan, 1995).

The lengthening of prison sentences, in addition, has had unintended ramifications by creating a pool of prisoners who have disabilities or chronic illnesses or are aged, or both (Coalition for Federal Sentencing Reform, 1998; Elser, 1998; Garcia, 2000; Maker & Stolberg, 2001). These new categories of prisoners have created stress for prison systems that were developed with younger and healthier inmates in mind and that stressed the importance of security rather than health care provision.

Increasing percentages of federal and state spending for prison construction and upkeep, as a result, have necessitated difficult budget choices at the state and local levels (Albanese, 2000). When inmates are terminally ill, as we are witnessing more and more, inherent mission conflicts become apparent. These conflicts are well articulated by a Maine sheriff (Dardis, 2007, p. 1): "I just feel it's inappropriate that someone should have to die or experience this level of disease while in a jail facility . . . We're not a hospice. We are criminal justice professionals asked to manage health care processes." Prisons no longer have the "luxury" of just being institutions that house those being punished by society. The twenty-first century has ushered in a new and multifaceted mission for prisons. This expanded mission has witnessed the emergence of prisoners as patients.

It has been projected that 600,000 or more inmates are due to be released from state and federal prisons every year for the foreseeable future (Butterfield, 2001a). However, many more, 15 million, are released from jails annually (Maeve, 2003). States currently are engaging in granting earlier paroles and reducing mandatory sentences as means of addressing elders and people who are terminally ill as well as general prison overcrowding (Butterfield, 2001c; Jonsson, 2003; Ostreicher, 2003; Zielbauer, 2003b).

Prison death rates are considerably higher than those of the general population, and there are no indications that they should not be higher after release. Although no studies were found examining the death rates of ex-inmates in the United States, a study which was done in Australia found that ex-inmates died at 40 times the rate of the general population, and drug overdoses, suicides, and accidents accounted for the majority of the deaths (Birnbauer, 2001). In another study, based in England but focused on ex-inmates under community supervision, ex-inmates had a higher likelihood of dying as a result of violence when compared to their counterparts still in prison (Satter, 2001).

The subject of health care of prisoners generally is viewed from either a prison or jail perspective. A prison is an institution that has a specific focus on incarcerating individuals convicted of violating state or federal laws; a jail is an institution that houses individuals sentenced for a relatively short period, usually less than one year, or who are being held pending trial.

The subject of incarceration historically has been viewed from the perspectives of public safety and the wellbeing of the community at large. These two perspectives, not surprisingly, are narrow in scope and quickly becoming dated. The early part of the twenty-first century has witnessed an embrace of a broader social, cultural, psychological, political, economic, and health understanding of what effect imprisonment has on communities and the nation. Two other "public" perspectives also have emerged. Public health and public works draw attention to the current and potential role of prisons in the health and economic wellbeing of communities (Berkman, 1995). Further, these perspectives highlight the broad reach of incarceration in this country.

The consequences of increased sentencing and the "causalities" of the nation's so-called war on drugs substantially have altered the broad reach of the nation's incarceration policies (Caukins et al., 1997). The war on drugs had a particularly devastating impact on the nation's communities of color. Prison populations increasingly are becoming racially and ethnically of color, primarily Black/African American and Latino, and are no longer largely restricted to males (Beatty, Holman & Schiraldi, 2000). The interplay of racial and health factors effectively has transformed the composition of prisons and, in the process, introduced a multitude of health and social challenges for correctional systems that will be felt well into the twenty-first century (Rhodes, Johnston, McMullen, & Hozik, 2000).

The long-term consequences of being a "felon" can be considerable in ways few in the general population possibly can realize. Federal law prohibits convicted drug felons, for example, from receiving federal money from Temporary Assistance for Needy Families (TANF) and food stamps. Although states may use state money to provide those benefits to convicted drug felons, sixteen states deny benefits entirely, eleven do so with a modified ban, twelve provide benefits dependent upon compliance with drug treatment, and twelve states have opted out of participating in the ban entirely (Sentencing Project, 2005a). Ex-felons also can be barred from employment in certain jobs, such as those providing education, drug counseling, home health care, and nursing care. The various consequences can affect the economic wellbeing of communities to which prisoners return.

Tonry and Petersilia (2000) identified six types of collateral consequences of imprisonment:

1. impact on prisoners' later lives through reduction of incomes and employment, loss of rights to vote and hold public office and certain types of employment, and break up of family
2. impact on prisoners' later physical and mental wellbeing in that the aging process within prison is significantly more rapid than for those not imprisoned, with all of its social and psychological consequences
3. impact on offenders' spouses/partners and children through breakup of family, or minimal or no contact with children
4. impact on prisoners' later crime involvement via higher likelihood to commit crimes and be re-imprisoned
5. impact on larger society when imprisonment is so prevalent as to lose its stigma within certain communities, lack of positive role models for youth, and loss of community-centered income
6. impact on prisoner while in confinement through trauma, separation from family and friends, or diseases obtained while imprisoned

These six areas are highly correlated and not confined to one time period; they can be immediate, near future, or far future.

Tonry and Petersilia (2000), however, have not touched upon the potential benefits of incarceration that include an opportunity to provide a service, health or otherwise, to an inmate in need. Stockett and Fields (1999, p. 2) argue this very point: "The unique circumstances of the prison environment offer the chance to provide effective health care, prevention, and education services to individuals who have been beyond the reach or resistant to interventions and services in the past. For many incarcerated persons, prison may be their first contact with medical and psychosocial interventions as well as their first opportunity for alcohol and drug treatment."

Various aspects of the correctional system in this country have been criticized. High recidivism rates have raised serious questions about the role of imprisonment in deterrence of crime (Langan & Levin, 2002). Life within prisons never would be confused with that of someone belonging to a country club:

> Living conditions within the prison system have never been pleasant or comfortable, but a harsher political climate now threatens to undo many of the reforms achieved through litigation and political advocacy over the past several decades. Congressional action in 1994 prohibited inmates from receiving Pell grants to continue higher education studies, while many states have passed their own legislation denying inmates access to various forms of recreation or cultural activities. Much of this legislation has been not just mean-spirited but counterproductive as well, by limiting prisoners' access to the acquisition of skills that might be used constructively upon their return to the community. (Mauer, 1999b, p. 2)

Prisons also are prime economic engines driving the economy of countless numbers of rural communities across the nation. Prison construction not only provides these communities with the potential to be a part of this building boom, but also provides them with opportunities to staff and service these institutions. The overall benefits, however, may be mixed for these communities (Kilborn, 2001).

If California were to be classified as a country, it would have the biggest prison system in the Western industrialized world, surpassing the entire federal prison system of France, Germany, Great Britain, the Netherlands, Japan, and Singapore combined (Schlosser, 1998). These nations combined have ten times California's population (*Pediatrics*, 2000). The necessity to construct new prisons in California to house inmates has resulted in more prison beds being built than university classrooms (Connolly et al., 1996).

California is not alone in experiencing this dramatic increase in prison construction. It is estimated that since 1980 prison expenditures in the United States increased 600 times faster than education (*Dollar & Sense*, 2001). Prisons increasingly are being built in rural areas of the state of California, just as they are in other states across the country. Marc Klass of California, whose daughter Polly Klass was murdered by a repeat offender in 1993, and who was a big supporter of the "three-strikes" movement, has had a change of mind on the subject (Fox, 2000, p. 40): "Trying to cure the disease of crime and violence just by building more prisons is like trying to cure cancer by building more cemeteries."

This book will touch only upon the topic of how public safety and public works are intertwined. When addressed, it will be as a means of contextualizing what imprisonment means for the disproportionate number of urban communities of color which "supply" the residents for these institutions in all regions of the United States. The primary focus of the book will be on public health and the current and projected state of health and long-term care in this nation's prisons. How government addresses public health within prisons, as a result, also will influence the public health of urban and rural America. "Benign neglect" will prove disastrous to communities and eventually the nation as a whole. This book also provides a set of recommendations for how best to develop and implement strategies for addressing the health needs of inmates.

HEALTH CARE NEEDS AND PRISON INMATES

Issues regarding health care in this country are manifested in a wide variety of spheres, particularly as they relate to health disparities in communities of color (Adams & Leath, 2002; Byrd & Clayton, 2002). Communities of color are overrepresented in prisons. Thus, it is not surprising to see correctional systems across all fifty states attempting to balance issues of provision of care and costs of health services to inmates (Abramsky, 2002). McKneally and Sade (2003) have categorized public responses to prisoners receiving extraordinary health care services into three types: (1) prisoners have violated the law and should not be awarded society's "most precious goods"; (2) providing high quality health care will serve to increase criminal behavior; and (3) why should prisoners receive health care when forty million law-abiding citizens have no insurance to pay for health care? These reasons serve to reinforce a stance that intensifies the outrage of awarding the "highest level of care" to felons at the public's expense.

The following letter to the editor of a newspaper (Stevenson, 2001) captures the public sentiment that believes prisoners are treated better than others in this country: "I was sickened at the proposed bus service for prisoners' relatives to be able to visit them in jail. My partner and I are on income support and my partner, aged forty-six, has severe dyslexia. For three years I have asked for a bus pass so that she can travel to and from Birmingham Central Library to obtain computer literacy and also to attend her dyslexic help group in the city . . . Prison inmates have computer access, educational tuition and rehabilitation. Perhaps my partner should take up robbery, mugging or some similar activity." Yet, is it true that prisoners have rights and access to services and care denied to most "ordinary" citizens? Are they in a position not only to advance their health status but also their education? In short, are they privileged? In addition, does society benefit from healthy and well-educated prisoners?

McMahon (2000) argues that the country's views toward prisoners cannot be separated from its views toward other marginalized and undervalued groups:

> In summary, the penal climate at the turn of the millennium is an exceedingly punitive one . . . Faith in the potential of rehabilitation has been seriously undermined since the 1970s, and the voices of those few who argue that treatment programs and penal reform can work tend to be drowned out in the public culture by media, and political and other sources advocating tougher measures against crime. In turn, this get-tough approach [is] associated with hardening attitudes more generally toward those in the poorer and vulnerable sections of society. Welfare status and social services were radically diminished in many countries during the closing decades of the twentieth century (p. 291).

Health care in prisons may be seen as too much of a luxury. Finn (1996) surveyed elected officials and found trends toward eliminating "frills" from prisons and jails such as weightlifting equipment, free coffee, television, hot meals, personal clothing, visitor-provided food, access to telephones, sporting activities, flexible visitations time, free medical service, and access to educational programs. He concludes that many of these efforts have been undertaken in an "information vacuum" or that decisions have been based on misinformation. He also suggests that the major force behind these efforts is legislators who believe that it will help them get elected or reelected by being "tough on crime." Interestingly, prison officials and guards do not share this enthusiasm for getting tough, because of safety concerns.

McMahon's (2000) perspective regarding marginalized and undervalued groups is compelling. Issues related to race and socioeconomic class permeate much of the country's perspective as to what constitutes "punishment" and what the rights of prisoners are to health care during their time in prison. Are prisoners receiving the best and most expensive treatments available? The answer is no. However, the public is misinformed. For every inmate who receives a heart or liver transplant, there are countless others receiving minimal or inadequate care. The thrust on the part of many correctional systems to have inmates co-pay for such things as doctors' visits, medication, or eyeglasses is a misguided response to punish them (Clines, 2000; *Plain Dealer*, 1997). Cutting down on "frivolous" visits to the infirmary may reduce costs in the short run, but at what cost to inmate health in the long run? In addition, the rapid expansion of the privatization of prisons is matched by the privatization of health care services for inmates. The emergence of private enterprise makes the introduction of humane health care difficult to achieve. When privatization is carried out with for-profit entities, quality of health care can be compromised by cost-saving to maximize profits. There is an inherent conflict of interests in the mandate of a for-profit corporation being responsible to stockholders to cut costs and maximize profits at the same time it is responsible to the government and its prisoners to provide good health care.

PURPOSE AND GOALS

The subject of imprisonment, trends, social justice, and the impact on communities and society is well addressed in the professional and popular arenas (Burton-Rose, Pens, & Wright, 1998; Harris & Miller, 2003; LeBlanc, 2003; Seymour & Hairston, 2001). The issues (constitutional, social, economic, political, and psychological) are profound, and this is why there are so many excellent books on those subjects. However, there are currently no books addressing both health and death. The projected number of inmates who are aging, have disabilities, or have chronic illnesses such as HIV/AIDS, and will live out their lives in prisons or under some other source of correctional supervision, will pose numerous challenges for this nation.

A focus on prisoners is justified based on this nation's propensity to incarcerate and the resulting crisis that state and federal prisons and jails face. Besides the issues within prisons, issues related to discharge planning for the return of inmates back to the community will be raised because they require careful planning on the part of correctional authorities. High-profile health issues such as pregnant inmates and inmates with HIV/AIDS will be addressed in the book. However, special attention will be paid to "less sensational" but just as challenging health issues, including inmates who have conditions such as blindness, deafness, amputations, quadriplegia, or paraplegia. These inmates require highly specialized treatment and pose challenging confinement and service delivery strategies. Since prisons are not just "graying," they also are "browning," special efforts will be made to highlight the needs of prisoners of color by addressing, for example, the issue of hypertensive heart disease in African Americans, and other diseases with high representation in these communities.

In addition, this book seeks to raise awareness about how health and death within the nation's prison system will have an impact on public health within prisons and on the larger society that includes providers of human services. Five major goals guide this book:

1. ground the reader in correctional trends with a special focus on the current health of prisoners
2. highlight key public health issues, challenges, and rewards of addressing the nation's prison population
3. examine the subject of death in prison, particularly because the number of prisoners sentenced to lengthy sentences means that they will die in prisons
4. provide "best practice" public health and social service models, and draw implications for planning and implementation of these model programs
5. highlight key health themes for policymakers, academics, and practitioners

This book will make extensive use of case examples, illustrations, and studies, which provide the reader with depth and details about prisoners' experiences. It is very easy to rely on statistics to paint a picture or tell a story about health care within correctional institutions. Cases, though, serve to humanize the issues and challenges prison inmates face in trying to obtain quality health care services, and to have their voices heard regarding their health needs. These cases also bring to light the complexities facing prison administration. Although the primary focus will be on state and federal prisons, jails will be included, where appropriate, to highlight the pervasive nature of the subject matter being addressed.

It is necessary for us to make a declaration that should help the reader better understand the authors' point of view on the subject of this book. Even though our perspective can be discerned very easily, it is important to make it explicit. The writing of a book on corrections in the United States raises many unsettling feelings because of how this system has touched the lives of so many people of color in this society, although these feelings do not come as any great surprise to us. One of the authors' first book on corrections (Delgado, 2001) brought up similar intense feelings. This second book, as a result, is both a continuation and a dramatic departure from the first book and has the added dimensions of health, and even the subject of death, for those inmates unfortunate enough never to leave prison alive.

Prevailing public and governmental official attitudes toward prisoners seriously have undermined any concerted effort at better understanding and meeting the health and rehabilitation needs of prisoners. Cases in point are the main federal public health agenda-setting publication, *Healthy People 2010* (U.S. Department of Health and Human Services, 2000) and its *Midcourse Review* (U.S. Department of Health and Human Services, 2005), which give scant attention to issues in prisons. We believe that the role and injustice perpetrated by prisons in the United States are summed up well by Cayley (1998):

> Crime must be answered in a convincing way; but imprisonment can accomplish this purpose only by generating new injustices . . . There is no frictionless medium in which retributive pain can be unproblematically delivered. Imprisonment is not just a neutral system of moral accounting, it is a violent ritualization of power, and, as such, it produces effects that undermine and overwhelm its capacity to represent justice (p. 347).

We cannot simply ignore these subjects within prisons, tempting as that may be. Denial, after all, is a very powerful defense mechanism. However, in the long run, at least as it relates to prisons, it will break down and place this nation in a very precarious position. This book is an attempt to bring the subjects of acute health care, long-term care, hospice care, and gerontology into the daily realm of the work we do. Issues related to aging, health, and dying get more complex within prisons because of the structure and processes used in these settings. An ability to contextualize the phenomenon of corrections is essential before a comprehensive solution to the roots of crime and requisite consequences can be found. This contextualization also serves to highlight the complexity of the subject matter.

This book is intended to help readers better understand key trends and approaches toward helping prisoners, particularly those who have an illness or are elders, and increase their quality of life in a total institution. Long-term care and death and dying are critical issues in this society; not surprisingly, they also are for the incarcerated. Bringing the element of incarceration into any discussion of health and death and dying makes the finding of "rational" and "fair and equitable" solutions arduous to achieve, however.

The field of criminal justice covers a broad arena, corrections being just one, yet a very prominent element. Criminal justice can be viewed best on a continuum in order better to appreciate its scope: arrest, arraignment, plea bargaining, diversion programs, trial, pre-sentencing, sentencing, probation, intermediate sanctions, jails and prisons, parole, or mandatory release. This book will touch upon most of these facets. However, the major focus will be on prisons. Prisons, by their unique structure and processes, wield a disproportionate role in how criminal justice policies are conceptualized in this society. Prisons, from a taxpayer perspective, represent the most expensive element.

All prisoners have the right to expect and receive quality health care while in prison. The impact of oppression such as racism, sexism, and heterosexism, is harsh in this society, though it increases in magnitude in total institutions such as prisons. Therefore, this book has a dual focus which is the need for quality for all prisoners, with particular attention to prisoners from undervalued backgrounds.

This book consists of three separate parts. Part 1, Context (chapters 1–4), includes an introduction; demographic information; social inequities; and political and ethical considerations. Part 2, Health Needs, Approaches, and Finances (chapters 5–9) covers the topics of high-profile health care needs; low-profile health care needs; death and dying; approaches and service delivery models; and financial cost considerations. Part 3 (chapter 10) discusses recommendations for the structure and delivery of health care to prisoners and ex-prisoners.

This chapter introduces the reader to the purpose behind the book and the contextualization of the subject matter. Health care needs are not homogeneous across different sociocultural groups in the nation, and neither should we expect the same in the nation's prison system. The system's graying cannot be separated from its browning, and it cannot be further separated from the feminization of the prison population. These distinctive and often overlapping trends provide a prodigious amount of challenges that have an impact on all aspects of health care delivery.

The early part of the twenty-first century represents a critical period during which the stance taken toward corrections will set the tone for an extended period of time. A fundamental decision about the future of prisons as a primary correctional strategy will need to be made. The federal and state correctional systems can continue to imprison record numbers and build prisons to house them, or a dramatically new approach will need to be created. Recent occurrences, such as California's passage of Proposition 36, which requires counties to focus on drug treatment over incarceration, offer much hope for a shift in state policies and, hopefully, will lead to changes in federal policies (Butterfield, 2001a; *Los Angeles Times*, 2001a; *New York Times*,

2001a; Nieves, 2000; *San Diego Union-Tribune*, 2001). However, a failure of this nation to reconsider current policies will have disastrous ramifications for current and future generations of prisoners and taxpayers alike.

Society's failure to meet the educational and health needs of inmates prior to their incarceration has presented prison systems with the challenge of meeting basic human needs within a system designed to provide punishment. The life experiences of inmates prior to their incarceration do not disappear upon their entry into prisons. In fact, they get further exacerbated. The development of any new models to effectively aid the health care needs of prisoners cannot succeed if they ignore the context in which inmates entered prison. The context in which these needs get expressed must be taken into account in any systematic effort at meeting them. There are other factors besides medical issues that must be weighed in any discussion of best strategies. These factors can be found in and outside of prison, and they certainly do not disappear at the gates of a prison. The manifestations of these factors, however, are shaped by the context of an institution such as a prison. The health conditions of prisoners cannot be understood by ignoring their health status prior to incarceration or their health after release.

This nation, to which this book attests, cannot turn its back on the health of inmates. Public health, in fact, has met public safety in jails and prisons. How soon and how effective we are in meeting the challenges of health needs will test this nation's will and resources. Ignoring these needs, however, only will postpone and increase the magnitude of health consequences for future generations, not to mention the financial costs to taxpayers.

It is fitting to end this chapter with a series of questions Mackenzie (2000) raises about the goals of correctional systems in this country:

> As we begin the 21st century, it is time [to] reflect on the goals of sentencing and corrections. What are the goals? Have we achieved these goals? What can we do to achieve them? Perhaps most important is to begin to ask what society expects from corrections? Are these expectations feasible? If not, can we educate the public to understand the challenges of sentencing and corrections? If yes, how will we go about meeting the expectations? (p. 39).

The answers to these questions undoubtedly also will address the graying and browning of the nation's inmate population, and test this nation's resolve as it enters a new millennium.

2

DEMOGRAPHICS

Any discussion of correctional health care requires grounding and understanding of the profile of who the prisoner is. Past, current, and future trends help one better understand how health care challenges have changed over the past few years and what challenges can be expected in the near future. Examination of the profiles at the state and local levels further illustrates their impact, and it sets the stage as to why prison health care has taken on such great significance at all levels of government.

There certainly is no lack of data on many of the characteristics of those who are under correctional supervision of various types such as in prison, on probation, and on parole. Each of these types of supervision has an influence on prison costs, health and otherwise, and brings with them challenges regarding how best to meet the needs of those correctionally supervised and how best to "protect" society. Important demographics to consider, and that are available, relate to gender, age, educational status, income, race, offense, and immigration status; others are important, but data are not gathered on them.

OVERVIEW OF THE NATION'S RECORD
NUMBER OF PRISONERS

At the beginning of 2008, there were 2,319,258 adults eighteen and over incarcerated, or an increase of 1.6% over the previous year (Pew Center, 2008). Out of this total, 1,596,127 were in state and federal prisons, with 723,131 in local jails (Pew Center, 2008). The actual incarceration rate was 1 in 99.1 adults (Pew Center, 2008). Women constituted 12.7% of the incarcerated jail population in 2005, compared to 10.2% in 1995, and 7.0% of all prisoners, up from 6.1% in 1995 (*Corrections Professional*, 2006a). Although males constitute almost 90% of jail inmates, women incarceration rates have increased at a faster pace between 1990 and 2005 (Bureau of Justice Statistics, 2006c).

There were over 4.9 million individuals on probation at the end of 2004, an increase of 0.5% from the previous year, and less than one-fifth of the average annual increase of 3.0% since 1965 (Bureau of Justice Statistics, 2005f, 2004f). There also were 764,400 people on parole. This followed the biggest increase in the number of parolees in at least one decade (Butterfield, 2004d). In 2004, Texas (534,280) and California (485,039) led the nation in the number of persons on probation and parole (Butterfield, 2004c). Women made up 23% of the nation's probationers and 12% of the parolees (Bureau of Justice Statistics, 2005f, 2004c). The majority of those on parole were white, non-Latinos (56%), followed by African American/Blacks (30%) and Latinos with 12% (Bureau of Justice Statistics, 2005f).

The United States leads the world in the rate of imprisonment (Kantor, 2006; *New York Times*, 2008; Pew, 2008; Powell, 2006). The record number of individuals under correctional supervision of various kinds translates into one out of every thirty-two adults (Associated Press, 2004). The increase in the prison population at the federal and state levels has been unprecedented in this nation's history and the subject of a considerable amount of analysis and debate (Gainsborough & Mauer, 2000). No significant sector of this nation's population has escaped this tendency to incarcerate (Mackenzie, 2000). However, some sectors have been overrepresented (Stone, 1999). For example, 60% of offenders in local jails were of color (*Corrections Professional*, 2006a). Further, no review of the literature or conversation about the status of incarcerated women could be complete without acknowledging the overrepresentation of women of color under correctional supervision and without highlighting the cultural considerations for provision of services in correctional settings. Women of color also face additional challenges upon reentry back into society due to racism, sexism, classism, and their offender status (Freudenberg, 2002a).

Although the number of men and women incarcerated slowed in 2003, it still had a 2.1 percent rate of growth, and this translated into millions of dollars needed to house and provide for basic needs, including health care (Butterfield, 2004d; Firestone, 2001a; Sentencing Project, 2001). Ironically, this growth continued, even though crime rates had decreased significantly from the 1980s (Blumstein, 2000; Butterfield, 2001a; Johnson, Golub, & Dunlap, 2000; Karmen, 2000). Between 2000 and 2001, the federal system grew 11 percent, largely as the result of mandatory drug sentencing and federal takeover of the Washington, D.C., prisoners (Firestone, 2001a). In 2007, thirty-six states had increases in their prison populations, although some had decreases. New York, Michigan, California, and Texas, among the largest state prison systems, were some with decreases (Pew, 2008). In addition, the New York City jail system experienced a dramatic decrease in the number of prisoners over several years, dropping from 21,449 in 1993 to 14,129 in 2006 (Powell, 2006). Still, the nationwide upward trend in incarceration remains very concerning.

Prisons for profit probably best exemplify the big business nature of imprisonment in this country (Stein, 2004). Prisons for profit enjoyed an incredible degree of popularity the last two decades of the twentieth century. In 1980, there were none in this country. However, fifteen years later, there were 104 housing 37,000 inmates, or 2% of the country's jail and prison population (Hallinan, 2001).

As of December 2003, according to the federal government, state prisons were operating between full capacity and 16% above capacity. Federal prisons were operating at 39% above capacity (Bureau of Justice Statistics, 2004d). Overcrowding of prisons has remained a reality in this country, particularly in the federal system, which has not constructed prisons at the necessary rate to accommodate the increase in incarceration rate.

Tough sentencing policies have made prison overcrowding a reality across the nation. For example, it is estimated that almost 10% of all inmates in state and federal prisons are serving life sentences, an increase of 83% from 1992. The percentage (20%) is even higher in New York and California state systems (Butterfield, 2004e). This has tremendous implications for health care services of the older adult prisoner.

PROFILE

The Correctional Association of New York developed a prisoner profile that reflects a national rather than a one-state profile, and it effectively grounds the demographics that follow in this chapter:

> He is a male of color in his early 30's, born and raised in poverty, unmarried, with children, and lacking a high school diploma. His educational deficiencies have likely resulted in low-paying or menial jobs. His history of substance abuse, parental neglect and high-risk behavior has compromised his physical and mental health as well as his ability to find and keep a job. Chances are strong that he supported his drug dependence by entering the neighborhood drug trade, which further exposed

him to life of violence and instability and prompted his decline into homelessness, joblessness and addiction (p. 23).

The Correctional Association of New York's perspective of health, health care, and inmate profile draws a stark view of the prison interactions and provision of care:

> He enters prison in poor health and withdrawing from drugs. Once the reality of his situation becomes clear, he will likely grow angry at "the system," frustrated by the rigidity of prison life and the remoteness of the facility that confines him, and depressed by the prospects of his life upon release. In the daily grind of prison life, the clinic may appear as a bright spot, a place where he will be cared for by nurses rather than confronted by "guards." Is it any wonder, then, that he might "play sick call" (inmate jargon for faking illness) because he is lonely and seeking attention? (More than likely, however, he is suffering from any of a host of ailments: asthma, diabetes, cancer or HIV). Is it any wonder that his social and coping skills are not as developed as those of his counterpart from a stable home and community? Is it any wonder that the abruptness of an overworked nurse—likely untrained in the psychosocial needs of inmates—is particularly distressing to him? (2000, p. 23).

The profile and assessment cited in the above quotes effectively grounds the subject of health care needs and services covered in this and the following chapters. The interaction of demographics and health are closely interwoven, to set a context that can be considered toxic to the health and wellbeing of inmates in the nation's prisons.

GENDER

Prisons are no longer the exclusive domain of men. The number of women, too, has experienced unprecedented growth in jails and prisons, although women do not approach the level of male representation (Belknap, 2001; George, 1999; Gilbert, 1999; Mullen, 1997; Owen, 1999; Sentencing Project, 2002a; Van Wormer & Bartollas, 2000). The female state prison population growth has far outdistanced that of males over the past twenty-five years, with the number of women serving sentences of one year or longer increasing by 757% between 1977 and 2004, or almost two times that of their male counterparts (at 388%) (*Corrections Professional*, 2006b).

As of May 2004, female federal prisoners numbered 12,104, or 6.8% of the total prison population. Males numbered 165,414, or 93.2% (Federal

Bureau of Prisons, 2004a). In 2003, there were an additional 87,583 women in local jails (Sentencing Project, 2005b). The increase in female inmates is not evenly spread across all state prison systems, however. Mountain states' prisons experienced a 1,600% increase; women in Oklahoma, for example, were ten times more likely to be incarcerated than their female counterparts in Massachusetts or Rhode Island (*Corrections Professional*, 2006b).

"Relative to the number of residents in the U.S. population, black women (375 per 100,000) were twice as likely as Hispanic women (142 per 100,000) and seven times more likely than white women (53 per 100,000) to be incarcerated in 1999" (Gaiter & Doll as cited in Kim, 2003). In addition, the disparity by race is evident when considering that two-thirds of the women on probation are white, while women of color are more likely to be under institutional supervision (National Institute of Corrections, 2003).

According to the Bureau of Justice Statistics, the total number of women under correctional supervision increased 81% from 1990 to 2000, while the number of men increased 45%. In 1980, women in state and federal prisons totaled 12,300. However, by 2004, their number had increased to 103,000 (Sentencing Project, 2002a). The average increase in female incarceration in the 1990s was 8.3%, and the annual rate of women sentenced to jails and prisons exceeded 10% in 18 states, led by Tennessee at 15%, North Dakota at 14.9%, Montana at 14.7%, and Idaho at 14.3% (Curry, 2001, p. 74).

Women's rate of incarceration has grown faster than that of men, at a rate 1.5 times higher (Women's Prison Association, 2003b). Women in 1980 had a rate of incarceration of 11 per 100,000 U.S. residents (males had a rate of 275), and by 1996 women had increased to 51 per 100,000, a 364% increase (Mackenzie, 2000). The adult female jail population has increased by 7% annually since 1990 while their male counterparts' rate has increased by 4.5%. Increased rates of arrests and incarceration among women are widely attributed to the "War on Drugs" (Kruttschnitt & Gartner, 2003). Women in prison are more likely than men (30% compared to 20%) to be incarcerated for a drug crime (Sentencing Project, 2005b). Approximately two-thirds of women arrested have used illicit drugs (Alemagno, 2001). The vast majority of female inmates are there as a result of drug abuse, and this is particularly the case with African Americans and Latinas.

The upsurge in the number of female inmates during the past decade brings with it a series of challenges that go far beyond security (Dreiling, 2003; Hoskins, 2004; Kruttschnitt & Gartner, 2003; Maeve, 2003; Pavello, 1999). Female inmates share many of the same challenges as their male counterparts and some that are unique to them (Severance, 2004). Women entering correctional systems generally come from impoverished communities, with fewer than half of them being employed full time at the time of their arrest. As a result, incomes among the correctionally supervised, prior to incarceration, are very low, with almost 37% of women and 28% of men having incomes of less than $600 per month (under $8,000 a year, assuming full employment) prior to arrest (National Institute of Corrections, 2003).

The term "feminization of poverty" has entered into virtually all discussions of poverty in the United States, and it has parallels in a discussion of prisons as well as links to incarceration of women. In fact, the "feminization of prisons" is probably the early twenty-first century's equivalent to poverty (Harden & Hill, 1998). The feminization of prisons and jails, unfortunately, does not refer to how prisons have changed to take into account female gender-related factors and needs (Henderson, Schaefer & Brown, 1998; Rathbone, 2005). The increasing number of women in the nation's prisons has created significant challenges for the delivery of health care and other services to them (Auerhahn & Leonard, 2000; Fogel & Belyea, 1999; Ross & Lawrence, 1998; Women's Prison Association, 2003b). For example, women inmates are three times more likely than males to be diagnosed HIV-positive (DeGroot, 2001).

Incarcerated women are more likely to have experienced physical and sexual abuse in comparison to the general population of women and in comparison to incarcerated men (Marcus-Mendoza & Wright, 2003). The Bureau of Justice Statistics reports a striking gender difference between female and male inmates, with more than 40% of the women reported being abused at some time in their lives compared with 9% of the men (National Institute of Corrections, 2003). Women prisoners with histories of violence perpetrated on them, as a result, generally still are dealing with the consequences of these experiences while in prison, requiring specialized care and services.

Correctionally supervised women are more likely than women in the general population to have grown up in a single-parent home, with 42% of women growing up in homes with only one parent. The majority (70%) of incarcerated women have at least one child under the age of eighteen. In comparison to the general population of women, incarcerated women are more likely never to have been married, with approximately half of women in jail and prison and 42% of women on probation reporting having never been married (National Institute of Corrections, 2003). In addition, in comparison with incarcerated men, incarcerated women are more likely to have at least one family member who has been incarcerated. While 37% of men had an immediate family member who has been incarcerated, about 50% of women had an immediate family member who has been incarcerated (National Institute of Corrections, 2003) These would make them more likely to have experienced poverty than others.

A number of correctional institutions have responded to the increased number of inmate mothers. Some prisons have responded by allowing inmates to have their children with them (Crary, 1999). California's East Bay community prison is such an example. To be eligible for this program, inmates must be in a regular state prison and serving a sentence of less than five years for a nonviolent offense. A program bed is more expensive than a regular prison bed because of the added services in place. It costs approximately $31,000 annually per participating mother as compared to $21,000 for a conventional prisoner.

AGE

The dramatic increase of elder inmates has turned correctional facilities into what critics call "Maximum Security Nursing Homes" and has raised serious concerns about the future of corrections in this country (Lang, 1999). The average age of a federal prisoner was thirty-eight years in 2004 (Federal Bureau of Prisons, 2004). In the same year, one out of every twenty-three inmates in prison was fifty-five or older, an 85% increase from 1995 (Sentencing Project, 2005b). A national estimate for the year 2025 has prisoners over the age of fifty-five at 50% of the total inmate population in the country (LaVecchia, 1997). In California, it is projected that while the prison population will increase by almost 16% between 1997 and 2020, prison population over the age of sixty will increase by 75% (Montgomery, 1997). By 2025, approximately 20% of its prisoners will be fifty-five or older, and this will translate into a budget of $4 billion just for older prisoners (Martin, 2003).

Macallar and Schiraldi (2000), in their analysis of California's massive increase in prison construction, note the influential role of the California Peace Officers Association (prison guard union) in lobbying elected officials for new prison construction. The new boom in construction resulted in an additional 26,000 new guard positions, with the nation's highest salaries. In 1995, the state of Ohio projected that it would require an additional 3,000 prison beds for older inmates by 2003 but exceeded that figure in 1997 (Holman, 1999).

The importance of having a detailed profile of the older inmate is critical in helping prison systems to develop appropriate responses (Wittmeier, 1999). Unfortunately, data related to the ethnicity and race of the elder inmate may be limited, and this seriously hampers any in-depth analysis of the graying of the nation's prisons. Most of the attention in the professional and popular media has been on youth and young adults because of their over-representation in prisons, probation, and parole.

Older inmates, of course, are not a homogenous group. Their offenses may be violent or nonviolent. Some are imprisoned for the first time, and some have extensive histories of incarceration. Some grow old while serving lengthy sentences but did not enter as elders. Their diseases and illnesses vary, as do their characteristics, such as race, ethnicity, gender, and sexual orientation. This heterogeneity complicates planning for this prison group.

Youth of color bear the brunt of this nation's policies toward juvenile justice (Building Blocks for Youth, 2000). African American youth aged ten to seventeen, for example, constitute 15% of their age group in the United States. However, they account for 26% of juvenile arrests, 32% of delinquency referrals to juvenile court, 41% of juveniles detained in delinquency cases, 46% of juveniles in corrections institutions, and 52% of juveniles waived to adult criminal court after judicial hearings. Between 1996 and 1998, Latino youth in Los Angeles were 2.3 times more likely than whites to be arrested, 2.4 times more likely to be prosecuted, and were imprisoned 7.3 times longer than white, non-Latino youth for the same crimes (Alexander, 2002). Consequently, the "browning" of this country's population also has been experienced in prisons and jails throughout the nation. Obtaining accurate numbers of Latino youth in the correctional system has been hampered, though, by states not having uniform definitions of who is Latino or Hispanic. Latino youth, as a result, are often counted as white (Alexander, 2002).

According to a Human Rights Watch and Amnesty International report, in 2005, there were twenty-six states where a life sentence without parole is mandatory for someone found guilty of first-degree murder regardless of age (Agence France Presse–English, 2005). The same report found that African American/Black youth are ten times more likely, when compared to white, non-Latino youth, to receive life without parole sentences. In California, however, they are 22.5 times more likely to do so. In Pennsylvania, Latino youth are ten times more likely than white, non-Latino, youth to receive this type of sentence (U.S. Newswire, 2005).

In 1992, African American youth were significantly more likely to be incarcerated in every offense group for both males and females (Males & Macallair, 2000). For crimes against persons, African American males and females were six times more likely than their white, non-Latino counterparts to be admitted to state juvenile facilities. For property crimes, African American males were almost four times more likely than white, non-Latino males, and African American females were three times more likely than white, non-Latinas, to be admitted to state juvenile facilities. For drug offenses, African American males were confined at a rate of thirty times that of white, non-Latino males. In addition, Latino youth were in custody in state public facilities on average 112 days more than white, non-Latino youth, and they had, on average, double the length of stay of non-Latino whites when admitted for a drug offense—306 days versus 144 days (Building Block for Youth, 2001).

EDUCATIONAL STATUS

The formal educational level of the nation's prisoners, based on a 2003 report (Harlow, 2003), is considerably lower than that of the general population. Sixty-eight percent of state prisoners, for example, do not have a high school diploma, although 26% had completed a GED while serving their sentences in a correctional facility. Latinos had the highest percentage (53%) of any group that had not completed a high school education, followed by African Americans/Blacks with 44%, and white, non-Latinos with 27%.

RACE

As noted in several of the previous sections, communities of color, particularly African Americans and Latinos, have been overrepresented in incarceration totals (Tuhus, 2001). By the end of 2004, there were an estimated 3,218 African American/Black males sentenced per 100,000 in the United States, compared to 1,220 for Latino males and 463 for white, non-Latino males (Bureau of Justice Statistics, 2006a). The Pew Center (2008), in a recent view of who is behind bars, highlights a very disturbing picture. African American/Black males ages twenty to thirty-four had the highest likelihood of being imprisoned with 1 in 9 being so, followed by African Americans/Black males age eighteen and older with 1 in 15 being incarcerated. White, non-Latino males eighteen or older, in turn, were 1 in 106. Latino males eighteen or older were 1 in 36. Among women, African American/Black women aged thirty-five to thirty-nine had the highest likelihood of being imprisoned with 1 in 100. White, non-Latinas in the same age category were 1 in 355. Latinas thirty-five to thirty-nine were 1 in 297.

African American males represent 49% of the incarcerated population, yet they only represent 13% of the nation's population (Mauer, 1999b). Prisoners of color comprised the majority of federal prisons in 2004: African

Americans/Blacks were 40.1%, and Latinos were 43.3%. Latinos, when counted by ethnicity (Latinos sometimes are counted as White or Black and sometimes as Latino), represented 32.1%. Asians and Native Americans represented 1.6% each (Federal Bureau of Prisons, 2004a). Latinos are considered one of the fastest-growing segments of the nation's prison population, increasing from 10.9% (state and federal inmates) in 1985 to 15.6% in 2001 (Sentencing Project, 2002b).

In 2004, African American male prison and jail inmates were incarcerated at a rate of 4,919 per 100,000, compared to 1,717 for Latinos and 717 per 100,000 for white, non–Latino males (Bureau of Justice Statistics, 2005a). An African American male born in 1991 has over a 29% chance of being incarcerated on any given day, or seven times that of a white, non–Latino male, who has only a 4% chance. Latinos, in turn, have a 16% chance (Mauer, 1999b).

Another perspective on the number of African American males who are incarcerated is to compare that number with the number enrolled in colleges or universities. In 1980, there were 143,000 African American males in correctional settings and 463,700 in colleges or universities. In 2000, there were approximately 800,000 African American men in either jail or prison and 603,000 enrolled in higher education (Butterfield, 2002a). The increase in imprisonment of African American men far outdistanced those enrolled in institutions of higher education between 1980 and 2000.

The impact of incarcerating nonviolent drug offenders has touched both males and females (Kelly, 2003). Ethnic and racial disparities in federal drug offense sentencing had a disproportionate impact on some groups (Lguchi, 2005; Pasko, 2002). However, it did particularly so on the African American community. In 1996, African Americans constituted 62.7% of all drug offenders who were incarcerated. Seven states had even higher rates, with 80–90% of all drug offenders incarcerated being African Americans. In fifteen states, African American males are being incarcerated at a rate of 20 to 57% greater than white, non–Latino males for the same offenses (Beatty, Holman & Schiraldi, 2000).

OFFENSE AND SENTENCING

Mandatory minimum sentences with guidelines requiring prisoners to serve 85% of their sentences, and legislatures passing laws on sentences without the possibility of parole, typify "get tough" policies. In 2004, there were 127,000 inmates serving life sentences, representing an increase of 83% since 1992

(Sentencing Project, 2005b). The average sentence served by newly admitted life-termers also increased dramatically from 21 years in 1991 to 29 years in 1997 (Sentencing Project, 2005b). The most common lengths of sentences in 2004 in federal prison were 5–10 years (28.9%), 10–15 years (17.4%), 3–5 years (16.1%), and 1–3 years (14.8%) (Federal Bureau of Prisons, 2004a).

Spending on incarceration reached nearly $40 billion during the year 2000. However, 60%, or $24 billion, went for incarcerating 1.2 million nonviolent offenders (Beatty, Holman & Schiraldi, 2000). In 2002, 55.7% of persons convicted of a drug offense fell into category 1, the least serious category of the sentencing guidelines, and 87% of these cases did not involve use of a weapon (Sentencing Project, 2004). In the year 1988, the number of drug offenders who were incarcerated exceeded the number of violent offenders for the first time in this nation's history, and between 1988 and 2000, it continued to do so (Beatty, Holman & Schiraldi, 2000). In 1986, there were eighteen persons per 100,000 who were incarcerated for drug offenses. However, by 1996, the rate had increased to 63 per 100,000, or a 24% increase. The estimated number of arrests for drug violations increased from 2002 to 2003, reflecting the continued trend toward incarceration for this category (Bureau of Justice Statistics, 2005e).

Fifty-five percent of federal prisoners are serving a sentence for a drug offense and 13% for a violent crime, with 72% of the prison population being considered nonviolent offenders with no history of violence (Sentencing Project, 2004). The increases in drug offenses have translated into almost half a million drug offenders being imprisoned, at a cost of $9.4 billion annually to taxpayers (Beatty, Holman & Schiradli, 2000). Only two states (Hawaii and West Virginia) did not increase the number of inmates due to drug offenses between 1986 and 1996. Another perspective on the magnitude of this trend toward incarcerating nonviolent drug offenders is that, in 2000, the United States had more prisoners for drug offenses (458,131) than the entire European Union (EU) with all offences combined (356,626), even though the EU had 100 million more people than the United States (Beatty, Holman & Schiraldi, 2000).

Drug offenses accounted for the largest number of inmates in federal prisons when offense-specific information has been made available. Drug offenses accounted for 54.3% in 2004. Weapons, explosives, and arson accounted for 11.9% followed by immigration violations (10.8%), robbery and burglary (6.4%), larceny (5.2%), and property offenses (4.4%) (Federal Bureau of Prisons, 2004).

Latinos are twice as likely as their white, non-Latino counterparts, and equally as likely as African Americans/Blacks, to be incarcerated for a drug offense (Sentencing Project, 2002b). However, in the federal system, they are half as likely as white, non-Latinos and less likely than African Americans/Blacks to receive treatment for substance abuse (Latinos, 19%, African American/Blacks, 25.7%, and white, non-Latinos, 39.5%) (Sentencing Project, 2002b).

Drug policies have had a disproportionate impact on both males and females of color (Delgado, 2004; Mauer, 1999). A Center on Addictions and Substance Abuse study found that 81% of state prison inmates, 80% of federal prison inmates, and 77% of jail inmates had used illegal drugs regularly (at least weekly for a minimum period of one month). These inmates had been imprisoned either for selling or possessing drugs, driving under the influence when they committed their crimes, had committed their crimes to obtain money for drugs, had a history of alcohol abuse, or had a combination of these characteristics (Belenko, Peugh, Califano Jr. & Foster, 1999). More than 50% of these inmates were first-time offenders, and most (97%) were considered nonviolent (Coalition for Federal Sentencing Reform, 1998). Older inmates (fifty-five or older) were less likely to commit crimes upon their release, with only 1.4% of those on probation or parole being reincarcerated for criminal offenses (Holman, 1999). Elder inmates, it should be noted, are generally male (Ornduff, 1996).

Incarceration and sentencing trends also reflect an increased tendency to imprison sexual offenders. This propensity, too, has had profound implications for the graying of the nation's prisons. The use of indefinite terms of "one day to life" for convicted sexual offenders necessitates that states be prepared for this group of inmates.

Elders convicted of sexual offenses are probably the only group of prisoners about whom most advocates of early release of inmates do not have a consensus (Krane, 1999f):

> And, contrary to popular impressions, most of the country's oldest prisoners aren't multiple murderers serving life sentences for heinous crimes committed in their youth. Often, the very oldest are sex offenders imprisoned relatively recently and considered too dangerous to parole . . . Parole boards treat sex cases gingerly, regularly denying release to infirm 80- and 90-year-olds. And, as states tighten anti-crime laws, sentencing statutes for sex crimes are getting special attention. For these reasons, aging sex offenders form the oldest bloc of prisoners in the country (p. 1–2).

One sex offender's assessment of his status touches upon the sentiments of the correctional system regarding these types of prisoners (Beyerlein, 1997):

"There's no rhyme or reason to the parole board," griped Donald Brunner, a 61-year-old sex offender from Chillicothe [Ohio]. "They keep them here until they're past the prime of doing anything (criminal), then they just put you out—$75 is what they give you." Brunner, who has emphysema and is in an assisted-living unit at orient, has been in prison since 1989 on a 3-to-10-year sentence for gross sexual imposition. He has been turned down for parole twice. Because he's a sex offender, he said, "I'm like the captain of a ship—I'm the last one to go" (p. 2).

The United States Supreme Court in an 8 to 1 ruling said that "sexually violent predators" could be imprisoned indefinitely.

IMMIGRATION STATUS

Almost 20% of all federal inmates are non-U.S. citizens, with approximately half of them being incarcerated for immigration violations and the remaining half for criminal violations such as drug offenses (VOA News, 2006). The number of detainees increased from approximately 20,000 annually in 1997 to almost 300,000 annually in 2007 (Block, 2007). A recent Government Accountability Office (GAO) report concluded that, in general, detainee facilities are both overcrowded and deficient in providing health care (Block, 2007). A lack of uniform standards on medical care also was cited as a cause of delayed medical testing and provision of treatment. It is important to note that immigrants have the lowest rate of incarceration for criminal offenses of any population group in the United States (VOA News, 2006).

As of May 2004, 71.2% of federal inmates were U.S. citizens. Four Latin American countries accounted for 22% of the remaining inmates: Mexico, 29,723 (16.7%); Colombia, 3,581 (2.0%); Dominican Republic, 3,502 (2.0%); and Cuba, 2,291 (1.3%). A total of 12,013 (6.8%) had other or unknown citizenship (Federal Bureau of Prisons, 2004a). These new inmates represent an upsurge in the number of unauthorized newcomers who have been caught and are awaiting hearings. According to Immigration and Customs Enforcement data for FY 2007, there were 164,000 immigrants with immigration violations, an important step in the process of deportation, with an additional 95,000 with criminal histories being deported (Preston, 2008).

The profile of the typical prisoner and the current and projected trends in this nation's prisons highlight how the prison system has challenged this nation's ability to pay for the costs associated with imprisonment. These costs, as noted in chapter 9, are not only projected to continue to increase, but also to wield considerable pressure on correctional budgets. The profile of the typical prisoner shows how certain groups and communities in this country have borne a disproportionate amount of the burden, highlighting significant prison racial disparities that only have gotten more pronounced in the past two decades.

3

SOCIAL INEQUITIES

There is wide acknowledgment that those currently in the nation's prison system have not been the healthiest segment of this nation's population, challenging prison systems to provide quality and cost-effective health care to a group that historically was in poor health and had limited access to quality care in its community (Allen & Bell, 1998; Conklin, Lincoln & Tuthill, 2000). Upon their entry into the prison system, overcrowding, exposure to other sick inmates, and inadequate systems of care exacerbate these issues (Ward & Bishop, 2001). The health status of "new" prisoners gets compromised in ways that extend far beyond the prisoners and includes their immediate family, neighbors, and community, and prison staff, and this is particularly the case with those inmates who have a long history of entering and leaving prison.

Given who enters prison in disproportionate numbers, a discussion of the context of prisons needs to explore social inequities such as racism and poverty. In addition, our society harbors other social inequities based on characteristics such as gender, sexual orientation, disability, and other areas of "difference" from a socially constructed norm. In fact, even the status of prisoner is a stigmatized identity. Therefore, it is important to consider issues relevant to various characteristics, as well as having more than one devalued identity, in addition to the identify of prisoner.

STATUS AS PRISONER

Going to prison marks one as a "deviant." The person enters a status in which he or she can be treated as different and unequal to others. As a result, the

31

conception of inmates as not human and evil and, therefore, needing social control, has compromised severely this nation's efforts to comprehensively meet inmate health care needs, and prevented the incorporation of prison health care services within a national public health agenda (Nadel & Travis, 1997). This categorization of inmates as less than human is reminiscent of the nation's views toward the enslavement of Africans between the 1600s and 1800s. The increasing "browning" of this nation's prisons brings race into any serious discussion as to why there is a prevailing negative view of inmates.

The public's characterization of inmates as undeserving facilitates the attempts of prison authorities and elected officials to severely limit basic health care services, not to mention extraordinary efforts to save inmate lives. Even the introduction of spirituality and religion within prison walls, which would seem to be viewed positively in current U.S. society, has raised safety concerns on the part of correctional officials (Niebuhr, 2001; Solove, 1996; Torok, 1999; Wilkinson & Unwin, 1999).

There are large numbers of medically uninsured people in the United States and wide disparities in access to health care (Becker, 2004; Fiscella, Franks, Doescher & Saver, 2002; Sered & Fernandopulle, 2005), so one cannot always say that a person who is not imprisoned has better health care than a prisoner. Outside a prison, though, there is at least the chance that one may have excellent health care and, perhaps, some degree of freedom in where to obtain health care. The prisoner lacks choice, and, in cases in which the prison provides inferior health care or none at all, the prisoner's situation is as bad as the person without health care on the outside.

The quality of health care and health care providers within prisons and jails has been criticized seriously (Arax, 1999; Dabney & Vaughn, 2000; Egelko, 2001; Rau, 2008; Russell, 2000; Skolnick, 1998; Wallace & Sward, 1994a,b; Sward & Wallace, 1994). This criticism generally has highlighted issues related to access, quality of services, qualifications of health care providers, and an overemphasis on security rather than health care provision. Yet, critics will argue that prisoners must pay their debt to society without compromise. One doctor's comments on the unpopularity of providing health care to inmates captures this sentiment: "'After all . . . many people say prisoners are scum . . . why should we provide free medical care for criminals when our own children can't get free medical care?"

The Institute of Medicine of the National Academies (IOM) (2006) recommends that prohibitions against use of prisoners in drug trials funded by the federal government should be lifted and that oversight should expand to all research, not just federally funded research, which has been the case. Loewenburg (2006) notes that the IOM sees potential health benefits to prisoners by their being part of research trials but that the practice of using prisoners had been prohibited after the massive and exploitive use of prisoners before the 1970s. As such, he cautions that "prisoner advocates and medical ethicists are still concerned about the possibility of the mistreatment and exploitation of vulnerable prison populations" (p. 1143). This is a proposed change in federal law that bears watching. While it is accurate that a person can benefit from a research trial, it also is true that one can be harmed. In addition, it is difficult to achieve truly informed consent with an institutionalized population.

RACE

A comprehensive grasp of the challenges inmates face in having their health care needs meet within a total institution such as a prison necessitates availability of data. Unfortunately, the prime source of data on inmates historically and currently comes from government or government-sponsored reports. These reports essentially have de-racialized and sanitized data on the disproportionate number of inmates of color in the nation's prisons. Results reported in these commissioned papers have done a disservice to the development of a better understanding of how social inequities have helped shape the profile of inmates and their health conditions. The *Washington Post*, in a 2005 editorial on Maryland's racial disparities in prison as a result of drug-offense sentencing, raised this issue for public scrutiny as one that is national in scope. Therefore, it is important to keep racial disparities at the forefront of any analysis of factors that affect prisoners.

There are two groups who receive inadequate or unequal treatment in reporting of federal data. These are Native Americans and Asian Americans. Generally, comparisons are presented among Whites, African Americans, and Latinos/Hispanics. There are some data on Native Americans and Asian Americans, but the data are not as available or as extensive as on other groups.

Race, according to Kerle (1998), is suggested through the use of code words such as "violent crime," "welfare reform," "illegal immigration," "drug problem, "and "youth delinquency" that find their way into policy decisions that have a severe and disproportional impact on certain racial and ethnic groups. Even the term "white collar" crime is devoid of associations of violence, despite the severe economic and psychological consequences it can have on victims' quality of life. One can postulate that, since it generally is not perpetrated by people of color, it is not treated with the seriousness with which other crimes or "social problems" are treated.

The manifestations of racism can be found in all sectors of this society. Perhaps nowhere is this issue more blatant than in the disproportionate number of men, women, and youth of color in the nation's federal, state, and county prison and jail systems (Blumstein, 2001; Delgado, 2001; Marable, 1999; Ness, 2001; Ruffins, 2002). Cook (2001) does a masterful job of tracing this country's recent ever-expanding use of, and fascination with, prisons and the significant social, political, and economic forces making changes in correctional policies difficult to achieve.

There is increasing evidence that disproportionate placement of people of color is expanding to include the Muslim population after September 11, with the introduction of the Patriot Act. Also, the abuse at the Abu Ghraib prison in Iraq goes well beyond the lack of provision of health care or negligence and into the realm of willful infliction of harm, and all known United States detainee prisons have had ethical questions raised about them (Miles, 2004; Okie, 2005). The impact of many of this nation's policies and actions toward people of color internationally seriously undermines this nation's claims of being a model democracy in the world.

United States immigration detention facilities' medical care is under serious scrutiny for its failings. These facilities often detain people of color and are another aspect of United States policies towards people from outside the country. Both houses of Congress have introduced the Detainee Basic Medical Care Act of 2008 to help ensure that detainees have basic medical services (ACLU, 2008).

During and after Hurricane Katrina in 2005, prisoners at the Orleans Parish Prison in Louisiana were trapped in horrific conditions. This prison incarcerates a disproportionate number of African Americans; although Orleans Parish was 66.6% African American prior to Katrina, the prison was 90% African American. Besides inmates being in lockdown as toxic floodwaters rose and created unsanitary, unhealthy, and dangerous conditions, food, potable water, and even medications for chronic illnesses and medical care for injuries were not provided for days after the storm (ACLU, 2006). This represented a failure to provide minimally decent care and protection to people who were trapped not only by the storm but also by a prison.

The nation's propensity to sentence men, women, and youth, particularly those of color to prisons, is not without its share of critics, however (Blumstein & Wallman, 2000; Chambliss, 1999; Currie, 1998; Daly & Maher, 1998; Dyer, 2000; Elikann, 1996, 1999; Mauer, 1999a,b, 2000; Parenti, 1999; Reiman, 1996; Rosenblatt, 1996; Skogan, 1990; Tonry, 1995; Zimring & Hawkins, 1991). Critics argue that this nation imprisons a disproportionate number of low-income people of color from urban communities and that the nation's law enforcement system specifically targets these communities, particularly in crimes involving substance abuse. In 2000, there were 36 states that had enacted mandatory minimum sentencing for drug offenses (Beatty, Holman & Schiraldi, 2000).

There were 3,470 Native Americans in 2007 in the federal prison system, representing 249 per 100,000 persons, a rate of incarceration higher than for the next most incarcerated group, African Americans. The U.S. criminal justice system treats Native Americans living on reservations differently than others. "For most Americans, routine felony offenses are prosecuted primarily by state governments; federal prosecutions occur only if there is a particular federal interest or a problem with national or international scope, such as terrorism or narcotics" (Native American Advisory Group, 2003, p. 1). Those who commit a felony such as murder, manslaughter, rape, assault with intent to kill, arson, burglary, or larceny on their reservation fall under the jurisdiction of the Federal Bureau of Investigation and the U.S. Attorney's offices. Putting Native American reservation felonies under federal jurisdiction dates to the 1885 Major Crimes Act. In addition, the 1825 Assimilative Crimes Act previously had designated state crimes on reservations also to be federal crimes.

Federal enforcement agencies often have harsher punishments than the state systems that geographically encompass the reservations. Therefore, a Native American who commits a felony on a reservation often will receive different and more severe punishment than someone else in the encompassing state receives. In addition, the federal system does not allow parole (Bureau of Indian Affairs, 2008; U.S. Department of Justice, 2008; *Wall Street Journal*, 2007).

Even youth of color are not exempt from the tendency to incarcerate people of color. Youth are overrepresented in the juvenile justice system and also have a higher probability of being waived to adult correctional systems when compared to white, non-Latinos committing the same crimes (Building Blocks for Youth, 1999; Males & Macallair, 2000). The results of these policies will have a far-reaching impact on the future of these youth within and outside of the criminal justice system. The health and educational needs of these new "types" of inmates will stress systems that have historically been developed to house adults.

A current case in California brings up the question of ethnic and religious discrimination within prisons, too. An Orthodox Jewish prisoner is suing to have himself labeled as something other than "White" because he has been forced to share a cell with inmates who are clearly anti-Semitic.

The prisoners have evidenced this by actions such as wearing swastika tattoos, and so the Jewish prisoner has asked for protection from having to share a cell with them (Eskenazi, 2003).

PRIMARY LANGUAGE OTHER THAN ENGLISH

Since the quality of access to services is very much dependent upon the communication skills of both patient and provider, having a primary language other than English becomes a barrier, and this communication gap takes on an even greater significance in total institutions such as prisons where inmates are restricted in where they access services. Communication barriers in general health care settings are well recognized, including cultural beliefs about illness. As a result, the same concerns or challenges can be found within prison walls.

The ability to use one's primary language during moments of crisis is invaluable in conveying a more accurate picture of one's needs and expectations of care. If that primary language is anything other than English, and the care provider speaks only English, then a major gap in communication exists that compromises the help-seeking process. Klein, Gieryic, O'Connell, Hall, and Klopf (2002), for example, found that one of the most significant barriers for HIV prevention services within New York State correctional facilities was the unavailability of prevention materials in Spanish.

POVERTY

It is a given in the United States that one's ability to buy "the best" legal representation can have a strong influence on the outcome of one's case. The quality of legal representation of poor and working-class defendants has left much to be desired (Fritsch & Rohde, 2001a,b,c). Therefore, it would be naïve not to acknowledge the inherent inequity in legal resources between lower-income and higher-income defendants.

Also, there are myths about criminals "getting rich." This is hardly the case with the people from low-income neighborhoods who so often go to prison. Among those who actually research crime, it is never thought of as an attractive career with unlimited potential for advancement. The Department of Labor does not include it in the careers, such as health service and information technology-related jobs, that will be in high demand in the early part of the twenty-first century. Rarely do young children, when asked what they want to be when they grow up, say that they aspire to be "habitual" criminals. One study of a gang (Levitt & Venkatesh, 1998) found that gang members who sold drugs tended to earn less than minimum wage doing so. Yet, the popular perception has those engaging in criminal acts as making a deliberate and strategic "career" move. This perception, or myth if you wish, makes the issuing of severe punishment that much easier to rationalize and for politicians to capitalize upon to pass punitive legislation.

Individuals committing crimes to support their drug habits, for example, do not view themselves as "professionals," "career-minded," or engaging in "career-advancement" work. Consequences of crime involvement behavior, as a result, take a secondary place behind the need to meet the body's craving for a drug. Imprisonment can be considered a sidetrack in an ever-constant path and push toward satisfaction of a need. The goal is not to earn money but to obtain drugs.

The high rate of poverty of those who go to prison also is reflected in their health status and issues. The typical prison or jail has an inmate population with high disease prevalence that enters the system with a history of inadequate health care utilization. A report by the Massachusetts Public Health Association (2003, p. 4) highlighted the profile of a correctional inmate that applies equally across the country: "The incarcerated population is sicker and much less likely to have received medical care in the community than those who have not been incarcerated. Risky behaviors, lack of access to health care, poverty, substandard nutrition, poor housing conditions and homelessness put this population at increased risk for many illnesses." When released from prisons, ex-inmates become carriers of various diseases back into their families, neighbors, and communities, and thus become a public health threat in addition to concerns about their public safety threat (Stockett & Fields, 1999). Given the fact that they so often come from low-income communities, that threat is especially evident in the low-income communities to which they return. However, there are very few programs that have as a goal follow-up of inmate health care after completion of their sentence.

As noted again in chapter 9 ("Financial Cost Considerations"), some states have attempted to address prison health care costs by charging inmates for services. Charging inmates for health service utilization has caused great concern on the part of inmate advocates. These fees can range from several dollars for visits to the infirmary to $60 for eyeglasses or several hundred dollars for dentures (Parenti, 1999). These fees have made it harder for inmates, particularly those with limited funds, to seek medical care (Gaseau &

Caramanis, 1999). As of 2000, thirty-eight states required payments from inmates, and the introduction of inmate fees has resulted in a significant reduction of sick call visits (Gaseau & Caramanis, 1999). However, the charging of fees has not resulted in significant financial gains for prisons.

The use of co-payments as a means of generating funding has raised important access issues and has not proven to generate sufficient funds to warrant the administrative costs of such a program. One study of California's co-payment program found that it generated $654,000 in income and cost $3.2 million to administer (Friends Community on Legislation of California, 2001). The question of fairness of asking a population group such as that found in prisons to pay co-payments when the level of income prior to incarceration was below poverty level must be raised. Lack of health insurance is a formidable barrier in accessing health care for these prisoners. A 1997 study in Massachusetts, for example, found that 97% of the state's prison population was not insured immediately before their arrest and incarceration (Elsner, 2004).

As the composition of prisons reflects inequities in society, the placement of prisons reflects inequities in which communities can profit from prisons. Huling and Mauer (2000) bring to the surface an often overlooked aspect of this nation's prison policies—rural areas have derived considerable benefits at the expense of urban communities:

> Not surprisingly, the benefits that rural communities derive from the census count come at the expense of urban neighborhoods, whose members represent a substantial portion of the inmates in rural prisons. In New York State, for example, while 89% of prisoners are housed in rural areas, three-quarters of the inmate population come from just seven neighborhoods in New York City. These neighborhoods and prisoners generally are disproportionately composed of low-income minorities— half of all inmates are African-American and one-sixth Latino. Thus, the urban communities hit hardest by both crime and criminal justice policies are similarly disadvantaged by losing funding and political influence through the reappointment process (p. 1).

The political and economic implications of this "redistribution" of resources from urban to rural areas are very difficult to reverse.

If one thinks of funds for social programs as a zero sum game, or even as a rather unlimited one in which society simply decides to fund one program and not another, comparisons between certain program expenditures are chilling. Between 1987 and 1995, state costs for prisons increased by 30%, while expenditures for universities decreased by 19%

(Drinan, 2000). Another perspective on this issue is that between 1980 and 2000 prison spending increased six times faster than higher education (*Dollar & Sense*, 2001). California has constructed twenty-one prisons and one state university since 1984. California could educate ten community college students, five state university students, or two University of California students for every individual incarcerated (Ambrosio & Schiraldi, 1997).

If one looks at the funding structures for prisons versus elementary and secondary schools, one also can see the inequities in spending on prisons. To a large extent, all society shares the costs of incarcerating people, often people of color, through state and federal taxes. In comparison, elementary and secondary education is largely funded by local property taxes, allowing and encouraging higher-income districts to have better resourced schools. Our society, therefore, provides unequal and inequitable resources for the children of color in the poorest districts by our funding structure for schools as well as our choice to spend large amounts of federal and state tax dollars on imprisonment.

GENDER

Women face special challenges as they enter a prison system that primarily has been geared to men. The nation's public health efforts at addressing the existence and need to eliminate health disparities hardly included prisoners (U.S. Department of Health and Human Services, 2000, 2005), and this oversight is nowhere more blatant than among incarcerated women who are, like their male counterparts, primarily African American and Latina (Allen, 2001). Like their male counterparts, they enter with a history of lack of access to, or utilization of, adequate health care. Many have histories of addiction, sexual and other kinds of abuse, and HIV infection. They also often enter as already a parent and/or pregnant. Zaitzow and Thomas (2003, p. 32) point out that women prisoners "are far more likely than incarcerated men to be the emotional and financial providers for their children." In addition, research in Massachusetts provides strong evidence that they often enter with a mental illness (Reuell, 2005).

Although women still are a much smaller proportion of the incarcerated population nationwide than men, Van Wormer and Bartollas (2000) predict that the increased presence of female inmates will result in the increased use of litigation as a significant strategy for equalizing services with their male counterparts. This use of litigation will focus not only on unequal access and treatment between women and male inmates, but also on the unique needs of women, such as pregnancy. In Missouri, for example, the American Civil Liberties Union has been arguing for the right of a female prisoner to have an abortion denied by the prison (Twiddy, 2005).

The anti-drug policies of recent decades have had a large effect on women, increasing their rates of incarceration, because they often tend to be imprisoned for drug offenses or other offenses that can be related to maintaining one's addiction, such as theft or prostitution. Rathbone (2005, p. 22), who tells the stories of prisoners in the Massachusetts women's prison, MCI Framingham, adds that "they are frequently mere accessories to their crimes: girlfriends, wives, or lovers of drug dealers, even lease-holders of apartments in which drugs are stashed." The corresponding lack of drug treatment options results in their not having options to deal with their addiction, too. Like men, their increasing numbers can result in the unhealthy condition of overcrowding in prisons, as it has in Pennsylvania (Smart, 2005).

Women in prisons may not receive the optimal preventative care for conditions for which they are at high risk by virtue of their histories, such as sexually transmitted diseases and cervical cancer. The Federal Bureau of Prisons says that it funds abortions only in cases of rape or those in which carrying the pregnancy to term would result in endangerment of the life of the mother (Federal Bureau of Prisons, 2004). In contrast, women may, however, sometimes be subjected to unnecessary and repetitive gynecological examinations, as was determined to have happened in a class action suit brought against Rikers Island Prison in New York. In that case, women had been told they had to have a pelvic examination, a Pap smear, and a breast examination, or be put into isolation, despite the fact that they actually had the right to refuse (Weissenstein, 2005). Therefore, their health needs as women per se will need to be addressed.

Women also are at risk for sexual assault by the male prison guards, who often work in women's prisons. In addition, male prison guards are not necessarily prohibited from invading women's privacy. At times, for example, they may conduct body searches and see women prisoners undressed (Rathbone, 2005).

SEXUAL ORIENTATION

Demographic data are not gathered on sexual orientation of prisoners, but prevailing social attitudes of homophobia and heterosexism are in evidence in prisons (Zielbauer, 2005g). These attitudes exist not just in men's prisons, but also in women's prisons (Bosworth, 2003). Human Rights Watch (2001) studied male rape in prisons. It reported that, among other factors, being gay or perceived as "feminine" correlates with prisoners being targeted for sexual assault; this includes transgender prisoners. In addition, this study pointed out that gay male prisoners are not likely to be perpetrators of sexual abuse and that the perpetrators do not view themselves as gay but rather as heterosexuals using another male to substitute for a woman.

Prison officials often do not protect victims of sexual assault (American Civil Liberties Union, 2002; Human Rights Watch, 2001, 2003). In the case *Johnson v. Johnson*, it was found that a young, gay, African American prisoner was left unprotected by Texas prison officials despite the fact that he was sold as a sexual slave to gangs, raped, and otherwise abused and degraded virtually daily. Unfortunately though, in what the American Civil Liberties Union called a "heartbreaking loss," his civil lawsuit against Texas prison officials for damages that cited discrimination based on race and sexual orientation was dismissed by a jury (American Civil Liberties Union, 2007, p.12).

Not only are prisoners who are targeted and assaulted inadequately protected by prison officials, but data gathered by the federal Bureau of Justice Statistics (2007) pursuant to the Prison Rape Elimination Act of 2003 documents sexual violence by prison staff on prisoners. In the case *Essary v. Chaney*, another Texas prisoner, a "slightly-built 22-year-old with very little prison experience and a history of mental illness," received monetary damages from the state of Texas and a prison correctional officer, after he was raped repeatedly by the prison correctional officer, and a warden failed to protect him (American Civil Liberties Union, 2007, p.12). Cases like these in Texas represent only those prisoners who manage to contact an outside advocacy agency such as the American Civil Liberties Union, which represented both of these prisoners, that helps them to gain some protection and then work their way through the legal system.

DISABILITY

Russell and Stewart (2001) raise ethical concerns about the treatment of inmates with disabilities within a system predicated on maintaining safety rather than providing care:

> Not surprisingly, once behind bars, prisoners with disabilities face even greater abuse and discrimination than they had encountered on the outside. For example, throughout the United States, guards are

known to confiscate from inmates with disabilities whatever will be most acutely missed: wheelchairs, walkers, crutches, braces, hearing aids, glasses, catheters, egg crates (special mattresses designed to prevent skin breakdown and aid circulation), and medications. Prisoners who require personal care or assistance—for example, quadriplegic inmates who need help with eating, dressing, bathing, etc.—are simply ignored (p. 62).

The types of concerns that Russell and Stewart have raised have led to many lawsuits using the constitutional arguments that inmates should not be subject to cruel and unusual punishment and that they have rights to due process and equal protection.

Suits also invoke the protection of the Americans with Disabilities Act (ADA). In the 1998 Supreme Court decision in *Yeskey v. Pennsylvania*, it was found that the ADA does apply to prisons as government agencies that are required by Title II of the ADA to make their facilities, programs, services, and activities accessible (Kreinut, Henderson, & Vandiver, 2003). In January 2006, the United States Supreme Court unanimously decided that Title II of the ADA does protect state prisoners from discrimination by state prison officials if it is conduct that could be challenged under the Fourteenth Amendment regarding due process and equal protection. This was decided in the case *Goodman v. Georgia* (The Bazelon Center for Mental Health Law, 2008). In that successful case, an inmate who was paraplegic said that he had suffered cruel and unusual punishment such as breaking bones when trying to use inaccessible toilet and shower facilities and having to sit in his own bodily waste (ACLU, 2007). These two decisions set positive precedents for certain protections of the ADA in prisons but do not necessarily answer all future questions about its application to prisons.

Prisoners who have severe and persistent mental illness also enter prison at a disadvantage because their psychiatric disability is a particularly stigmatized one even before they enter prison. As Kupers (1996) points out, prisoners with severe and persistent mental illnesses have been particularly vulnerable:

> Prison overcrowding makes life inside miserable for everyone, but especially for prisoners suffering from (or prone to suffer) severe and chronic mental illness. Rape is a serious trauma for everyone, but there is a subgroup of mentally ill prisoners who are much more likely than the average prisoner to become a victim . . . and to suffer a serious psychiatric decompensation or breakdown as a result of trauma (p. 15).

The health and mental health consequences of overcrowding can be both profound and extensive.

Several successful federal class action lawsuits have been brought against the California prison system. Two current disability cases are *Coleman v. Schwarzenegger* regarding mental illness and *Armstrong v. Schwarzenegger* in which the certified class of prisoners includes those with mobility, sight, hearing, learning, or kidney impairments. Therefore, it is clear that persons with disabilities of various types are not receiving needed services. In a separate case, *Plata v. Schwarzenegger,* California's prison medical system was placed in receivership in October 2005 by a federal district court judge. In that case, medical care in California's adult prisons was found to be unconstitutional. Subsequent to the receivership, the medical case, the two disability cases, and a fourth case focusing on dental care, *Perez v. Tilton,* were kept separate but coordinated under direction of the court. The coordination aims to carry out remedies efficiently and address costs effectively (California Prison Health Care Receivership Corporation, 2008; Urban Strategies Council, 2008; Washington University School of Law, 2008).

Some of the same issues within the California prison system affect persons who need medical or dental care as well as those who need services related to their disabilities. In addition, though, each group needs remedies that are specific to their needs. In the *Coleman v. Schwarzenegger* case, it was found that inmates with mental illness were subjected to cruel and unusual punishment because of lack of mental health services. In *Armstrong v. Schwarzenegger,* it was found that there were ADA violations at parole hearings such as making a prisoner who used a wheelchair crawl upstairs to the hearing; shackling a prisoner who was deaf, resulting in his not being able to communicate with his sign language interpreter; and not helping a prisoner who was blind read complicated written materials (Urban Strategies Council, 2008). Clearly, these violations show that prisoners with disabilities are at a serious disadvantage even in being able to get out of prison, in addition to experiencing degrading and demeaning treatment while in prison.

PRE-EXISTING HEALTH CARE NEEDS

It would be foolhardy for prison officials, legislatures, and health care providers to ignore how the browning of the prison system brings with it a new set of conditions, challenges, and dilemmas. The prevalence of certain illnesses and diseases commonly found within the communities in which inmates lived prior to their incarceration does not magically disappear when they enter prison. In fact, health conditions get worse due to the stress associated with leaving family on the outside, disruption of daily routines, and the uncertainty that awaits an inmate upon entering prison.

The poor health status of prisoners is not a recent occurrence. A 1971 publication of *Medical World News* noted: "At the outset, the prison population is not healthy . . . the 'typical' inmate enters prison with a 95% chance that he needs medical care and a 66% chance that the care he receives will be the first contact with professional medical attention. Furthermore, he has a 50% likelihood of drug use, a 5% chance of severe psychiatric disturbance, and a 15% possibility of having serious emotional problems" (p. 26). The health status of inmates upon entering prisons in many ways not only has gotten worse in the past thirty years, but it now applies even more to women as they now have an increased presence in correctional systems across the country.

As commented on throughout this book, the new profile of the nation's prisoners highlights that they are primarily of color—African American/Black and Latino—and have entered the correctional system with high pre-existing rates of heart disease, cancer, diabetes, and asthma, to list but four very common health conditions.

Heart Disease

Heart disease is the number one killer in the United States, and it kills more women than men every year. It is estimated that 500,000 women die every year from heart disease. It is further estimated that 1 out of every 3 women will die from heart disease, with 1 out of every 11 women getting breast cancer (Sinatra, 2000). African Americans, as a group, have a higher morbidity and mortality rate than White, non-Latinos, due to hypertension and related cardiovascular disease. Hypertension, as a result, takes on added significance within prisoner populations in this country (Tomlinson & Schechter, 2003). Although estimated prevalence rates for hypertension are lower for prisoners than the general population (18% versus 24%), this chronic disease is still a burden among inmates (*Health & Medical Weekly*, 2003). Hypertension increases in prevalence as an individual ages (National Commission on Correctional Health Care, 2003d), and prisoner rates are "relatively high given that the prison population is younger as a whole" (Rand Corporation, 2003).

Over the past thirty years, the African American/Black, non-Latino ratio of coronary heart disease (CHD) has increased steadily. It is estimated that anywhere from 40% to 60% of the CHD mortality risk among African Americans is attributed to the prevalence and severity of hypertension

(Jones et al., 2002). Delayed treatment of hypertension in African Americans results in an increased mortality rate anywhere from five to seven times that of White, non-Latinos.

CHD is rated the number one cause of mortality, disability, and health care costs in the country (Schneider, 2001). Hypertension and hypertensive heart diseases place African Americans at a distinct disadvantage. African American women, as a group, are considered to have the worst health status of any group on almost all of the major health indices. Heart disease, and its related illnesses, is at the top of the list among the biggest killers of African American women. African American women have a 1.4 times higher likelihood than White, non-Latinas, and a 2.1 times higher rate than that of Latinas (*Ebony*, 2001). High blood pressure and higher cholesterol levels, diet, smoking, and obesity, combined with hereditary factors, are the primary reasons for African American women (and men) to have high rates of heart disease (Schneider, 2001). It is estimated that over half of the general population in the United States are overweight (54.3%), with African American women being the most overweight subgroup, followed by Latinas (Hughes, 2000).

Cancer

Cancer—and more specifically lung, breast, and colorectal cancer—is prevalent among African American women. Pneumonia, influenza, asthma, and bronchitis also rank among the top killers of African American women (*Ebony*, 2001). It is estimated that more than 186,000 women per year are diagnosed with breast cancer in the United States, and over 45,000 women die from this disease (Williams, 1998). African American women's breast cancer incidence is lower than White, non-Latinas, yet they die at a higher rate.

Deaths from breast cancer decreased from 1973 to 1995 for White, non-Latinas (7.1%), but increased 19.4% for African American women during that period (Griffin, 1998). In 1995, for example, 31.9 African American women per 100,000 died from breast cancer, while 24.8 per 100,000 White, non-Latinas, died. Older low-income African American women have been found to have the highest rates of not following breast cancer screening guidelines (Williams, 1998).

The prison experience compounds breast cancer detection and treatment (Williams, 1998):

> There are many diseases that women are screened and treated for while in prison because of the risk of spread in the outside community when

the inmate is released; however, this is not the case with breast cancer. Women entering a state prison system are given a brief physical examination without the benefit of a clinical breast examination or instruction on breast self-examination practice. (p. 22)

In addition, Mathew, Elting, Cooksley, Owen, and Lin (2005) found cancers with unique epidemiology and high associated mortality to have emerged among incarcerated populations.

Availability of prescription drugs has historically posed a challenge for prison officials. Cancer pain management in prisons, for example, has been identified as a key emerging problem because of the unique challenges prisons present, not the least of which is drug misuse/diversion and the lack of inmate credibility (Lin & Mathew, 2005). Greater recognition of cancer has resulted in the need for new methods for prevention and early intervention in the case of women inmates. An increased risk for cervical cancer among women inmates increases the importance of a Papanicolaou (Pap) test and requisite follow-up treatment (Magee, Hult, Turalba & McMillan, 2005).

Diabetes

Diabetes is a major killer among African Americans and the general population, claiming fifth place among the former and sixth place among the latter (Byrd & Clayton, 2002). Stroke and diabetes are the second and third leading causes of death among African American women (*Ebony*, 2001). There are three types of diabetes. Type 1, insulin dependent, which once was known as juvenile-onset diabetes, accounts for 5 to 10% of all diagnosed cases. Type 2, non-insulin dependent, once known as adult-onset diabetes, is the most common form and accounts for 90 to 95% of all diagnosed cases. Gestational diabetes, the third type, occurs during pregnancy and disappears after birth and can occur in anywhere from 2 to 5% of all pregnancies (Cortes, 2002). Risk factors for type 2, the most common form of diabetes, are family history, old age, race/ethnicity, gestational diabetes, compromised glucose tolerance, being overweight, and physical inactivity. Like hypertension, diabetes is underrepresented in the prison population, with 4.8% versus 7% for the general population (National Commission on Correctional Health Care, 2003d). However, like hypertension, diabetes increases in prevalence as individuals age and places an undue burden on prisoners.

It is estimated that over 15.7 million individuals have diabetes but only two-thirds have been diagnosed (Cortes, 2002). Diabetes disproportionately affects people of color. Of the total number of individuals twenty and older who have diabetes, diagnosed and undiagnosed, it is estimated that 11.3 million (7.8%) are White, non-Latinos, followed by African Americans with 2.3 million (10.8%), and Latinos accounting for 1.2 million (10.6%).

In 2000, there were over 11 million (4.4% prevalence) people in the United States diagnosed with diabetes, with a 165% projected increase to 29 million in 2050, or a prevalence of 7.4% (Boyle et al., 2001). Changing demographic characteristics during the next fifty years will account for 37% of the increase, with 36% being the result of increased prevalence rates and 27% due to population growth (Boyle et al., 2001).

African American males are expected to experience the greatest increase (363%) in diabetes during this fifty-year period; African American women, in turn, are expected to be the second-fastest-growing group with 217%, followed by White, non-Latino males with 148%, and White, non-Latinos with 107% increase. Among Latino subgroups aged forty-five to seventy-four, Puerto Ricans had the largest proportion with diabetes (26%), followed by Mexican Americans (24%), and Cubans with 16% (Cortes, 2002).

The National Commission on Correctional Health Care estimates that about 5% of prisoners have diabetes, or 74,000 (*Health & Medicine Week*, 2003). Prisoners with diabetes face considerable challenges within prisons, as noted by a California corrections official: "Some of these guys are very sick . . . Diabetes is especially problematic because non-medical prisons rarely cater to those with special dietary needs. Prisoners with diabetes usually eat the same food as other inmates, meals full of sugar and carbohydrates" (Pfeiffer, 2002, p. 3). Yalamachili, Babu, and Sukhija (2005) strongly recommend that correctional institutions develop policies and procedures for the management of diabetes. Further, training of medical and correctional staff in diabetes care practices also is recommended, as well as prompt diagnosis and treatment as a means of reducing mortality and morbidity resulting from diabetes.

Asthma

Asthma is a chronic inflammatory disease of the airways that is found in between fourteen to fifteen million persons in the country (Hornung et al., 2003b). White, non-Latinos have the highest prevalence rates with 9.1 per 100, followed by African Americans/Blacks with 8.8 per 100, and Latinos with 6.1 per 100. Females, with the exception of Latinas, generally have higher rates when compared to males. African Americans/Blacks have a rate of 8.5 per 100 (males, 7.3), and White, non-Latinas, have a rate of 8.3 per 100 (males, 7.6). Latinas, however, have a rate of 6.1 per 100 compared to Latino males with 6.2 per 100 (Hornung et al., 2003b).

Hornung, Anno, Greifinger, and Gadre (2003b) developed a model that predicts an asthma rate of 7.2 per 100 inmates, or 118,461 in state and federal prisons and local jails across the United States. This figure, however, is 15,000 greater than the number of cases that have been identified. The National Commission on Corrections Health Care estimates are higher at 8 to 9% or 140,000 cases in the prison system (*Health & Medical Week,* 2003). Almost 93% of the cases are predicted to occur among males, with White, non-Latinos, and African American males following suit, and Latino males representing the third-highest number. Fewer than 10% of the asthma cases in prisons and jails are predicted to be women, however.

It is impossible to look at the subject of incarceration and health care without grounding it within a social context to better understand why correctional institutions have failed at providing basic health care. Correctional institutions have slowly been transformed from places that were predominantly established to punish young white males, to places where they are increasingly housing a population of color. Prisons also are places where the number of women and elder inmates constitute an increasing proportion of the population.

The "isms" of society can be found in one place, namely prisons. To ignore this fact, makes understanding society's proposals to address health care needs of inmates impossible. Solutions to the nation's prison health care crisis necessitate that solutions be grounded within the reality that these inmates face, both within and outside of prison.

4

POLITICAL AND
ETHICAL CONSIDERATIONS

It is necessary to develop a better comprehension of how health needs get manifested and the numerous factors that either facilitate or hinder the service delivery of health services to prison inmates (Walker, 1995). Since different perspectives have been expressed over time, it would be simplistic to jump into any discussion of health care issues in the nation's prisons without a historical context from which to examine current-day issues. Such a context provides a better understanding not only of the forces that led to health care service provision but also of how they helped shape current services, dilemmas, and strategies.

HISTORICAL OVERVIEW

Prisons and jails were attempts to reform earlier colonial practices that had "reflected British insistence on severe and cruel punishments" (Rothman, 1971, p. 39), such as hanging and whipping. Kneeper (1993, p. 1) notes: "Colonial jails amounted to local lockups for the detention of suspects awaiting trial and convicted lawbreakers sentenced to corporal punishment." Initially, prisons and jails, which were unhealthy environments (Jordan, 1969), tended to be used only for pretrial detention, witnesses for trials, debtors, heretics, slaves who had escaped or were being punished by their owners, or to house prisoners of war, including Native Americans, but the actual punishment after trial was done by various other means, including corporal punishment, peonage, and deportation (Barnes, 1922; Feer, 1961; Hirsch, 1992; Jordan, 1969; Morris, 1950; and Wood, 1987). England also sent convicts to the colonies where their punishment was doing

49

forced labor under a bondage contract that had been bought by a colonist (Morgan, 1989).

Under the slave codes that began in the colonial period, slaves could be incarcerated, but their incarceration for long periods was seen as not economically good for either their owners or society and, in addition, might allow them to exchange "potentially dangerous ideas and information" (Wood, 1987, p. 248). When various prison laws were reformed, the slave codes were not similarly reformed, and punishments for slaves remained harsher than for whites with similar offenses.

To substitute for other severe and cruel punishments, though, during and after the colonial period, states began to use prisons, jails, and houses of correction for incarceration that was "certain but humane" as the actual punishment (Rothman, 1971, p. 39). In the late 1600s, in West Jersey (later part of New Jersey), William Penn and the Quakers advocated that workhouses be used there instead of corporal punishment. Penn, soon after, also advocated the same method for Pennsylvania, but this method was not permanently or uniformly used in either place. Despite the workhouse concept not being sustained, "the real center from which the modern prison and its accompanying system of discipline and administration" derived "was the system introduced in Philadelphia by Quakers following 1776" (Barnes, 1922, p. 259). These prisons used solitary confinement, especially so that prisoners would have time and privacy to reflect on their morality and thus become reformed.

Later, in the nineteenth century before the Civil War, reformers came to believe that specialized institutions of various types could be places of reform by which individuals could be changed for the better and that could maintain the social order (Axinn and Stern, 2008). There was a belief in a kind of rehabilitation called "moral treatment" that would teach residents of institutions ways to behave that eventually would make them disciplined, contributing members of society. Part of this movement for specialized institutions was the penitentiary movement that looked to ordered architecture, discipline, and routines that separated inmates not only from the society that might corrupt them but also, to varying extents, from each other. The solitary confinement of the Pennsylvania system, however, gave way before the Civil War to the Auburn system, which did not isolate prisoners totally from each other; the post–Civil War Elmira system also did not use total isolation as a practice. Houses of refuge for children seen as in need of supervision and as threats to the community were developed, too; these often were both racially and gender segregated by design or practice.

Another aspect of the specialized institution movement was the mental hospital. It is ironic that over 160 years ago prison reformers successfully advocated getting people with mental illness out of jails and almshouses and into then new institutions specifically created to take care of them, but today people with mental illness, again, make up a large portion of the prison population. Advocates such as Dorothea Lynde Dix strongly believed that it was unethical, inhumane, and impossible to treat persons with mental illness successfully while in prisons or in the early "catch all" almshouses. Prisons were considered institutions that would exacerbate mental illness symptoms. The birth of mental hospitals ushered in a new era for treating people with mental illness who were improperly incarcerated in prisons. By 1880, there were seventy-five mental hospitals in this country, and it was estimated that less than 1% of all prison inmates were suffering from severe mental illness (Ort, 1999). Dorothea Dix's reform efforts had proved quite successful for a time.

After the Civil War, however, institutions such as penitentiaries and mental hospitals lost their focus on reform and strengthened their characteristics of warehousing with discipline, resulting in custodial care without a focus on rehabilitating the person. Social Darwinism had emerged as an accepted sociological theory, which stood in stark contrast to a belief in people's ability to change through the influence of an orderly, benign environment. Despite the fact that various institutions were no longer being used for rehabilitation, the large structures built continued to be used as the method of warehousing prisoners, people with mental illness, and others. Prisoners in several southern states, primarily African Americans, both male and female, began to be forced to do dangerous work for factories, plantations, and mines under the convict lease system and in chain gangs, and this system continued throughout the first half of the twentieth century.

By the turn of the twentieth century, the eugenics movement was well accepted within various institutions in society. People who believed in eugenics, and the believers included those at universities and elsewhere, saw prisoners as a class of people to be put into institutions or even to be sterilized. It was not until 1942 that the United States Supreme Court ruled that forced sterilization of prisoners was unconstitutional. Within the eugenics movement, there was a highly classist, nativist, racist approach to "purging" society of people of various types who were seen as inferior. Lest one think this period was not a truly pernicious one, one should keep in mind that Hitler's Germany explicitly drew on sterilization policies of the United States as at least partial support for Germany's policies.

In 1968, a ruling on racial segregation in prisons said that racially segregated prisons were unconstitutional. This was in response to a case brought by the American Civil Liberties Union (American Civil Liberties Union, 2005).

Recognition of prison administration in this country as a distinct profession did not occur until the 1940s and 1950s, according to Lindenauer and Harness (1981). A thrust toward rehabilitation in the 1960s witnessed an increased recognition of health care as an instrumental part of rehabilitation. The initial thrust of correctional health care efforts in the 1970s sought simply to introduce health care services into correctional settings because relatively few settings had any in place (Anno, 2001). It was during the 1970s, too, that attention began to be paid to women, who were recognized as the "forgotten offenders" (Thomas, 2003, p. 5). In the early part of the twenty-first century, the focus has shifted from introducing health care to improving health care, through the establishment of minimum standards, ethical codes, and improving the training of health care personnel. The provision of health care within correctional institutions has, not surprisingly, paralleled trends in criminal justice theory and practice.

Thorburn (1995) traces the establishment of health care as a constitutional right to the 1970s and the U.S. Supreme Court case of *Estelle v. Gamble* (429 US97 [1976]), in which the court found that "deliberate indifference to the serious medical needs of prisoners constitutes the unnecessary and wanton infliction of pain." This constitutes a violation of the Eighth Amendment. In *DeShaney v. Winnebago County DSS* in 1989, the court stated: "When the state by affirmative exercise of its power so restrains an individual's liberty that it renders him unable to care for himself, and at the same time fails to provide for his basic human needs—e.g., food, clothing, shelter, medical care, and reasonable safety—it transgresses the substantive limits on state actions set by the Eighth Amendment and the due process clause" (Thorburn, 1995, p. 189).

These Supreme Court decisions, in combination with the involvement of organized medicine in 1972 by the American Medical Association (AMA), served as an impetus for correctional systems to pay closer attention to inmate health needs. The AMA's survey and establishment of standards for correctional health services led to the development of a pilot health care project (Thorburn, 1995). This pilot program, in turn, became the precursor to the establishment of the National Commission on Correctional Health Care.

The profile of an incarcerated person during the 1970s was that of a relatively young male who might have been either white or of color. Young inmates were not high users of health services outside or inside of prisons. Access to prison health care was based on a demand basis, with a triage system dictating level and type of service needed (Thorburn, 1995). The 1980s witnessed a shift in philosophy toward punishing criminals rather than seeking to rehabilitate them. This shift largely was fueled by a belief that nothing could be done to rehabilitate prisoners successfully. However, the demographic profile of the nation's prisoners has shifted dramatically. The "browning" of the correctional system occurred, sentencing policies resulted in longer prison terms, women entered the system in unprecedented numbers, and the problem of substance abuse increased. Further, the introduction of inmates with HIV and AIDS, not to mention other diseases such as hepatitis B and C, dramatically changed the nature of health care needs, costs, and service delivery systems.

Ironically, inmates are the only population group in the United States with a constitutional right to health care. The important point needs to be reemphasized that inmates have greater access to health care when compared to those sharing a similar sociodemographic profile in the general population (Petersilia, 2003). Tremendous advances have been made in the medical field, and with these advances, there have been ethical dilemmas. It seems that there is no lack of health care dilemmas when addressing this nation's prison inmates (Anno, 2001).

The early part of the twenty-first century only promises more questions than answers on how best to provide quality and cost-effective health services to prisoners. For example, does the right to health care include access to clinical trials such as for HIV/AIDS (De Groot, Bick, Thomas & Stubblefield, 2001)? The increased need to address health needs of prisoners also has resulted in potential ethical conflicts for health care personnel (Coyle, 1997). There are few, if any, businesses in this country that have a continuous stream of revenue, steady work for health personnel, and a diverse patient mix (Shinkman, 2000). Prison health care is booming and projected to continue to grow well into the early part of the twenty-first century.

GOALS OF INCARCERATION

Prisons fulfill a variety of roles in society, depending upon the political premises and analysis used (*Social Justice*, 2000). Proponents of the nation's correctional policies would stress the importance of punishment as a means of deterrence and say that being "soft" on crime leads to lawlessness. A more progressive, or radical, perspective assesses criminal justice policies as a means by which society disempowers marginalized groups such as communities of color, by taking adult members out of the community and placing them in total institutions (Barry, 2000; Codd, 2001; Lafer & Confessore, 1999; Light, 2000; Malveaux, 2001; McCormick, 2000).

Tensions among punishing, controlling, and caring for prisoners are inherently contradictory in the nation's correctional system, and this compounds the delivery of quality and comprehensive health services within prisons (Adams, 1995; Brown, 1998; Harding, 2000; Ornduff, 1996). O'Connor (2003, p. 1) sums up these tensions quite well: "The topic of prison health care raises the hackles of others who see no fairness in the system, including those who work in corrections. Meanwhile, prisoner rights advocates cite the constitutional and moral obligations the state has in providing for the well-being of those incarcerated. Before these tensions can be resolved society must have an in-depth profile of how health issues get manifested within the nation's prison systems and possible trends for the early part of the twenty-first century."

Garland (2001) posits that, as a result of major social and economic structural changes in society, crime and punishment have taken on significant symbolic meaning for the public. Rehabilitation and reform play no role in this meaning, but incarceration and punishment satisfy public demands. All criminals are considered to be rational human beings who consciously prefer to engage in criminal activity, not requiring any special motivation or disposition. Society's effort to control these individuals gets manifested in longer prison sentences, limited parole opportunities, and "hard" time while in prison. In addition, it seems as if no age group has escaped this nation's tendency to imprison. Florida, for example, opened what is considered to be the nation's first geriatric work camp (Chattahoochee) and houses men who are "able to work" but not older prisoners who are in failing health (Pendleton, 2000).

Increased efforts to shame prisoners have been coupled with decreased efforts to rehabilitate and increased efforts to take away privileges (Boxer, 2001; Gordon, 2000; Stockman, 2001). The emergence of the concept of no-frills prisons and jails typifies the trend on the part of the public and government toward punishing rather than rehabilitating inmates (Finn, 1996). The introduction of chain gangs and the reduction of certain amenities and privileges such as eliminating weightlifting, banning electric equipment in cells, monitoring telephone calls, restricting exercise time, to list but a few, are meant to eliminate comforts in prisons and reemphasize the punishment aspects of incarceration.

Most prisoners have not committed violent acts. In fact, most prisoners have been sentenced for drug violations of various kinds, and critics would argue that the punishment does not fit the crime. For example, disempowerment can result even after one has served one's sentence. This may be accomplished by taking away one's ability to influence events within one's community by prohibitions such as losing one's right to vote and to hold certain jobs (Jackson, 2001). The psychosocial consequences of imprisonment truly only can be calculated and appreciated within a long-range viewpoint. A short-term perspective does not do justice to their impact on the lives of juvenile or adult inmates. Still, there is a slow, but nonetheless important, shift toward rehabilitation that must be acknowledged. The term "rehabilitation" is receiving greater attention in such significant states as Texas, Pennsylvania, and Ohio. Yet, a more comprehensive view of rehabilitation will require increased expenditures and changes within prison structure of activities, staffing, and attitudes about what constitutes prison time. When rehabilitation is mentioned, however, it is operationalized more commonly as job training. There is no denying the importance of gainful employment for ex-convicts. Yet, a broader definition of rehabilitation is in order, one that takes into account a comprehensive range of health, social service, and education perspectives.

Although prison time provides an opportunity for inmates to start on a path toward rehabilitation and hopefully, eventually, have it hold, it only can happen if correctional institutions accept rehabilitation as part of their mission. This requires adoption of a philosophical foundation and specific allocation of resources.

This nation's propensity to incarcerate nonviolent women and men is compounded further by the conditions they face once they are imprisoned. Prisons, due to increasing overcrowding and their toxic environment (emotional and physical), further undermine communities of color across the United States, and serious questions are raised about the intent of this society toward these undervalued groups (Butterfield, 2003a; Thorburn, 1998). Murphy (2001, p. 131), in an article in *Fortune* magazine, comments on this matter:

> Make no mistake: A large proportion of inmates thoroughly deserve to be exactly where they are. Incarceration is an effective way to isolate really awful people. But too many prisons stuffed with nonviolent, idle inmates is simply wasteful, of both people and money. We should do better to learn from several states that have lowered the crime rate without substantially raising prison populations . . . Instead of being excepted for its willingness to jail its citizens, the goal for America should be to become excepted in the application of wisdom to its criminal population. At the moment, it is not even close.

Kerbs (1999) also argues that there are several significant justifications for releasing older prisoners before their sentence is completed: (1) states will save taxpayers considerable money because of the high costs associated with incarcerating these prisoners; (2) elder inmates have low recidivism rates; (3) prisons are not designed to house elders; and (4) prison programs cannot provide adequate care, safety, and special accommodations for elders who have disabilities as per the mandates of the Americans with Disabilities Act (ADA).

ATTITUDES TOWARD HEALTH CARE FOR PRISONERS

Access to health care is a universal right in industrialized societies other than the United States. However, since access to health care is not necessarily a goal they or taxpayers have embraced in this society even for the general population, they may not have embraced this goal for prisoners, either. Still, a public health perspective that emphasizes prevention, early intervention, containment of communicable diseases, and safe and healthy environments often is advocated by critics of current health care efforts in correctional systems and represents a dramatic departure from more conventional perspectives that stress punishment and control of inmates (Glaser & Greifinger, 1993; Harding, 2000; Marquart, Merianos, Herbert & Carroll, 1997; Martin, 2001). Prisons present public health challenges because of both their being total institutions (Goffman, 1961) and the circumstances of individuals entering these systems. The pressing nature of these challenges necessitates screening, diagnosing, and treating diseases as rapidly as possible. Public health and public safety historically have not intersected, and this is likely the result of public health services being perceived possibly as a threat to prison security and routines. In addition, public health services in the general population have been a neglected area in the United States historically.

The aging population, combined with prisoners with debilitating diseases such as hepatitis C, will result in an increasing need for various types of transplants, heart and liver being but two highly publicized types. Any form of organ transplant, however, will galvanize attention on the inmates who receive them and the correctional systems authorizing them. Transplants in many ways symbolize "what is wrong" with current prison health policies. Nevertheless, these transplants are few and far between, not unlike what is experienced by the general population.

The shift in roles from that of a prisoner to that of a patient necessitates a corresponding change in cultural values. An inability of correctional staff to allow this shift in roles makes it impossible to both punish and heal at the same time in a setting much more comfortable doing the former. Prison administrators worry about inmates who fake illnesses in order to obtain favorable treatment of various kinds: "Health care workers in many of the nation's prisons and jails view inmates as notorious fakers. Some convicts . . . do it for the chance to escape. More often, prisoners wheedle for painkillers, syringes and supplies for the prison black market. Male inmates fake illness so they can talk to—and possibly feel the touch of—a female nurse. Others want to avoid work or get out of their cell for a few hours. The trick for health workers is to be aware of those techniques, without losing the ability to care for the prisoners" (Bell & Allen, 1998, p. 1). Inmate efforts to fake illness do not have to be motivated by a desire to escape work details, however. They may need to share material with health care staff that may be too sensitive to share with prison staff. They also may be bored with daily routines, and a visit to health services is one constructive way of dealing with boredom. Health services also provide inmates with an opportunity to be themselves and exercise a certain degree of control over their lives (Anno, 2001).

Although the possibility of inmates "faking" health care needs is present, just as it is in any health system serving the general population, the health needs of prisoners are real and represent a reality upon which advocates and critics of current correctional health care systems can agree. In fact, the suspicion about "faking" actually has resulted in denial of access to health care that has caused prisoner disabilities and deaths. How to address these issues is where major disagreement exists.

Anno, Faiver, and Harness (1998, p. 69) pose several provocative questions that highlight the complexity of health care provision within correctional institutions in this country: "How badly is the care needed? How quickly is it needed? What will happen if it is not provided? How much does it cost? How long has the inmate had the condition? How did it happen? How long will the inmate remain in the correctional system? What other treatments are available? How effective are they? How much does the patient want the care? What evidence has the patient shown that he or she will cooperate in the treatment process? Will the intervention bring significant improvement? How old is the inmate? Is it a prison or a jail?"

PRISONS AS TOXIC ENVIRONMENTS

Prisons can be viewed as toxic places based on a number of measures. A case in New York City is an excellent example of toxic correctional facilities. New York City, twenty-two years after settling an inmate federal suit in 1978 on eliminating inhumane and unconstitutional conditions, still had not made significant progress in addressing the foul air and extremely cold and unsanitary conditions that led to the lawsuit (Lipton, 2001). One study found soon-to-be-released prisoners to be considerably sicker on average than the general population. They had a four times greater risk for tuberculosis, a nine to ten times greater risk for hepatitis C, a five times greater risk for AIDS, an eight to nine times greater risk for HIV infection, a three to five times greater risk for bipolar disorder, and an equal chance for major depression (Rand Corporation, 2003).

Prisoners are rightly concerned about infectious diseases within prisons, as evidenced in a class action lawsuit against the California Department of Corrections. In 2002, a federal lawsuit sought to prohibit California prisons from cutting inmates' hair with unsterilized clippers (Reich, 2002). A heightened awareness of the risk of contracting HIV and hepatitis from haircuts led to this lawsuit.

Correctional institutions are frequently overcrowded, have poor air circulation, and are places where unhealthy hygiene practices often are the norm. Any one of these conditions increases the likelihood of a contagious disease spreading. When combined, prisons and jails are toxic environments (Faiver, 1998d; Kerbs, 2000a).

Overcrowding of prisons has remained a reality in this country, particularly in the federal system, which has not constructed prisons at the necessary rate to accommodate the increase in incarceration rate. Prison overcrowding, however, only touches upon a narrow dimension: the availability of beds. It does not touch upon quality of life, treatment programs, and educational programs.

Prison overcrowding also has an impact on staff, particularly newly hired prison guards. High turnover rates in prison guards have resulted in the lowering of the age of guards from 21 years to 18 years of age in some states as a means of staffing prisons. However, since prisoners are serving longer mandatory sentences, there is minimal incentive for good behavior. Combined with guards' poor working conditions, a competitive economy, and increased number of positions to be filled due to an increased number of prisons, an explosive situation exists in many of the nation's prisons (Alpert, 2001; Arax & Gladstone, 1998; Belluck, 2001; Clary, 1999; Conover, 2000; Glionna, 2001; Hurst & Morain, 1994; Jones, 2001; Kerle, 1998). These conditions seriously compromise both safety and health within prisons. For example, the lack of attention to inmate rape has raised serious concerns for the physical and emotional health of victims (Lehrer, 2001; Lewin, 2001).

RIGHTS ISSUES

Federal legislation, particularly the Americans with Disabilities Act (ADA), has played an important role in ensuring the rights of prisoners to access health care. State prisons, for example, must comply with the ADA and make "reasonable accommodations" for inmates with documented disabilities (Murray, 1998). "Reasonable accommodations" easily can translate into significant changes in prisons, such as building ramps and doing away with steps, removing structures to increase access and minimize falls, widening bathroom stalls to allow wheelchair accessibility, increasing access to eating areas, increasing climate control, regulating light, reducing crowding, and introducing relevant social, educational, and rehabilitation programs, to note but a few of the changes that may be required (Baker, 1999; Florida Corrections Commission, 1999; Starr, 1999; Stashenko, 1999). Structural changes that are retrofitted to old construction can be expensive but also allow jails and prisons to carry out for prisoners with disabilities what many perceive to be the primary mission of prisons and jails, namely, insuring the safety and wellbeing of the general population.

The financing of correctional health care is not just a correctional system responsibility. It is also an instrumental part of American society and a constitutional right (Bell, 1992; Glaser & Greifinger, 1983; National Commission on Correctional Health Care, 1993b; Weiner & Anno, 1992). Elsner (2004, p. 103) notes: "It is perhaps unfair to expect prisons to act as a front line in the nation's battle against infectious diseases when nobody is willing to give them the money to do so. But prisons still have the duty to care for the general health of their inmates, which in itself is a formidable challenge."

Anno (1993) goes so far as to argue that if correctional institutions are to serve as health facilities, then they should be founded as such. This, however, will necessitate radical changes in the current prison system or the creation of separate prisons that have as a central purpose provision of care rather than safety of society. These types of prisons would be unlike anything known in the history of this country.

An often overlooked issue in prison health care is the role of informed consent and prisoners' right to refuse treatment (Failing & Sears, 2001; Parker & Paine, 1999). Informed consent is best thought of as a process rather than a single event resulting in a signature on an official piece of paper. Like any meaningful process, decision making is based on the existence of dialogue, mutual respect, and trust, qualities that often are absent in correctional setting relationships between staff and inmates.

Zimring and Hawkins (2004) note that it has been only in the past three decades that penal reforms have been significantly included within a broader and more encompassing human rights agenda. The authors go on to note: "The strategic role of the criminal offender is in defining the absolute minimum obligation of state to citizen, so that adequate provisions for prisoners is a defensible necessity" (2004, p. 177). Provision of health care as a right has taken prominence within this rights agenda.

The fight for inmate rights to quality health care, not surprisingly, has dominated the work of prison reformers and inmate advocates. However, the circumstance under which prisoners legally and ethically can refuse treatment in prisons is complex, like that of their rights to receive treatment. The right of inmates to refuse treatment, like in the general population, is not absolute and must be balanced with the state's interest in requiring treatment (Failing & Sears, 2001).

In 2003, a federal appeals court in St. Louis issued a dramatic ruling on a case involving an Arkansas inmate's right to refuse medication. The case of Charles Lauerne Singleton, a death row inmate who refused to take antipsychotic medication to make him sane, and therefore able to be executed, struck at what many critics contend is an impossible and unacceptable ethical dilemma. A 1986 U.S. Supreme Court decision held that it was unconstitutional under the Eighth Amendment to execute inmates if they were declared insane (Liptak, 2003a). Psychiatrists, according to the American Medical Association (AMA) are prohibited from providing treatment for the sole purpose of executing an inmate. In essence, the federal appeals decision weighed society's interest in punishing an inmate over his unwillingness to take medication. The latter perspective won.

Parker and Paine (1999) pose various circumstances, or questions, that raise issues of prisoners' rights to having control over their own bodies:

> For example, can it be said that the state has a 'legitimate penological interest' in providing medical treatment to a competent inmate who withholds consent even though he reasonably is expected to die without it? Or do broader societal concerns come into play? Does it matter if the inmate is terminally ill, though death is not imminent, and the medication or surgery will only prolong his suffering? What if death is on the horizon and the treatment will postpone it only for a very short time? On the other hand, what if the inmate has been injured in an accident and would die without treatment, which in all probability would restore him to health? Finally, what right does the state have to treat a competent inmate who is terminally ill, but who has expressed the desire to die? (p. 241)

Being totally dependent upon the government severely compromises an inmate's ability to exercise his or her judgment, and this cannot be ignored in any discussions of ethics and health care. There is little doubt the future will witness an increasing number of cases in the court system, and eventually in the Supreme Court, addressing the issues associated with inmate rights to refuse treatment.

ETHICAL ISSUES

The increase in prison populations during the 1980s and 1990s resulted in an increase in the number of violations of prisoner rights, reflecting both overcrowding and a shift in attitudes toward prisoner rights. These ethical and legal violations have spurred the creation of ethical codes involving prisoner care (Reams, Smith, Fletcher & Spencer, 1999). The following four stories raise ethical dilemmas that increasingly will be found in correctional systems across the country. The "solutions" to these four cases, however, are not without controversy and considerable economic and social costs to the nation. These stories raise key questions that strike at the heart of society's responses to the health and welfare of inmates in its care. These case examples, in addition, emphasize the need for prison systems to individualize their health services at considerable financial costs to the public.

CASE EXAMPLE 1. "INMATE'S TRANSPLANT PROMPTS QUESTIONS OF COSTS AND ETHICS" (STERNGOLD, 2002)

A California inmate received a heart transplant that was expected to cost California taxpayers approximately $1 million. The initial surgery cost $200,000, but the total bill would add up to $1 million. The courts have determined that inmates cannot be denied medical treatment just because they are incarcerated. Lengthy prison sentences combined with inmates with chronic diseases are expected to place greater demands upon correctional systems providing organ transplants in the foreseeable future. Should inmates be recipients of health services that effectively are limited to a relatively small percentage of the general population?

CASE EXAMPLE 2. "PRISONER WANTS TO DONATE HIS SECOND KIDNEY" (JOSEFSON, 1999)

An inmate offered to donate his remaining kidney to his daughter. He had donated his first kidney to his estranged daughter in 1996. David Patterson was currently serving a 13-year term for burglary and heroin possession. Giving his second kidney effectively would shorten his life. However, doing so also would cost the state of California taxpayers $50,000 per year for dialysis. Do prisoners have ultimate control over their bodies? A related question is, can the state effectively terminate the life of a non-inmate by limiting the donation of the inmate's organs?

CASE EXAMPLE 3. "DO PRISON INMATES HAVE A RIGHT TO VEGETARIAN MEALS?" (OGDEN, 2001)

In an effort to keep costs down, prison dieticians provide uniform meals. Therefore, providing certain inmates with special meals has tremendous implications for systems predicated on serving thousands of inmates efficiently and effectively. Is provision of "special" meals a right or privilege? Must vegetarian meals be specific to religious or health demands? The consequences of individualizing meals require that prison systems both acknowledge the rights of inmates to request "special" treatment and, in the process, change important prison routines.

CASE EXAMPLE 4. "INMATE'S SUIT ASKS STATE TO PAY FOR SEX CHANGE" (ASSOCIATED PRESS, 2002A)

Robert Krosilek sued the Massachusetts Department of Corrections in federal court to have the state pay for a sex-change operation and hormone therapy to allow him to live as a woman. He contended that the department was violating his civil rights and subjecting him to cruel and unusual punishment by refusing to provide this service. Court prison policy in Massachusetts does not allow male inmates to commence female hormones while in prison. The response from District Attorney John Moses was, "Here is a guy who's been convicted of brutally murdering a beautiful young woman and he's been ordered to serve the rest of his life without parole in prison, and we're supposed to be concerned about his sexual orientation and give him a free sex-change operation? It doesn't make any sense to me." The financial costs of this service were not provided in the article, but can be considered to be well into the thousands of dollars, not to mention the legal precedent it would set in the state.

U.S. District Court Judge Mark L. Wolf found that Mr. Krosilek was entitled to psychotherapeutic treatment for his "gender disorder." The Court, however, did not recommend hormone therapy or a sex-change operation (Cambanis, 2002). Yet, if a doctor providing treatment to Mr. Krosilek recommends either hormone therapy or the sex-change surgery, prison officials only can deny such treatment for security reasons. Then, the matter will ultimately have to be returned and settled in court and a decision rendered based on a determination of whether or not withholding of treatment is unconstitutionally cruel and unusual punishment and a violation of the Eighth Amendment. The significance of the decision was not lost on Judge Wolf: "'The idea that an imprisoned male murderer may ever have a right to receive female hormones and sex reassignment surgery may understandably strike people as bizarre,' Wolf wrote in his ruling. But he said, prison officials can't prevent Kosilek from getting treatment, including hormone therapy or surgery, out of 'a fear of public and political criticism.'" (Cambanis, 2002, p. B5)

Faiver (1998e) notes that it has been arduous for health care personnel not to breach ethical and legal rights:

> Despite their initial strong commitment to ethical principles, many health professionals after some time in corrections begin to experience a lessening of sensitivity and a blunting of these ideals. The erosion is a gradual process, and often appears to be proportionate to the degree of direct contact with inmates. The erosion also will be greater the more the professional is isolated from his or her peers. (p. 253)

The authors have touched upon a subject that is not popular with the general public, yet it cannot be ignored without great costs to the public. Institutions wield tremendous influence over the behavior of people who work within them. Total institutions, however, wield even greater influence, and this must be taken into account in the hiring, training, and supervision of staff.

There is a wide failure to understand that a set of ethical principles and an ethical decision-making process benefit both prison officials and inmates alike. Hornblum's 1998 book detailing the abuses and exploitation of inmates in the name of medical science chronicles the potential for abuse of inmate rights by the absence of a bioethical code of ethics with specific considerations of prisoners in the United States. The American Correctional Health Services Association Code of Ethics is one example of an effort to institute a bioethical code of ethics within correctional health services (Reams, 1998, p. 62).

THE AMERICAN CORRECTIONAL HEALTH
SERVICES ASSOCIATION CODE OF ETHICS

1. Inmates shall be evaluated as a patient or client in each and every health encounter.
2. Medical treatment shall be rendered only when it is justified by an accepted medical diagnosis. Treatment and invasive procedures shall be rendered after informed consent.
3. Inmates shall have the right to refuse care and treatment. Involuntary treatment shall be reserved for emergency situations in which there is grave disability or immediate threat of danger to the inmate or others.
4. Health care services shall be provided with respect to sound privacy in all cases and sight privacy, regardless of custody status.
5. All inmates shall be provided health care services regardless of custody status.
6. Correctional health professionals shall be identified and shall not represent themselves as other than their licenses permit.
7. Correctional health professionals shall collect and analyze specimens only for diagnostic testing based on sound medical principles.
8. Body cavity searches shall be performed by those health professionals who have received training in proper techniques and who are not in a patient-provider relationship with the inmate.
9. Health professionals shall not be involved in any aspect of execution of the death penalty.
10. All medical information shall be confidential and health care records shall be maintained and transported in a confidential manner.
11. Health professionals shall honor custody functions but shall not participate in such functions as escorting, forced transfers, security supervision, strip searches or witnessing use of force.
12. Correctional health personnel shall undertake biomedical research on inmates only when the research methods meet all requirements for experimentation on human subjects and when individual inmates or prison populations are expected to derive benefits from the results of the research.

The bioethical code of ethics listed above represents an important step in the process of ensuring inmates receive needed health care by helping health providers better understand their responsibilities and potential ethical dilemmas.

Reams, Smith, Fletcher, and Spencer (1998, p. 112) present two case studies of inmates to illustrate the bioethical dilemmas often found in prisons:

J. W. is an HIV-positive inmate whose illness is progressing steadily. The infectious disease consultant recommends an expensive "cocktail" of medicines that are now J. W.'s only hope of survival. The warden warns that the prison cannot afford this treatment regimen. J. W. and his lawyer argue that he is entitled to health care in prison. Is J. W. entitled to these expensive medicines? What if paying for this treatment means that other prison programs must be cancelled? Is it in society's best interest to prolong J. W.'s life? Suppose J. W. is a convicted murderer serving a life sentence?

S. M. is an inmate who is suspected of concealing matches in her vagina. The warden asks the nurse to perform a pelvic examination. S. M. refuses. Should the nurse force S. M. to undergo the examination? Does the nurse have a greater duty to her supervisor or to the autonomy of her patient? If she does not perform the examination, will her job be in jeopardy? If she does force it, will she be an effective health care provider for S. M. in the future? Can S. M. charge the nurse with assault? What if S. M. has threatened to harm herself or others with the matches?

J. W. and S. M. are not atypical cases in today's prison system. Health care providers, not surprisingly, often encounter ethical dilemmas unlike those found by their colleagues who are not in prison settings. Ethical decision making pertaining to resource rationing, inmate rights, confidentiality, informed consent, and divided loyalties is commonplace and indicative of why a bioethical program is essential in prisons (Reams, Smith, Fletcher & Spencer, 1998). However, some of the inherent contradictions, or tensions, make the introduction of a bioethical program difficult to accomplish.

Of special concern is access to, and quality of, health care in privatized prisons, that is, those that are operated under contracts by private, for-profit corporations. Concerns were sufficiently severe to influence many states to roll back or rescind contracts by 2000 (Greene, 2003). However, some state and city prison systems have continued to award contracts to private companies even though there have been serious problems in the delivery of quality health services (Zielbauer, 2005a,b).

Nowhere is the death of the American dream more apparent than among this nation's correctional prisoners (Ratcliff & Craig, 2004). The loss of opportunity to achieve and contribute most often is mentioned when discussing prisoners. However, the long-term care needs of these prisoners and the likelihood of death behind bars compound the prospects of life behind prison walls (Allen & Bell, 1998; Conklin, Lincoln & Tuthill, 2000). This is not unique to the United States. Britain, too, is facing similar challenges (Katz, 2001).

This nation has faced numerous challenges in its history, one of which has been reconciliation of the presence of racism in the world's "leading democracy." Reverend Jesse Jackson (2001) was quite eloquent in stating this very point:

> America, known the world over as the land of the free, was founded on the principle of liberty and justice for all. Our freedoms are to be envied in many respects . . . Yet, at the same time, some 2 million of our citizens are denied their freedom . . . We incarcerate more of our citizens than any other nation. At some point we must ask ourselves: What is the moral price we pay as a nation for locking up our youth rather than lifting them up? Until something is done about this staggering practice we can no longer claim to be "the land of the free." (p. 1)

Striving to be a world leader naturally results in other nations carefully weighing whether or not this is truly the case, or simply public relations "spin."

II

HEALTH NEEDS,
APPROACHES, AND FINANCES

5

HIGH-PROFILE
HEALTH CARE NEEDS

The health issues, diseases, and illnesses covered in this book do not exist in isolation from each other, and this compounds any efforts to address the health needs of prisoners in this country (Davis, 2002; Watson, Stimpson & Hostick, 2004). For example, those with HIV/AIDS also may have histories of substance abuse, physical and sexual abuse, dual diagnosis (mental illness and substance abuse), tuberculosis, or hepatitis B or C. Their health status may be compounded by racism, sexism, heterosexism, learning disabilities, poor history of receiving quality health care, or functional illiteracy. Sociodemographic factors such as gender, age, and race and ethnicity, in turn, further challenge health care delivery within prisons (Davis, 2002). One prison health researcher, speaking in *World Disease Weekly*, summed up how prison conditions can exacerbate the health issues of incoming inmates:

> And once they're incarcerated, they're more likely to get other diseases. It makes correctional facilities into ticking time bombs. Many people crowded together, often suffering from diseases that weaken their immune systems, form a potential breeding ground and reservoir for diseases. (2006b, p. 160)

Over ten years ago, the New York City Department of Corrections that housed 18,000 inmates per day identified the complexity of health needs that confronted correctional systems across the country (NYC Department of Corrections, 1997). One in eight male inmates and more than one in four females was HIV positive, one in eight inmates had a sexually transmitted disease (STD), and one out of six New Yorkers diagnosed with tuberculosis (TB) was a former or current jail inmate. One out of four inmates had some form of mental illness. One out of ten had severe and persistent mental illness. The vast majority of city inmates (75% to 95%) had a history of substance abuse. The New York City Department of Corrections was not unique in this country, and many of the issues faced in this system could be found in other regions. No place in the country is immune from the challenges facing correctional systems as they very often struggle to carry out a multifaceted mission in the twenty-first century (Davis, 2002).

Taking a holistic approach means to appreciate the interplay of these and other factors. Yet, each illness has unique aspects and deserves individual attention. Therefore, this chapter examines several high-incidence illnesses or subgroups that proliferate in prisons. High-incidence diseases also tend to be those for which there is a consensus as to their seriousness. In essence, they become "high-profile" health care needs within correctional systems. Low-profile needs will be addressed in chapter 6.

Often, advocates' efforts have put these issues onto the national landscape, and their prominence beyond prison walls, therefore, represents the end result of a concerted political campaign. Unfortunately, successful efforts at making an issue "high-profile" through reports, research publicity, and litigation ultimately may mean that other issues are overlooked, making them "low-profile." In addition, being well known as illnesses of prisoners may tend further to stigmatize those people with the illnesses among the larger population as well as among prisoners.

Co-morbidity between certain types of illnesses or diseases such as substance abuse and HIV, or mental health and substance abuse, are not well addressed among the general population and, as a result, are even more difficult to address within a total institution such as a prison (Davis, 2002). Acknowledging this does not mean, however, that we can therefore repeat society's mistakes within prisons. We do not have the luxury, or the right, simply to take the easy way out. Golembeski and Fullilove (2005) point out that the "prison-industrial complex" only has increased in size since the 1970s, and they argue for a more humanistic and community-centered approach to incarceration and community reentry. Not surprisingly, disproportionate rates of incarceration, as already noted in chapter 2, result in disproportionate health disparities involving low-income populations of color (Gaiter, Potter & O'Leary, 2006).

SUBSTANCE ABUSE

We purposefully start addressing high-profile health issues by starting with substance abuse. The subject of substance abuse certainly has garnered its share of attention in both the public and scholarly spheres. There is little dispute that substance abuse is a major social issue in this country. Its high-profile nature is evidenced by how the nation's presidents have addressed the subject in policies, including the creation of the Office of National Drug Policy, otherwise known as the Office of the Drug Czar. The rate of drug-involved prisoners must be seen as a health issue within the nation's prisons, necessitating the availability of programs and services to help inmates with substance-abusing histories to obtain rehabilitation (Blint, 2001; Inciardi, Martin & Butzin, 2004; Marks, 1999; McCaffrey, 2000; Welsh & Zajac, 2004; Zielbauer, 2003a). Narevic and colleagues (2006) found that inmates with substance-abusing backgrounds reported more episodes of serious illness, more mental health problems, and poorer self-rated health.

Virtually no subgroup of inmates has escaped involvement with drugs. Older offenders, for example, are no exception. Arndt, Turvey, and Flaum (2002) report that 71% of older inmates (fifty-five and older) have had a substance abuse problem, yet treatment is rarely tailored for the age of the inmate. In 1996, anywhere from 70 to 85% of prison inmates were in need of some type of substance abuse treatment (Belenko, Peugh, Califano Jr. & Foster, 1999). Belenko and Peugh (2005), using data from 1997, estimated that one-third of female inmates and one-half of male inmates needed residential treatment, and half of males and one-third of females may need no treatment. It is estimated that states spend approximately 5% of their overall state prison budgets on substance abuse treatment (Belenko, Peugh, Califano Jr. & Foster, 1999). Daley and colleagues (2004) concluded, based on a study of Connecticut's in-prison substance abuse treatment program, that treatment is cost-effective. Belenko and Peugh (2005), however, have concluded that treatment capacities in state prisons are inadequate to meet the needs at all stages and levels of care. Federal prisons do not fare as well, with spending estimated at 0.9% of the total federal prison budget going for such treatment.

The relationship between substance abuse and multiple health issues such as HIV, hepatitis B and C, and mental illness is very strong. Co-occurrence of any illnesses or diseases raises incredible issues in structuring delivery of services within and outside of prisons. Hartwell (2004), in a study of offenders with mental illness only and offenders with a dual diagnosis of mental illness and substance abuse, found that substance abuse was an "important feature" that influences both real and perceived levels of functioning, engagement with the criminal justice system, and reliance on social service organizations in the community.

Varghese and Fields (1999) specifically address the close relationship between substance abuse and infectious diseases within correctional settings and note their high correlation. Programs must be tied actively to other health, education, and social services to be effective and need to be coordinated with outside resources, too (Belenko, 2000).The health consequences associated with injection drug use are well known, and HIV is not the single concern. For example, hepatitis C (HCV) is a highly transmittable disease through injection drug use. It is estimated that anywhere from 70 to 89% of individuals who inject drugs become infected within a one-year period (*Positive Populations*, 2003e). The physical health status of inmates with substance abuse histories very often has deteriorated over the years and has taken a secondary role to drug use. Consequently, prison health personnel are confronted with severe health conditions that compound detoxification and recovery from substance abuse (Belenko, Peugh, Califano Jr., & Foster, 1999).

Nowhere is this need considered greatest than with the dually diagnosed (substance abuse and mental illness) prison population (Wexler, 2003). Dual diagnosis of substance abuse and mental illness, unfortunately, is not uncommon (Gaseau, 2001a; Hellard & Aitken, 2004). Reynolds, Mezey, Chapman, Wheeler, Drummond, and Baldacchino (2005) found high rates of co-morbid, post-traumatic stress disorders (PTSD) and associated distress, and substance dependence and misuse. Missina and Grella (2006), in turn, in a study among female inmates, found a high prevalence of childhood trauma.

Inmates who have serious mental illness and substance abuse problems face incredible challenges in having their health needs met within and outside of prisons (Maue, 2001). It is not unusual to have one problem identified and the other overlooked. (National Alliance for the Mentally Ill, 2001). The American Psychiatric Association (2000) estimates that 75% of those inmates with serious mental illnesses also have co-occurring substance abuse disorders, and they are more likely to be incarcerated four to five times longer than those inmates without mental illnesses.

Fiscella, Pless, Meldrum, and Fiscella (2004) raise ethical and constitutional questions about how alcohol and opiate withdrawal are addressed in jails. Further, it would be a serious mistake to think that prisons are drug-free settings and that, therefore, prisoners naturally will detoxify during the incarceration. Prisoners rarely are able to remain drug-free or achieve rehabilitation while incarcerated. On the contrary, the availability of low-quality, and sometimes toxic, drugs perpetuate drug-using habits (Mahon, 1996). The use of inhalants in prisons is almost impossible to prevent because of the availability of cleaning fluids of various kinds. One Tennessee state prisons study found that approximately 28% of inmates reported injecting drugs while in prison (*New York Times*, 2001b).

Efforts to escape the harsh surroundings of prisons lend themselves to a search for mind-altering substances and efforts to self-medicate (Cook, 2001). One survey of former prisoners found that 88% said they could obtain drugs easily during their sentences, and 46% reported that their imprisonment made them more likely to use drugs than had they not been imprisoned (*Los Angeles Times*, 2000; *New York Times*, 2001b). Increased engagement in other risk-taking behaviors such as tattooing and gambling, for example, also represents efforts to deal with boredom.

According to the Bureau of Justice Statistics, the overwhelming majority (83%) of incarcerated women have substance abuse problems and/or were using alcohol, drugs, or both during the commission of their crime or in the month prior to their incarceration (Kim, 2003). "Nearly one in three women serving time in state prisons reported committing the offense to obtain money to support a drug habit" (National Institute of Corrections, 2003, p. 6). In contrast, a survey completed by the Substance Abuse and Mental Health Services Administration indicates significantly lower rates of alcohol and/or drug use among the general population of women older than twelve. Specifically, 2.1% of females surveyed had engaged in heavy alcohol use within thirty days preceding the survey, 4.1% had used an illicit drug, and 1.2% had used a psychotherapeutic drug for a nonmedical purpose (National Institute of Corrections, 2003).

Langan and Pelissier (2001) note that almost all prison-based substance abuse treatment programs have been designed with male prisoners as the primary population group in need, neglecting the special health and social needs of female inmates. This male-focused model neglects to also take into consideration that female inmates with drug histories have used drugs more frequently, used "harder" drugs, and used them for different reasons than their male counterparts. That drug abuse often occurs along with other issues is especially evident for women prisoners (Sterk, Theall & Elifson, 2005).

Incarcerated women with substance-abusing backgrounds have more and different treatment needs from their male counterparts (Fogel, 1993; Kelly, 2003; Smith & Dailard, 1994; Singer, Bussey, Song, & Lunghofer, 1995). According to Peters, Strozier, Murrin, and Kearns (1998), women more often than men have histories of depression and emotional, physical, and sexual abuse. They also are more likely to have used cocaine (90% versus 80% for men), more likely to have used it in the thirty days prior to incarceration (76% versus 61% for men), and more likely to have used it on each of the prior thirty days (58% versus 12% for men). Blitz, Wolff, and Paap (2006), on a positive note, report on how women inmates in New Jersey state prisons have been able to improve their access to treatment.

HIV/AIDS

HIV/AIDS in prisons is a public health concern in this country that cannot continue to be ignored (Bureau of Justice Statistics, 2008; DeCarlo & Zack, 1996; Hellard & Aitken, 2004; MacGowan et al., 2006; Moseley & Tewsbury, 2006; National Commission on Correctional Health Care, 2005a; *New York Times*, 2001b; Stone, 1997; Zaitzow, 2001). MacGown and colleagues (2006) note that early diagnosis of HIV infection has tremendous medical and public health benefits. Myers and colleagues (2005), for example, stress the importance of comprehensive service delivery planning for returning inmates, such as men and women at risk for contracting HIV, who further compromise the health of their communities. It is estimated that a lifetime treatment cost of $186,900 can be saved by preventing HIV infection, raising the fiscal importance of prevention (Varghese & Peterman, 2003). A 2001 estimate of the costs of providing care to inmates with HIV or AIDS placed the amounts at $80,396 per year for those inmates who were HIV-positive and $105,963 for inmates with AIDS (*The Body*, 2001b). These costs can be expected to increase as overall prison populations increase, even if percents of inmates with HIV/AIDS decrease, particularly in systems that have a high disproportionate number of inmates of color.

There is a lack of consensus on the need for, and importance of, mandatory testing of prison inmates, though (Amankwaa, Amankwaa, & Ochie, 1999; Spaulding et al., 2002). Reliance on inmates asking for an HIV test, versus mandatory testing, is one reason for the lower percentage of inmate testing in states that have only voluntary testing (*AIDS Alert Archives*, 2000). One Wisconsin state prison study found that nearly one-third of HIV-1 seropositive inmates refused to be tested voluntarily for HIV (Hoxie et al., 1998). Testing, of course, facilitates the early identification and treatment of those with the virus (Byrne, 1997).

In 2005, the National Commission on Correctional Health Care (2005a) estimated that as many as 17% of all HIV-positive people in the United States were processed through the criminal justice system every year. Between 20–26% of people with HIV/AIDS have spent time in correctional systems (Kantor, 2006). Despite the unreliability of prison statistics on HIV/AIDS, it generally can be assumed that HIV/AIDS is represented disproportionately within the prison population (Blankenship, Smoyer, Bray, & Mattocks, 2005; Collica, 2002; Gibson, 2005).

Prison statistics on HIV and AIDS may not reflect the full extent of infection because a lack of uniform policies on testing makes statistics on prison infection rates unreliable. In 2006, only twenty-one states tested all inmates at admission or at some time during imprisonment. Forty state prison systems and the federal prison system tested if inmates had symptoms; requested a test; or were involved in an incident of possible transmission. Sixteen states and the federal prison system tested what the Bureau of Justice Statistics called persons in "high risk" groups (Bureau of Justice Statistics, 2008).

Yet, it may be dangerous for a prisoner to be known as having HIV/AIDS. Pugh (1998) provides one such illustration:

> During his seven years in prison, Marco Fernandez has explained his weekly trips to the pharmacy and 27-pill-a day drug regimen as the down side of a long battle with liver disease. It's a ruse that allows the former drug dealer from Miami a strange measure of credibility and security from harassment. There's no honor in picking on a sick man at Coleman Federal Correctional Institution in Florida's Sumpter County. Unless, of course, that man has AIDS. "You've got ignorant individuals in here, and they can sabotage you if they know you're got HIV," said Fernandez, who spoke freely. "They'll burn up your room or stick a knife under your bed or plant some marijuana so the guards can find it and put you in the hole," he says. "It's a dirty business in here" (p. 1).

The growth in the number of inmates who are HIV-positive has slowed and even decreased, and, between 2002 and 2003, that number decreased by 1% (Bureau of Justice Statistics, 2005b). Between 2003 and 2004, the number of prisoners who were HIV-positive continued to fall, from 23,663 in 2003 to 23,046 in 2004 (U.S. Newswire, 2006). This decrease was reflected in twenty states. However, twenty-four states and the federal system reported increases during the 2003 to 2004 period (U.S. Newswire, 2006). From 2005 to 2006, there was a 3.1% decrease in the number of HIV-positive prisoners, even though the prison population grew by 2.2% in that period (Bureau of Justice Statistics, 2008). Nevertheless, 1.6% of male and 2.4% of female state and federal prisoners tested HIV-positive or had AIDS at the end of 2006. This reflected an increase for females but a decrease for males from 2005. At the end of 2006, New York, Texas, and Florida had nearly half (46%) of all prisoners who had either HIV or were confirmed to have AIDS. New York reported that over 5% of its male inmates were HIV-positive. Three states had more than 7% of their women inmates known to be HIV-positive; New York reported 12.2%, and both Florida and New Jersey reported 7.6% (Bureau of Justice Statistics, 2008).

Women inmates often have higher rates than their male counterparts, particularly for those under the age of twenty-five (Bureau of Justice Statistics, 2008; Fogel & Belyea, 1999; Palevitz, 2001). Women in state and federal prisons had a rate of 2.4% compared to 1.6% for men (Bureau of Justice Statistics, 2008). HIV-positive women in prisons also are most likely to be of color. In 2000, in Texas, which had the second-most incarcerated women in the country behind California, 72.4% of the women who were HIV-positive were African American, and 2.4% were Latinas (Onorato, 2001).

African American women, as a subgroup, are experiencing a dramatic increase in HIV/AIDS. According to the Centers for Disease Control and Prevention, they accounted for 64% of all new HIV/AIDS cases among women in the United States; unprotected sex with men was responsible for 75% of the new infections, with sharing needles during drug taking accounting for 25% (Ballard, 2001). The development of new testing methods, such as the use of oral HIV testing, have been found to promote voluntary testing in prisons, however, particularly among males and African Americans (Bauserman, Ward, & Swetz, 2001).

Women inmates are particularly vulnerable to the consequences associated with improper treatment for HIV and AIDS while incarcerated. The National Commission on Correctional Health Care (2005a) recommends, for example, that all pregnant women inmates be tested for HIV. Female inmates with HIV have a higher injection drug use rate than their male counterparts (Centers for Disease Control, 2001c). The AIDS virus makes infected women more susceptible to cancer (Hader et al., 2001; Palevitz, 2001). This susceptibility, it is speculated, is due to elevated secondary infections with human papillomavirus (HPV). HPV is the major cause of cervical cancer and also may play a role in some other cancers (National Cancer Institute, 2004).

Franklin, Fearn, and Franklin (2005) comment on the implications of an increased risk for HIV/AIDS for female inmates:

> This risk presents a significant public health concern as the majority of female offenders receive limited screening, treatment, education, and counseling related to HIV/AIDS infection and transmission while in prison. Additionally, when these women return to their communities, they are generally ill-equipped to prevent the transmission of their disease (p. 99).

The increased number of inmates with histories of substance abuse has resulted in an increased number of HIV-positive cases in prisons (Frank,

1999; Moseley & Tewsbury, 2006). For example, one estimate has 4% of women in prison and 18% in New York state prisons as being HIV-positive (Women's Prison Association, 2003a). Overall, prisoners with HIV or AIDS entering correctional institutions most likely contracted the virus through the use of injection drug use. According to the Centers for Disease Control and Prevention, 61% of all inmates have injected drugs compared with an injection drug rate of 27% among nonincarcerated people with AIDS (Dean-Gaitor & Fleming, 1999).

Inmates with HIV bring with them a host of health care needs that go beyond just the physical (National Commission on Correctional Health Care, 2005a). Zinkernagel and others (2001), for example, found that HIV infection often is associated with serious mental health problems such as anxiety and depression. Women who are HIV-positive often go without receiving needed mental health counseling (*Mental Health Weekly*, 2001b). African American women as a subgroup are even more likely to go without mental health services or needed psychotherapeutic medications.

The overall rate of prisoners confirmed to have AIDS (0.46%) was more than two and a half the rate of that of the general population (0.17%) (Bureau of Justice Statistics, 2008). Massachusetts and New York reported the highest percentage of confirmed AIDS cases with 1.3% each, followed by Maryland (1.2%) and North Carolina (1.1%). In 2006, there were 5,674 inmates in state (5,018) and federal (656) prisons with confirmed AIDS (Bureau of Justice Statistics, 2008).

AIDS is the second-leading cause of deaths in all prisons, following natural causes, and is about three times higher than in the total U.S. population, 20% versus 6% (AIDS in Prison Project, 2001). AIDS is the leading cause of death among women prisoners (Fogel & Belyea, 1999). By 2006, the number of AIDS-related deaths in state prisons had decreased substantially, to 155 from 176 in 2005, and over 1,000 in 1995. The decrease went from 100 deaths per 100,000 in 1995 to 25 per 100,000 (Bureau of Justice Statistics, 2001a, 2008). One study comparing prison and total AIDS-related deaths found that African Americans comprised more than two-thirds of prison cases, compared to 39% of total cases (Kantor, 2006). The three state prison systems with the highest number of inmate deaths from AIDS in 2006 (Bureau of Justice Statistics, 2008) were Florida (28), New York (14), Pennsylvania (13), Georgia (10) and Louisiana (10).

Significant progress has been made in reducing AIDS-related deaths in prisons. In 2006, as already noted, New York reported fourteen deaths due to AIDS. In 1996, 907 New York state prison inmates died as a result of AIDS, or 29% of all deaths of state prisoners (Altman, 1999). AIDS accounted for two-thirds of all deaths during the decade of the 1990s in New York state prisons (*AIDS Alert* Archives, 2000; Centers for Disease Control and Prevention, 2001).

MENTAL ILLNESS

The subject of mental illness is complex regardless of the population group being discussed, and its complexity only is increased when discussing prisoners. The broadness of the subject matter necessitates that it be examined from a variety of subareas. For the purposes of this chapter, the authors have elected to include a variety of conditions that have received what we believe to be the greatest attention.

Public discussion or debate about mental illness in the past often resulted from communities resisting the placement of residential settings within their community. However, the discussion of mental illness slowly but quite dramatically has changed to that of prisons and the incarceration and treatment of inmates. This shift, which some would argue has been slow in coming, only can be understood fully or appreciated through a multifaceted set of lenses. The processing of the "mentally ill" through the criminal justice system rather than the mental health system represented a significant shift in policy in this country and can be traced back to the early 1970s (Dike, 2006; Harcourt, 2007). In 1959, it was estimated that there were 559,000 patients in the nation's state mental health hospitals; by the late 1990s this number had decreased significantly to approximately 70,000 (Doherty, 2002). Public concern about violence and potential violence by individuals with mental illness largely has fueled this shift (Lamberti, Weisman & Faden, 2004; Monahan, 2004).

Inmates with serious and persistent mental illnesses have a higher likelihood of being imprisoned for violent offenses when compared to their counterparts without mental illness, and they are twice as likely to have been homeless twelve months prior to their arrest and incarceration (Ortiz, 2001). Watson, Simpson, and Hostick (2004) concluded that having a mental health problem is a causative factor for imprisonment. Feller (2006), in turn, raises serious concerns about the interplay between inmates with mental illness and the role that prisons play in exacerbating their conditions.

There is a considerable range in the reported prevalence of mental illness within correctional facilities, and this may well be due to differences in defining mental illness and because these statistics are based on service utilization (Anno, 2001; Fazel & Lubbe, 2005; Veysey & Bichler-Robertson, 2003a). Also, mental health needs often do not occur in isolation from other health needs. For example, it is estimated that one in three inmates with HIV also can suffer from anxiety disorders. If untreated, the risk of depression and suicide also can increase (National Commission on Correctional Health Care, 2005a).

In 2000, approximately 10% of state inmates received psychotropic medications, and 12.5% received mental health therapy or counseling (Bureau of Justice Statistics, 2001b). The American Psychiatric Association (2000) estimates that 20% of the nation's prisoners have serious mental illness, and 5% are actively psychotic. The National Commission on Correctional Health Care estimates that 18% of state prisoners have major depression, and 22–30% have an anxiety disorder (*Health & Medicine Weekly*, 2003). According to the Bureau of Justice Statistics (2006), 64% of jail, 56% of state, and 45% of federal prisoners had a "mental health problem" in the twelve months prior to the research that was conducted.

The National Commission on Correctional Health Care (2005b) found that the prevalence of female offenders with mental illness paralleled that of men and that women offenders were more likely to have histories of dual diagnoses. A 1994–1995 study of female inmates in California, Connecticut, and Florida found that 31% of the inmates receiving treatment for mental health disorders reported that they were not receiving medical supervision (Acoca, 1998). The Department of Justice estimates that female inmates are treated for mental illness at a higher rate when compared to males; 25% of the female inmates receive treatment compared to 10% of male inmates (*USA Today*, 2001).

Roskes, Feldman, Arrington, and Leisher (1999) note in their assessment of the challenges faced by offenders with severe and persistent mental illness that, as a group, they are probably the most stigmatized mental health population group in society:

> The need for treatment of the mentally disordered is no less, and perhaps much greater, than the need of the average non-forensic community mental health client. In addition to carrying the burden of severe and persistent mental illness, often with co-morbid addiction, these people

suffer the added stigma that society attaches to the convicted criminal. Psychiatrists and other mental health professionals are not immune to fear of and distaste for these clients. In addition, treating professionals have the added concern of liability exposure when working with a clientele that has a history of dangerous behavior (p. 471).

For persons with co-occurring disorders, their frequency of contact with the criminal justice system increases dramatically when compared to persons with just mental illness or substance abuse (Redlich, Steadman, Robbins & Swanson, 2006; Shafer, Arthur & Franczak, 2004).

Inmates with severe and persistent mental illness represent a group that often is denigrated by both prisoners and guards alike (Edwards, 2000; Fellner & Abramsky, 2003). Their "unpredictability" makes them dangerous within prisons and jails where dependability and control of behavior are valued. Petersilia (2003), in a book specifically devoted to released inmates, found that inmates with mental illness were 1.4 times more likely to be injured while imprisoned and three times more likely to be sexually assaulted during their incarceration when compared to inmates without mental illness. Human Rights Watch (2003), in a rare study of suicide and self-mutilation in this nation's prisons, drew a direct association between an increase in self-injury behavior and an increased prevalence of mental illness among the incarcerated and inadequate provision of quality mental health care. Further, these inmates face a fearful community upon their release, and this increases the likelihood of their return to a life behind bars.

Torrey and colleagues (1993) pointed out in the early 1990s that criminalizing persons with severe mental illness would result in turning jails and prisons into de facto mental hospitals. There are a number of prisons that have claimed the distinction of being the "largest mental health hospitals" in the country. Rikers Island prison in New York City is widely considered to be this nation's largest mental hospital, and this reflects how the inmate profile has changed over the years. Barr (1999), in an extensive review of the New York State and City correctional systems, found that these institutions have replaced mental hospitals for New Yorkers with mental illness. It was estimated that the New York correctional system had 8,000 inmates with mental illness on any given day. In 1997, 15,000 New York City jail inmates were treated for mental illness with an additional 33,000 requiring some form of mental health service.

In late 2006, Florida experienced a constitutional crisis when the state courts threatened to fine the Florida Department of Children and Families over their unwillingness to follow the law and transfer inmates found incompetent to stand trial from county jails to psychiatric hospitals within a fifteen-day period (Goodnough, 2006). State officials argued that psychiatric hospitals did not have beds to accommodate these inmates. These inmates (averaging 300), in the meantime, stayed in county jails without receiving needed mental health treatment. During a one-week period, there were 307 inmates with mental illness to be transferred, including 72% who had waited past the fifteen-day period.

The term "criminalization of the mentally ill" first appeared in professional literature in 1972, coined by Marc Abramson (1972), and it captured the emergence of the trend to incarcerate the violators of the law who were suffering from severe and persistent mental illness (Lurigio, 2000). Lindeman (2000) uses the term "transinstitutization of the mentally ill" to explain the emergence of correctional institutions as the psychiatric hospitals of the twenty-first century. This trend, incidentally, is not restricted to the United States, with worldwide estimates placing prisoners with serious mental illness into the millions (Reuters Health Service, 2002).

The movement toward deinstitutionalizing the nation's state mental patients has resulted in over 90% of all psychiatric beds being eliminated nationwide without needed community supports being developed. It is estimated that the United States currently has more persons with mental illness in prisons and jails than in all of the state mental hospitals combined (Sigurdson, 2000). One estimate puts it at three times that of psychiatric hospitals (Satel, 2003). The nation's three largest "mental health" facilities are the Los Angeles County Jail, Rikers Island in New York, and Cook County Jail in Chicago. Critics of how this nation meets the needs of inmates with severe and persistent mental illness are quick to point out that prisons have de facto replaced mental hospitals (Kupers, 1996). In 2000, it was estimated that approximately 10% of all state inmates were receiving psychotropic medication, with Hawaii, Maine, Montana, Nebraska, and Oregon reporting 20% rates for their inmates (CNN.Com, 2001).

Hospitalized mental patients in the general population numbered 80,000 in 1999 from a high of 560,000 in 1955 (Harcourt, 2008; Kupers, 1999). In comparison, a U.S. Department of Justice study estimated that, in the year 2000, there were 191,000 state prisoners, or 16% of the total inmate population, who could be classified as mentally ill (*Mental Health Weekly*, 2001a). When taking into account jail and federal prisoners, the number increases to 250,000 (U.S. Department of Justice, 2001). A comparative study of the United States and the United Kingdom found that U.S. prison inmates were two to four times more likely than the general population to be psychotic or seriously depressed, and ten times more likely to display antisocial behavior (Reuters Health Service, 2002).

The interrelationship between mental health and other factors, such as substance abuse, HIV/AIDS, suicide, and aging, is unmistakable and results in increased challenges to providing effective therapy/counseling (Goulet et al., 1998; Maue, 2001; Watson, Simpson & Hostick, 2004). In a study of great relevance for prison inmates, although it took place in a public mental hospital, researchers found that mental health patients were also at greater risk for contracting HIV, tuberculosis, and hepatitis B and C than the general population (Mozes, 2000). Patients were four to five times more likely to get hepatitis B and twelve times more likely to get hepatitis C. Approximately 20% tested positive for tuberculosis, and 3% tested positive for HIV. Homelessness prior to incarceration often is associated with mental health issues and many different types of illnesses. Kushel, Hahn, Evans, Bangsberg, and Moss (2005), for example, concluded that the health risks among ex-inmates who were homeless prior to incarceration were higher when compared to counterparts who were not homeless. Further, almost one-forth of the homeless (23.1%) had a history of imprisonment. Increasingly, these inmates are older adults (Shah, 2006).

A 1994–1996 Connecticut prison study of female inmates found that they have a high prevalence of mental illness, which places them at an increased risk for contracting HIV because of a history of substance abuse and risky sexual behavior (Goulet et al., 1998). In part due to their histories of physical and sexual abuse, incarcerated women are also more likely to have higher rates of mental health issues than women in the general population and than male inmates. Depression, post-traumatic stress disorder (PTSD), and substance abuse are the leading mental health diagnoses of incarcerated women (National Institute of Corrections, 2003). When compared to the general population, although female inmates have lower rates of anxiety-related disorders, they have higher rates of substance abuse, antisocial disorders, borderline personality disorders, and symptoms of post-traumatic stress disorder (Henderson, Schaeffer & Brown, 1998). When they are compared to male counterparts in prison, they are more likely to have used cocaine and heroin, have a coexisting psychiatric disorder, and a history of sexual and physical abuse (Henderson, Schaeffer & Brown 1998). However, depressed female inmates are less likely than male inmates to use mental health services for their depression (Baskin, Sommers, Tessler & Steadman, 1989).

Successful treatment of inmates with mental illness increases the likelihood of safer and healthier prison time for inmates with serious mental illness as well as those without this health condition (Veysey & Bichler-Robinson, 2003b). Elsner (2004) specifically comments on the challenges these inmates face while incarcerated:

> The mentally ill are some of the most tragic cases inhabiting the U.S. prison system. They are particularly poorly equipped to survive in the brutal prison world . . . may find it almost impossible to hide their fear and weaknesses. Antipsychotic medications may slow their reaction times, which makes them more vulnerable to being attacked and raped, which in turn exacerbates their mental state (p. 79).

Inmates with mental illness also have a greater chance of getting into fights, when compared with those who are not mentally ill.

Kupers (2000) raises serious questions about current correctional strategies and goals pertaining to inmates with mental illness:

> Instead of drawing the obvious conclusions that widespread overcrowding and forced idleness make prisons more dangerous, drive prisoners mad and reduce the chances for released felons to succeed at going straight, corrections authorities have resorted to a strategy involving much more punitive segregation, especially in supermaximum or maxi-maxi prison units (p. 8).

Metzner and Dvoskin (2006) advance the notion that mental health services within supermaximum security prisons need to take into account the unique context of these settings in the conceptualization and delivery of mental health services.

Also, inmates with severe mental illness rarely get released from jail or prison before their sentence is completed. One study in 1997 found that only one in five inmates across the country actually do so. These types of inmates generally are not considered good candidates for work-release programs or community alternatives to incarceration (Harrington, 1999). Once released following incarceration, most do not receive follow-up care, increasing the likelihood of returning to prison (*San Francisco Chronicle*,

2000). One prosecutor in Maine summed up quite well the revolving door that these inmates face (Harrison, 2005):

> I've been a prosecutor for 20 years and seen a fair number of mentally ill criminal defendants . . . I see a treadmill where mentally ill people go from the jail to the courthouse to the jail to the courthouse. Nothing thus far seems to have made a difference . . . If we can get them off the treadmill and plugged into services, everybody wins (p. B1).

The case of Charles Stevens, an inmate at Rikers Island in New York City, illustrates how this "revolving door" phenomenon is put in motion and what consequences it can have for both inmates and society alike:

> Nadine Stevens doesn't want her son released from jail—not unless the city can help him with his psychiatric troubles . . . Diagnosed as a para- noid schizophrenic, Stevens, 38, is one of 20,000 inmates Rikers Island treats for mental illness each year. As inmates, they receive medication and some therapy. But as soon as they are released, the mentally ill with- out family are typically dropped off in the middle of the night at a sub- way station with $3 in tokens or MetroCard fare . . . The city offers dis- charge planning for a small number of mentally ill inmates. But thousands of others receive no medication, no help getting Medicaid, no housing and no referral to mental health services (Hackett, 2000, p. 12).

It should be noted that the browning and feminization of prisons also can be found in New York City's correctional system in that 50% of the prisoners are African American and 35% are Latino. Women, although constituting 10% of the jail population, account for 17% of those utilizing mental health services (*Mental Health Weekly*, 2001a).

The Los Angeles County Jail system, with 16% of its inmates requir- ing mental health services on a daily basis, also is claimed to be de facto the largest mental hospital in the United States (Torrey, 1997). In addition, Cook County Jail in Illinois houses the county's largest population of per- sons with mental illness (Lyderson, 2000). In 2000, the state of Tennessee estimated that there were 3,500 inmates, or one in every five, who were mentally ill (Snyder, 2000).

SUICIDE

Daniels (2006) refers to the act of suicide within prisons as a "sentinel" event that requires a collaborative deterrence strategy across all sectors of a prison (administrative, custodial, and clinical staff). Hall and Gabor (2004) would extend this collaboration to include prisoners themselves. Not surprisingly, suicide is a significant cause of death in jails and prisons (Center on Crime, Communities & Culture, 1996; *Corrections Professional*, 2005k; Daniel & Fleming, 2006; Hanser, 2002; Hayes, 1999). It is ranked as the third leading cause of deaths for inmates, behind natural causes and AIDS (Bureau of Justice Statistics, 2005c).

Suicide rates in the nation's prisons have declined since the early 1980s. In state prisons suicide rates fell from 34 per 100,000 in 1980 to 16 per 100,000 in 1990, and have stabilized since then. In 2002, the average suicide rate in state prisons was 14 per 100,000 (Bureau of Justice Statistics, 2005c). Jail suicides, too, have declined from 129 per 100,000 in 1983 to 47 per 100,000 in 2002 (Bureau of Justice Statistics, 2005c). Suicide rates in jails historically have been much higher than that of prisons (*Corrections Professional*, 2005k).

There was wide variability among states, though, ranging from a low of no suicides (three states) to a high of 71 per 100,000 during the 2001 to 2002 period (Bureau of Justice Statistics, 2005c). Four states accounted for 42% (142 out of 337) of all suicides in state prisons in 2002 (Bureau of Justice Statistics, 2005c): California (52), Texas (49), New York (21), and Illinois (20). California experienced a 17% increase between 2005 and 2006, and Texas suicides increased 22% during the same period (Johnson, 2006).

Connecticut state prisons recorded fifteen inmates who committed suicide from 2000 through 2002. Between 1993 and 1999, there was an average of three suicides per year. In 2003, there were four suicides. In 2004, the number increased to nine, and, in the first ten months of 2005, the number stood at seven (Truzzi, 2005). The high number of Connecticut suicides per 100,000 resulted in the state Office of Protection and Advocacy requesting documentation about individual suicides and the American Civil Liberties Union National Prison Project, based in Washington, D.C., opening an investigation. Lawsuits have resulted, too. In March 2003, for example, Connecticut paid the family of one inmate who committed suicide a sum of $750,000 as part of a settlement.

There was also wide variability in suicide rates based on race and ethnicity. During the 2000 to 2002 period, White, non–Latino inmates were six times more likely to commit suicide than African American/Black inmates and three times more likely than Latino inmates (*Corrections Professional*, 2005k). Further, inmates with a history of violence had a suicide rate three times that of their nonviolent counterparts (*Corrections Professional*, 2005k). Females' suicide rates are generally much lower than that of their male counterparts. Older inmates have a higher likelihood of committing suicide. State prisoners age forty-five or older, constitute 17% of inmates but represent 66% of all suicides (*Corrections Professional*, 2005k).

It has been speculated that suicides are probably the result of increased numbers of inmates with mental illness entering correctional institutions (Blint, 2003; Gusafson, 2007; Johnson, 2002). A 2002 New York state prison suicides study found that 70% of all prisoners who successfully committed suicide had histories of mental illness, with 40% having received mental health services within three days of their suicide (Correctional Association of New York, 2004). A Pennsylvania study found that 56% of the inmates who committed suicide in 1997, and 64% of those in 1998, were receiving mental health services at the time of their suicides (Couturier & Maue, 2000). Further, inmates are at increased likelihood of committing suicide when in segregated cells as a form of punishment. These cells are smaller, personal possessions are not allowed, and recreation time is curtailed (Gustafson, 2007; Welsh-Huggins, 2005).

Daniel and Fleming (2006) studied suicides in Connecticut's state correctional system between 1992 and 2002 and highlight the importance of correctional systems doing the following:

1. systematic screening and evaluation of suicide risk
2. obtaining mental health information from community sources and jails
3. being aware of the increased risks posed by administrative segregation and interfacility transfer
4. increasing the role and importance of clinical monitoring
5. recognizing and tracking communication of intent to commit suicide

Although Daniel and Fleming (2006) are making a specific reference to one state system, their recommendations have relevance throughout the country.

The typical profile of a suicide victim is that of a young, White, non-Latino, male who has been incarcerated for nonviolent offenses and was intoxicated when arrested (Bonner, 2000; Hayes, 1999). However, there are high, and increasing, rates of prison suicides among life-sentenced prisoners (Liebling, 2000). This trend has resulted in efforts to assess suicide risks better (Correia, 2000; Winter, 2003). The first twenty-four hours of incarceration are considered to be the most important in preventing suicides (Bender, 2003). Inmates who perceive themselves as having no viable future or support system, along with inmates who are depressed and articulate thoughts of suicide, are at high risk for committing suicide. Kurta, Mrvous, and Krenzelok (2006), in a rare study of poison center utilization by correctional facilities in Pennsylvania, found that intentional exposure was the most common (53.2%) reason for contacting the center, with suicide attempts accounting for almost half of these exposures.

Failed suicide efforts can have far-reaching ramifications on a prison system, as in the case of Troy Christian Davey, a California state prisoner whose failed suicide resulted in his being given a compassionate release:

> His story is one of a prison health care system that went awry with tragic consequences that will require the state to support Davey for the rest of his life. He entered that state prison system in December 1989 at age 21. He was emotionally unstable with low intelligence and a history of suicidal tendencies, but physically able-bodied. He was released in March 1993 at 24. He is totally disabled, both mentally and physically. Simply and bluntly, he is curled up in a ball and helpless (Walsh, 1996, p. 8).

The state of California must pay a $1.5 million malpractice legal settlement.

The American Academy of Pediatrics (2001) found that adolescents who are incarcerated in juvenile facilities may be at higher risk when compared with youth in the general population to have STDs, drug use history, issues regarding pregnancy and parenting, HIV infection, and various preexisting mental health disorders. Inpatient psychiatric hospitalization rates prior to incarceration ranged from 12% to 26%, with 38% to 66% reporting outpatient contacts or treatment.

Another study (National Commission on Correctional Health Care, 2001) has 73% of all youth in juvenile facilities reporting mental health problems during sentencing and 57% having received previous treatment. Fifty-five percent had symptoms associated with conduct disorders, and up to 45% had a diagnosis of attention-deficit/hyperactivity disorder. Multiple diagnoses were not uncommon. Approximately percent had schizophrenia and other psychotic disorders. Finally, approximately 19% were suicidal, and 50% had mental illness co-occurring with substance abuse (National Commission on Correctional Health Care, 2001).

OLDER INMATES

The older inmate prison population overlaps considerably with the chronically ill and the terminally ill population (Anno et al., 2004; Watson, Simpson, & Hostick, 2004; Shah, 2006; Yorston & Taylor, 2006). Although each of these population groups can coexist, in reality, they often are one and the same. Yorston and Taylor's (2006) review of the literature on older offenders found that they bring a host of mental health needs and challenges to prison systems. According to Baker (2005), inmates with severe and persistent mental illness also suffer from high rates of co-morbid medical illnesses that can go undiagnosed, and thus, untreated. This condition compounds further decision making pertaining to inmates with terminal illnesses.

Holman's (1997) following detailed account of the ailments of Gustave Karpanty, sixty-years old and serving a five-to-fifteen-year sentence in the Regional Medical Unit at Coxsackie Correctional Facility (New York), illustrates the challenge that correctional facilities face in treating ailing aging inmates:

> Bedridden for more than a year, he's unable to care for himself. He has a laundry list of ailments: asthma, deafness, schizophrenia, anemia, ulcers, high blood pressure, diverticulitis, [and] arthritis. Last year guards shuttled him to an outside hospital for surgery to remove a serious intestinal blockage (p. 33).

It is recognized widely that the fastest-growing segment of the U.S. correctional system is middle-aged "baby boomers" (Anno et al., 2004; Gubler & Petersilia, 2006; Price, 2006). Older adults are not "invisible" or new within correctional systems and will continue to demand considerable attention in the twenty-first century (Aday, 2003; Fazel et al., 2001; Gallagher, 2001). In the late 1980s, Chaneles (1987) identified older prisoners as a growing population group. One projection has older adult prisoners constituting one-third of the U.S. prison population by the year 2030 (SeniorJournal.Com, 2006).

Their numbers tripled between 1990 and 2001, and their proportion of the total prison population increased from 4.0 percent to 8.2 percent during that period (Yorston & Taylor, 2006). In 1997, there were an estimated 800 inmates, one author called oldest of the old (seventy-five or older) in prisons across the nation (Krane, 1999c). A 1999 nationwide records search found thirteen prisoners in their 90s, including one who was ninety-four years old, who was not scheduled to be released until 2006, at the age of one hundred (Krane, 1999f). Another estimate has the increase in the older prisoner population at 750% in the past twenty years (Guber & Petersilia, 2006).

Alabama typifies this trend. In the mid-1990s, almost half of the state's inmates were under the age of twenty-eight. In 2006, that age has increased to thirty-seven or older (Crowder, 2006). An increase of almost ten years in average age translates into a prison population that not only has gotten older, but also gotten unhealthier. Arizona, in turn, is expected to experience a doubling of its older adult inmate population between 1998 and 2009, with health care costs skyrocketing in the process (Villa, 2005). In 2005, almost half of the new admissions to Arizona's prisons were fifty-five or older, constituting almost 5% (1,569 inmates) of the prison population (Villa, 2005). North Carolina, too, has shown a dramatic increase in the number of older adult inmates (Price, 2006).

Older adult inmates can be found in other industrialized nations. Japan, for example, is a society that is experiencing graying of its general population. Japan's prison inmates aged sixty-five and older is the fastest-growing sector of the prison population (Onishi, 2007). Older adult inmates account for 12.3% of the total Japanese inmate population, representing an increase from 9.3% in 2000. Crawley (2005), in a unique study of older adult male inmates in England, details the everyday consequences of imprisonment for this group. The author concludes that older adult inmates are largely "invisible" within prison systems and that this failure to differentiate the needs of this group from young inmates, under the pretense of equality, is largely unfair in nature and has deleterious health and social consequences.

The public's conception of a prison or jail inmate's profile rarely conjures up elders who are frail, immobile, heavily dependent upon medications, and not a threat to society. Pollak (1941, p. 213) summed up academic perceptions quite well in explaining why older adult inmates generally were overlooked in scholarly papers: "Old criminals offer an ugly picture and it seems as if even scientists do not like to look at it for any considerable amount of time." Further, the general public imagines males as constituting older inmates.

However, females, too, are increasing in representation. In California, for example, older female inmates have increased 350% between 1995 and 2005 (Williams et al., 2006). Yet, very little is known about their functional impairment. Reviere and Young (2004), in a rare article specifically focused on older female inmates, note that prisons are failing to provide for many of the unique health needs facing this population group. The National Commission on Correctional Health Care (2005b) singles out failure of correctional systems to prepare for the specialized needs of older female inmates.

Warren (2002), in analyzing California's aging prison population, argues that the state has not developed a systemwide plan that takes into account an ever increasing number of older prisoners. In 2002, approximately 4% of California's prison population was fifty-five or older. In 2003, there were 6,400 older prisoners, with projections of this group reaching 30,200 by the year 2022 and even 50,000, or one-third of the total prison population, by 2025 (Guber & Petersilia, 2006; Thompson, 2006). Ironically, California was the first state in the nation (1954) to operate a prison exclusively devoted to geriatric prisoners, but it was closed in 1971 when the prison population declined (Kobrin, 2005; Unknown Author, 2002).

Wisconsin, a state generally not associated with prison populations, typifies low-profile states regarding older adult prisoners. In 1995, there were 165 prisoners older than sixty; in 2005, it had increased to 492 prisoners (*Capital Times*, 2006). Officials are considering the aging prison population as the primary reason for prisons' tripled cost from $28.5 million in 1998 to $87.6 million in 2005. The case of Juan Rivera brings the statistic of the aging inmate population to life in the Wisconsin prison system:

> Juan Rivera's hair went grey long ago. He has dentures but seldom wears them because they hurt his gums. At 89, he struggles to remember and tends to repeat a story he told you just minutes before. His wrinkled face has become nondescript with time. But state prison officials recognize his face too well. Rivera, a repeat child sex offender, is the oldest inmate in the Wisconsin prison system, where faces like his are becoming more common every year (Purvis, 2006, p. 1).

The importance of planning for an aging prison population is well recognized in the field (Mare, 2004). The increase in age also results in increases and incidences of chronic illnesses and disabilities (Anno et al., 2004). High-profile illnesses are often accompanied with worsening eyesight, arthritis, seizures, respiratory problems, diabetes, and hearing losses of varying degrees (Villa, 2005). Further, older inmates also face health consequences from being victimized by younger prisoners, as noted by Turley (cited in Gubler & Petersilia, 2006, p. 6): "We all know grandparents who complain they're afraid to walk at night because of crime. Imagine being a geriatric in a neighborhood where everyone is certifiably violent."

There is no facet of the correctional system that has escaped the increase of older inmates. The health needs of older prisoners, regardless of correctional setting, exceed that of the general population and younger prisoners (Fazel et al., 2001; Kulmann & Rudell, 2005; Tarbuck, 2001).

The following four case vignettes put a real face and name to prison statistics related to elder inmates, one of whom is only 50 years old, but with severe health care needs. These raise for the reader the incredible challenges inherent in provision of health care within prisons for an increasingly aging population

FRANK ASHTON, COLORADO (FRIEDBERG, 1999)

Frank Ashton is 62 years old and in lousy shape. He suffers from hypertension, has had a heart bypass, needs medication five times a day for diabetes and must use a wheelchair since his right leg, amputated at the knee, no longer can handle a prosthesis. Grizzled, soft-spoken and articulate, Ashton is in state prison. He's been there since 1979, when he was sentenced to 25 to 35 years for his involvement in a drug deal that ended with two women dead.

CHARLES MCCLELLAND, NEBRASKA (TYSVER, 1998)

Charles McCellard was 21 when he entered into a Nebraska prison in 1948. Fifty years later, the three-time killer is tied to an oxygen tank in a prison hospital with wheezy lungs and a bad heart. Around-the-clock nurses mingle with his guards. His three life sentences have been topped by a terminal diagnosis. The 71-year-old McClelland, with his walker and old-man shuffle, serves as a harbinger of the escalating health-care costs to the nation's prisons.

CLARK TIPTON, OHIO (BEYERIEIN, 1997)

Clark Tipton used to be a tough guy. Now it's tough for him to walk to the bathroom. "I can walk . . . I just can't breathe when I do." A 61-year-old emphysema suffer, Tipton lives in a special kind of nursing home—one with locks on the heavy iron doors, bars on the windows and razor ribbon around the perimeter. Tipton isn't a very sympathetic character. He'd already been to prison twice by 1970, when he killed his wife and stepson and critically wounded his stepdaughter. He was sentenced to life in prison, and that's exactly what he's doing—along with hundreds of other inmates who are spending their retirement years in lockup.

AMELIA "MOLLY" REYES, CALIFORNIA
(SWARD & WALLACE, 1994)

Prisoners of Central California Women's Facility, Chowchilla, said Molly Reyes had been trying to get medical care for several weeks in early 1993. "She had been trying to see the doctor in sick call for about a month and a half, constantly stating that she was sick, having dizzy spells and chest pain and in need of attention," said Reyes'cellmate . . . . . Late on February 24, Reyes began spitting up blood in her cell . . . another cellmate, heard her retching into the toilet at 11:20 P.M. Rico awakened the others in the cell, and they called out for help and cradled Reyes, swabbing her face with wet towels. A guard made repeated calls for a medical aide . . . but nearly an hour passed before the aide arrived to summon an ambulance. During the wait, Reyes continued to vomit and cry out in pain. According to prison staff, Reyes did not leave for the hospital until an hour and 20 minutes after her bleeding was discovered. She was pronounced dead of severe gastrointestinal bleeding a few hours later, she was 50 years old. . . . In March, Reyes was buried in a Bakersfield cemetery. At her funeral, 9-year-old granddaughter Rochelle Munoz tearfully read a poem in her memory. "Even though I miss you . . . I know you will still be here with me/Love you with all my heart."

Kuhlmann and Ruddell (2005, p. 51), in summarizing the literature on the health status of older inmates, identified the following range of serious health problems: "dementia, cancer, stroke, incontinence, arthritis, ulcers, hypertension, chronic respiratory ailments, chronic gastrointestinal problems, prostate problems, heart disease, and deteriorating kidney functions." They also have a higher propensity to have functional disabilities than younger inmates. In addition, they have greater need for dental prostheses and continued dental care due to lack of previous dental care (Florida Corrections Commission, 1999; Ornduff, 1996).

One Federal Bureau of Prisons study (Falter, 1999) found that inmates over the age of fifty (average age was 57.2 years old) make increased use of health care services due to hypertension (19%), atherosclerotic heart disease (5.4%), diabetes (3.4%), and chronic obstructive pulmonary disease (2.5%). One California study of older inmates' health needs found that 80% had at least one chronic condition, 38% had hypertension, 28% had heart disease, and 16% had cataracts (Sizemore, 2000); older inmates, on average, have three chronic illnesses (Aday, 1994).

In 2003, Michigan had 5,570 (11.4%) of its prisoners aged fifty or older, up from 3,359 (7.0%) in the year 2000 (Heinlein, 2003). An average day in a Michigan prison would find between fifty-five to sixty prisoners on daily kidney dialysis. This constitutes part of an annual $170 million spent on health care, up from $157 million in 2002, with prescription drugs accounting for $5 million of this budget increase.

Their social and health needs slowly but surely will surpass their security needs within prisons and jails (Carroll, 2001; Marquart, Merianos, & Doucet, 2000; Yorston & Taylor, 2006). How these systems address their needs will have a profound impact on the mission of correctional institutions for many decades. Inmates who have quadriplegia, have paralysis due to strokes, use wheelchairs, or have Alzheimer's disease that requires twenty-four-hour health care will not be unusual in this nation's prisons (Krane, 1999f).

The topic of Alzheimer's disease, for example, has received considerable national attention as the baby-boom generation approaches old age. However, a parallel process also is taking place in this nation's prisons without corresponding national attention. The case of Stanley Wilson in many ways is not uncommon now and will be much more common in the future, if projected demographic trends are realized:

> Stanley Wilson can no longer recall his age or why he was sent to prison. Alzheimer's has stolen his memory. His hazy mind wanders through space much more freely than his body these days, and he believes he will be released from his prison in the rolling hills of western Pennsylvania "this weekend." Mr. Wilson is 59 years old, though he looks at least 70 (Butterfield, 1997b, p.E3).

Caldwell, Jarvis, and Rosefield (2001), in a rare article specifically focused on older female inmates, note that the dramatic increase in incarceration of women will necessitate gender-specific planning of health care services, and the costs for these services will be far greater than for their male counterparts. They estimate that, since women usually present more health care needs than men, this will translate to prisons, too. They note that illnesses such as HIV, heart disease, primary coronary artery disease and congestive heart failure, cancer, diabetes and its complications, kidney and peripheral vascular disease, vision problems, cerebral vascular accidents, arthritis, and dementia stand out as health needs for women. Specialized gender-specific programs also translate into hospice care.

As of 2005, there were 120 older women in the California correctional system, with over 50% being sixty or older, of whom thirteen were over the age of seventy (Strupp & Willmott, 2005). The majority (82 or 68%) were white, non-Latinas. Strupp and Willmott (2005), in a comprehensive examination of the health care needs of older women in California's state correctional system, make recommendations that have applicability across the nation:

Given the failed medical system, the enormous cost to the state, extremely low recidivism rates and the numerous violations of basic human dignity that remain part and parcel of the imprisonment of elderly persons, the primary recommendations of this report centers on reducing the number of older prisoners in California through a combination of early release programs and expansion of community-based alternatives to incarceration. Releasing older prisoners and caring for them in the community could potentially save the state millions by reducing the hefty custodial costs associated with guarding incarcerated elders. Additionally, the state could save money because many released seniors could access federally funded services such as Medicare and Social Security (p. 60).

Finally, older prisoners have a significantly higher proportion of mental illness when compared to young inmates, with approximately 15% to 25% of older inmates having some form of mental illness. The Florida Corrections Commission (1999) reports that depression is the most common form followed by dementia, substance abuse, organic brain disease, personality disorders, functional psychosis, and paranoid schizophrenia. As with elders in the general population, it is important to have expertise in geriatric medicine to know how to differentiate mental illness from the effects of other conditions, such as thyroid disorders, medication interactions, or medication side effects.

FEMALE INMATES

The term "correctional facilities as social safety net" has emerged, particularly regarding the mentally ill and the homeless. A social safety net attempts to capture the potential role institutions can play to help individuals, male or female, receive needed services. One inmate stated this very point (Fearn & Parker, 2005, p. 15): "Prison was their 'big chance' to get healthy." It is not unusual for female inmates to have minimal or no health care prior to their incarceration (Baldwin & Jones, 2000; Fearn & Parker, 2005; McDonald, 1995; National Commission on Correctional Health Care, 2005b). Failure to redress years of health neglect, however, can be compounded by immersion into a toxic environment and, in the case of female inmates, further contribute to failing health.

The profile of the typical woman entering this nation's correctional system is of an individual of color, living in poverty, having a high risk of having experienced trauma, and with limited or no access to health care (Anderson, 2003; Fearn & Parker, 2005; McClellan, 2002; Kim, 2003). Jails and prisons often represent the only health care that incarcerated women will receive, and they subsequently enter jails and prisons in poor health and experience more serious and frequent health problems than their male counterparts (Braithwaite, Treadwell & Arriola, 2005; National Institute of Corrections, 2003; Williams & Schulte-Day, 2006). Incarcerated women historically have utilized health care services much more than their male counterparts (Demars & Walsh, 1981; National Commission on Correctional Care, 1994c). Not surprisingly, it is estimated that 20% to 35% of women go to prison sick call daily compared to 7% to 10% of men (National Institute of Corrections, 2003). Female inmates also bring with them unique health care needs that their male counterparts do not share, or if they do share, not to the same degree (Collica, 2002; Watson, Simpson, & Hostick, 2004; Young, 1998). Women who are HIV-positive, for example, are more susceptible to cervical cancer, possibly due to elevated secondary infections with human papillomavirus (Fearn & Parker, 2005; Palevitz, 2001).

Watterson's (1996) assessment of the health status of female inmates is poignant and highlights how their health needs overlap with their male counterparts but stand out as unique:

> Getting reliable health care for prisoners is a big problem. Most of the women who wind up in prison didn't have healthy diets, good nutrition, or patterns of adequate rest, fresh air, and exercise even before they were incarcerated. For the most part, they lacked the training, the resources, and self-esteem to have taken good care of themselves. They don't have medical insurance and haven't had regular checkups, Pap smears, mammograms, or necessary dental care. If they're pregnant, they most likely haven't had adequate nutrition or prenatal care, and if they've recently given birth, they are probably lacking the necessary vitamins and nutrients they need for postnatal recovery. A surprisingly large number never saw an obstetrician during their pregnancy. (p. 253)

In a study of 151 women prisoners completed by the National Council on Crime and Delinquency (NCCD) in 1996, 61% required medical treatment for one or more physical problems, and 45% required mental health treatment (Acoca, 1998). Additionally, "According to the women interviewed, access to all services (particularly to psychological, substance abuse, and acute medical treatment) was extremely limited. They also reported that even when care was initially made available, ongoing medical supervision and follow-up were often lacking" (Acoca, 1998, p. 51). Macalino, Vlahov, Dickerson, Schwartzapfel, and Rich (2005) found the incidence of hepatitis B and C infections among reincarcerated women to be high, making correctional institutions settings that could fulfill important public health functions such as testing, treatment, and prevention of infectious diseases.

Young (1997) found in a study of Washington state female inmates that over 50% were on some form of medication prior to their incarceration, and almost three-quarters smoked, or three times that of the general population. Over 60% indicated having at least one major health problem (asthma, back and neck pain, or a heart condition) and almost 20% had a physical limitation. Asthma was reported by 18% of the women, considerably higher than the 4.7% reported by the general population. Almost 90% reported serious dental problems. Mortality rates of female inmates, not surprisingly, are higher than that of females in the general population. For example, women inmates in New York state prisons in 1994 had a morality rate twice that of their counterparts in the general population (Ross & Lawrence, 1998). They are more likely than males to be HIV-positive or have AIDS, adding to the likelihood of increased death rates in the not too distant future (Franklin, Fearn & Franklin, 2005; Ross & Lawrence, 1998).

Historically, the subject of inmates who are pregnant has not been seen as a major correctional issue (Williams & Schulte-Day, 2006). The 1980s, though, brought about major changes in sentiments concerning pregnant offenders (Daane, 2003). First, it was rare for women to be imprisoned. Second, it was even rarer for those who were pregnant to be imprisoned. Consequently, if it was an issue at sentencing, it was possible for correctional systems to find "alternatives."

In the early 1990s, approximately 6% of all women entering prison were pregnant (Martin et al., 1997). A 1993 study found that approximately one in four female inmates were either pregnant or postpartum when they entered prison (Smith, 1993). Two-thirds of all female inmates were mothers to children under the age of eighteen. Seventy percent of these inmates lived with their children prior to incarceration. In 1997–1998, there were an estimated 2,200 pregnant women who were incarcerated in the United States, and over 1,300 gave birth to their babies while imprisoned (Amnesty International, 2000). In 1998, 80% of all women who were incarcerated were mothers, with an average of between two and three children (Kauffman, 2001). In 2000, an estimated 10% of all women prisoners were pregnant, reflecting a continued increase in this population group (Bureau of Justice Statistics, 2002).

Information on the effects of incarceration on pregnancy outcomes is conflicting. Some critics argue that prison-induced stressors increase health risks for newborns and their mothers. Others, however, argue that incarceration may promote health outcomes through provision of care, proper diet, and changes in risk-taking behaviors. Kyei-Aboagye, Vragovic, and Chong (2000), for example, found that birth outcomes in incarcerated women with substance-abusing histories were improved, particularly when adopting a health-promotion lifestyle.

Women, as a result, constitute what is often referred to as a "special population" necessitating special initiatives (Ortiz, 2000). Since their representation in prisons is increasing at a record pace, they present correctional institutions with unique and pressing health problems, especially inmates who are pregnant (Crary, 1999; Dressel, Porterfield & Barnhill, 1998; Flanagan, 1995; Lowenstein, 2001; Williams & Schulte-Day, 2006).

The high-profile health needs addressed in this chapter are certainly well known in society and are not restricted to those who are imprisoned. These needs are complex and very often are co-occurring, making treatment that much more arduous and costly to achieve. These health needs usually have been conceptualized as being "prison related," with minimal attention to the impact they will have on society once inmates are released back into the community. In the case of pregnant inmates, for example, prisons are cast into a role that they historically have not had to encounter, namely, provision of child care. Prisons historically have been structured to house male adults and not women and children.

Ironically, access to mind-altering drugs may have led many inmates into a life of crime to support their habits, and they still can continue their drug-taking habits within prisons, making rehabilitation impossible and increasing the risk of contracting hepatitis B and C and HIV. Once released, risk-taking drug and sexual behaviors often lead former prisoners into continuing a lifestyle that not only will put them in harm's way but also will do so to their families. The social, economic, psychological, and political costs are immeasurable to their communities and society in general. Thus, it is not an unreasonable conclusion that prison is the "drug treatment" of choice in the United States.

6

LOW-PROFILE HEALTH CARE NEEDS

There is little disputing that certain groups have gotten their share of national public and scholarly attention in any serious discussion of prison-related health care services. "High-profile" health issues, as addressed in chapter 5, have proven particularly challenging for prison authorities in their quest to provide society safety from prisoners. Like schools, prisons have been asked to do more and more in their mission, and high-profile health care needs reflect how society's expectations have changed over the years.

At the same time, other "low-profile" health issues do exist, and it only may be a question of time before they move up and occupy a high-profile status (McKinley, 2007). Several issues will be addressed in this chapter, some of which may come as a surprise to the reader. Some readers may well argue that some of these do not belong in this chapter and instead should be presented in chapter 5 alongside other "high-profile" issues. Nine issues have been selected to be included in this chapter:

1. Hepatitis B
2. Hepatitis C
3. Tuberculosis
4. Sexually transmitted diseases
5. Methicillin-resistant *Staphylococcus aureus* infections
6. Prison injuries
7. End stage renal disease
8. Head injuries
9. Disabilities

These low-profile issues are not considered "low-profile" to those inmates who have one or multiple types, however (Fuhrman, 2002).

Each of these issues will be treated as if it existed in isolation from others. Needs are rarely that simple though. The challenge for prison health care services is compounded by the close relationship or interplay among these various issues and the importance of prevention, early detection, and treatment. Further, although this chapter focuses on how these low-profile issues have impacts on prisoners, they also have impacts on prison health care staff. For example, Gaseau (2001c), in a National Institute for Occupational Safety and Health study of correctional health care staff exposure to infectious disease, found staff to be at high risk for exposure to hepatitis B and C.

HEPATITIS B

In 2000, there were an estimated 73,000 individuals in the United States who were newly infected with hepatitis B (HBV) (*IDU/HIV Prevention*, 2002a). It is estimated that the prevalence of HBV among prison inmates can range from 13% to 47% and two to six times that of the general population (Centers for Disease Control and Prevention, 2004). HBV is preventable through the use of a vaccine. An estimated 5,000 die nationally every year from illnesses caused by HBV infection (*IDU/HIV Prevention*, 2002a). The costs of treating HBV are estimated at $6,000 per case. According to the Centers for Disease Control, it is cost-effective to vaccinate for HBV (Pisu, Meltzer & Lyeria, 2002), which can be overlooked because it may be asymptomatic. It is most commonly contracted through sexual contact, and its highest concentration can be found in blood, saliva, and semen. Hepatitis B generally causes a limited infection that the body successfully can fight off within a few months (Beck & Maruschak, 2004).

HBV infection in U.S. prisons is not a new phenomenon. Bader (1986), in a study published over one decade ago, found prisoners to be a high-risk group for infection. One survey by the California Department of Corrections in 1995 found that 50% of incoming women inmates and 33% of incoming male inmates tested positive for HBV (California Study, 1995). California, it should be noted, is not unique in the nation. In 1996 alone, it was estimated that 155,000 prison inmates with current or chronic HBV were released from prisons into the community (*Health & Medicine Weekly*, 2003). Kahn and colleagues (2005) have documented the transmission of HBV within prisons and advocate for vaccination of inmates as a means of reducing the potential epidemic of this form of infection. High infections of HBV and HCV represent a significant community health threat (Beck & Maruschak, 2004; Macalino et al., 2004).

It is estimated that almost 30% of all new HBV infections have been uncovered in individuals with a history of incarceration (Buck et al., 2006). One estimate says that transmission of HBV infection within prisons can range from 0.8% to 3.8% per year (Centers for Disease Control and Prevention, 2004). Further, one Rhode Island study of male inmates found that HBV and HCV infections were significantly associated with drug injection histories (Macalino et al., 2004).

It is estimated that 50% to 60% of adults with HBV infection show no signs or symptoms in the initial stages of infection. Those with symptoms generally experience jaundice, fatigue, stomach pain, loss of appetite, nausea, vomiting, and joint pain. Estimates have one-third of chronically infected persons developing a mild to moderate form of liver disease that can turn into fibrosis (scarring of liver tissue). Another one-third of infected persons develop severe liver disease that can turn into cirrhosis (severe fibrosis) or liver cancer. Anywhere from 15% to 25% of this last group will die from complications of chronic liver disease (*IDU/HIV Prevention*, 2002a). Those with HBV are twelve to thirty times more likely to develop hepatocellular carcinoma, the most common form of liver cancer in adults, than noncarriers. Prisons, as noted in the California study cited earlier, have a population that is considered at high risk for contracting HBV.

Charuvastra and colleagues' (2001) study of state and federal prison vaccination practices found that many states do not vaccinate even the most high-risk inmates for HBV. In 2000, almost one-third of all state prisons reported doing no HBV vaccinations. By midyear 2000, only 1,033 state facilities reported that they provided HBV vaccinations as a matter of policy (Bureau of Justice Statistics, 2004b). However, 401 facilities actually administered the vaccination, with 13,655 inmates completing the three-dose series of vaccinations for HBV (Bureau of Justice Statistics, 2004c).

One Rhode Island study found that 93% of inmates studied between June and August 2002 said they would voluntarily agree to take a hepatitis B vaccine while incarcerated (News-Medical.Net, 2004). However, this does not mean that there are no additional vaccination barriers on the part of inmates. Obstacles to vaccination during imprisonment include fear of needles and distrust of prison staff, and after release, time and cost appear as significant barriers (Buck et al., 2006). Not surprisingly, addressing HBV from a prevention or early identification perspective results in a net savings to prison systems and society (Pisu, Meltzer & Lyeria, 2002).

HEPATITIS C

Hepatitis C (HCV) was first identified in 1989 (Reuters, 2003). It is estimated that 175 million people worldwide have HCV (Reuters, 2003) and that there are four million Americans infected, or approximately four times those who are infected with HIV (Talvi, 2001). The American Public Health Association (2003) estimated that 2% of the general population was infected. It is found largely in persons between the ages of twenty to thirty-nine (Cowley, 2002; Fackelmann, 1999b; Grodeck, 1999; Munoz-Plaza et al., 2005; Reuters, 2003). However, this estimate does not include those who are institutionalized, homeless, or incarcerated. Approximately 30,000 new infections occur every year in the United States (Cowley, 2002). Estimates place the number of Latinos who are HCV positive at 2 percent, with a projection of 4% by the year 2028 (Delgado-Vega, 2003). Other countries have not escaped either. In Ireland, for example, inmates with HCV are more common than those who are HIV-positive (O'Morain, 2000). HCV is a potentially fatal disease that is considered an imminent crisis in the nation's prisons (Cassidy, 2003; Cowley, 2002; Centers for Disease Control and Prevention, 2003; Varghese & Fields, 1999).

The relative ease through which HCV can be transmitted increases the chances of major epidemics occurring within prisons (Editorial, 2000; Vlahov, Nelson, Quinn & Kendig, 1993). It is a blood-borne disease that can exist outside the human body. Transmission can occur through the sharing of things such as razor blades, nail files, scissors, and toothbrushes, and by sexual transmission through rashes or sores. Tattooing and body piercing frequently are prohibited within prisons, so inmates hide the requisite equipment and share it secretly (Braithwaite et al., 1999). Therefore, these practices also increase the likelihood of transmission.

Intravenous (IV) drug users are a population overly represented in the nation's prison population. The HCV virus prevalence in the incarcerated population is especially acute among persons infected with HIV and injection-drug users (Hammett, Gaither & Crawford, 1998). Studies highlight that approximately 80% of IV drug users have, contracted HCV when sharing needles tainted with blood (Fackelmann, 1999b). It is estimated that almost 60% of HCV is transmitted through the sharing of needles, with the remaining percentage through other contact (Isaacs & Hammer-Tomizuka, 2001). The Centers for Disease Control and Prevention (1998) estimates that over 20% of the cases may have occurred through sexual contact. Macalino, Dhawan, and Rich (2005), however, caution that, although a definition of "high-risk" for HCV often involves IV drug users, this must be reexamined. The authors found in a Rhode Island study that 66% of inmates who were HCV positive did not report a history of IV drug use.

In 2000, 31.4% of all prison inmates tested positive for HCV, with estimates ranging from 12% to 31% (Spaulding et al., 2006). However, estimates have anywhere from 20% to 60% of the prison population having this disease, or 400,000 to 1.2 million inmates (Cassidy, 2003; Fackelman, 1999a,b; Rohde, 2001c; Talvi, 2001). In 1997, an estimated 300,000 prisoners had HCV, a prevalence nine times that of the general population, or 33% of all those infected in the United States (Altman, 1999). Approximately 38% of Texas, 22% of California, 32% of Maryland, 70% of Connecticut, and 46% of Virginia inmates, for example, had HCV (Bureau of Justice Statistics, 2004b). In New York state prisons, it has been estimated that 9,000 to 10,000 inmates are infected with HCV (Pfeiffer, 2003). One 2002 estimate has 12% to 39% of released prisoners nationwide having chronic hepatitis B and C (Salcido, Chen, Whitley & D'Amico, 2003).

Women (53.5%) are more likely than men (39.4%) to be infected (Fackelmann, 1999a,b). California found that 54% of the incoming female inmates and 39% of the incoming male inmates were infected with hepatitis C (Fox et al., 2005). California, as a system, has an estimated 33% of all male, and between 25% and 39% of all female, inmates as having HCV (Munoz-Plaza et al., 2005). The prevalence was even higher (65.7%) among inmates with a history of IV drug use, compared to those without drug use histories (Fox et al., 2005). In Massachusetts, it was estimated that 27% of males and 44% of females in jails and prisons were infected with HCV (Massachusetts Public Health Association, 2003; Salcido, Chen, Whitley & D'Amico, 2003). HVC, as a result, is probably the most prevalent bloodborne infection among prisoners in the United States.

It is estimated that 80% of persons with HCV infection display no physical signs or symptoms during the initial phase of the infection. HCV can exist within one's body for 10 to 30 years before symptoms appear, with 90% of HCV carriers not being aware they are infected. It was not until 1993 that HCV screening in blood banks began. Those who develop symptoms usually experience jaundice, fatigue, dark urine, loss of appetite, and nausea. Approximately 50% to 60% of chronically infected persons develop a mild to moderate form of chronic liver disease, with 10% to 20% developing severe liver disease that can result in cirrhosis or liver cancer (*IDU/HIV Prevention*, 2002b). One estimate says almost 85% of those infected will suffer a chronic infection and that, anywhere from ten to forty years after the infection, liver failure and death may occur (Fackelmann, 1999b). Of those infected, 15% eventually recover, and 5% die. It is estimated that HCV kills approximately 8,000 to 10,000 people every year (Cowley, 2002). Applied to 156,000 California inmates, for example, approximately 3,200 will eventually die as a result of HCV (Cowley, 2002).

In 1998, the Centers for Disease Control and Prevention estimated that approximately 25,000 deaths occur annually in the United States as a result of chronic liver disease, with HCV accounting for 40% of the death total. The death rate is expected to triple to almost 30,000 by the year 2008 (Cowley, 2002; Grodeck, 1999). HCV also has been identified as the leading indicator for liver transplants in the United States, with an estimated cost of $300,000 each (Massachusetts Public Health Association, 2003).

For women inmates who are more likely than the general population to be HIV-positive and to have ongoing substance abuse issues, HCV is widespread. "Strikingly, a 1994 study by the California Department of Health revealed that 54% of women entering state prisons tested positive for HCV—a potentially fatal disease with no known cure—compared to 39% of incoming males" (Acoca, 1998). Another study in California found that, of women who were HIV-positive, 85% were also HCV-positive, considerably higher than men, who were at 61% (Dey, 2003; Hoskins, 2004).

A 2000 census of state prisons found 79% reported having some form of testing policy for HCV. Thirty-three percent of tests in state prisons that tested only targeted groups were positive compared to 27% of those in facilities that conducted random tests or all inmates (Bureau of Justice Statistics, 2004b). The high incidence of HCV among the incarcerated should encourage correctional institutions to undertake HCV antibody screening and behavioral interventions (Fox et al., 2005). Cost estimates in Texas, for example, approximate $65 million for a "minimum" treatment program (*New York Times*, 1999).

One study of treatment costs of diagnosis to completion of evaluation or treatment estimated that it would cost between $646,768 to $2,706,740 (Paris, Pradham, Allen & Cassidy, 2005). The introduction of a needle exchange program and professional tattooing have been recommended as potentially effective methods for reducing the risk of contracting HCV in Australian prisons, but carries implications for prisons in other countries such as the United States (*Canberra Times*, 2006). One Canadian study of federal prisoners found that HCV treatment outcome was feasible and effective (Farley et al. 2005).

TUBERCULOSIS

Although tuberculosis (TB) cases in the United States have fallen to approximately 4 cases per 100,000, it is still overrepresented in the prison population. By mid-2003, the incarcerated population was over three times (3.2%) more likely than the general population (less than 1.0%) to be TB-positive (Hall, 2006). TB is still considered the leading cause of deaths among prison inmates worldwide (Hall, 2006). It is not a disease of another era. Worldwide 2 million people died from this disease in 2000 (*Houston Chronicle*, 2001). TB is considered the primary cause of death in HIV-infected people (*Corrections Professional*, 2005h).

Prisons and jails are acknowledged widely to be a prime source for TB transmission in this society (Bock, Reeves, LaMarre & DeVoe, 1998; MacIntyre et al., 1999; Roberts et al., 2006; Wilcock, Hammett & Parent, 1995; Zack, Flanagan & DeCarlo, 2000). Experts would be hard pressed to design facilities that more efficiently transmit airborne diseases than what is currently found in this nation's prisons (Centers for Disease Control and Prevention, 2006; *Corrections Professional*, 2005h; Gostin, 1995; Harding, 2000; Taylor & Nguyen, 2003). MacNeil, Lobato, and Moore (2005) concluded that inmates with TB were less likely than non-inmates to complete treatment, raising important public health implications for ex-inmates returning to their community. The public health concern is such that it is recommended that new skin test conversions in inmates must be treated as a new infection, regardless of any identifiable exposure to tuberculosis, because of the highly contagious nature of the disease (MacIntyre et al., 1999).

Outbreaks of tuberculosis are not uncommon in prison systems, with both inmates and prison guards having a higher incidence than the general population (Centers for Disease Control, 2004; Centre for Infectious Disease Prevention and Control, 2001; Jones et al., 1999; Mueller, 1996), and the likelihood of contracting tuberculosis in prisons increases with length of time in prisons (Centers for Disease Control, 1995; Kendig, 1998). Studies have found a positive relationship between rates of positive tuberculin skin-test results and length of incarceration, strongly indicating the possibility that transmission may have occurred during incarceration (Bellin, Fletcher, & Safyer, 1993; Stead, 1978). Not surprisingly, staff and visitors to prisons can be infected from prisoners with TB (Garcia, 2000; Hegstrom, 2001; Laniado-Laborin, 2001). The potential for correctional health care workers to contract tuberculosis has raised the importance of continued vigilance to control occupational exposure (Mitchell et al., 2005).

The incidence of tuberculosis within prisons generally is estimated to be three to ten times higher than that of the general population (Bock et al., 1998; Centers for Disease Control, 1995; Laniado-Laborin, 2001; Ridzon, 2003). In one California prison, the tuberculosis rate was 184 per 100,000 in 1991, or ten times that of the state rate (Braithwaite, Braithwaite & Poulson, 1999). However, the national incidence of tuberculosis in persons with AIDS is approximately 500 times that of the general population (Thorburn, 1995, 1998). In the early 1990s, researchers found a positive association between past exposure to tuberculosis and HIV in male inmates (Salive, Vlahov, & Brewer, 1990).

A twenty-nine-state survey of tuberculosis in nursing homes and correctional facilities found that the aggregate tuberculosis incidence rate for nursing home residents was 1.8 times higher than the rate seen in elders in the general population, and the rate for prisoners was considerably higher at 3.9 times that of the rate for nonincarcerated counterparts (Hutton, Cauthen & Bloch, 1993). There are instances, however, in which 50 times the national average has been recorded.

Mutation has resulted in some strains of TB resistant to treatment. In some instances, inmates with tuberculosis have strains of Mycobacterium tuberculosis that are multidrug resistant (Laniado-Laborin, 2001). One study found that 80% of all new multidrug-resistant TB cases in New York City could be traced back to jails and prisons (Petersilia, 2000a). In the mid-1990s, there was a prison epidemic of multidrug-resistant tuberculosis in New York State. It, for example, had a rate of 15.4 per 100,000 in 1976 and 1978, which increased dramatically to 105.5 per 100,000 in 1986. By 1993, it further increased to 139.3 per 100,000. In 1992, New Jersey state prisons had a rate of 91.3 per 100,000 with 12.6 per 100,000 in the general population (Centers for Disease Control, 1995, 1996). In the late 1990s, approximately 9% of a sample of female inmates admitted to New York state prisons tested positive for tuberculosis, and 2% showed signs of active disease (Ross & Lawrence, 1998).

Studies of tuberculosis transmission within prisons, not surprisingly, have shown a high degree of case clustering; more than 25% of the cases show a unique fingerprint (Chaves, Dronda, Cave, et al., 1997). Several factors interplay to spur the spread of drug-resistant TB:

1. infection with HIV or hepatitis B and C viruses
2. improper nutrition
3. poor ventilation
4. overcrowding
5. history of substance abuse
6. history of limited access to health care prior to incarceration

7. high proportion of inmates from high-incidence countries
   (Laniado-Laborin, 2001; Greifinger, 2005)

It is estimated that approximately 92% of prisons and 51% of jails screen all incoming inmates for TB (Hammett, Harmon & Maruschak, 1999). However, in the case of jails, many inmates are released before skin-test results are read (*Health & Medicine Weekly*, 2003). Hayden and colleagues (2005) note that TB prevention efforts in jails, for example, are hampered by short jail sentences and poor completion of treatment among prisoners released prior to completing treatment regime. Standard early intervention treatment costs are low, when made available (*Houston Chronicle*, 2001). However, the National Institute of Corrections estimates that it costs $56,000 to $90,000 to treat one tuberculosis patient in a correctional setting.

SEXUALLY TRANSMITTED DISEASES

The subject of sexually transmitted diseases (STDs) in this country has not received the attention it deserves, despite the prevalence of STDs. That prevalence is alarming, with five STDs accounting for five out of the ten most frequently reported diseases in the United States in 1995 (SIECUS Report, 1997); STDs accounted for 87% of all cases of diseases in that year.

Despite the prevalence, health consequences, and economic costs of STDs, they generally are not recognized sufficiently when discussing health care needs and services, in or out of prison. This lack of recognition translates into minimal funding for screening and early identification, and it makes STDs an invisible threat to health within correctional institutions (Kraut, Haddix, Carande-Kulis & Greifinger, 2003). Nelson, Friedman, and Gaydos (2005), in a federal prison study of the potential benefits of screening women at entry, recommend that women thirty and younger should be screened. Bernstein and colleagues (2006), too, suggest screening, particularly in jails, which often present the earliest opportunity to identify and treat STDs.

Syphilis is the most commonly screened-for STD; 90% of federal and state facilities screen for it, but only 55% of county facilities screen for syphilis (Hoskins, 2004). Parece and associates (1999), in their study of city and county jails, found that 52% to 77% had a policy for STD screening based on symptoms or by arrestee request. However, only 0.2% to 6% of these institutions offered routine testing. One recent estimate reported that 6% of all newly admitted inmates had recent syphilis infection, 6% had chlamydia, and 4% had gonorrhea (Abramsky, 2002). In examining released prisoners in 1997, between 202,000 and 322,000 prisoners were likely to be carrying syphilis, 77,000 had gonorrhea, and 186,000 had chlamydia (Hammet, Harmon & Rhodes, 2003). One study of Chicago's Cook County jail found that it accounted for approximately 25% of all newly diagnosed syphilis cases in the city of Chicago (Skolnick, 1998b).

However, the costs of testing for chlamydia and gonorrhea, for example, often are noted to be a significant barrier for routine screening. Screening women for chlamydia and gonococcal infection by using urine tests has been found to be feasible and acceptable for female inmates (Mertz et al., 2002). These diseases, if left untreated, will seriously compromise the health of those infected and that of their partners. Initial screening, as a result, takes on added significance within total institutions such as correctional facilities (Kraut-Becher et al., 2003).

The prevalence of STDs is high among women who are incarcerated (*Morbidity and Mortality Weekly Report*, 1999). In 1999, 3% to 28% of female inmates had syphilis, 1.4% to 6% had chlamydia, and 0.7% to 7.4% had gonorrhea (*IDU/HIV Prevention*, 2001a). The Centers for Disease Control's study of adult correctional facilities found that 10% to 13% of female inmates tested positive for chlamydia, and 5% to 9% tested positive for gonococcus. In another study of juvenile correctional institutions, 16% to 27% tested positive for chlamydia, and 6% to 17% for gonococcus (*Family Practice News*, 2000).

Occurrence of STDs also is high among gay male inmates. In a 2000–2001 study of a Los Angeles County jail, in a section composed of gay males, STDs were alarmingly high. Over a ten-month period, 14% of 723 screenings given to male inmates showed them to be HIV-positive; twenty-seven inmates had chlamydia; sixteen had gonorrhea, and several had syphilis (Shuster, 2001).

Outbreaks of infectious diseases within prisons are not restricted to tuberculosis and HIV. The case of the outbreak of syphilis in Alabama is such a case in point (Wolfe et al., 2001). In 1999, a syphilis outbreak was reported in three Alabama state men's prisons. The causes were traced to mixing of prisoners with unscreened jail populations, transfers of infected inmates between prisons, and multiple sexual partners. STDs within correctional institutions present a very real potential for an epidemic.

METHICILLIN-RESISTANT
STAPHYLOCOCCUS AUREUS INFECTIONS

Prisons and jails in several states have experienced outbreaks of a Staphylococcus infection (Goldstein, Hradecky, Vilke & Chan, 2006), methicillin-resistant *Staphylococcus* aureus (MRSA), which commonly is carried on the skin or in the nose of the infected person. Although resistant to a commonly used drug, methicillin, the infection can be treated successfully with other antibiotics, if identified as MRSA. If left untreated, or if it occurs in people with other conditions such as HIV or diabetes, it can be very serious or even fatal.

Crowded conditions in prisons are a factor in passing on MRSA, as are poor hygiene and uncleanliness (*World Disease Weekly*, 2006a). A study of the Texas prison system (Baillargeon et al., 2004) found that inmates with circulatory disease, cardiovascular disease, diabetes, end-stage liver disease (ESLD), end-stage renal disease (ESRD), HIV/AIDS, or skin diseases had elevated rates of MSRA infection; infection was particularly high for those with HIV/AIDS, ESLD, and ESRD. In addition to prisoners, MRSA has been passed to employees and then to others outside prison (Lindt, 2005). The Federal Bureau of Prisons has acknowledged its seriousness by selecting it for inclusion in its *Clinical Practice Guidelines* (2005). Recommendations for addressing this disease are:

- staff education and precautions
- sanitation and hygiene
- surveillance and infection control measures
- inmate containment and transfer policies
- outbreak management
- specific antibiotic guidelines
  (Goldstein et al., 2006)

PRISONER INJURIES, RAPES, AND SELF-MUTILATION

The subject of health care in prison covers a wide range of diseases and physical conditions. The subjects of injuries, rapes, and self-mutilation often are not considered when discussing prison health care. These subjects, however, are an integral part of any inmate health status and must, as a result, receive the attention they deserve.

Injuries

There are very few advocates of current correctional system policies who would argue that life within prisons could be considered safe from psychological and physical harm. Injuries within prisons, as a result, must be

considered in any systematic attempt to provide health care services. Injuries can occur in a variety of circumstances, with each requiring a specific approach to prevention: prisoner to prisoner, prisoner to guard, self-
inflicted, guard to prisoner, and as a result of accidents related to carrying
out prison-related responsibilities. However, any search of professional literature on prison injuries will find very few references to this subject, and
there is no systematic reporting protocol for injuries in prisons. Nevertheless, one recent estimate of serious injuries placed the figure of injuries per
year at 26,000 (*Prison Issues*, 2004).

Wees (1995) found that violence in prisons had increased dramatically
between 1993 and 1995, resulting in an increased number of prisoner injuries. Thorburn (1999), in one of the few studies specifically focused on
prison injuries, found that it is a serious health issue. Two state studies
(Michigan and Hawaii) reported by Thorburn highlight the extent of this
problem. Michigan reported 505.7 injuries per 1,000 inmates per year, and
Hawaii reported 683 per 1,000.

Prison-related injuries increase with length of time served in prison
and are highly correlated with a number of factors (Maruschak & Beck,
2001). Approximately 22% of all inmates can expect to be injured during
their sentence. A Federal Bureau of Prisons study in 1999 found that injuries resulting from accidents during work or recreation, or other types of
accidents, were the most frequent sources of injuries (25,975), with 3,134
injuries resulting from assaults and fights (Maruschak & Beck, 2001). When
the injured inmate also is severely ill, an elder, or both, the health consequences of such acts are much more serious when compared with younger
and healthier inmates.

Still, inmates 34 years or younger more often than inmates 45 years or
older experience injuries; men are more likely to be injured than women,
regardless of time served. Those with mental illness are twice as likely as
their counterparts without mental illness to be injured in a fight, and violent offenders have a higher likelihood of being injured in a fight than nonviolent offenders (Maruschak & Beck, 2001).

Rapes

It is recognized widely that nonconsensual sexual encounters are one of
the health risks associated with increased imprisonment rates (Bureau of Justice Statistics, 2007; McGuire, 2005; Zweig, Naser, Blackmore & Schaffer,
2006). However, obtaining documentation on the extent of this prison-related
problem has been difficult, seriously compromising any national efforts to de-

termine the prevalence of rapes within prisons. Feelings of shame, guilt, embarrassment, and stigma, and concerns about retribution, all combine to make reporting of rapes difficult for the victim. McGuire (2005, p. 73) notes, "Acquiring the 'punk' or 'queer' label in a male prison frequently results in additional victimization, further motivating victims to conceal their victimization." Hensley and Tewsbury's 2005 study of state wardens' perceptions of prison sexual assaults found it to be relatively rare within their respective institutions. The authors, however, advocate for training to better inform wardens on this subject: "Understanding and being prepared to respond to real and perceived incidents of sexual assault and their resulting consequences is critically important for efficient and effective correctional institutional management" (Hensley & Tewsbury, 2005, p. 195). Robertson (2003) points out that prison rape has social, physiological, and psychological dimensions for the victim as well as public health consequences for the community upon release because of the risk of the inmates acquiring STDs from rapes.

The passage of the Prison Rape Elimination Act of 2003 effectively placed corrections officials on notice by requiring the Department of Justice to study the problem of sexual assaults in prison and develop a strategy for addressing this problem (*New York Times*, 2005d). This law is in response to what was perceived to be a national correctional crisis. An early 1990s *New York Times* article (Donaldson, 1993) noted that the problem of prison rapes was quite extensive, with approximately 290,000 male and 135,000 female inmates per year being sexually assaulted. Another more updated estimate puts unwanted sexual acts at 60,000 per day (*Prison Issues*, 2004). According to the Bureau of Justice Statistics (2005c), there were 8,210 allegations of sexual violence, or 3.15 allegations per 1,000 inmates, in 2004. The largest proportion (42%) involved staff sexual misconduct, followed by 37% inmate-on-inmate nonconsensual sexual acts, 11% staff sexual harassment, and 10% involving abusive sexual contact. In 2007, 4.5% of federal and state prisoners reported being sexually victimized (Beck & Harrison, 2007). It was estimated that in 1999, 30% of new Texas inmates could be expected to be sexually assaulted within their first forty-eight hours inside a prison, with 237 inmate-on-inmate sexual assaults being formally reported to prison officials. In 2002, this number increased to 460 (Ward, 2005b).

Self-mutilation

Human Rights Watch (2003) was unable to locate any national or statewide data as part of their study on self-mutilation in prisons. Self-mutilation can take a variety of forms, such as cutting, inserting foreign objects under the skin, overdosing on medicines, and swallowing objects, to list the most common forms. A 2001 prison study of female inmates in Holloway, England, who injured themselves while in prison found that 12% reported they injured themselves while attempting suicide. Eighty-eight percent stated that self-injury represented an attempt to relieve tension, anger, and feelings of depression (Centre for Evidence Based Mental Health, 2001).

END STAGE RENAL DISEASE

End stage renal disease (ESRD) is a major health issue in this country for the general population and one that has received increasing attention, particularly regarding kidney transplants. Even for Medicare-eligible younger persons, not just elders, Medicare is available for people with ESRD. The lack of Medicare coverage for prisoners, however, results in federal and state correctional systems paying the total cost of such health care, since inmates lose Medicare coverage while in prison.

In 2007, there were approximately 300,000 patients in the general population who were on hemodialysis, with an estimated 95,000 receiving kidney transplants. More recently, over 38,000 people were on waiting lists for a donor kidney. African Americans accounted for almost 33% of all patients with kidney failure, but only 13% of the U.S. population (U.S. Renal Data Systems, 2002).

Advances in health care have made kidney transplants, as opposed to hemodialysis, the preferred medical treatment (Ozgen & Ozcan, 2002). It is estimated that the death rate for hemodialysis patients is approximately 23% per year, but kidney transplants reduce the risk of death to almost 3% per year. The medical preference for kidney transplants is obvious. However, if the patient is a prison inmate, medical decisions are much more complex.

The Federal Bureau of Prisons had 134 inmates on dialysis and, as a policy, has not approved transplants in over one decade except in special circumstances. Inmates with kidney failure can be part of a clustering program strategy (housing together) as a means of containing prison costs. Inmates with kidney failure requiring dialysis have been housed in one of three federal prisons in the United States: Otisville, New York; Springfield, Missouri; and Lexington, Kentucky. In 1998, California had ninety-one dialysis patients and last approved a kidney transplant in 1989. Maryland had thirty inmates with kidney failure and does not permit transplants. Florida had fifty inmates on dialysis and approved one transplant when the inmate's family agreed to pay for the costs. Virginia is one of the few states that by policy refers inmates for kidney transplants. Virginia considers this policy to be both cost-effective and compassionate. Nevertheless, most states do not share Virginia's philosophy (Okie, 1998).

HEAD INJURIES

Head injuries can result in a variety of impairments and can precede entering prison or occur in prison. The subject of head injuries among prisoners, although of critical importance, largely has been overlooked in corrections literature, with some notable exceptions that occurred in the 1990s. Templer and colleagues (1992) found a higher rate of permanent injury from head trauma in prisoners than other populations, and Sarapata, Herrmann, Johnson, and Aycock (1998) found a higher likelihood of head injury in incarcerated persons than nonincarcerated persons in very small compared samples. Merbitz, Jain, Good, and Jain (1995) touched upon the subject of communications impairments in their study of head-injured inmates in a midwestern state prison. Morrell and Merbitz (1998) found that inmates with head injuries were twice as likely as those without to be involved in disciplinary infractions, and they have a higher rate of head injury (83%) preceding imprisonment for felons than was found in nonincarcerated populations (5% of a college sample and 15% of a community sample). This is a health care need that deserves further study (CDC, 2007).

DISABILITIES

Inmates with disabilities are at a distinct disadvantage within correctional systems and are often a target for other inmates. Providing specialized services for inmates with disabilities, however, is not without controversy. Still, they have the same right to health care as all inmates have and, in addition, have protections under the Americans with Disabilities Act (ADA) of 1990.

Despite some studies, the exact number of prisoners with disabilities is not known. Not all prisoners may be identified, such as when a person with an intellectual disability or a learning disability may be assumed not to have a disability. There may be inadequate identification policies and procedures, a current egregious example of which has been described regarding the Los Angeles County Jail and its failure accurately to identify prisoners who use wheelchairs for the purposes of necessary accommodations (Disability Rights Legal Center, 2008; Winton, 2008). Data on physical disabilities may be gathered differently by different prisons or not gathered at all (Krienert, Henderson, & Vandiver, 2003). Even data gathered by the Bureau of Justice Statistics (BJS) may not be comparable over time (Maruschak, 2008). In some cases, too, the inmate may prefer not to self-identify into a stigmatized status. It would, however, be important to have consistency in identifying inmates who have disabilities and in providing them accommodations because their ability to communicate within and access their environments effectively plays an instrumental role in helping them mediate the vicissitudes of prison life. Furthermore, the continued graying of the prison population can be expected to place greater pressure on prison systems to meet the hearing, speech, visual, and cognitive needs of older inmates.

Paz (2008, p. 50) advocates for granting prisoners with disabilities their rights under the ADA and says: "If it is not feasible to treat disabled prisoners fairly and without discrimination in prison settings, then alternative settings should be considered." Preston (2003) reports on a Pennsylvania survey focused on determining support for a separate justice system for special needs populations and found support for a separate system for those with "mental disabilities" but less support for those with physical disabilities. There was little support for a system for older adult inmates, too. In addition, upon release from prisons, inmates rarely are placed in specialized caseloads or provided with extra assistance to help them reenter into society and access needed services. Therefore, despite legal protections of the ADA, specialized needs do not necessarily result in appropriate accommodations. Inmates with disabilities even often elicit extremely negative reactions from public officials and the general public in a way similar to how the budgetary needs of students receiving special education services elicit negative reactions from some school administrators and local taxpayers.

Disabilities among prisoners, like the general population, can occur in childhood or have an onset in adulthood. Although they can begin at any time in adulthood, elders certainly will have a disproportionate share. Disabilities can result from a variety of causes, such as a traumatic brain injury or a chronic illness such as diabetes or Alzheimer's, or they may be of unknown cause. They can have an impact on intellectual, mental, or physical functions. (Mental illness, which is a disability, is discussed separately in chapter 5 as a high-profile need.) One's life is less stressful and less restricted, though, when the social and physical environments provide accommodations for individuals' needs, or those environments are created using universal design principles that provide inclusion, comfort, and accessibility for people of diverse experiences and abilities. Essentially, universally designed environments are not "special" but accommodate the full range of people in society.

In one of the few systematic efforts to compare the speech, hearing, and visual status of state prison inmates with that of the general, non-incarcerated population, significant differences were found between the two groups in a 1997 BJS study of inmates' self-reports (Maruschak & Beck, 2001). Speech disabilities in state prison inmates were more than three times higher than in the general population (3.7% versus 1.0%). The state inmate with visual impairment, too, had higher prevalence rates, more than twice that of the general population (8.3% versus 3.1%). In contrast, the prevalence of hearing impairment among state inmates was surprisingly lower than that of the general population (5.7% versus 8.3%). In a 2004 systematic BJS study (Maruschak, 2008), which was pointed out as not comparable to data in the previous BJS study, state prison inmates reported speech impairments at a rate of 3.8% and federal inmates at a rate of 1.5%; vision impairments at a rate of 10.3% for state inmates and 8.6% for federal inmates, and hearing impairments at a rate of 7.0% for state inmates and 5.0% for federal inmates.

Other estimates, however, have been higher for those with deafness or hearing impairment. Vernon (1995), estimated that anywhere from 13-20% of all inmates had significant hearing loss. Miller (2001) cited estimates of 30–40% of inmates in correctional facilities having "significant hearing loss." Twersky-Glasner and Sheridan (2005) pointed out that no federal agency requires and compiles data on prisoners who are deaf from states and localities. Whatever their numbers may be, inmates who are deaf or have hearing impairments face considerable challenges in the criminal justice system (Miller, 2004; Vernon & Miller, 2005; DePree, 2006). One of those challenges is in literacy, a lack of which makes it more difficult to understand one's environment and promotes isolation and boredom in an already isolating and boring environment. A Texas study (Miller, 2004) found that more than half of the inmates who were deaf had functional literacy levels below grade three. Vernon and Miller (2005) pointed out that inmates who are deaf can find themselves violating prison rules because of a lack of awareness of verbal orders and auditory signals such as buzzers and doors rolling and even be at risk of rape and other assaults because of limited awareness of their surroundings. Also, Miller (2001), in analyzing twenty-two court cases after the ADA and a survey of forty-six professional sign language interpreters working in criminal justice settings, raised serious concerns about due process rights for defendants and inmates who are deaf or have hearing impairments.

A 1990 study of state and federal prisons found that the percentage of the inmate population with ambulating problems ranged from 0.04–0.05 percent. A 1992 study found the percentage of inmates with mobility impairments and who used wheelchairs in state prisons ranged from 0.12–1.35 percent (Gardner, 1998). A 2004 BJS study (Maruschak, 2008) found 1.4 percent of state prison inmates and 1.6 percent of federal prison inmates to have paralysis and 2.5 percent of state inmates and 2.3 percent of federal inmates to have mobility impairments (which was described as use of a cane, wheelchair, walker, hearing aid, or other aids in daily activity).

The controversy surrounding the decision to deny Rudolfo Hernandez, aged fifty-two, a prosthetic limb to enable him to walk to his execution received national news (Jorden, 2002). The cost of the prosthesis (approximately $15,000) was not the reason for denial, since one firm offered to donate the prosthesis. A Texas correctional department spokesperson noted:

> The prison system has clinics for inmate-amputees and policies for inmates who may need an artificial limb. One requirement is that the limb be "necessary for safe performance of major functional activities" like movement, self-care and balance . . . After Hernandez's left leg was amputated four inches below the knee . . . because of complications from the diabetes, he developed a staph infection that won't clear up so that he can be fitted . . . We can't do it as long as an infection is here" (Jorden, 2002, p. 1).

Although physical disabilities and chronic illnesses are not well counted in prisons, they may be able to be counted more easily than disabilities that are related to intellectual, learning, or cognitive functioning. Disabilities related to intellectual functioning of prisoners generally have been discussed under the rubric of "mental retardation and death row," clearly an important topic. In June 2002, the Supreme Court ruled in the case *Atkins v. Virginia* that executions of prisoners judged to be "mentally retarded" cannot be allowed because the Eighth Amendment prohibits cruel and unusual punishment (Davis, 2005; Ho, 2003). The discussion of learning needs and special education of prisoners, however, has not received as much attention as it warrants. Nevertheless, any examination of health care in prisons cannot be accomplished without also taking into consideration learning needs of various types.

The assignment of diagnoses or the use of categories such as "learning disability," "learning impairment," "intellectual disability," "mental retardation," "lower functioning," "developmental disability," "emotional disturbance," or "attention deficit/hyperactivity disorder" are complex, subjective, and controversial. One major controversy is the use of the term "mental retardation," which is seen by advocates and self-advocates as demeaning and stigmatizing. It is recognized that long-term damage and low expectations are caused by the assignment of such an antiquated, pejorative label. This is important to note here in and of itself but also to assert that, where the term is used in research that is described, this is not the preferred term of the authors, who prefer the term "intellectual disability." Furthermore, controversy exists about the assignment of the diagnoses of "mental retardation" versus "learning disability." In fact, in 1969, the American Association on Mental Retardation changed the criterion for "mental retardation" from an intelligence quotient (IQ) score of 85 to an IQ score of 70 (Harry, Klingner, Sturges, & Moore, 2002). This change cast serious doubt on the "scientific" nature of the diagnoses and raised the issue that they are socially constructed, if persons who one day were "mentally retarded" were the next day "learning disabled."

The long overdue move away from the term "mental retardation" is evident from a social policy perspective in the name changes of various public agencies and advocacy groups. Examples include the name change of the President's Committee on Mental Retardation to the President's Committee on People with Intellectual Disabilities in 2003; the removal of the term "mental retardation" from the mission statement of the Arc (at one time known as the Association for Retarded Citizens) in 2005; the name change of the 130 year old American Association on Mental Retardation to the American Association on Intellectual and Developmental Disabilities in 2006; the fact that only ten states still use the term "mental retardation" in their state service agencies for persons with disabilities; and the legislation that is progressing in 2008 in Massachusetts to change the name of its Department of Mental Retardation to the Department of Developmental Services (Berry, Spilka, & Sarkissian, 2008).

The value of IQ tests has long been questioned. The strengths and "multiple intelligences" these tests miss were identified more than twenty years ago (Gardner, 1985). The racial bias in the overall special education evaluation process has been identified, too (Losen & Orfield, 2002). African

American students are more than twice as likely as White students to be put into special education "mental retardation"programs, and they are two-thirds more likely than White students to be put into special education "emotional disturbance" programs (Children's Defense Fund, 2007). Also, students of color, especially African American and Latino students, are less likely than White students to be educated in fully inclusive settings and more likely to be educated in segregated, restrictive, separate settings than White students (Fierros & Conroy, 2002). To these controversies and concerns within the general population, one needs to add the further issue of the assignment of such diagnoses to an already stigmatized prison population. One issue is that prisons are not known for their careful assessment and addressing of prisoners' learning needs. They also are not known for their skill in assessing and addressing legitimate needs for protection of prisoners who have any difficulty negotiating the prison setting. Furthermore, prisons serve a disproportionate number of people of color, who often do not receive the benefit of the doubt in the assignment of stigmatizing labels. Finally, schools systems are a part of the trajectory that has been identified by the Children's Defense Fund (2007) as the "cradle to prison pipeline."

Nevertheless, prisoners are categorized as having various intellectual, cognitive, or learning issues, sometimes using demeaning diagnostic labels. At times, these labels are used by legal advocates to attempt to protect prisoners with a diagnosis of "mental retardation" from the death penalty. At times, labels serve to provide protection to prisoners who may be preyed upon by other inmates or staff. In addition, labels are used in the special education system that give youth sentenced to adult prisons legal rights to special education services within prison walls. Therefore, researchers who use terms with which the authors take issue often use those terms as they find them assigned within prison systems. Nichols, Bench, Morlok, and Liston (2003), however, caution that assignment of diagnoses in correctional settings may not reflect an inmate's true capabilities. In addition, terminology differs from study to study, so one must strive to understand what issues any particular terminology in a study denotes. Still, even doing that does not negate the fact that "definitional and terminological variation" makes research itself and the comparison of studies problematic (Hassan & Gordon, 2003, p. 29).

The term "developmental disabilities" that is used in some studies is an umbrella term that denotes disabilities that begin at birth or in childhood and can include a variety of diagnoses. The United States Administration on Developmental Disabilities (2007, p.1) which is responsible for the implementation and administration of the Developmental Disabilities Assistance and

Bill of Rights Act of 2000, defines developmental disabilities as "severe, life-long disabilities attributable to mental and/or physical impairments, manifested before age twenty-two." It further states that developmental disabilities result in substantial limitations in three or more areas of major life activities: "capacity for independent living; economic self-sufficiency; learning; mobility; receptive and expressive language; self-care; and self-direction." The Centers for Disease Control and Prevention (2007, p. 1) provides several examples: "autism spectrum disorders; cerebral palsy; hearing loss; mental retardation; and vision impairment."

State developmental agencies have similar, but not necessarily as broad, definitions, with the Massachusetts Developmental Disabilities Council (2007, p. 1) adding that developmental disabilities are "attributable to a mental, emotional, sensory, and/or physical impairment that is apparent before the age of twenty-two. People with developmental disabilities often need a combination of special services, support, and other assistance that is likely to continue indefinitely." The agency also asserts that persons with developmental disabilities in the general population are the most severely underserved population in Massachusetts.

Historically, the term was coined as part of an effort to bring advocates for people with various disabilities together to effect policy change. Although a person with a developmental disability does not necessarily have an intellectual disability, in order to avoid stigma of the term "mental retardation," some advocates and researchers use the umbrella term "developmental disabilities" as a proxy for intellectual disabilities, or the use of the term may not be entirely clear. Nevertheless, the term certainly can be assumed to mean people who may benefit from certain assistance, accommodations, or education in prison.

Petersilia (2000b) used the term "developmental disabilities" to describe people with intellectual disabilities. She cited national estimates that say that prisoners with this diagnosis account for 4–10% of the prison population, greater than the general population, with an estimate of 2–3%. In California, she estimated conservatively that there were 15,518 individuals with such disabilities in jail or prison or on probation or parole. Many will not be recognized as having intellectual disabilities while in prison and, further, will be victimized by other prisoners (Arrayan, 2003; Petersilia, 2000b).

Some sources that have used the term "mental retardation" have cited varying estimates: 2.5% (McCarthy, 1985); 4% (RAND Corporation, 1997); 3–9.5% (Russell & Stewart, 2001); and 10% (Anno, 2001). Ho (2003) pointed out that determining the prevalence rate is extremely difficult and that there is a lack of standardized screening processes across jurisdictions as well as possible racial bias in assessments. Whatever the numbers of prisoners with intellectual disabilities are, RAND Corporation (1997, p. 2) expressed the concern, based on its study, that "whether states take action to save money or to comply with a court order, much more needs to be known to ensure that the actions taken will serve justice, the taxpayer, and the offender with mental retardation."

New York State, in one of the earliest studies on developmental disabilities, found that 2% of state inmates had such disabilities in 1991 (New York State Correctional Facilities Commission, 1991). It was estimated that as many as 15% of the inmate population experienced some form of limitation in basic life skills (basic job performance skills, personal hygiene and health care, meal preparation, and home budgeting) for successful reentry into the community. Specialized units were created in New York State to protect inmates when they were at risk for potential harm from other inmates (Ray, Harmon, & Trojnor, 1991).

Unfortunately, there has been a lack of uniform assessment of inmates at entry into prisons with a specific focus on uncovering "learning disabilities," too. In one analysis in the 1990s, such prisoners were speculated to account for approximately 30% of the prison population (Sturmski, 1996), and the National Institute for Literacy (2002) has used the estimate of 30–50%. A 2004 BJS study (Maruschak, 2008) in which state and federal prison inmates were asked to self-report on having a "learning impairment" found that 23.3% of state prisoners and 12.7 percent of federal prisoners noted they had this. Prisons have been criticized for having inadequate resources, training, and equipment to meet the needs of inmates with learning disabilities, though (National Adult Literacy and Learning Disabilities Center, 1996).

Although the focus of this book is on prisons, which largely incarcerate adults, some juveniles are sentenced to adult prisons and jails. It is not possible to determine their specific rates of various disabilities because data on disabilities are not gathered and reported routinely from prisons by age. The latest relevant survey by BJS (Maruschak, 2008) did report age categories, but the youngest category was "24 or younger." (In fact, the only category for elders was "45 or older.") Also, nationwide statistics on disabilities or special education needs that juveniles have who enter correctional facilities encompass the many types of juvenile correctional facilities in which youth are incarcerated as well as adult prisons. "Incarcerated youths with disabilities may be housed in jails, detention facilities, group homes for young offenders, adult or juvenile prisons, camps, ranches, private programs, or treatment facilities" (National Center on Education, Disability and Juvenile Justice, 1999, p. 2).

There are, however, some general estimates that have been made about juveniles with disabilities in the criminal justice system. One estimate was that 55% of incarcerated juveniles had learning disabilities (Russell & Stewart, 2001). Those classified as having some form of "mental retardation" have been estimated to range from 10–30%, compared to 1–3% of the general population (Glick, Sturgeon, & Venator-Santiago, 1998). A study in the 1980s of fourteen juveniles condemned to death found that all fourteen had multiple disabilities such as neurological impairment, mental illness, and cognitive deficits, and most suffered from central nervous system injuries resulting from physical and/or sexual abuse in early childhood (Lewis, 1988). Another study estimated disabilities among juveniles as follows: 45% with specific learning disability; 42% with emotional disturbance; 7% with "mental retardation;" 3% with speech or language impairment; and 3% with other disabilities (visual impairment, hearing impairment, other health impairment, orthopedic impairment, autism, traumatic brain injury, multiple disabilities, or deaf-blindness) (National Center on Education, Disability and Juvenile Justice, 1999).

The provision of educational services to juvenile inmates with disabilities is required primarily by the federal Individual with Disabilities Education Act (IDEA) for youth through age twenty-one, although Section 504 of the Rehabilitation Act and the Americans with Disabilities Act also provide protections and access. There are some exceptions within IDEA, though. For example, for youth ages eighteen through twenty-one who had no finding of a need for special education services before imprisonment, states are not required by federal law to provide them with special education services while incarcerated. While special education is provided to youth in correctional settings, lawsuits indicate that this does not always happen (Burrell & Warboys, 2000; National Center on Education, Disability and Juvenile Justice, 2005; Quinn, Rutherford, & Leone, 2001). These lawsuits can take years to resolve, whether against juvenile facilities or adult facilities to which youth are committed, rather than result in timely provision of educational services. It is very unfortunate that incarcerated youth and their advocates have to bring lawsuits to obtain education or that the youth have to wait so long for an education that they might have been provided on the outside in a more timely and less adversarial manner.

CONCLUSION

Health and disability issues rarely are simple to identify or define, let alone successfully address. This occurs in the general population and in the inmate population, too. However, solutions to problems within prisons are complex because of the status of the "patient" or, in the case of special education, "student." Is the inmate a patient or student first? Is the inmate an inmate or someone who happens to have needs related to illness or disability? The stance taken in answering these questions dictates the approach correctional systems take toward provision of services.

The "low-profile" needs and issues identified and addressed in this chapter are certainly not minor for the inmates who have them—or for society, for that matter. Many of these are co-occurring and substantially affect inmates' lives within and outside of prison upon their release, with far-reaching consequences for their families and communities. Prison officials also have serious concerns about these issues and needs, particularly since they involve prison officials delivering new forms of care or services. Further, the associated financial costs are significant. In short, these issues and needs are legitimate concerns for society. If not taken seriously, then it will be only a question of time before they are "promoted" to high-profile status. The "low- profile" nature of these needs and issues does not equate with a low level of necessary attention.

7

DEATH AND DYING

The last several decades have brought the subject of death and dying onto the national scene. Major organizations either have developed or expanded significantly in their scope and influence on this subject. This increased attention has translated into an increased awareness of this phase of the life cycle and in greater organizational resources for helping the dying and their loved ones with grieving. Society has started to embrace the concept of compassionate end-of-life care, although with great debate from a religious and social standpoint, and the economics of the subject taking secondary status. The subjects of death, dying, and compassion, however, have been slow in working their way into this nation's prison systems (Baker, 2005; Byock, 2002; Levine, 2005; O'Connor, 2006; Tillman, 2000).

The early twenty-first century has ushered the subject into the nation's prisons and, with it, questions of how best to meet the needs of dying inmates within a total institution with a primary mission of maintaining safety (Linder et al., 2002; Linder, Knauf, Enders & Meyers, 2002; Shimkus, 2002). Humanitarian end-of-life care requires that dying inmates be cared for and be comfortable in the process. Both care and comfort are of equal importance in guiding end-of-life care (Zimmermann, Wald & Thompson, 2002). Prison administrators find themselves fulfilling roles of funeral directors, cemetery operators, and grief counselors, for which they have not been prepared properly (McMahon, 2003).

The likelihood of inmates actually dying in prison while serving their sentence has increased significantly in the last two decades, with an initial recognition in the early to mid-1990s (Duggar, 1995; Zimmerman, Wald & Thompson, 2002). Willmott and Olphen (2005) note that inmates often enter prison systems with acute health conditions that eventually turn into chronic illnesses, with incarceration effectively turning into a death sentence. A recent *New York Times* survey of forty states (data unavailable for ten states) found that two-thirds witnessed at least a 50% increase in the number of inmates with life sentences between 1993 and 2004 (Liptak, 2005b,d). This translates to 10% of a total prison population of 132,000. With this projected increase in the number of inmates who eventually will die in prison, there has been a greater awareness of the costs associated with this phase in their lives and the need for model programs to bring a cost-effective and more humane treatment in end-of-life care.

What does it mean for an inmate to realize that he or she will not only age in place but also will, in all likelihood, die in place? The prospect of actually dying in prison is probably one of the most depressing thoughts for an inmate, as well captured by Williams (2001):

> I was surprised when a fellow inmate said he was opposed to state-sanctioned executions in one breath and in the next wished a death sentence on himself. He has served 20 years of a life sentence and said he couldn't accept growing old and dying in prison. He cited the severing of familial ties, the inadequate medical care of older inmates and the treatment they endure from the younger ones who have a blatant disregard for their elders or for life itself . . . "Before reaching that point of hopelessness, uselessness," he said, "I would rather get a lethal substance, a syringe, make my peace with God and release the substance into my veins. I would close my eyes and welcome death." . . . But why? To circumvent the final indignity exacted upon a lifer by the state. The humiliation of dying alone, slowly and painfully, in a prison hospital ward and then having his emaciated body shipped to the state morgue where the unclaimed are unceremoniously cremated. By injecting himself with a lethal substance, his will to be free would be executed on his own terms. (p. 9A)

This chapter examines statistics and trends, provides case examples, and highlights how changes in prison population profiles and correctional policies bring relevance to the subjects of death and dying and hospice care in prisons. Death and dying classes and workshops are no longer the exclusive domain of hospitals and geriatric settings; prisons are the new frontier for these subjects. Yampolskaya and Winston (2003), in a study of the components and outcomes of prison hospice programs, concluded that these programs not only increase the quality and comfort of care, but do so in a cost-effective manner.

Dying in prison requires the development of innovative and compassionate strategies and program models; it also very often necessitates that correctional institutions develop a multifaceted set of policies and programs, since the range of issues and health needs within prisons are complex (Zimmermann, Wald & Thompson, 2002). These new initiatives being accepted and successful, however, will necessitate that a consensus be reached on key ethical questions, financing, and safety compromises (O'Connor, 2006). In essence, society must confront the essence of what punishment means and at what point compassion and forgiveness enter into decisions. The decisions related to this and other questions will form the philosophical underpinnings of a comprehensive strategy for end-of-life care within prisons.

RATES AND REASONS FOR INMATE DEATHS

Institutions such as hospitals and nursing homes historically have dealt with the subject of death almost on a daily basis, and the professional literature on this subject reflects this reality. However, death and mourning are increasingly commonplace in today's prisons and are no longer restricted to inmates on death row or those serving life sentences (Levine, 2005; Maull, 1998; Pfeiffer, 2005a,b). The state of Kansas, for example, experienced forty-six inmates' deaths during the January 2003 to July 2004 period; twenty-eight were the result of natural causes, twelve were suicides, and six were under investigation (Associated Press & Local Wire, 2006a). One county jail, Sedgwick, experienced twenty-six suicide attempts over a 12-month period. The Pendelton Correctional Facility in Indiana experienced three deaths over a two-month period, two of which were due to drug overdoses and one of which was an apparent suicide (Associated Press, 2006b).

Misdiagnoses of serious illnesses also have to be considered in the case of inmates dying from natural causes, as in the case of Lloyd Martell in Michigan, although this dimension often is overlooked in discussions of prison deaths:

> Lloyd Martell knows that he soon will be dead from the colon cancer that has spread to his lymph nodes and lungs. What bothers him is he could have gotten treatment that may have saved his life if a prison doctor had told him the polyp removed from his colon in December 2004 was cancerous. At 41, he still could look forward to a full life, still could watch his two sons, ages 6 and 7, grow up. . . . Martell serving one to four years for fleeing Detroit-area police, who tried to stop him while

he was driving on a suspended license, asked a prison doctor to remove what he thought was a hemorrhoid. . . . [the doctor] assured him it was a benign polyp and sent him back to his cell, Martell said. Eleven months later, in November 2005, Martell began bleeding from his rectum and was admitted to . . . [the] . . . hospital. That's when a doctor showed him a pathology report written when the polyp was removed nearly a year earlier. "She told me it was stage-four colon cancer," Martell said, "I had 20 months to live. My life changed dramatically at that moment. That's when I realized I was facing a death sentence for fleeing and eluding." In August [2006], Martell was granted a medical parole and sent home to die. (Shellenbarger, 2006, p. 1)

Dying in prison is what most inmates fear the most. They are separated from family and friends (those who matter most in their lives) and are in a setting that symbolizes what for many is a low point in their lives. Inmates are no different than the general population (80%) who want to die at home (Byock, 2002). The case of Bill Gause in Arizona State Prison illustrates this point:

Bill Gause, who has spent half his lifetime behind bars, expects to die in prison. Now 72, Gause came to prison in 1969 for killing his estranged wife. Years ago, he was a prison trustee who even managed a bus garage for a school district. Now, he picks up cigarette butts. Gause's left leg, ravaged by arthritis, doesn't hold him anymore, so he is in a wheelchair. The arthritis also is in his elbows where the pain is so intense it burns. He has kidney stones that double him over and three stents in his heart after two heart attacks. His bifocals changed almost constantly as his eyesight worsened. He pops 10 pills twice a day and uses an inhaler for his emphysema. "I think they brought me here to die," Gause said from his dormitory-style housing unit for disabled inmates at the Tucson prison. "I'm not too far from it." (Villa, 2005, p. 1)

The increased prevalence of deaths within correctional institutions such as prisons has placed a tremendous amount of strain on systems that are overcrowded and ill equipped to address the needs of dying prisoners. Cahal (2002), in tracing the origins of one hospice prison movement, noted that one study of forty-three inmate deaths in the Oregon prison system, between 1993 and 1996, found that thirty-four inmates died of natural causes, and twenty-six had a terminal prognosis at least three months prior to their death. This made a prison hospice program at one site viable, once institutional and inmate bias had been addressed. For example, one inmate referred to the infirmary as the "death house."

Deaths can be the result of natural causes, suicide, drug overdose, or inmate-on-inmate violence. Killings within prisons are not uncommon. Recently, over a seven-month period during 2003–2004, there were five killings in the Los Angeles County Jail. San Quentin had fewer killings covering the last eight-year period (LeDuff, 2004).

Deaths also can be the result of substandard health care practices (Pfeiffer, 2005a). The number of AIDS-related deaths has decreased to go along with the number of HIV-positive inmates. In 2003, there were 282 deaths resulting from AIDS, decreasing to 203 deaths in 2004 (U.S. Newswire, 2006). The rate decreased from 21 per 100,000 to 14 per 100,000.

It is estimated that from 2,500 to over 3,000 inmates now die of natural causes in the nation's prisons every year, an increase from an estimated 727 in 1980 and 1,500 in 1999 (Byock, 2002; Kolker, 2000; Stolberg, 2001). In 1999, natural causes were the leading cause of death in jails (385), followed closely by suicides (324) and AIDS-related deaths (222) (Bureau of Justice Statistics, 2001a). In Florida, in 1989, for example, a total of seventy-nine prisoners died in prison. However, in 1999, a total of 225 died, almost a 300% increase. The example of Huntsville, Texas, also illustrates this trend. In 1977, three inmates were buried in its cemetery. In 1987, the number increased to nineteen. In 1995, 102 inmates were buried there (Krane, 1999a). Nationally, in 1997, there were 824 terminally ill inmates placed in regular department of corrections infirmaries or prison hospitals, 152 placed in formal hospice settings within the system, and ninety-six who received compassionate release (U.S. Department of Justice, 1998).

The subject of death in prisons historically has been viewed from the point of view of the murder of inmates. Clashes between rival gangs, drug overdoses, vendettas, and deaths resulting from failed escapes as well as suicides usually are thought of when discussing inmate deaths, too (Dowdy, 1997; Theis, 1996). However, the introduction of HIV/AIDS into the prison system by inmates who are infected, and the deaths resulting from inmates with severe health problems, have brought a new dimension to this subject (Minkowitz, 1989). Although the trend toward a decreasing mortality rate as a result of better drug regimens for AIDS is promising, one never should lose sight of the fact that each death represents a person. Deaths due to medical reasons have cast death and dying within prisons in a totally new light by asking to what extent society is willing to allow circumstances surrounding the death of inmates to dictate the introduction of compassion within a punishment paradigm. Levine (2005) notes that less than 1% of inmates have advance directive discussions and even fewer complete an advance directive. These, incidentally, usually involve a do-not-resuscitate order.

The case of Dean Mallis puts a human face to those inmates with AIDS who will die while serving their sentences in prison:

A county jail in Maine is wrestling with a problem prisons throughout the United States are beginning to face: how to deal with seriously ill and dying inmates. Maine's Cumberland County Jail houses 26-year-old Dean Mallis, who is dying of complications from AIDS, in an 8-foot by 10-foot cell. He weighs just 62 pounds and is so weak he rarely gets up to walk across his cell to use the toilet. He scarcely has energy to eat, but he can summon up enough strength to say he does not want to die in jail. He has but six weeks to live. "When you look at his condition, his criminal behavior becomes moot . . . We have a human being. What do we want to do with him that's appropriately humane and meets our legal responsibility around custody? That's the balancing act." (Dardis, 2007, p. 6)

The state of Maine is certainly not alone in struggling with finding a balance between security goals and caring goals. The costs will be staggering in terms of economic, political, and social consequences. In 1995, the Florida corrections system, for example, estimated that treating the 2,171 state prison inmates who were HIV-positive or had AIDS cost the state $7.8 million (Pfankuch, 1999).

It is not unusual to find cases involving terminally ill inmates that defy conventional reason, such as that of the California state prison in which the state spent $900,000 to maintain twenty-four-hour coverage for six months over a dying inmate (Anonymous, 1997). Ellis's (1997) description of this terminally ill inmate raises possible end-of-life and compassionate release questions, including the role of hospice care:

For seven months, convicted burglar Frederick Lopez lay dying of AIDS in a bleak prison hospital while a warden's request "strongly urging" that he be allowed to spend his last days in the care of his family languished in the Orange County courthouse. "He suffers from dementia," said his sister. "He cannot walk. He cannot dress himself. It's hard for him to feed himself. He's dying, and I think he deserves to die outside prison near his family." . . . a judge . . . finally ordered Lopez's release to a hospice near his family. . . . His care in the final six months of life ultimately cost the state $888,709, including more than $200,000 for armed correctional officers while he lay immobile in a Marin County hospital. (p. A3)

Prisons have responded in a variety of ways to the increased number of deaths, and their responses have elucidated the conflicted nature of correctional systems toward dying inmates. Some simply have ignored this trend and either made no changes or made minimal changes in policies and procedures. Others have made more formal attempts, such as development of hospice programs, or allowed indigenous efforts to thrive, such as special burial rituals (Shimkus, 2002). As of 2000, there were twelve states with formal hospice programs, including California and Texas, and twelve states considering establishing such a program (Kolker, 2000). Many of these programs systematically have incorporated current prisoners and volunteers (Danton, 2001; Kolker, 2000; Williams, 2001). Having inmates work in these programs has been found to be beneficial to both patients and those assisting.

Death is becoming a greater reality in today's prison systems (Ratcliff, 2000; Steiner, 2003). No state has escaped this phenomenon. The cases of Gloria Broxton and Betty Jo Ross at the Central California Women's Facility at Chowchilla are excellent examples and bring to the foreground the importance of prisons having a set of guiding principles to help them address the needs of dying inmates.

THE CASE OF GLORIA BROXTON (MORAN, 2001)

Deep within the state prison, Gloria Broxton lies on a hospital bed, the life slowly ebbing out of her body. Her life can be measured in weeks, or perhaps, a handful of months. No one knows, but this much is for sure; Broxton, serving a six-year term . . . for dealing drugs, won't finish her sentence. The cancer inside her body is moving quicker than the calendar marking the remaining days of her prison term. . . . Broxton . . . wants her final breaths to be drawn outside the prison walls. Her hopes are lodged in a file stuffed with records, diagnoses, analyses and recommendations. It is her application for compassionate release, an obscure and rarely invoked proceeding that each year allows a few dozen terminally ill prisoners to be released before their prison term expires. It is a process that weighs medical, legal and even moral issues, and can be both grindingly bureaucratic and intensely emotional.

THE CASE OF BETTY JO ROSS (ARAX, 1994)

A 35-year-old woman dying of AIDS has been released from state prison after a three-month campaign by other inmates and AIDS activists who demanded her freedom on grounds of compassion. Betty Jo Ross, who suffers from AIDS-related dementia and blindness was released . . . from the Central California Women's Facility at Chowchilla after serving four months of a two-year sentence for assault with a deadly weapon. Ross's mother picked her

---

up at the prison 35 miles northwest of Fresno and drove her home to East Palo Alto. Doctors have told Ross, a mother of three, that she has less than six months to live. "It feels so good to have my child home with me . . . I can see her perking up a little bit. But she's a pretty sick girl. I took her to the hospital today and they want to keep her for awhile." . . . Even before her sentence, Ross had been found to have AIDS. Shortly after arriving at the prison . . . Ross became so weak that other inmates had to carry her to the dining hall. . . . The HIV-positive section of the prison, in which 52 infected inmates live, lacked a wheelchair. Ross spent a month in the prison infirmary, where the staff determined that she was in the final stages of AIDS.

Gloria Broxton and Betty Jo Ross are just two of hundreds who currently are dying in prison. Efforts to provide them with a compassionate release are often to no avail because prison bureaucracies and the courts are not fast enough to grant permission in a timely manner. These systems historically have not had to work together to release dying inmates.

Enders, Paterniti, and Meyers (2005) raise questions about advance-care planning and end-of-life decisions for female inmates. Prisons challenge effective communication between patients and health care personnel, making decision making difficult to achieve. The authors, in turn, emphasize the importance of female inmates having health information and providing all parties involved in decision making with requisite communication skills to reduce stress and vulnerability in this population group.

PRISON RESPONSES TO DEATHS

Byock (2002) raises a common and prevailing rationale that informs whether and how prison systems should respond to dying inmates:

> Why should we care where and how inmates die? This question is implicit whenever prison hospice or compassionate release is discussed in the media and with politicians. Many people would respond that we should care simply because prisoners are human beings and humane treatment is simply the right thing to do. Many Americans, however, feel that convicted murderers, rapists, child molesters, and drug dealers deserve whatever they get. If they die suffering, in pain and alone, so be it (p. 2).

Prison systems, as already noted earlier in this chapter, are being forced to decide how and when they must respond to dying inmates, or what is often referred to as "the least amongst us."

Rideau and Wikberg (1992) provide vivid details and chronicle the lives and deaths of numerous prisoners in a state prison in Louisiana and identify the loneliness, fears, sadness, and tragedies associated with the prospect of dying behind prison walls. O'Connor (2006), in turn, chronicles the case of a terminally ill inmate, covering a six-month period, and makes recommendations for the role of therapy and the presence of ethical dilemmas in helping an inmate in this stage. Once death occurs, it is rare to see visitors to a prison grave site. Prisoners, particularly those who have spent most of their lives behind bars, rarely have family and friends who maintain contact with them over the years. Death, in many ways, represents a continuation of this disconnect. Prisoners, being part of a prison community, witness these events and fear that they, too, will have a similar ending.

Ironically, death and dying within prisons generally is approached from the point of view of the inmates, and in unusual circumstances, their families, despite the fact that so much else about prisoners is viewed from the vantage point of security. When families of inmates suffer losses, they must address grief without the benefit of the individual who is incarcerated, which brings an often overlooked dimension to death. However, as noted by a warden of a geriatric nursing facility for prisoners, staff, too, are affected:

> Many old prisoners are lost to age, too. And losing them is tough on the people who guard and feed and counsel them . . . It's such a small place, everyone knows everyone. That's the hardest thing for my staff . . . the death and dying process (Porterfield, 1999, p. 3).

Taylor (2002) addresses the importance of training, mentoring, and nurturing for staff as they are called upon to address death: "Our own human experience of grief can cross the lines separating inmates, inmate families on the outside and within the prison system, victim families, and correctional staff" (p. 173).

Prison personnel now must be prepared for the phenomenon of death to occur for reasons other than violence or state-mandated executions (Bolger, 2005). Few personnel, however, are prepared emotionally for this experience. Correctional institutions, as a result, must institute training, consultation, and other forms of support to better prepare staff for what has become a more and more common occurrence, namely, losses.

The increased health complications that some dying prisoners face have raised important social, ethical, cost, and programmatic questions for this society and its correctional system (*AIDS Policy & Law*, 1997; Bauersmith & Gent, 2002; Betteridge, 2001). O'Connor (2004) raises the need for correctional systems to reexamine and institute new policies and procedures for pain management, use of existential therapy (review of meaningful events in the lives of inmates), and use of compassionate release. Steiner (2003), in turn, raises the possibility of prison systems instituting compassionate release policies to help dying inmates and relieve prison systems of the burden of meeting the needs of these inmates.

Institutional responses to the increased number of inmates dying while serving their sentence have not been restricted to correctional administration, with inmates, too, responding. The increased number of deaths occurring within prisons has necessitated that prisoners develop rituals to help them grieve the loss of their fellow inmates. These inmates help with grief before and after the death of an inmate, which usually is the role of hospice services, when available. These developments easily can be subsumed under the construct of "culture."

Increases in prison deaths have resulted in some prisons developing their own funeral industry, as in the case of Angola, Louisiana (Cobb, 1997; Schindler, 1999; Tillman, 2000). Prisoners build the coffins and have ritualized burial ceremonies such as having a horse-drawn hearse. One prisoner commented on the importance of the rituals for the entire community:

> Somebody's got to bury these guys. . . . It's not just a case of throwing them in the ground. We have a group of inmates who sing songs and pray over the guys, to give them a little respect, a little dignity (Krane, 1999a, p. 2).

The parallel with religious services is no mistake.

Inmates, too, have been called upon to serve as hospice caregivers. One inmate hospice volunteer described his experiences eloquently:

> When I first joined the hospice program, I didn't fully understand who we were going to help. . . . I didn't realize how many people here in the prison were dying. . . . I originally joined the program because I saw it as a way to atone for the things I've done, but I've learned a lot about myself in the past year. . . . I have found abilities and strengths that I didn't know I had (Cahal, 2002, p. 128).

Inmates assuming the role of hospice caregivers must meet established criteria to be a part of a program. Inmates convicted of sex or drug crimes, for example, are disqualified from participating. Inmates with serious violation of prison rules, too, are excluded (Shimkus, 2002). Once they pass an initial evaluation, they undergo training with a hospice trainer and can attend periodic meetings. Byock (2002) argues that there is much to be learned as to why inmates seek to work together without recognition or material reward, to care for one another and in the process create a civil community in one of the most inhospitable settings in the world.

ASSISTED SUICIDE

We can think of few topics that can be as controversial as physician-assisted suicide. The nation as a whole has in no way arrived at a consensus on terminal illness and suicide, although the subject is not alien to most people, and it is systematically being addressed in other countries. However, taking this controversial subject to the nation's prisons brings up many of the same issues encountered outside of prison walls and some additional ones, too. We broach this subject here with great trepidation. Nevertheless, broach it we must because the subject is not without some advocates as well as critics.

Hudson and colleagues (2006), in an Australian nonprison-based sample of health staff working with patients with advanced disease—with implications for the United States—put forth the use of guidelines to assist staff with "desire to die statements," or DTDS. The authors' guideline recommendations are intended to help health professionals with patient decisions for euthanasia or physician-assisted suicide. Prison health care staff working with inmates with advanced disease face many of the same issues raised by Hudson and colleagues, and additional ones due to the nature of the setting within which inmates find themselves.

The case of Lewis Roger Moore, a Colorado state correctional inmate, succinctly brings the issue of assisted suicide to prisoners and in the process also raises for scrutiny potential ethical breaches and dangers:

> A convicted paraplegic murderer who is serving a life prison term has asked that the state put him to death in an act of assisted suicide. Lewis Roger Moore said "lifers" should be allowed the option of assisted suicide as they grow older because "prison conditions often can be torturous on aging infirm lifers. There is no right for prisons to impose unbearable torture, especially perpetually—for the life of the prisoner." Moore wrote in a motion filed in Denver District Court, "By unbearable, this is the sole definition of the prisoner, no one else. When the prisoner decides prison is unbearable, he has the right to end life with suicide." Moore, a 48-year-old in a wheelchair, was found guilty in July 1981 of murdering his roommate . . . Moore claims there is no constitutional ban to suicide, and that no law prohibiting assisted suicide as applied to a "lifer" could possibly be constitutional . . . Moore's terrible injuries were no fault of his own. He was the innocent victim of a prison riot, in which he was stabbed and his spinal cord severed. (Pankratz, 1998, p. B4)

Clearly, this example illustrates not only the ethical issue of assisted suicide but also the risk of serious injury from violence in prisons. In addition, it raises the question whether quality of life, in prison or through compassionate release, could be improved so that a prisoner sees life as worth living. Levine (2005) concluded, based upon a study of end-of-life care of prisoners, that removing systematic barriers can be considered a starting point toward development of more consistent advance directive discussions and implementation of end-of-life care. A process that is normally difficult to address may be compounded further by confusion related to mental illness and competency and staff biases about end-of-life care. Baker (2005) raises the fact that there is a lack of literature on severe and persistent mental illness and palliative and end-of-life care, and this makes development of programs that much more difficult to develop for this population group within prisons.

There has been remarkable progress in introducing the subject of death and dying into the nation's prisons as the result of incredible pressures because of the rising number of inmates who have died while serving their sentences. As a result, the past decade or so has witnessed significant changes in how this subject is considered and acted upon in many of this country's prisons. This progress will, no doubt, not only continue but also will accelerate in the next decade because of the changing demographic profile of inmates and the increased economic and social costs associated with their imprisonment. The issues and approaches addressed in this chapter will not be resolved anytime soon. However, the questions are being asked, and that is the first critical step in developing appropriate responses to death and dying in prisons.

Some suggestions will be controversial, such as compassionate release and assisted suicides, clearly two ends of the spectrum as to how to allow prisoners to exit prison before completion of their sentences. As controversial as assisted suicide is outside prison, obviously it is as controversial with a person incarcerated for life. Compassionate release is controversial as well, because it contrasts with the ethics of punishment. Correctional systems likely increasingly will face ethical questions because there will be an ever-increasing number of inmates who will not see their freedom outside of prisons in the next two to three decades.

8

APPROACHES AND SERVICE
DELIVERY MODELS

The subject of long-term care in the United States has received and will continue to receive national attention because of the graying of this country's population, although there is no long-term care system in place now. This is not surprising, because there is no national health insurance, even for acute health care needs. For the general population, the cost falls on families, with some costs going to Medicaid for those who are eligible through poverty or "spending down." For people who are incarcerated, the government must pay for long-term care. Long-term care of prisoners is receiving attention in the hopes of developing new models that not only will save the country tax dollars but also can meet the ever-increasing needs of the patient, who also happens to be a prisoner, and doing so in a manner that, at least, addresses minimal health standards (Anno et al., 2004).

The health care needs and challenges facing this nation's prison population are considerable in nature and share much in common with health care needs of the general population. Nevertheless, there are a set of challenges that are specific to correctional health settings. The solutions to these challenges, in the eyes of many critics of the current system, are public health centered:

> The challenges for public health and corrections policymakers to address the threat of communicable diseases adequately will require deliberation and established policies on screening and testing protocols, compassionate release, isolation procedures for TB, and harm-reduction procedures (related to availability of condoms and sterile syringes). Proactive health education and prevention programs with emphasis on peer education warrants concerted attention by program planners. Moreover, collaboration with community agencies and health departments also will reduce

the public health threat to the community (Braithwaite, Braithwaite & Poulson, 1999, p. 5).

Braithwaite, Braithwaite, and Poulson (1999), like many of their colleagues in the field, advocate an expansion of a system of health care that brings prisons within the context of community through contracting and coordinating with community service providers. The isolation of prisons from the rest of society effectively has limited the resources and political and social capital that can be marshaled to assist in health care delivery. All parties benefit from an inclusion strategy. Nevertheless, such an approach brings prisons into direct contact with sectors of the community that not only do not have a history of contact with prisons but also possess negative stereotypes of prison personnel and inmates.

Watson, Simpson, and Hostick's (2004) review of national British and international literature on prison health care concluded, not surprisingly, that there was no one model that was applicable, but there were six cross-cutting themes that needed to be considered and incorporated into any model:

> Health promotion as a unifying concept for health care in prisons incorporating health needs assessment. Health screening on arrival in the prison system incorporating standardised protocols and validated instruments with an emphasis on mental health. Partnership between prison systems and the NHS [National Health Service]. Telemedicine as one mode of delivering health needs in prisons. Education of prison staff, including health care staff, about the health needs of prisoners. Developing a model of prison health care which looks beyond the prison environment to the communities which the prison serves (p. 126).

This chapter provides the reader with a perspective on different service delivery models currently in operation. Consolidated specialized units in prisons and early conditional medical release or compassionate release are examples that will be explored (Aday, 1994; Anzel, 2000; Brown, 1998; Lundstrom, 1994) as well as other examples.

WORTHINESS VERSUS GREATEST NEED

The debate between who is worthy enough to get services and who is unworthy is as old as this nation. The answer to this question has profound consequences for the nature and extent of services made available to prisoners. Although controversial, the U.S. Supreme Court has provided this nation with a clear and unequivocal stance on the rights of prisoners to receive the health care services they need. (Interestingly, the general population has no such right to either acute or long-term care, unlike all other industrialized nations.)

The moment the correctional system takes on the responsibility for the health and welfare of inmates, though, it assumes the role of administrator of punishment that is not cruel and unusual (Maroney, 2005). Inmates do lose some of their rights while they are incarcerated, and in some states, increasingly so. Upon release, they also may lose their right to vote and to hold certain employment positions. However, while they lose some rights, they also inherit a right to be cared for while under the supervision of the state, city, county, or federal government (Kay, 1991).

The National Commission on Correctional Health Care (1993b) put forth an argument for making third-party reimbursement for correctional health care that, unfortunately, still is relevant 16 years later:

> As a vital component of the community public health program, the financing of correctional health care is a responsibility that all in society must share. In the free world, private (i.e., health insurance and out-of-pocket expenditures) and public (i.e., Medicare and Medicaid) programs pay for this health care. The health care provided to those in jail or prison, however, is not included in these expenditures. Those who are incarcerated lose eligibility benefits even though they may have been eligible prior to arrest. Upon arrest, detention, conviction and sentencing, the burden of providing health care falls upon counties (i.e., jails) and the states (i.e., prisons, p. 1).

Fung (2002), in quoting the United Network of Organ Sharing Ethics Committee, argues this very controversial point. Fung states that:

> convicted criminals have been sentenced only to a specific punishment, and have not been sentenced by society to an additional punishment of an inability to receive consideration for medical services . . . and that absent any societal imperative, one's status as a prisoner should not preclude them from consideration for a transplant; such consideration does not guarantee transplantation (p. 2).

PROGRAMMATIC APPROACHES

Efforts to deliver acute health care and long-term care and to address public health concerns while containing costs in correctional facilities generally can fall into six types: (1) Consolidation of specialized medical care; (2) Managed care; (3) Use of telemedicine; (4) Compassionate release; (5) Hospice care; and (6) Continuity of care.

1. Consolidation of Specialized Medical Care

The development of specialized units in prisons has gained considerable momentum across the country in the past decade and has encountered numerous challenges along the way. This movement has been fueled, not surprisingly, by correctional systems trying to be more effective in provision of health services and trying to cut costs. Housing inmates together who are chronically ill or terminally ill and, in many cases, also aged, has allowed these systems to free prisons to carry out their primary mission of providing security by consolidating inmates who are too ill to be a security risk and who have needs that are not typical of the general prison population.

Elders, in similar fashion to other inmates who have physical or mental disabilities, HIV/AIDS, or other types of chronic illnesses necessitate specialized housing and health care and can be expected to continue to present unique challenges to prison systems in the early part of the twenty-first century (*Arizona Republic*, 2005; Clemmitt, 2007; Gubler & Petersilia, 2006; Haggerty, 2000; Kuhlmann & Ruddell, 2005; Perez, 1997; Rikard & Rosenberg, 2007; Rosenfield, 1993). Consequently, there is an increasing awareness of the need to provide alternatives to conventional prison beds for elder and "infirm" inmates (Abner, 2006; Adams, 1995; Lundstrom, 1994).

Flanagan (1992) argued for a new perspective or framework for more effectively addressing the needs of elder and special health care inmates, because the nature of corrections has changed over the years, and so has the profile of the population in prisons. The lengthening of prison sentences has resulted in creating unique problems and needs of long-term inmates. A new framework, or paradigm, is required for understanding the new and expanded roles of prisons in this country. Warehousing, although attractive to "hard-core" punishment advocates, is not a humane or even legal option. Improved management, however, directed by clear and ambitious goals, is the future for corrections. Better management of long-term prisoners advances the "state of the art" for correctional systems.

The consolidation of specialized medical care as a primary cost and service delivery strategy offers the most hope for prison health care, although not without controversy (Cropsey, Wexler, Melnick, Taxman & Young, 2007; Gubler & Petersilia, 2006; Warren, 2002). In a 1997 U.S. Department of Justice survey (Thigpen & Hunter, 1998), thirty-nine departments of corrections had consolidated portions of their medical services in one or multiple sites, and five were in the process of doing so at the time of the survey. At least twenty-seven departments had consolidated medical care for elders and/or terminally ill inmates, the most expensive sectors of the prison population.

Critics of this strategy of specialized settings have raised serious concerns about what it means to isolate chronically and/or terminally ill inmates from other inmates within the prison system. One criticism has been that older inmates are, in fact, respected by younger inmates because of their life experience, and this "stabilizing" influence is lost when they are segregated from younger prisoners (Wittmeier, 1999). Critics also have pointed out the tremendous economic costs of such efforts. However, they fail to take into account that people with chronic illnesses or disabilities in the general population who need long-term care services are economically costly to society, too, and it would be unfair to expect inmates to be any less costly (Holden, 2001).

Moving those prisoners from prisons to nursing homes, for example, where the state can get reimbursed can translate into significant savings, not to mention increased quality health care when compared to prisons. This move to nursing homes also makes inmates eligible for Medicaid, Social Security, pensions, and other potential benefits for which they would not be eligible by being in a prison (Beyerlein, 1997). Holman (1999) advocated the use of nursing homes in the community while still under correctional supervision ($32,000 annually) and, if needed, intensive probation supervision ($6,500 annually) for elder inmates in need of long-term care. The cost is still considerably lower than the estimated $69,000 for a nursing home prison cell. Further, in cases where elder inmates are honorably discharged military veterans, the Veterans Administration can meet their health care needs.

The 1980s witnessed a number of states responding to the needs of older adult inmates and inmates with disabilities through specialized housing. A landmark lawsuit in 1981 forced the state of Alabama to create a new form of prison specifically designed to address "infirm" older inmates (Krane, 1999b). In 1984, North Carolina developed the McCain Correctional Hospital as an inmate nursing home for frail elders and those with disabilities. South Carolina, Tennessee, and Kansas also established special facilities for older inmates or inmates with disabilities in the 1980s (Black, 1984).

In 1997, the state of Washington opened an assisted living prison, Ahtanum Heights, at a cost of $7 million to construct and an operating cost of $2 million per year to house 120 inmates (Porterfield, 1999). It had more in common with a nursing home than a correctional facility. The inmates, none of whom were terminally ill, all had chronic illnesses. The facility's focus was less on security and more on services, as evidenced by some of the operating rules:

> DeJonge [superintendent] runs his prison with a few simple rules. Everyone must have a job, from tending the garden to running the elevator. Everyone must do his own laundry, no matter how old he is. And if you don't have a high-school education and don't have any cognitive problems, you must work toward a high school equivalency diploma, even if you're 70 or older. The rules come as a shock to many of the elderly inmates used to quietly mildewing in their previous prison (Porterfield, 1999, p. 1).

In 1999, Virginia constructed a prison focused on providing assisted living care for inmates (Aoki, 1999). Wayne National Forest in Ohio, too, developed a 450-unit institution, at a cost of $10 million per year, or $22,000 per prisoner. Prisoners averaged fifty-nine years of age, with the oldest being eighty-seven (Krane, 1999b). Kentucky has two special units, one of which is considered the only licensed unit in a nursing care facility inside a medium security correctional facility in the United States (Ackerman, 2008). By 2002, over 50% of the state correctional systems had introduced some form of age-segregated accommodations (Yorston & Taylor, 2006). In 2005, there were sixteen states with special housing units for geriatric inmates (*Arizona Republic*, 2005). In the same year, Massachusetts became the first state in New England to provide an assisted-living facility for inmates (Belkin, 2005). In 2007, New York opened a thirty-bed unit specializing in treating inmates with dementia (Hill, 2007). The unit is housed in the third floor of Fishkill's medical center, with the average age of an inmate being sixty-two years, or twenty-six years older than the system-wide average.

The following are other examples that indicate that the movement toward separate units is shaping the correctional prison system across this country. Arkansas has two special housing areas for the most chronically ill inmates near its hospital in Pine Bluff, and an eighty-bed unit at the Jefferson County Correctional facility. Georgia has a 165-bed Men's Correctional Institution at Hartwick. Illinois has a specialized unit at the Dixon Correctional Center. Indiana has two facilities for inmates with special needs and older inmates. Louisiana has four programs. Maryland has special floors or hospital units. The Minnesota Correctional Facility Stillwater Senior Dormitory houses twenty-three men aged fifty or older. Mississippi has two special units at the Mississippi State Penitentiary at Parchmond. Missouri has a twenty-two-bed unit at Moberly Correctional

Center. New Jersey maintains a sixty-four-bed extended care unit for the most seriously ill inmates, including geriatric inmates. Nevada maintains a seventy-five-bed unit for older inmates at the Nevada Correctional Center in Carson City and a 100-bed unit at the Southern Nevada Correctional Center in North Las Vegas. Oklahoma opened a geriatric 250-bed unit at the Joseph Hart Correctional Center at Lexington. Pennsylvania opened the Laurel Highlands State Correctional Institute for older and "physically challenged" inmates. Texas has a sixty-bed geriatric facility at a regional medical center. West Virginia has a forty-five-bed unit at "Old Men's Colony" and a 450-bed unit conversion of a former "mental retardation" institution to a prison facility. Wyoming has special units at the Wyoming State Penitentiary (Alpert, 2001; Aoki, 1999; Baker, 1999; *Baton Rouge Advocate*, 1998; Florida Corrections Commission, 1999; Foster, 2000; Gaseau, 2001b; Jones, 2001; LaVecchia, 1997; Pendleton, 2000; Sheeler, 2001; Sizemore, 2000).

These "special" units inadvertently may result in elder inmates being removed further from their families as well as from other prisoners because of increased distances, though, thereby doubly isolating them "for their own good." However, in contrast, by 2005, only Alabama tested and placed all inmates with HIV in segregated housing, representing the trend away from segregation and toward a case-by-case determination (Kantor, 2006).

These "special prisons," some of which have been converted from state mental hospitals, and in the case of North Carolina, from a tuberculosis hospital, were supposed to lower medical costs by placing all geriatric prisoners in one setting (Black, 1989; *Keeper's Voice*, 1997). These specialized settings may not result in cost savings, though, particularly in the case of inmates over the age of sixty (Yorston & Taylor, 2006).

Prison inmates, as already addressed, have health-related problems at an earlier stage of their lives than others and are considered by many to be "elderly" at age fifty-five, fully ten years before the general population (Adams, 1995; Schreiber, 1999). Classification of "elderly" inmates, in turn, is difficult to do. Based on a 2001 study, only twenty-two of forty-nine state prisons that responded had a working definition of the term "elderly" (Shimkus, 2004).

Despite the considerable efforts prisons are making in several states to meet elders' needs, prisons often are ill equipped to address the multifaceted needs of older inmates:

> Still, many experts say U.S. prisons aren't ready to handle large numbers of elderly prisoners. There is a crisis in the making. The national prison

population is graying at an unprecedented rate, and the prison system is
simply not prepared to deal with gerontological disease and geriatric care
. . . . The geriatric prison population has very specialized needs that
most facilities are very poorly suited to handle. The result is that most
gerontological problems go untreated until they are chronic (Schreiber,
1999, p. 1).

Another issue is that special units in prisons can bring with them special issues, or tensions, as in the example of Alabama's segregated units for
HIV-positive inmates. Alabama's Limestone Correctional Facility houses
over 200 prisoners who are HIV-positive. These inmates are segregated
twenty-four-hours a day and do not participate in programs offered to non-
infected inmates. Prison concerns over the spread of AIDS weigh more
heavily than inmate access to programs available to noninfected inmates
within the prison system. Alabama's Tutwiler Prison for Women also has a
segregated unit for women, thirty in number. They, too, have no access to
educational and vocational programs offered to other female inmates.
Blumberg and Laster (1999), however, argue that segregation of prisoners,
in this case those with HIV/AIDS, provides a false sense of security for
those prisoners in the general population that the threat of HIV/AIDS has
been removed from their surroundings. Thus, efforts to do prevention and
education are seen as not necessary because it is believed there is no threat
of infection.

Special units also have been established to address the needs of inmates
with intellectual disabilities. A national survey of program characteristics for
"lower-functioning" and "mentally retarded" offenders (Nichols et al.,
2003), in which forty-one states participated (with California, Florida, Illinois, Indiana, North Dakota, Oklahoma, Texas, and Wisconsin not participating), found that only eighteen states indicated that they had a program
or living units specifically designed for "lower-functioning" inmates. The
remaining twenty-three states indicated that they did not offer such programs but tended to combine those inmates with inmates with mental illness if such a program existed for that group.

Texas, which did not participate in the survey, has developed two specialized housing units (731 beds) to "mitigate the negative effects of incarceration and to promote successful reintegration into the community for inmates with mental retardation" (Texas Department of Corrections, 2000,
p.1). The New York State Developmental Disabilities Planning Council
(2007) has a project called Person-Centered Planning for Inmates with Developmental Disabilities, which was designed "to lead to productive and ha-

bilitative incarceration for inmates with disabilities and significantly reduce recidivism rates" (p. 8). This project takes place under the supervision of the New York State Department of Corrections and the Division of Parole in the special units of Wende, Arthur Kill, and Sullivan. Cornell University provides training and technical support (Blessing, Golden, & Ruiz-Quin-tanilla, 2005).

2. Managed Care

The use of managed care to hold health care costs down also has found its way into the nation's correctional system. The rush toward managed care only can be appreciated fully within the context of the dramatic increase in the costs associated with health care provision:

> To harried prison officials, the arrival of HMOs must seem like a dream come true. Read their spiels: "We take full responsibility for all operational, financial, and legal responsibilities, so you can concentrate on the important duties of running a first-rate facility," coos Prison Health Services Inc., of Brentwood, Tennessee. Not to be outdone, Correctional Medical Services of St. Louis promises: "Contracting means you relinquish the hassles of managing your health care unit . . . when it comes time to pay for in-mate health care services, you'll receive only one bill.". . . For now, the list of questions outweighs the answers. But one thing is clear: Things are changing fast in the prison world, and privatization may well be the future of prison HIV care (Maddow, 2000, p. 1).

Managed care is a subject of intense debate regarding its use by the general population and, with an incarcerated population, it also raises issues such as quality of care.

3. Telemedicine

The potential of telemedicine programs only recently has started to be explored in the delivery of prison health services (Aoki et al., 2004; Doarn, Justis, Chaudhri & Merrell, 2005; Gailium, 1999), and it has gained popular-ity in the past several years as a result of an increased need within prisons (*Corrections Professional*, 2005i; Doarn, Justis, Chaudhri & Merrell, 2005; Tucker et al., 2006). Telemedicine can be defined as "the delivery and provision of health care and consultative services to individual patients and the transmission of in-formation related to care, over distance, using telecommunication technolo-gies" (National Commission on Correctional Health Care, 1997a, p. 1). The use of telecommunications technology to deliver health care can be traced back to the 1920s when radio was used to connect physicians at shore stations with ships at sea during medical emergencies. The remote location of most prisons makes accessibility to health care specialists arduous and expensive.

It has been estimated that twenty-seven states use telemedicine in their correctional programs (Laidler, 2001). One state program estimated that it cost the department $300 to transport one prisoner to an external-based health appointment. Overall, savings of $102 per patient contact were achieved by avoiding inmate transportation outside of the prison facility (Healthcare Info Tech Business Report Archives, 1999). Savings resulting from not having to transport prisoners to outside facilities increase the attractiveness of methods such as telemedicine (*Corrections Professionals*, 2005j).

Yet, the costs of establishing and maintaining a prison telemedicine program may make it too expensive to be cost-effective. Third-party payers do not cover related costs for professional fees or the purchase and implementation of the technology (Charles, 2000). Cost-effectiveness is also very much dependent upon the medical service being provided. One evaluation of a prison telemedicine program found significant cost savings in cases where inmate transfers via airplane charters were avoided and in-prison consultations were substituted by telemedicine conferences. However, modest cost savings resulted when trips to local medical facilities were averted (National Institute of Justice, 1999). Aoki and colleagues (2004), in a cost-effectiveness analysis of telemedicine evaluating diabetic retinopathy in a prison population, found that this method holds great potential for reducing costs of care and the consequences (blindness) of type 2 diabetes.

The possibility of alternating telemedicine with on-site visits by health care staff is one way of increasing access to health care and cutting costs in the process. Telemedicine can involve a variety of approaches: video, audio, and conference calls. Examinations, consultations, and patient records can be transmitted through telemedicine equipment (Slipy, 1995; Sit-DuVall, 2000). Also, transporting prisoners to community-based health care facilities, in addition, is a significant security risk (May, 2001). Telemedicine addresses issues of inconvenience, cost, and safety (Doarn, Justis, Chaudhri, & Merrell, 2005). It can be thought of as an auxilliary approach to other "in-house" approaches (Meystre, 2006).

Telemedicine, however, is not restricted to physical health care. Mental health services, too, have been delivered through this method (Fitzgibbons & Gunter, 2000). Tucker and colleagues (2006) found that telemedicine psychiatric services were favored by some inmates for evaluation of safety and sexual issues, although some inmates preferred the use of on-site mental health staff.

Although there is a considerable amount of capital investment up front in establishing a telemedicine program, the cost savings over time can be sufficient to use this approach to medical care delivery for some needs (Doarn, Justis, Chaudhri & Merrell, 2005). Shea (2006) predicts that the benefits of telemedicine will far outweigh the financial costs, particularly because the availability of software associated with this service facilitates access to data. However, it would be a serious mistake for prison officials to think that telemedicine will result in substantial savings or replace any in-house staffing of health care services. Still, it can serve a variety of important functions. For example, palliative care telemedicine has been proposed as an effective means of providing assessment and therapy for prisoners, as well as education for correctional staff on end-of-life treatment (Justis & Lyckholm, n.d.).

Although the potential of telemedicine for reducing costs and increasing access to health care has been identified, Anderson (2003) raises the possibility that this form of health delivery has issues when addressing women inmates:

1. Women's prisons are often more remote than men's.
2. Women's prisons are more lacking in medical facilities.
3. Women inmates have more health care needs that require expensive outside contractors. (e.g., childbirth) (p. 54)

Thus, reliance on telemedicine has the potential to place women inmates at a distinct disadvantage in receiving necessary health care when compared with their male counterparts. In addition, as is the case outside prisons, telemedicine raises confidentiality issues specific to the use of technology that transmits information from one facility to another.

4. Compassionate Release

The subject of compassionate release is complex and controversial (Kaplan, 1999; Steiner, 2003). Beck (1999) asserts that compassion cannot possibly be legislated or mandated by administrative decree. However, humane and compassionate care can be seriously thwarted by lack of standards or inhumane legal and administrative policies or by the way prison personnel elect to interpret laws and policies.

The important role litigation plays in helping to ensure inmates receive needed care is evident. With some exceptions, this litigation has taken on provision of health care through the use of the Eighth Amendment, which prohibits cruel and unusual punishment. However, liability of correctional systems for post-release health care has not received the attention it warrants. Yet, the role and responsibility of prisons to released or paroled prisoners has started to be raised in litigation efforts regarding health care:

> Many prisons have found the cheapest way to deal [with] these problems is to parole or discharge the prisoner on a "compassionate" release. Since most prisoners have no money, insurance, or community resources, the effect is often to deny them care or at least delay it (LSU Law Center, 2001, p. 1).

The increased presence of defendants who are HIV-positive or have AIDS, and who eventually will be imprisoned, has raised arguments for and against decreased sentencing. The arguments for extraordinary circumstances generally are based on four key criteria (Hansell, 1998):

1. Does the condition severely and predictably impair a defendant?
2. Is the prison system able to provide requisite health care?
3. Will incarceration worsen the health status of the defendant?
4. Would the health condition result in exposing the defendant to victimization?

These four criteria also can be applied to compassionate release cases.

Compassionate release, although increasingly being considered a viable option that is both humanitarian and cost-saving, is still controversial, and critics of these types of programs are getting organized politically. In the case of Louisiana's Victims and Citizens Against Crime, Executive Director Sandy Krasnoff stated its position on compassionate release quite clearly: "We don't want to hear all this baloney about how when they get old and sick we need to let them out" (Stolberg, 2001, p. A1). Critics of compassionate release contend that punishment must not be circumvented by extenuating circumstances and that these efforts not only do a disservice to victims, but also undermine the resolve of the country to extract justice.

The costs of housing dying prisoners can be considerable, with estimates of up to $75,000 per year (Anonymous, 1997). The costs of having prisoners released prior to completion of their sentence or their death can be both lowered and shared with other public systems. Having eliminated security costs allows for a focus on end-of-life care; prisoners moved out of a prison system can be covered by other governmental sources or even private insurance where applicable. However, sadly, it is not unusual to have inmates dying while they await processing of their medical parole (Kaplan, 1999).

Russell (1994), however, argues that although compassionate release programs are increasing in number, much progress needs to occur before they can accomplish the goals that led to their creation:

> The mechanisms for compassionate release of terminally ill prisoners now operating in the United States are many and varied. These mechanisms share some common features, and they certainly exist with a common purpose. It is unfortunate, therefore, that much of the compassionate release programs are inefficient in accomplishing these laudable humanitarian goals. It is of even greater concern that some jurisdictions and the federal system are essentially devoid of compassionate release mechanisms. The creation of systems that operate expeditiously and fairly is essential for success in the endeavor to extend humanitarian assistance even to those we have imprisoned. Ultimately, society itself is served if our compassionate impulses can reach beyond the issues of crime and punishment to serve all people as human beings (p. 836).

5. Hospice Care

The terms "palliative care" and "hospice care" often are used interchangeably. However, Byock (2002) differentiates these two terms: "Palliative care is a discipline; hospice is a way of delivering that discipline" (p. 4). Death often is considered the final stage of a prisoner's sentence as the result of the interplay of various factors addressed in this book (Dubler, 1998). Therefore, hospice care is an important option for many prisoners.

The first hospice program in the United States was established in New Haven, Connecticut, in 1974 (Griffith, 2001; Williams, 2001). Hospice programs now are in more than 4,160 locations across the country (Scheffenacker, 2007). The number of prison hospice programs has increased in the past decade (Wright & Bronstein, 2007).

In 1998, a survey was conducted of fifty-three correctional systems (forty-seven states, Bureau of Prisons, Philadelphia, Guam, Virgin Islands, and Washington, D.C.) to identify current and projected end-of-life programs (Ratcliff & Cohn, 2000). It found that nineteen systems did not have any form of hospice or palliative care program or any plans to develop one. Twelve were seriously considering establishing a program. Nine provided some form of palliative care but did not have a formal hospice, and twelve had a formal hospice program.

In 2000, the National Prison Hospice Association (NPHA) found that there were approximately twenty to twenty-five active hospice programs in prisons out of a total of 1,300 state and federal prisons (*Arizona Republic*, 2005; Hot Topics in Healthcare, 2000). A 2004 survey (Maull, 2005) found that thirty-five state prisons and the federal prison system had formalized hospice programs. Therefore, hospice is not widely used in prisons, although its use is emerging. Its use in the general public is larger but still not necessarily the first choice of persons who are terminally ill. Its compassionate principles may serve an aging population well, though, if prisoners are given the choice to use it.

The projected increase in the number of inmates who will die in prison prior to completion of their sentence raises many of the same issues and dilemmas found in the general population as that group grays, too. Advance directives, for example, are no longer within the exclusive domain of the general population and are also applicable to the incarcerated. The use of a living will, do not resuscitate orders (DNRs), health care proxy, and durable power of attorney are applicable within prisons, although the nature of the confinement can make carrying them out and monitoring them quite arduous and possibly compromising (Levine, 2005).

Advocates of humanitarian end-of-life care would argue that it is at this stage that the goals of health care and incarceration are more likely to clash:

> The antagonism, suspicion, and fear that have governed the relationship between inmate and authorities prior to the last stage of illness continue to define and constrain that relationship during the inmate's dying. For this reason, among others, compassionate release of dying inmates is such an important part of planning for terminal care. (Dubler, 1998, p. 152)

Introduction of compassionate end-of-life care in prisons will require dramatic changes in the structure of hospice services along with an equally dramatic change in prison culture. Mara (2004), for example, discusses the fact that hospices in prisons have the special requirement of security and so may prohibit the use of volunteers from outside the prison. Instead, volunteers may be drawn from the inmate population, as has been done in the Louisiana State Penitentiary in Angola.

In many prisons, there has been a slow but no less dynamic shift in culture regarding death and dying (Kolker, 2000). This shift is nowhere more pronounced than in the attention paid to the physical and emotional needs of dying inmates. The establishment of prison-based hospice programs provides staff and inmates with an opportunity to refocus from concerns about safety and punishment to humanistic concerns for the dying. The hospice movement in the United States has made tremendous progress over the past several decades, and this progress is evident in the correctional system.

6. Continuity of Care

Continuity of health care after prisoners are released is inadequate and is especially important for people with long-term care needs, such as severe and persistent mental illness or AIDS. For example, failure to provide medications upon release is now common practice because of concerns about inmates selling their medications. There is also an unwillingness of doctors to release with prescriptions because these imply a responsibility for follow-up care once in the community. In contrast, one study of New Jersey jails found that three-quarters of administrators believed that providing inmates with two weeks of medication at release is very or extremely important to their health (Wolff & Veysey, 2001). The court system can help ensure that released inmates have medications or prescriptions for medications by ordering treatment as a condition of release or actually releasing inmates to the custody of a mental health provider (Wolff & Veysey, 2001).

Continuity of care as a guiding programmatic principle is predicated upon active collaboration between correctional systems and community services. The National Commission on Correctional Health Care (1995) took a stand that inmate health care was part of a national public health continuum. The dynamic nature of incarceration in which 10 million are processed into jails annually and eventually released, and 850,000 are released from prisons annually, causes inmate health problems to become community health problems and thereby society's health problems (Kahn, 2000).

The expansion and development of continuity of care models will necessitate creation of new partnerships between prisons and community-based organizations (Laufer et al., 2002). Establishing effective partnerships between correctional settings and community settings is challenged by the nature of the patient population though:

> The past behavior and present circumstances of inmates also create problems when trying to connect them back to services in the community. Some of the problems [are] . . . lack of insurance coverage, history of violence, and history of incarceration. Shelters often will not take people with criminal histories, and service providers will not take people without insurance coverage. In addition, some inmates have strained relations with some programs and providers and, as such, have burned service bridges, making it more difficult to find treatment services and housing for them. (Wolff & Veysey, 2001, p. 10)

Still, continuity of care benefits both released prisoners and the community.

CONCLUSION

There is little question that the subject of correctional health care is getting national attention at the federal and state levels. The spiraling costs and the dilemmas associated with inmate health care delivery, including the end-of-life stage, have prompted policymakers and elected officials to develop and implement a variety of approaches toward America's inmates. The approaches highlighted in this chapter represent an ever-expanding arena that will only continue to expand into the immediate future.

These approaches must not only contend with provision of quality care within a correctional setting, but must also prove to be financially prudent in an age where elected officials are increasingly more reluctant to increase taxes, or admit that this nation's experimentation with incarceration has failed, and the price of this failure is increasing dramatically with no end in sight.

9

FINANCIAL COST CONSIDERATIONS

The sensational attention that prison health care has received at the national and local levels is probably primarily the result of the "low incidence" cases, such as those involving heart and kidney transplants or sex reassignment surgeries. However, these high-profile cases mask other forms of attention, particularly on the part of elected officials and policymakers and prison administrators, namely, the high costs of health care and the challenges in providing this service within a correctional system. Potter (2002) notes that prison health care primarily is discussed as a "budgetary" or "logistical" nightmare rather than as a public health concern. The subject of correctional health care costs, however, is difficult to disentangle from society's values pertaining to crime and punishment. Further, determining the financial costs of prison health care is difficult under the best of circumstances, and not within the grasp of "ordinary" citizens, elected officials, and policymakers.

Provision of health care in correctional systems and the costs of doing so necessitate a multifaceted perspective. This chapter attempts to provide the reader with such a perspective, including:

1. the prison health care industrial complex
2. challenges in determining costs
3. fiscal costs
4. impact of litigation and sentencing policies
5. expensive treatments
6. managed care: salvation or illusion?
7. cost containment

The above seven categories highlight both the importance and the challenges facing elected officials and policymakers in better addressing correctional health care. However, the "average" taxpayer ultimately must make the decision about how this country will respond to current and future challenges in this arena. After all, taxpayers ultimately pay for these decisions, which often get framed in a zero-sum fashion that pits public safety against public health and education.

PRISON HEALTH CARE INDUSTRIAL COMPLEX

There is little disputing that prisons in general, as well as health care have emerged as a "growth industry" in the United States. Thus, it is appropriate to examine health care costs within this context. Christie (2000) views the costs of prisons and imprisonment from an economic and capitalistic perspective and brings into focus a prime motivator on the part of stakeholders: to maintain and expand the "prison-industrial complex." He states (2000, p. 13):

> Societies of the Western type face two major problems: Wealth is everywhere unequally distributed. So is access to paid work. Both problems contain potentialities for unrest. The crime control industry is suited for coping with both. This industry provides profit and work while at the same time producing control of those who otherwise might have disturbed the social process (p. 13).

The market value of the incarcerated only recently has started to receive attention from both scholars and the popular press. Taylor (1997), for example, makes this observation concerning juvenile detainees:

> Detained youth have a market value. They provide caseworkers, probation officers, detention staff, and others with employment. When youth realize that they are being used as a commodity, they begin to question both their value as human beings and the legitimacy of a mainstream culture that allows and encourages employers to treat individuals in this way. Decreased self-value, distrust of society's structure, and feelings of helplessness prevail (p. 7).

Hallinan's 2001 book *Going Up the River* specifically explores how rural and small towns, left behind by the most recent economic boom, actively have sought prisons to replace jobs and contracts lost by the closing of factories and military bases; it will remain to be seen how the closings of military bases in 2005 will affect the prison industry. The addition to the "military-industrial complex" of a "prison-industrial complex" represents a shift in how prisons have become big business in this country over the last twenty years and how vested interests in maintaining this financially lucrative enterprise can be quite formidable.

The increased number of prisoners, combined with those who are aging and/or have special medical needs, has resulted in a huge increase in funding for correctional systems across the United States. Increasing rates of incarceration, not surprisingly, result in dramatic increases in prison-related expenditures. "Big government," at least when referring to corrections, is accepted by elected officials and those who elect them (Drinan, 2000). In fiscal year (FY) 2003, local (city and town) governments spent more ($93 billion) on criminal justice than state ($61 billion) or federal governments ($30 billion) (Bureau of Justice Statistics, 2006b).

The increased costs of incarceration, however, have put many states at odds with the federal government and its tendency to toughen prison sentences because of the increased costs to taxpayers at the state level (Butterfield, 2003c; Zielbauer, 2003a). Critics of these expenditures argue that older prisoners cannot harm anyone, yet cost taxpayers millions of dollars by remaining in prison, as if they were a threat, and further contributing to the overcrowding of prisons (Anderson, 1998; Ratcliff & Craig, 2004; Ornduff, 1996).

CHALLENGES IN DETERMINING COSTS

Determining actual costs and who really pays often is not an easy task in health care. This certainly is the case when discussing health care and correctional systems (Stana, 2000). Prison health care costs have increased at a dramatic pace in the past two decades and were estimated to be $3.3 billion in the year 2001, or 12% of prison operating expenses (Bureau of Justice Statistics, 2004e). Jacobs (2004) holds the position that financial resources do not guarantee decent prison conditions and operations. However, lack of resources assures that the opposite occurs.

The consequences of shifting the financial burden from communities to state and federal governments are projected to be immeasurable and quite complex to calculate. Sigurdson (2000) states that:

> This local cost saving is only an illusion. We seem to forget that we pay for incarceration with taxes. We also take individuals, jobs and resources

out of our communities and move them to central facilities (prisons), in which adequate care is very expensive because of the added cost of incarceration. We have not saved money overall; we have only shifted where we spend it . . . The resultant cost in suffering to patients, families and victims of crime is arguably unmeasurable. (p. 74)

Simply stated, someone must pay for the costs of incarceration.

The process of determining the actual costs of prison health care is challenging for a variety of reasons, one of which is the lack of data regarding cost categories such as provision of guards for inmates receiving health care outside of the prison confines. Costs associated with providing guards for hospitalized inmates is a category that increasingly gets overlooked in efforts to cost out prison health care and develop a more accurate picture. California, for example, spent $19 million in guarding hospitalized inmates in 1999 and was projected to spend $31 million in 2005 (Gladstone, 2005).

FISCAL COSTS

Prevailing wisdom on slowing correctional health care budgets has identified six strategies (*Corrections Professional*, 2005c,d):

1. outsourcing or privatizing care
2. "pulling back" on private health care contracts as a result of lawsuits and increased costs
3. charging inmates fees as a way to reduce unnecessary clinic visits
4. creating diversion programs
5. creating and enforcing policies to deal with communicable diseases
6. developing programs and facilities specifically focused on inmates who are aging and those who have a chronic mental illness

One estimate by the Government Accountability Office shows that prison medical costs are rising at a rate of 21% per year (*Corrections Professional*, 2006c). Awofeso (2005a), in an extensive review of the literature on prison health care, concluded that correctional health care is becoming increasingly more difficult to fund around the world and not just in the United States. States are struggling with balancing budgets as correctional costs, particularly health care, continue to absorb a greater portion of the overall budget (Perez, 2005). Efforts to shift indirect costs, as a result, are becoming more prevalent (Domino, Norton, Morrissey & Thakur, 2004).

The financial costs and burdens of imprisoning older adults, for example, are staggering to governments and will continue to be so in the future. The case of the following inmate highlights why their health care costs are high and will only continue to escalate in the future (Korbin, 2005):

> It's still dark when inmate No. 41465 wakes up to begin her day. The shrunken 82-year-old changes from her pajamas and pink house coat into jeans and a denim short labeled *California Prisoner* and begins her drill: breakfast at 6, sack lunch pickup at 6:30, infirmary at 7, where she acquires an ankle chain, belly chains and handcuffs. She then hobbles to a van for the 40-minute ride to Riverside Hospital for dialysis beginning at 8. Helen Loheac suffers from chronic renal failure, a condition that she figures costs the state $436,000 a year, not counting the two $24.75-an-hour armed corrections officers who guard her, all 5 feet and 90 pounds, for up to eight hours a day three times a week (p. 1).

Nationwide, jails and prisons employed 747,000 people in 2001 (Butterfield, 2004a). California, according to the organization Families to Amend California's 3-Strikes (2001), recently spent approximately $5.7 billion on its prisons and jails, with $4.5 billion on youth and adult corrections and $1.2 billion on county jails. It employed over 46,000 personnel (*Los Angeles Times*, 2000). This staggering sum of tax dollars placed corrections at a higher spending level than higher education ($4.3 billion). In 2002, corrections consumed 6% of the state's budget (Ziebauer, 2003b). Although projected to stabilize, California's prison population still is growing at a rate that could fill two new prisons every year, with each new prison costing $280 million to build and $80 million to operate. It was estimated that 67% of those sent back to prison in California were parolees who violated a condition of their release, which cost the state $900 million a year, with an additional $465 million spent on supervising parolees (Butterfield, 2003d).

According to the U.S. Department of Justice, in 1996, a total of $40 billion a year was spent on federal, state, and local prison construction and operation. State prisons accounted for more than half ($22 billion). In FY 1996, states spent almost $2.5 billion on inmate medical and dental care, or 11.8% of prison operating budgets (Stephan, 1999). According to the Bureau of Justice Statistics (Stephan, 1999), six states had correctional budgets over $1 billion in the late 1990s (California, Florida, Michigan, New York,

Ohio, and Texas). California led the nation with a budget of $3 billion. In 2005, thirteen states had correctional budgets over $1 billion (Pew Center, 2008). Another perspective on costs is that, for every $100 million spent on new prison construction, there is a long-term commitment of $1.6 billion over the next thirty years (Ambrosio & Schiraldi, 1997).

In 1975, California's state correctional system employed 6,000, and twenty-five years later it had grown to 41,000 employees (Wacquant, 2000). In the late 1990s, California spent $475 million to provide medical, dental, and psychological services for inmates (Krane, 1999b). In 2003, California spent $1 billion, of which $4.5 million went for hearing aids and $108,000 for sixty prosthetic eyes. The system had 27,000 or 27% of its inmates who were considered mentally ill, 1,300 with AIDS, 150 on daily dialysis, eighteen who had paraplegia, and seven who had quadriplegia (Thompson, 2004).

In 2005, there was general agreement that California's costs for contracted health care and pharmacy services were "out of control" at $74.6 million, up from $14.8 million five years earlier (*Sacramento Bee*, 2005). There was one California inmate who had survived four types of cancer and a stroke. His medication of twelve pills per day cost $1,800 per month, or $21,600 per year (Guber & Petersilia, 2006). Furthermore, estimates for upgrading this system's health care are $100 million a year, or about a 10% increase over the $1 billion California currently spends on correctional health care (Furillo, 2005; Sterngold & Martin, 2005).

Prison deaths due to poor quality of health care are one of the primary reasons why California's correctional health care was placed in receivership. However, inmate deaths related to poor health services are not unique to California. New York State, for example, between 2004 and 2005, had twenty-three inmate deaths because of substandard medical care provided by a private company (Pfeiffer, 2005a).

The City of New York Department of Corrections spent, on average, almost $59,000 per inmate during FY2003. However, the costs did not take into account insurance and pension costs for guards or medical care, estimated at $150 million, or "fixed" costs such as bus fleets, building maintenance, heating fuel, and food service. These added costs raised the "actual" costs to almost $100,000 for each inmate (Zielbauer, 2004). One New Jersey study of correctional health care in jails estimated that the average pharmacy cost per month for an inmate who is HIV positive was $1,000. HIV medications and mental illness medications accounted for approximately 50 percent of New Jersey's annual pharmacy budgets (Wolff & Veysey, 2001).

Wisconsin has seen its correctional health care budget go from $10 million in 1992 to $61.4 million in 2003, primarily as a consequence of a growing inmate population and rising costs of drugs (Marley, 2005). Maryland's correctional health care budget was expected to increase by 60% 2005 and 2006, accounting for an estimated $110 million a year. This projected increase in costs was largely the result of adopting federal treatment protocols for treatments for inmates with AIDS and hepatitis C (Sentementes, 2005). The New Hampshire Department of Corrections health care costs exceeded the budget for FY2005 by $1.63 million. However, the correctional medical costs have exceeded the budget by 25%, or $25 million, over the past five years (Moskowitz, 2006). Louisiana, too, is facing similar challenges (Pitchford, 2005).

North Carolina's prison health costs were $138 million in 2004–2005, and this did not include dental or mental health services (Associated Press State & Local Wire, 2005a). The emergence of "meth mouth," a dental condition caused by use of methamphetamine, has been recognized as a key factor in rising dental care within prisons (Sullivan, 2005). Minnesota's correctional dental health costs nearly doubled between 2000 and 2004 ($1.19 million to $2.01 million), largely as a result of this health condition (Brunswick, 2005).

Prison inmates share many of the same ailments that others have in this society, and may be in even poorer health (Krane, 1999b):

> As prisoners age, they wade into the same morass of ill health as the general population: disorientation, heart disease, diabetes, asthma, emphysema and terminal illnesses such as AIDS, cancer and tuberculosis . . . Unlike the general population, however, prisoners aren't responsible for finding the special care their deteriorating bodies and minds require. The burden falls upon the jailer—and ultimately the taxpayer (p. 1).

Krane (1999b) gives an example of a California prisoner who received a heart transplant at an estimated cost of $1 million.

Elder prisoners have been identified as a key element behind the dramatic increases in state prison health care budgets (Colimore, 2005a & b). Nationally, in the year 2000, the costs associated with elder inmates were $2.8 billion, and 125,000 were aged fifty or older, with 35,000 to 50,000 over the age of sixty-five (Adams, 1995; Coalition for Federal Sentencing Reform, 1998; Florida Corrections Commission, 1999; Kerbs, 1999). Virginia spent approximately $61 million annually on 891 elder inmates who accounted for 3% of the state's prison population (Lang, 1999). This figure translated into $69,000 per inmate, or two to three times the costs of incarcerating other inmates (Holman, 1999). A more recent estimate has these prisoners costing $70,000 per year, at more than 300 percent of the costs of housing a younger inmate (Gubler & Petersilia, 2006). The additional expenses are largely attributable to health care needs. One estimate has the costs of incarcerating California's older inmates at $4 billion by the year 2025 (Guber & Petersilia, 2006).

Arizona's prison health care budget increased over 78 percent in the 1995 to 2005 year period, with Arizona spending almost $36 million a year more on health care than it did ten years ago. This increase largely is due to the increase in elder prisoners (Villa, 2005). The state projects that the number of elder prisoners will increase to 2,000 by 2009, or double the number in 1998. Alabama, in turn, estimates that aging prisoners are largely responsible for health care costs, making up 20 percent of the state's prison budget, and this is a state that spends the lowest amount on inmates per capita in the country (Crowder, 2006). Nebraska's cost of housing an inmate over the age of sixty is estimated to be $70,000 per year, or three times the costs of an average inmate (Hicks, 2005). These costs are only expected to increase as inmates age in place.

Unfortunately, health care costs have taken an immense hold on current discussions of prisoner health care rights and unduly have shaped how state legislatures have responded to the challenges. The introduction of managed care has been one response to the escalating costs of health care. However, prisoners do not utilize health care services in the same manner as the general population, since the nonincarcerated can be more mobile in their search for care. Health care costs can be addressed successfully only within the broader backdrop of prisoner rights to quality health care. This backdrop is laden with biased perceptions of the "easy life" inmates enjoy while in prison with taxpayers paying the bill. Taxpayers at the local, state, and federal level are the ones who do pay. Efforts to shift costs from one level to another are generally no more than shell games or illusions used by prison officials and elected officials. Ultimately, we the taxpayers must pay.

IMPACT OF LITIGATION AND SENTENCING POLICIES

The use of the judicial system arguably has been the primary strategy used by inmates and their advocates to obtain health care (*Corrections Professional*, 2005f; Hill, 2005; Hurley, 2005; *New York Law Journal*, 2005; Scheffey, 2005; Zielbauer, 2005c). The Eighth Amendment has been used to ensure that inmates' rights to care are not violated. McGrath (2002), however, notes that, as a result of qualified immunity granted to correctional personnel, prisoners cannot bring a claim for negligence or medical malpractice, necessitating reliance on violation of constitutional rights by cruel and unusual punishment, which is viewed as a higher legal standard to achieve.

The U.S. Court of Appeals for the Second Circuit held that prison health care providers cannot deny adequate health care to prisoners because of financial costs (Robbins, 1999). The Eleventh Circuit decided that a managed care organization providing health care to inmates would violate the deliberate indifference standard by prioritizing costs ahead of medical costs. Also, the United States Supreme Court ruled unanimously on January 9, 1999, that the federal law barring discrimination against persons with disabilities applies to inmates in state prisons (Mauro, 1999).

Faiver (1998e) traces part of the dramatic increase in health care costs (doubling between 1982 and 1989) to prisoner litigation. There is little dispute that litigation by HIV-infected prisoners played an influential role in serving as a venue for the introduction of health care within correctional institutions in the past fifteen years or so (Potter, 2002). It remains to be seen how much further the courts will shape health care services within correctional facilities (Albert, 2002). Passage of the Prison Litigation Reform Act of 1996 effectively has curtailed federal court involvement in prison and jail operation and reduced the number of lawsuits filed by inmates (Collins & Grant, 1999). Similar efforts targeting health care will no doubt create pressure for the scaling back of services to prisoners. Nevertheless, the sheer magnitude of the number of lawsuits will overcome greater restrictions in using the courts as vehicles for change within prisons. Access to the courts by inmates to redress perceived injustices, although curtailed, still is assured under the Constitution (McClain, Sheehan & Butler, 1998).

In 2005, the state of Ohio settled a class action lawsuit that claimed that the prison health care system was unconstitutional and that poor-quality correctional health care was cruel and unusual punishment (Ludlow, 2005a). As a result, Ohio's health care system was to increase the number of doctors from thirty-two to fifty-three by 2007, or one physician per 900 inmates, and provide 275 additional nurses. It was expected to cost the state $7 million during the first year (Ludlow, 2005b).

The Department of Justice has initiated a formal inquiry into Delaware's state prison system's health care services in review of allegations of inadequate health care and civil rights violations (Associated Press & Local Wire, 2005b). Since the passage of the Civil Rights of Institutionalized Persons Act in 1980, the Justice Department has initiated more than 300 investigations of jails and prisons in thirty-nine states (Associated Press & Local Wire, 2005b).

Tougher sentencing policies such as California's three-strike policy will have a profound impact on costs to correctional systems. For example, unless California significantly alters its three-strike policy, it is estimated that it will increase its three-strikes felons by 1,200 per year, and it is estimated that by the year 2026 there will be 30,000 inmates serving sentences of twenty-five years to life in the state. This translates into an annual cost of $750 million a year (Pfeiffer, 2002).

EXPENSIVE TREATMENTS FOR HEALTH CARE: ARE THEY A PRIVILEGE OR A RIGHT?

Lundstrom (1994), like Anno, Faiver, and Harness (1998), echoes a common argument pertaining to expensive health care for prisoners that will need to be resolved in the not-too-distant future. Expensive treatments present both a medical and moral values problem for society. Should prisoners receive treatments such as transplants (heart, bone marrow, or kidney) when "law abiding" citizens may not be able to because of costs or access to quality care? The concept of "equitable access" has emerged to help frame the issues and considerations that must be addressed in providing health care to prisoners. Equitable access refers to the guarantee that all people have the same level of health care; there also needs to be a minimum level of health care to which everyone in this society is entitled.

In FY2005, the state of New Hampshire had thirty-seven inmates with health care bills of over $10,000 or more, with four inmates having bills exceeding $100,000 each. For example, it spent $730,000 on dialysis for four inmates, with one inmate being flown to Oregon for treatment costing over $285,000 (Moskovitz, 2006). Another perspective on costs is that 1.5% of the state's approximately 21,000 inmates accounted for more than 20% of the medical costs. In another example, in 2002, Georgia spent $4.1 million on thirty-seven inmates whose conditions were classified as "catastrophic." One inmate alone, who had lupus, diabetes, and kidney failure and who subsequently died, cost the state $340,000 that year (Elsner, 2004). Levine (2002) sums up the challenges facing correctional systems:

> The trick seems to be setting a standard of care for prisons somewhere between the absolute best and the minimum threshold, while controlling costs and toeing legal lines. It's largely an uncharted area—and one that constantly triggers lawsuits. (p. 104)

MANAGED CARE

Robbins (1999) notes that managed care in prison must not be confused with its conventional counterparts outside of prison because the circumstances surrounding who the patient is and the goals of the health care provider are substantially different:

1. Prisoners invariably are considerably less healthy than the general population
2. The quality of health care in prisons can be considered "minimal" in quality and amount when compared to that received by the general population covered by managed care
3. Patients in a prison setting do not enjoy the freedoms associated with an open marketplace for selecting health plans, since they get what they get
4. If the health care provider in the prison refuses to provide treatment, prisoners' options are very limited to go elsewhere for care

Efforts to introduce managed care in prisons have not been successful in providing quality care because of an overemphasis on costs, raising serious questions about violations of the Eighth Amendment:

> In an effort to cut costs, many state and county incarceration facilities have turned to private managed health care organizations to provide health care for their prisoners. Despite—or, perhaps, because of—the money saved by the government and the money made by managed care organizations, the level of health care in prisons has resulted in inmate injuries and deaths, many of which have been are being challenged on Eighth Amendment grounds. (Robbins, 1999, p. 205)

The potential for economic profit in serving the nation's prison health care needs has not gone unnoticed. Corporations such as Correctional Medical Services Inc., St. Louis (the largest private provider in the country), provide health services to more than 268,000 inmates in thirty states. It is estimated that over $3.75 billion a year is spent on correctional health care, with private managed care companies accounting for 25% of this budget (Allen & Bell, 1998). Prison Health (American Service Group corporate parent) provides medical care for 175,000 inmates (Lipton, 2000). New York City was negotiating a new three-year $313.7 million health services contract with Prison Health Services Inc. (Lipton, 2000). Wackenhut runs the nation's only privatized mental health prison (Mississippi) in the country; it also operates a 520-bed drug treatment facility in Kyle, Texas (Slevin, 2001).

In 2000, thirty-four states had some form of privatized health care for prisoners, with twenty-four states having this service completely run by private contractors (Montague, 2003). Wyoming is one of the most recent states attempting to cut costs of prison health care by contracting to a private health care provider (Associated Press, 2005). In addition, some states privatize not just health care but the entire prison. In late 2005, a Colorado State audit of private prisons found that they fell short of what can be considered minimum standards for safety and medical care (Associated Press State & Local Wire, 2005c).

The case of Billy Roberts illustrates the pitfalls of introducing managed health care in the nation's prisons:

> Billy Roberts, a prisoner in an Alabama state prison, had a history of severe psychiatric disorders. He was ordered put on suicide watch, and received large doses of psychotropic drugs. A managed health care company, Correctional Medical Services (CMS), was responsible for the health care at the prison. After Roberts had a suicide episode, CMS's statewide mental health care director reportedly put Roberts in an isolation cell rather than a psychiatric care unit. The mental health care director also ordered that Roberts' medication be discontinued pursuant to an alleged policy of CMS to get as many prisoners off psychotropic drugs as soon as possible in order to keep costs down. Six days later, Billy Roberts hanged himself. (Robbins, 1999, p. 26)

An overemphasis on cost cutting raises serious questions about quality of health care decisions that can prove personally costly.

The United States Supreme Court ruled in the 2001 decision *Correctional Services Corporation v. Malesko* that "for profit corporations like CSC who run prisons under contract with the federal government are protected from suit for their constitutional violations" (Alexander, 2003, p. 67). This case overturned a lower court's decision that would have allowed a prisoner, John Malesko, to obtain remedies when he suffered a heart attack climbing a staircase in a facility in New York run by Correctional Services Corporation. The lawyers for the corporation argued successfully that "like the United States government itself, the corporation was not subject to suit for any violations of Malesko's right to health care" (Alexander, 2003, p. 67). Although private corporations' primary purpose is profits, essentially the Supreme Court extended a protection of government, whose primary purpose is not profits, to a profit-making corporation by virtue of that corporation being a contractor for the government.

COST CONTAINMENT

The Federal Bureau of Prisons examined efforts to contain the costs of providing health care to prisoners in federal prisons (Government Accountability Office, 2000). This study focused on answering four specific areas:

1. the impact on co-payments of frivolous health visits
2. staff reduction activities
3. development of intermediate care facilities for inmates with long-term care needs
4. the impact of the Federal Prisoner Health Care Copayment Act of 1999

With the exception of intermediate care facilities, which have the potential to result in significant savings but require further study, the other efforts resulted in limited savings.

Some correction systems, in an effort to avoid excessive health costs, actually have mounted campaigns to improve the health of inmates:

> "Preventive care, we're into that big time," said Dr. Kenneth Moritsugu, an assistant surgeon general and medical director of the Federal Bureau of Prisons. "We're not going to prevent every single disease, but we certainly can inhibit that disease." Before long, the wiffle ball and horseshoes played at Hocking Correctional Facility, Ohio's over-50 special prison in Nelsonville, may be as widespread as basketball and weight-lifting. The prison's classes on death and dying are as commonplace as those on reading. (Montgomery, 1997, p. 2)

Other correctional systems, like New Hampshire for example, have enacted medical-parole laws that free inmates with high medical care bills (Moskowitz, 2006). However, as is the case of New Hampshire, the laws rarely are used since only one or two inmates generally get released per year.

There have been other efforts at containing costs such as having inmates co-pay a fee each time they seek medical care. Arkansas, for example, instituted such a system in 2005 (Bauman, 2005). Arkansas state inmates are charged $3 per sick-call visit, to the infirmaries. The primary intent of this payment was to curtail inmate visits, and this has resulted in about a 25% drop over the course of one-year period (22,665 compared to 30,021). Research is needed to determine the consequences of this policy in deterring inmates from seeking care because of lack of funds to pay the fee.

Pennsylvania's Carbon County Prison Board currently is considering billing prisoners for fake health and medical problems, as a means of cutting health care costs (Fullon, 2005). However, in 2004, Carbon had two inmates suffer heart attacks resulting in $100,000 costs, but only $50,000 had been allocated for medical costs for the entire year. Therefore, early signs of illness must not be interpreted as being fake. Awofeso (2005a), in reviewing the cost-effectiveness of co-payment policies and prison health care, concluded that the policy compromises inmate access to health care while not significantly reducing prison health care costs in the process.

The subject of smoking by inmates has started to receive increased attention. California (Drucker, 2005) and North Carolina (Associated Press State & Local Wire, 2005a), for example, recently enacted legislation to make prisons smoke-free to reduce the health care costs of inmates who smoke and nonsmoking inmates exposed to secondary smoke.

It is estimated that elders cost above 300% more to house than average prisoners (Krane, 1999c). Average prisoner costs are $20,000 per year with geriatric prisons costing $69,000–$70,000 per year because of health care needs. These costs are projected to continue to increase dramatically in the early part of the twenty-first century with health costs far outstripping average prisoner expenses. One corrections official captured the reality of aging prisoners quite well when stating: "As people get older and older, you expect their medical-needs level will increase . . . when it reaches a critical level, they need to be in an area with more facilities and nursing services" (Friedberg, 1999, p. 2). Elder prisoners experience even greater health care needs than the general elder population, and this group is causing great concern as the nation looks toward cutting health care benefits of government programs.

Health, health care, and costs cannot be understood successfully in isolation from each other. Further, ethical issues and considerations cannot be separated from the shadow of a total institution such as a prison. The consequences of illnesses do take on various manifestations based upon the sociodemographic characteristics of the person. Health disparities are a fact of life in the general population and nowhere more so than within prisons. Serving time in a correctional institution presents an opportunity to intervene in an inmate's life and provide needed services. However, prisons and jails are also places where lack of quality health care can combine with a toxic environment to compromise further the health status of inmates. In cases where inmates enter prison in relatively healthy conditions, the diseases and illnesses awaiting them will increase the likelihood that they do not remain healthy for a long period of time (McQueen, 1992; Russell, 2000). Prisons, in essence, are toxic environments.

We would like to believe that reform of the nation's correctional health care system would be initiated by the emergence of a greater consciousness of how inadequate care is cruel and unusual punishment and that this perspective has no place in a democratic nation. Unfortunately, health care reform will be brought about by litigation and concerns about how health care budgets are taking a greater share of national and local tax dollars.

The subject of health care costs is one that easily can have a series of books devoted to it, and this chapter only provides a glimpse of how difficult and controversial this subject is in the country. Nevertheless, difficulties and controversies aside, the costs of health care will not simply go away as more and more class action suits are initiated, argued, and eventually won in the nation's courts, California being such a case example. Further, it is impossible to separate costs from a fundamental philosophy that views provision of health care to prisoners as a "frill" or "luxury" within which taxpayers should not be burdened. The values expressed in provision of inadequate correctional health care up to this point have resulted in the creation of a crisis that only will increase in magnitude the longer we continue to neglect this subject. The financial costs of health care in the near future will make the costs at this time pale by comparison. The projected costs of California's prison health care system being under receivership (estimated at over $1 billion over ten years) only will be duplicated in various degrees across the entire nation's prison system, resulting in increased taxes or cuts in health, education, and human service budgets for noninstitutionalized populations.

III

RECOMMENDATIONS

10

RECOMMENDATIONS

We hope the reader has developed an in-depth appreciation of the magnitude of the challenge health care provision is for the nation's correctional system. The challenge is multifaceted and increasingly growing in complexity (Davis, 2002). The urgency of this challenge necessitates that the nation, and not just the correctional sector, undertake immediate and bold steps to ameliorate this crisis (McTighe, 2004; Williams, 2007). Society's negative views toward criminals effectively were translated into national and state legislation which, in turn, has resulted in a massive buildup in the construction of prisons and requisite staffing of them. In short, it is a crisis of such proportions that it will not disappear if not discussed.

In an assessment of correctional health care in the United States, Anno (2001) identified the multitude of complexities that compound a rational approach to service provision within prisons. These complexities have long historical life and shape current efforts to meet the health needs of prisoners. The subject of correctional care and health care cannot be artificially separated since the significance of the intersection between corrections and illness is unmistakable. Inmates or former inmates account for 35% of tuberculosis, 12% of hepatitis B, 29% of hepatitis C, 17% of AIDS, and 13% of HIV-positive known cases in the United States (National Commission on Correctional Health Care, 2003d). The interplay of several factors compound delivery of quality correctional health care. The absence of guidance on legal issues, ethical concerns, custody-medical interfaces, staffing, inmates' special health needs, and cost containment all play prominent roles in hindering the delivery of quality health care within correctional institutions (Anno, 2001).

Correctional institutions represent a largely untapped opportunity to protect the public health of the nation, particularly urban residents, since the majority of inmates originate in this nation's cities (National Commission on Correctional Health Care, 2003e). This chapter draws on and synthesizes recommendations from a variety of sources. These comprehensive and strategic recommendations address field practices as well as policy and professional education.

The enormity of the challenges facing the country's prison system as it attempts to address a multitude of health needs will require a systematic and comprehensive approach. The financial costs to government will be staggering, although the alternatives of ignoring this crisis only will exacerbate the financial and social costs to the nation. This "comprehensive" perspective toward recommendations purposely attempts to provide readers with concrete actions they can take to better serve the target populations in prisons. Special attention also will be paid to how culture, race, class, and gender affect delivery and acceptance of services. Clearly, major reforms at all levels of the correctional system are in order, and these will necessitate a working and positive relationship among the public, government, and the correctional system itself.

Marshall, Simpson, and Stevens (2000) put forth the argument that prison health care services must respond to changing times and challenges for a variety of reasons:

1. Historically, provided health services were not need based.
2. There has been an emergence of new illnesses and shifts in patterns of diseases.
3. New medical advances have occurred, making treating illnesses more promising.
4. Increased medical knowledge facilitates treatment provision.
5. Dramatic changes in societal expectations pertaining to health coverage and rights have resulted and also must apply to prison populations.

The reasons bring to the forefront the need for correctional systems to update their medical services to take into account twenty-first century goals rather than nineteenth century goals that stressed punishment and confinement.

As already noted in chapter 8, Watson, Simpson, and Hostick (2004) identified six cross-cutting themes related to development of models for health service delivery in prisons. The following twelve categories build upon these cross-cutting themes. These categories and recommendations, however, are not prioritized in order of importance:

1. Rethinking of access
2. Importance of oversight organizations
3. Standards and protocols
4. Initial screening, testing, and health status
5. Realistically assessing the costs of imprisonment
6. Partnership with community-based organizations
7. Specialized training for health care providers
8. Provision of care (substance abuse, mental health services, HIV/AIDS, and end-of-life)
9. Special populations (elders, women, and youth)
10. Preventing and containing communicable diseases
11. Promotion of healthy lifestyles
12. Health status of soon-to-be-released inmates

Further, in the above we have avoided developing a laundry list of recommendations in the hopes of emphasizing the importance of a shift in philosophy concerning prison health care and the interrelationships between countless numbers of illnesses. After all, it is the rare inmate who has but one illness, just like it is rare to find one noninstitutionalized citizen with just one challenge in life.

RETHINKING ACCESS

Access to services or care is a multifaceted issue and, as a result, quite complex. Thus, starting the recommendations chapter with a discussion of access represents a logical first step in better understanding the challenges facing prison health care in the nation.

Access can be conceptualized as consisting of four interdependent but interrelated domains:

1. geographical and physical
2. psychological
3. cultural
4. operational
(Delgado, 2000)

Geographical and physical accessibility necessitates services being easily reached within an institution or community. In the case of prisons or jails, this form of accessibility is highly regulated, monitored, and controlled. A primary purpose of a prison or jail is to restrict mobility. Consequently, although services may be geographically accessible, they may be physically inaccessible because of confinement of the prisoner and denial of access by prison decision makers.

Psychological accessibility examines to what extent the service is stigmatizing or nonstigmatizing. Some diseases such as HIV and AIDS historically have been very stigmatizing within and outside of prisons. If inmates must self-identify by visiting a place within a prison associated with HIV and AIDS, they may well be reluctant to do so. A poignant example of this stigma was captured in a book titled *AIDS Counseling Education Program* (1998), about Bedford Hills Correctional Facility, New York. Women inmates diagnosed with HIV and AIDS faced hostility from other inmates when it was discovered that they were infected. This education program served to empower women prisoners by providing education and roles for prisoners to play in helping fellow prisoners who had HIV/AIDS. Their sensitivity and knowledge about HIV/AIDS allowed them to be effective health educators and advocates.

Cultural accessibility refers to the nature and process used to deliver services. These services must be attuned to the culture, language preference, and background of inmates in an effort to minimize barriers between service provision and service utilization. Various approaches can be used to minimize cultural barriers, such as hiring staff who represent the ethnic and racial backgrounds of inmates, making forms and reading materials available in the language preference of inmates, or disseminating information in accessible formats for those who have a disability or are illiterate.

Finally, operational accessibility addresses the importance of having hours, days, and procedures that facilitate service provision on demand. Operational procedures that are cumbersome or invasive may discourage use of services by prisoners. Co-payment of fees by inmates for health care is an example of an operational barrier to accessibility. Avoidance of seeking medical care because of the costs associated with co-payments represents a significant barrier for inmates with limited financial resources. Interestingly, it was estimated that the California Department of Corrections' annual co-pay program would generate $1.7 million per year. However, it actually generated $654,000 and cost the state $3.2 million, or almost 500% of the annual collections, according to a report to the Congressional Judiciary Committee Report on H.R. 1349.

All four types of access domain are important within correctional settings. A prison having three out of four still seriously limits access and proper utilization of health care by inmates, yet gives the illusion of having access readily available. Nevertheless, each of the four arenas of accessibility is by their very nature alien to total institutions such as prisons, and they make carrying out health care programs difficult. Goffman's classic book, *Asylums: Essays on the Social Situation of Mental Patients and Other Inmates* (1961), provides important insights into how total institutions effectively seek to institute total control over inmates and patients by limiting access along a variety of dimensions such as the ones addressed in this section.

IMPORTANCE OF OVERSIGHT ORGANIZATIONS

Murphy (2005) raises the importance of an independent advocate to help ensure that health care rights of prisoners not be compromised. This advocate ideally should be someone or an organization outside of the prison system who can facilitate the right to timely and adequate medical care. Even with the best of intentions, due to the population and the political nature of prisons, there will continue to be a role for advocacy groups such as the American Civil Liberties Union and Human Rights Watch.

Oversight organizations historically have played important roles in this nation, and prison health care is just one of the latest challenges facing the country. Currently there are essentially four major organizations that are national in scope and address correctional health from a comprehensive rather than a specialty perspective (Anno, 2001):

1. American Correctional Association (ACA)
2. American Public Health Association (APHA)
3. Joint Commission on Accreditation of Healthcare Organizations (JCAHO
4. National Commission on Correctional Health Care (NCCHC)

The American Public Health Association's third edition of *Standards for Health Services in Correctional Institutions* (2003a) is based upon fundamental principles of public health and the legal guidelines of the U.S. Constitution, court rulings, and international treaties. This latest edition has an expanded section on mental disorders to take into account how this topic has increased in importance since the last edition. Further, this edition also brings into the forefront the importance of health promotion as a vital component of any health care delivery model. The APHA recognizes the importance of prisoner rights to quality health care and the interrelationship between prison health and public health.

These four accrediting bodies arguably have the most comprehensive coverage of health services within correctional institutions. Anno (2001) provides a detailed assessment of each of the strengths and weaknesses of these accrediting organizations. The role and function of oversight organizations, as a result, cannot be minimized because they are in a unique position to report on conditions and have the political capital to mobilize requisite resources to address the unique needs inmates present this nation's health care system. California's correctional health system, which is currently under receivership, has been ordered by the court to receive accreditation from the National Commission on Correctional Health Care and the American Correctional Association, in an effort to establish standards and have external review, as a means of improving its health care (*Sacramento Bee*, 2005).

STANDARDS AND PROTOCOLS

Establishment of standards for health care within prisons represents an initial and critical step in the development of quality health care, but standards by themselves are not sufficient to ensure delivery (Miller, 2006; Stone, Kaiser & Mantese, 2006). California is a case in point. By law, all state prison hospitals and infirmaries were supposed to have been certified by the California Department of Health Services by 1996. However, only five out of thirty-three had obtained their licenses by 2001. According to the governor's office, only sixteen facilities were expected to obtain licenses within the next two years (*San Francisco Chronicle*, 2001). Not unexpectedly, failure to make progress on this and other factors resulted in the California correctional health care system being placed in receivership in 2005 (Moore, 2007). This move by the federal courts is considered unprecedented in scope affecting all thirty-three of the state's prisons, representing a judicial effort to stop the needless deaths of inmates as a result of medical malfeasance (Sterngold, 2005).

Accreditation standard lapses are not unique to prison correctional health care. According to the American Correctional Association, only approximately 5% of all jails, or 150, are accredited by the organization (Tanner, 2002). Generally, states develop their own standards, which, expectedly, vary considerably between states. The American Jail Association notes that ten states have no statewide inspection system (Tanner, 2000).

Reams, Smith, Fletcher, and Spencer (1998) raise concerns about this very point in their assessment of the problems with the content and implementation of minimum standards developed by the American Correctional Association and the National Commission on Correctional Health Care.

The authors identified five key problems with the implementation of these standards:

1. There are very few correctional institutions certified by national organizations to provide health care, thus few can be held accountable to abide by these standards.
2. As with most standards, these prioritize procedural regularity without equal emphasis on promoting performance, resulting in a situation where compliance does not necessarily equate with improved care.
3. The standards are not equally high across all aspects of health care.
4. These standards do not embrace a common perspective on ethical problems.
5. Ethical decision making needs to be outlined to address ethical dilemmas, and this is missing.

There are, however, several organizations that provide guidelines for a variety of health issues correctional facilities face. The Centers for Disease Control and Prevention (CDC) has established a Web site (www.cdc/gov/ nchstp/od/ccwg/default.htm) specifically dedicated to public health and criminal justice:

> The mission of this website is to foster collaboration between public health organizations and the criminal justice system by providing information on correctional health care issues to health care providers, the people they serve, and the general public.

As part of this mission, CDC has established treatment and clinical practice guidelines for juveniles, women, mental health, and infectious and chronic illnesses.

The National Commission on Correctional Health Care's Standards for Health Services provides guidelines in general areas of care and treatment, health records, administration, personnel, and medical–legal issues. These guidelines were developed specifically to assist correctional health care professionals to manage diseases commonly found in jails, prisons, and juvenile confinement facilities. The guidelines were the result of clinical guidelines recommended by other organizations, including the National Institutes of Health, the American Diabetes Association, the National Heart, Lung, and Blood Institute, and the U.S. Department of Health and Human Services, and were the result of a study on the health needs of soon-to-be-released inmates, which was released to Congress in 2002. Finally, the

Federal Bureau of Prisons developed clinical practice guidelines (CPG) on the following:

- asthma
- coronary artery disease
- detoxification of chemically dependent inmates
- diabetes
- gastroesophageal reflux disease (GERD)
- dyspepsia and peptic ulcer disease
- headache
- high cholesterol
- HIV infection
- hypertension
- major depressive disorder
- methicillin-resistant *Staphylococcus aureus* (MRSA) infections
- preventive health care
- tuberculosis
- varicella zoster virus infections
- viral infections

Therefore, there are sources for advice and up-to-date information to improve health care for prisoners. The challenge is to consult and use the guidelines as part of a comprehensive and coordinated system of health care within any particular setting. Otherwise, the sources serve to identify and document health care issues but are limited in their value for shaping service delivery.

INITIAL SCREENING, TESTING, AND HEALTH STATUS

A distinctive and disturbing pattern can be discerned throughout this book, namely, the absence of a systematic process for screening and testing for illnesses and diseases (Miller, 2006). In essence, the current system of health care needs to shift from a reactive "sick call" system to one that is proactive and emphasizes prevention and health promotion, screening, early detection, and early treatment (Harding, 2000; Howell, 2002; Marshall, Fordyce & Rich, 2008). The Commission on Safety and Abuse in America's Prisons, after a fifteen-month study, issued a report with a series of recommendations. Two of these recommendations were development of a uniform data-reporting requirement and the extension of Medicaid and Medicare, without co-payments, to eligible inmates (Slevin, 2006).

The results of a recent national survey of correctional systems are not surprising, concluding that, "Many State prison systems cannot report detailed, accurate data on the prevalence of medical problems or mental disorders within their inmate populations" (Hornung, Anno, Greifinger & Gadre, 2003a, p. 10). For example, 17% of jails and prisons do not screen systematically for mental illness, and 40% of jails and 17% of prisons do not provide mental health services (National Commission on Correctional Health Care, 2003d). Screening for tuberculosis in jails and following up in clinics after release also have been recommended strongly as a means of reducing outbreaks of tuberculosis (Hayden et al., 2005; Tulsky et al., 1998). One study of nineteen nations prepared for the World Health Organization found the United States to be one of four nations that did not have a national policy on HIV management in prisons (Kantor, 2006). Binswanger and colleagues (2005) recommend systematic screening for cancer for high-risk inmates. Correctional institutions, in this case jail, have been found to be excellent settings for screening. Magee and colleagues (2005) echo this call for cancer screening among female inmates.

The subject of cost-effectiveness of early screening and prevention has received considerable research attention in the past few years and has raised important considerations in the development of prison health care (Hornung, Greifinger, & Gadre, 2003a; Kraut, Haddix, Carande-Kulis, & Greifinger, 2003; Lyerla, 2003; National Commission on Correctional Health Care, 2003f; Taylor & Nguyen, 2003; Tomlinson & Schechter, 2003; Varghese & Peterman, 2003). Findings have stressed the cost-effectiveness of early screening and prevention of illnesses for prisoners and the general population. For example, the cost-effectiveness of universal screening for chlamydia and gonorrhea is significant (Kraut-Becher et al., 2004).

Another key theme that has appeared throughout this book has been the importance of accurate and ongoing data collection, and the role of data in influencing decision making pertaining to health care policies and services. The Massachusetts Public Health Association (2003) identified accurate data gathering as a key factor in improving correctional health care:

> Accurate data that record and track inmate health history, current health status, and movement through the criminal justice system are needed for appropriate care and to determine health status indicators of the incarcerated population in aggregate. These data are also necessary to conduct the evaluation research necessary to determine which inmate programs are most effective in improving health outcomes (p. 24).

Prison officials must consider several issues, for example, how injuries are recorded and services are provided to address them.

A number of significant barriers and challenges make following a prescribed regimen of medication adherence outside and inside of prisons arduous at best (Frank, 1999):

1. High rates of illiteracy and primary language other than English make following instructions challenging.
2. Stigma leads to a fear of being labeled and the consequences of being a scapegoat within prisons.
3. Costs of treatment create financial liability for providers and contractors and serve as a disincentive to identifying and treating HIV-positive inmates.
4. Inadequately trained staff cannot respond to rapid changes in treatment, and so training and consultation to insure delivery of the most effective treatment are necessary.
5. Multiple presenting problems, such as HIV and substance abuse, place tremendous pressure on staff being able to address problems simultaneously.
6. Cultural issues can result through a lack of staff awareness of cultural belief systems and values of inmates of color.
7. Security and control can stand in the way of effective treatment that is dependent upon individualization of services, a practice that often is eschewed by prison administrators.

Allison and Clark (2001) stress the strategic function of information systems in helping correctional systems meet the ever complex and changing health care needs of inmates. The importance of a medical information system is borne out by the Los Angeles County Sheriff's Department (LASD) jail system, which is considered one of the largest in the world. The medical challenges posed by the approximately 20,000 average daily sentenced and pretrail inmates, or 165,000 inmates per year, can be overwhelming (Allison & Clark, 2001). There are 500 inmates with AIDS; 3,000 inmates with mental illness; 100 prescribers of medication; 400 nurses; 150,000 medical charts filed annually; 4,600 charts created monthly; and 9,500 requests for charts per month. The upgrading of information systems brings with it a set of pressures upon correctional systems in that, once the information is gathered and "legitimized," prisons and jails cannot simply ignore it and can be held legally and politically accountable for not meeting the needs of inmates.

Obtaining a comprehensive and accurate health status of prison inmates is logically the first step to developing a comprehensive health care system that accurately can profile current inmate needs and project into the future as the age of an inmate increases (Anno et al., 2004; Parece et al., 1999). A 1998 survey of state prisons found that these systems lacked "comprehensive and accurate" data on inmate health status. Only twenty states had information systems with capabilities of identifying inmates with physical disabilities at admission; twenty-two systems had the ability to identify inmates with mental and emotional problems; and twenty-two states could identify inmates with specialized medical conditions. Eighteen states had this medical information electronically on three-quarters of their inmates (Maruschak & Beck, 2001).

Obtaining an inmate health status, as a result of information-gathering limitations, necessitates a greater emphasis on the use of inmate self-reports. Self-reports, however, have serious shortcomings, particularly in cases where inmates may not have the ability or willingness to report on their health condition. Further, inmates may underreport on health conditions that are not diagnosed easily or are stigmatizing, such as HIV/AIDS or other sexually transmitted diseases. Consequently, in situations where inmates are sentenced for a long period of time and are infected, prison systems will be faced with providing health care at a late stage in disease development, increasing the costs of services and effects in the inmate. Early identification, as a result, will play a critical role in addressing illnesses in the early stages.

REALISTICALLY ASSESSING THE COSTS OF IMPRISONMENT

The nation's buildup of prisons has resulted in an increased concentration of individuals with high risks for contracting many different types of health ailments. The passage of a federal crime bill during President Bill Clinton's administration in 1994 provided $10 billion to states for construction of new prisons and jails for jurisdictions that qualified. Unfortunately, localities that took advantage of these funds failed to take into account the long-term fiscal costs of maintaining these correctional institutions once built (Anderson, 2003; Butterfield, 2003b). In addition, the impact of this new prison construction boom had a disproportionate impact on urban communities of color. Inmates are not counted as living in their respective communities. Instead, they are counted as residents where the correctional institutions are located. This shift in residence effectively takes government-allocated resources based upon population away from urban communities of color to rural communities that are primarily White, non-Latino.

It is of critical importance that efforts to estimate the costs of prison health care take into account a broad rather than narrow perspective of what items constitute costs. Prescriptions are but one problem. For example, in 2001, the state of Wisconsin approved an additional $5.67 million in emergency funding to get prisoners medicine and health care. Increased drug costs accounted for 50% of the health care budget deficits. Drug costs averaged $457 per inmate (Jones, 2001). Wisconsin, needless to say, is not alone in struggling with increased health care costs. Wolff (2002, 2005), in turn, suggests that prisoners be viewed from a social capital perspective, making investments in their health ultimately beneficial for society and also resulting in reduced costs. Howell (2002) argues that early screening is cost-effective. Furthermore, estimating the medical costs for inmates cannot be based soley on the prevalence of diseases of those entering prisons. Rhodes, Johnston, McMullen, and Hozik (2000) found that the age of the male inmate at imprisonment becomes the factor most likely to predict costs.

Wacquant (2002) identified four primary strategies for reducing the spiraling correctional costs in this country:

1. lowering the level of living standards, which entails doing away with "frills" such as educational programs, sports, and other entertainment activities, and reducing efforts to rehabilitate inmates
2. harnessing technological innovations such as minimizing transportation of inmates for appearances in court and health settings through use of video and telemedicine, greater use of electronics to trace inmates, and minimizing contraband
3. transferring costs of incarceration to inmates and their families, including charging prisoners for room and board or meals and co-payments for health care
4. using inmates as contract workers to private industry

These strategies have been used in part, whole, or combination to address costs as well as to ensure that a punishment theme remains for incarceration. Each of these strategies, however, is controversial and raises serious questions about the role and costs of incarceration in a democratic society.

Failure of the courts to provide a ceiling on minimal health care has provided pressure to raise costs and quality of health care during a time when law-abiding citizens have had difficulty meeting health care needs of their own. Morash, Haarr, and Rucker (1994) predicted in the early 1990s that the increased presence of women in correctional systems only will add to the pressure to use class action litigation to bring equality for women and, in the process, further increase the costs of health care in prisons and how they get structured. Improving health care in prisons is an important and humane goal for a population that has no other alternative. Still, it highlights the piecemeal approach to health care in the United States, still the only industrialized country without universal health insurance.

The ever-increasing costs of prison health care have resulted in prisons turning to reduce costs through managed care and other strategies. Since the primary goal of a managed care health system is to cut costs, prisoners are at a distinct disadvantage in securing quality health care. Inmates are not "paying customers," and they do not have the option of selecting a health care plan, making them more vulnerable to prison health care providers delivering the cheapest service rather than the most appropriate care.

In 1997, twelve states had contracted with private health care firms to provide health care to all inmates, with another twenty states contracting for part of their health systems. It was estimated that those states saved 10–15 percent in health care costs as a result of contracting. However, the quality of health care varied considerably, with some states having to terminate their contracts because of poor quality health care. Savings, as a result, were achieved in the short-term at the expense of quality. Long-term savings, however, will no doubt be compromised (Council of State Governments, 1997). A 2003 study found that twenty-four states had privatized inmate health care systems, with an additional ten states having some privatized health care (Washington Policy Center, 2003).

The consequences stemming from imprisonment have far-reaching impacts on communities, particularly those of color throughout the nation, for this and future generations. These ramifications can be felt in overt and covert ways (Lincoln, Miles & Scheibel, 2008). Taxes, for example, are one way that corrections have an impact on every man, woman, and child by diverting funds from initiatives that can better day-to-day living. State and local governments are faced with zero-sum decisions about how to allocate tax dollars. Schools, parks, recreation, and street repairs, for example, compete for the same dollars as prisons (Hallinan, 2001). Advocates of community alternatives to imprisonment argue that this nation cannot build its way out of prison overcrowding (Hengesh, 1996; Hughes, 1996). A focus away from imprisonment to other fiscally wise and rehabilitative alternatives does not necessarily reflect being "soft"-on-crime (Larivee, 1996). However, it reflects a strategic and rational position that actively seeks to differentiate between violent criminals and nonviolent criminals. The former can best be housed in prisons, and the latter in community alternatives (Larivee, 1996).

PARTNERSHIP WITH
COMMUNITY-BASED ORGANIZATIONS

The immensity of the challenges of meeting the health care needs of prisoners, particularly those who are severely ill or dying, requires the marshalling of resources beyond those usually found in prisons (LIS Inc., 2003; Macher et al., 2005; Watson, Simpson & Hostick, 2004). Eliason, Taylor, and Williams (2004), Heines (2005), and Klein and colleagues (2002) argue for the "critical" need to establish a comprehensive community health system to meet the health needs of reentering women inmates and safeguard the health of their community in the process. A similar call to action also can be made for all other subgroups of returning former inmates.

Shah (2006), in turn, raises the need for correctional systems to develop a comprehensive care system network for older adult inmates while they are in prison and upon their release. The Robert Woods Johnson Foundation recently provided a $7.4 million grant to the Hampden (Massachusetts) County Correctional Center to undertake an ambitious correctional health initiative for released inmates involving community-based organizations and correctional institutions (Donnelly, 2007).

Fagan (2004) makes an important observation pertaining to prison health care when noting that hospitals in this society are not stand-alone institutions. They are frequently a part of a broader system of care with partnerships with public health, outpatient clinics, home care, nursing homes, and so forth. Thus, it would be unfair to look at correctional health as a stand-alone system. Applebaum, Manning, and Noonan (2002) address this very point and highlight the role of university hospitals in partnerships with prison systems to provide mental health services.

When prison health care is conceptualized as part of a broader fabric of health care, the enormity of the task facing prisons is shared with the broader community, making the effort of addressing health care easier to propose and implement (Hammett, 2002; Greifinger, 2008). Further, the coordination between prisons and community-based organizations—when thought of as a transitional phase for newly released prisoners—decreases the deleterious impact unhealthy prisoners can have on the broader community (Flanagan, 2004). Freudenberg and colleagues (2005) advance the importance of a comprehensive, including health care, perspective on inmate reentry into the community. Wolff (2002, 2005), in turn, conceptualizes this transitional phase as a public investment phase in ensuring healthiness for the community as a whole.

A Federal Bureau of Prisons study on the skill sets and health care needs of released offenders identified the importance of newly released inmates departing with specific skills and the importance of breaking down external barriers to health care (Gaes & Kendig, 2003). Hammet, Gaiter, and Crawford (1998) note:

> An important factor in the improvement of treatment and prevention services in correctional and criminal justice settings is expanding and strengthening collaborations among public health departments, correctional and criminal justice agencies, and community-based organizations. (p. 104)

Belenko, Langley, Crimmins, and Chaple (2004) have identified probationers and parolees as a "hidden risk group" in need of HIV education and prevention interventions that are community-based. Sowell and colleagues (2001) stress the importance of case management as a vehicle for improving the health care of returning inmates who are HIV-positive.

Data play an increasingly important role in helping to shape correctional health care in the twenty-first century (Mellow, 2008; Woodward, 2008). Hammett, Harmon, and Rhodes (2003) propose a two-part strategy for increasing the recognition of correctional health as a national public health problem—development and dissemination of quantitative estimates of the impact of infectious disease of the correctionally involved and quantitative analyses of the costs and benefits of prevention and early intervention of infectious diseases. Creating public awareness of how prison health care affects the entire nation and not just the incarcerated is a fundamental step in the direction of legitimating correctional and community partnerships.

Thorburn (1995) issues a similar challenge in bringing together correctional and public health systems:

> This national health problem should be a shared responsibility. It requires coordinated planning and initiatives with communities, as well as shared resources. It is time for correctional health care to be recognized as an integral public health sector. Both State and local health departments need to join with correctional health professionals in preventing the spread of infectious disease within corrections and to the public (p. 560).

One federal demonstration program based in California that focused on men and women leaving California state prisons (Get Connected) typifies the importance of case management of inmates leaving prisons. A central focus of this program is on HIV prevention and facilitates linkage with community-based organizations (Myers et al., 2005).

Nevertheless, the call for a coordinated campaign is not without challenges, and for collaborations to succeed it is essential to have a mutual recognition of how different organizational cultures and contexts (environment) influence corrections and public health views of health care (*IDU/HIV Prevention*, 2001b). A recent study by the U.S. Department of Justice (LIS Inc., 2003) identified barriers that prevent collaboration, in this case between public health and corrections: (1) the importance and need of establishing mechanisms for dialogue to identify common interests; (2) differences in agency missions and goals; and (3) the lack of initiation on the part of departments of corrections. The Public Health and Corrections Association (2002) identified four additional challenges: (1) lack of leadership; (2) logistical barriers; (3) limited resources; and (4) ineffectual or lack of comprehensive correctional policies.

Community-based resources in the form of organized programs, volunteers, and interns, to list but three, must be a part of any systematic and comprehensive effort. It is imperative that the point-of-cost savings should not be stressed in advocating changes that are more humane, although cost savings will occur over the long haul. The primary purpose of these forms of collaboration is the provision of quality and compassionate care. Unlike the mental hospital deinstitutionalization movement that was advanced with the promise of greater fiscal savings, this movement must hinge on the critical importance of care.

Collaborations take on added significance regarding women (Kates, Ransford & Cardozo, 2005). Overall, the literature reviewed consistently recommended bolstering reentry/aftercare programs, increased rigorous medical research specific to women, evaluation of interventions, and multidisciplinary collaboration. These collaborations, in turn, actively must help these women reunite with their children, in cases where they are mothers.

Freudenberg (2002a), in an extensive review of the literature on inmates who are women of color and their reentry into society, draws conclusions that have general applicability to all inmates regardless of their gender and ethnic/racial background, and highlights the importance of coordination of service provision between prisons and community-based organizations:

> Common characteristics of such (successful) interventions include the following: pre-release as well as post-release services, integration of drug treatment, health care, employment and vocational training, social services, mental health, and housing; activities conducted at the client, community, and policy levels; and strong partnerships among correctional and public health agencies and community organizations (p. 1897).

Community-prison partnerships throughout all facets of prison health care delivery, as a result, are predicated upon mutual understanding of needs, a willingness to enter into working relationships, and the working out of cost sharing so that neither system is left totally with the onus of supporting a population group with high health needs.

Hammett, Gaiter, and Crawford (1998) identified six key factors that were associated with the most effective reentry programs, and they provide an outline of a model of service delivery predicated on a close working relationship between prisons and community organizations:

1. staff training and skills
2. case management
3. network of referral services
4. client participation in discharge planning
5. former inmates as service providers
6. the understanding, support, and cooperation of administrators, wardens, sheriffs, and correctional staff (p. 109)

Health care delivery, as a result, no longer should be conceptualized as exclusively taking place within prisons to the exclusion of follow-up within the community upon release from prisons (Stack, 2000).

The lack of community-based treatment programs to prevent incarceration is widely considered to play a prominent role in why offenders with mental illnesses get sentenced to jails or prisons. Inmates suffering from mental illness are most often incarcerated for relatively minor offenses such as trespassing, failing to pay for a meal, vagrancy, disorderly conduct, or alcohol-related charges (Center on Crime, Communities & Culture, 1996). A 1995 study in New York City found that 43% of all defendants with mental illness were homeless at the time of their arrest; there were 3,800 on any given day (Barr, 1999). Systematic efforts to help newly released inmates avoid a return to drug use and crime are highly recommended (*IDU/HIV Prevention*, 2001c). Thus, efforts to prevent incarceration through diversion programs will go a long way toward reducing incarceration numbers and, in the process, meeting the health needs of a population group at high risk for illnesses.

The emergence of compassionate release in the case of inmates with terminal illnesses and who do not pose a threat to society further enhances the importance of discharge planning and case management once the offender leaves the prison system. These services will require transitional programs with extensive community-based organizations and close watching of ex-offenders' access to a multitude of health and social services. The staffing of these transitional programs necessitates highly trained and motivated staff to work with this client population.

Compassionate release will represent a subsection, and one that will only grow in importance in an ongoing debate of early-release initiatives, in an effort to stem correctional costs, particularly for high-cost-type prisoners such as those who are terminally ill. In 2002, France enacted what is probably the most compressive system for early release for seriously ill and elder prisoners in the world, and it is being viewed as a possible model for similar efforts in Europe and North America (Steiner, 2003). Human rights rather than costs guided this effort. The French introduction of a new system of medical parole represents a systemwide approach to an increasingly significant problem in France. This phase of health services is extremely costly and will require the creation of innovative and cost-sensitive programs.

Finally, coordination between prisons and community-based organizations should be seen within the context of a wealthy nation that lacks a national health insurance, an optimal public health infrastructure, and an adequate long-term care system. Coordination is more difficult when the general population lacks these and is competing with prisoners for the limited resources that do exist. When the United States finally develops a national health insurance, a strong public health system, and a strong long-term care system, care should be taken to include the needs of prisoners as well as the needs of released prisoners in these structures. Although prisoners cannot wait for these resources to be improved, or provided humane care, it is probable that they will be less likely to be begrudged services when the full U.S. population has a right to health care, public health services, and long-term care.

SPECIALIZED TRAINING FOR HEALTH CARE PROVIDERS

There is little argument that very few health care personnel have received adequate training to prepare them to work within correctional institutions such as prisons and jails, and that there is a desperate need for this field to attract highly qualified and motivated staff (Anno et al., 2004; Baker, 2005; Levine, 2005; Willmott & Olphen, 2005). Some would argue that no formalized training possibly could prepare anyone for work behind bars. Specialized training can help better prepare providers for the experience and, in the process, create a cadre of staff with both the preparation and the willingness to embrace a mission focused on correctional health care (Alemagno, Wilkinson & Levy, 2004; Goldkuhle, 1999; Macher et al., 2005; Raimer & Stobo, 2004; Strupp & Willmott, 2005; Taylor, 2002).

Ironically, the introduction and expansion of health care personnel has not been accepted widely within correctional systems, and health personnel can be viewed as causing trouble rather than alleviating it, thus compounding others' jobs (Harding, 2000). The marginalization of health care staff, particularly those who are considered to be "soft" on inmates, causes a tremendous amount of strain and easily can lead to burnout and staff turnover, complicating service delivery. Attracting and preparing staff for roles of health care providers within correctional systems will not succeed if their mere presence is viewed as either a security risk or a detriment to law enforcement.

Initiatives to attract and keep staff within prisons represent a dramatic departure from the usual hiring practices. Prisons no longer must be viewed as employers of the last resort for health personnel. Attracting staff to these systems, in turn, can be facilitated through extensive use of internships for allied health professionals. Internships historically have played important roles within helping professions, particularly social work. Placement in organizations provides students with an opportunity to learn through hands-on experiences what it means to work in a particular field. Internships, too, have allowed organizations access to university/college resources and to recruit a future workforce. This workforce, then, would be better able to enter the field with minimal efforts to orient them to the scope of practice within the field. Thus, internships represent a win–win situation for both the field and higher learning institutions.

A community perspective on specialized training is also in order. It would be inaccurate to think that health care and social service providers have the requisite training to meet the unique challenges posed by returning ex-inmates. Health and social service staff can play influential roles in helping former inmates to reclaim their self-esteem, in addition to helping them secure health and social services. Empowering these individuals will represent a critical component of any effort to provide continuity of care. Low self-esteem is often an overlooked element in any health care delivery system, particularly one that is prisoner-focused; therefore, it takes on great significance in the case of ex-inmates (Willmott & Olphen, 2005). Health and social service personnel, in addition, must incorporate advocacy roles as part of their work with ex-inmates.

PROVISION OF CARE

The actual provision of health care for incarcerated patients represents the intersection of policy and the beneficiaries of the decision-making process. This section will focus on four health care problems that we believe will continue to play prominent roles in the near future. Substance abuse, mental health, HIV/AIDS, and end-of-life services increasingly will become cost categories representing significant parts of prison health care budgets.

Faiver (1998f) notes the ideal conditions that must be present for inmates to receive quality health care:

> For inmates . . . access to the health care system and to needed care essentially must be unimpeded. This means that the inmate, without risk of interference by anyone and without fear of reprisal, must be able to alert health care staff of a health need, to receive a timely professional evaluation of that need, and to receive treatment in a manner prescribed by a competent provider (p. 101).

It is doubtful that there is a prison system in this country that can lay claim to having these conditions.

A. Substance Abuse Services within Prisons

It is no mistake that substance-abusing inmates represent a significant sector of the prison population. Thus, any serious efforts to keep these individuals from reentering prisons must address the problems associated with abusing drugs (Leukefeld et al., 2006). The area of HIV/AIDS, for example, has shown great promise in leading the way for collaborative partnerships between corrections institutions and communities in addressing substance abuse and HIV/AIDS (*Public Health & Corrections*, 2003).

The dramatic increase in imprisonment rates for drug offenders resulted in the following statement by Barry R. McCaffrey, then director of the Office of National Drug Control Policy:

> It is clear that we cannot arrest our way out of the problem of chronic drug abuse and drug-driven crime. We cannot continue to apply policies and programs that do not deal with the root causes of substance abuse and attendant crime. Nor should we expect to continue to have the widespread societal support for our counter-drug programs if the American people begin to believe these programs are unfair (Beatty, Holman & Schiraldi, 2000, p. 1).

The increased availability of substance abuse treatment where it currently is being offered and introduction of treatment where it is not available represent the cornerstone of any effective prison-related initiative to address the health care needs of prisoners. The role of substance abuse in increasing the nation's incarceration rates is well recognized, particularly within communities of color. Unfortunately, as the number of prisoners in need of treatment has increased in tandem with the overall prisoner population, the proportion receiving treatment has declined. Between 1995 and 1996, the number of inmates in treatment decreased by 18,360 as inmates needing treatment increased by 39,578 (Belenko, Peugh, Califano Jr. & Foster, 1999).

According to a 2000 Substance Abuse Treatment and Mental Health Services Administration (SAMHSA) report, fewer than half of the nation's 7,564 adult and juvenile treatment facilities provided treatment to inmates. Although low, this figure represents an increase from 40% in 1997. In 1999, a total of 173,000 inmates, or approximately 10.5% of all inmates, were in substance abuse treatment programs—12,500 in federal prisons, 99,000 in state prisons, 34,000 in jails, and 27,000 in juvenile facilities. Turvey and Flaum (2002), in a rare study specifically focused on elder inmates, found that 71% of older inmates had a history of substance abuse problems, more likely alcohol, when compared with younger inmates, and longer histories of problems. Nevertheless, less than one-third had ever received any form of treatment. A recent metastudy of coercive treatment, though, has raised questions about the effectiveness of this form of treatment within correctional settings (Norland, Sowell & DiChiara, 2003).

As already noted, women under correctional supervision are more likely than women in the general population and than their male counterparts to have histories of substance abuse. Programming for incarcerated women, however, has four main deficiencies: drug treatment is not offered; drug treatment is not women-specific or drug-specific; the delivery of treatment programming is significantly lower than demand; and follow-up is limited or nonexistent within the correctional setting and postrelease. "It is estimated that no more than 10% of drug-abusing women are offered drug treatment in jail or prison, and most jails lack comprehensive discharge planning or aftercare programs" (Freudenberg, 2002a, p. 1895).

The Office of National Drug Policy estimated that 57% of all of those in the general population who need drug treatment do not receive it. In 1998, there were approximately 5 million drug users who needed treatment, but only 2.1 million received it (National Drug Control Policy, 2000). Treatment effectiveness can be measured in a variety of ways. However, one study shows a 64% decrease in arrests with treatment—a powerful indicator of treatment effectiveness (Center for Substance Abuse Treatment, 1997). Treatment, in addition, has been found to be ten times more effective for reducing societal costs when compared to interdiction (stopping of drugs such as heroin and cocaine at the nation's borders) (Rydell & Everingham, 1994). Prisons, however, generally have done a poor job of addressing drug treatment (Tonry, 2004), and news stories often highlight this fact. Ironically, access to drug treatment may be increased greatly once an individual gets arrested (Twedt, 2005).

It recently has been estimated that there are 14.8 million illicit-drug users in this country and approximately $11.9 billion spent on treating drug addiction (Gutjrie, 2000). The relationship between crime and substance abuse is beyond dispute in many academic and policy circles. However, efforts to stem the number of drug-related crimes generally have focused on incarceration, interdiction, and mandatory sentencing (Fehr, 2000; Seyfer, 2000; Tierney, 2005). Needless to say, these efforts largely have resulted in failure. Milton Friedman (1998), an internationally known conservative economist, has criticized this policy on both moral and pragmatic grounds. The criminal justice system and the alcohol and other drug abuse treatment systems have not developed effective working relationships. The parallels with the criminal justice and the mental health systems are striking (Mauer, 2000).

Approximately 33% of state prisoners and 20% of federal inmates said they committed their offenses for which they were sentenced while under the influence of drugs. Approximately 50% of those on probation and parole have substance-abusing backgrounds (*San Francisco Chronicle*, 2000). Cook (2001) points out the need for alternate methods to incarceration for those convicted of drug-related crimes, particularly those that are nonviolent in nature:

> Greater provision of substance abuse treatment programs before incarceration could go a long way toward lowering the rates and costs of the criminal justice system. There is a growing awareness that unless drug cases are handled alternatively, the entire system will collapse due to sheer volume. (p. 179)

B. Provision of Mental Health Services

Mental health as a health condition brings with it a host of unique challenges for prison health care (Patterson & Greifinger, 2008). However, when mental health is combined with other illnesses, particularly among inmates of color, it presents a set of challenges with which systems of care outside of prisons also are struggling (Peters & Bekman, 2008). The value of culturally competent services generally has found acceptance in noninstitutional populations. However, this has not been the case for the incarcerated. Primm, Osher, and Gomez (2005), commenting on the importance of cultural competency in correctional systems, raise concerns about the general absence of mental health services for an increasingly multicultural inmate population.

Wolff (1998), in examining the interactions and formal relationships between mental health and law enforcement systems, identified a series of challenges, or barriers, to effectively meet the needs of inmates with severe mental illness. Ironically, neither system wishes to be held fiscally and clinically responsible for the needs of prisoners with severe mental illness, compounding service delivery during preincarceration and postincarceration.

Correctional systems have been slow to recognize the unique challenges that inmates with severe and persistent mental illness present (Hoge, 2008). Colorado, for example, has built a facility to house inmates with severe mental illness (Stahl & West, 2001). This facility has space specifically designed for medical operations, work, and training programs.

The subject of mental illness usually elicits three questions from prison officials (Maue, 2001):

1. Why should prisons treat this condition?
2. If so, what services should be offered?
3. How much should be spent on this service?

Nevertheless, the mandatory provision of services for inmates with mental illness has been well established by the nation's highest courts. Yet, the questions of how best to provide services and in the most cost-effective manner have not been answered to the satisfaction of all concerned. It remains to be seen, however, if the assumptions underlying the questions and answers really can be agreed upon. Jails and prisons generally are ill equipped either to recognize or treat mental illness, which represents a critical element in any successful effort in this area. In 1997, there were sixty-seven correctional institutions under investigation by the Department of Justice, and forty-six were correcting problems with their mental health services to avoid pending lawsuits (Sigurdson, 2000).

A 1999 U.S. Bureau of Justice study found that sixteen departments of corrections (DOCs) make no special distinction between inmates with or without mental illness (U.S. Department of Justice, 2001). Thirty-three do make operational distinctions. Also, a majority of DOCs (twenty-eight states and the Federal Bureau of Prisons) do use formalized assessment findings to determine inmate mental health status. The study of found that 70% screened inmates for mental illness at intake, 65% conducted psychiatric assessments, 51% provided twenty-four-hour mental health care, 71% provided some form of therapy or counseling, and 66% offered psychotropic medications. It also found that 13% of all inmates received therapy or counseling, 10% received psychotropic medications, and 2% were placed in twenty-four-hour mental health units. However, 20% of the inmates with mental illness went untreated in the prisons. These inmates upon release generally received no follow-up or treatment. Out of 70,000 state prison inmates, 7% to 8% were considered mentally ill, and 15,000 to 20,000 mentally ill state prisoners were being released into New York City alone on a yearly basis.

Inmate access to mental health services is guaranteed by the Eighth Amendment of the United States Constitution. The 1980 Fifth Circuit Court decision of *Ruiz vs. Estelle* established minimum requirements for mental health services in prisons that include:

1. screening and evaluation to identify those needing mental health services in prisons' care
2. a treatment plan for identified problems
3. qualified mental health staff sufficient to treat the population
4. a health records system
5. a suicide prevention and treatment program
6. the appropriate use of behavior-altering medications
   (National Commission on Correctional Health Care, 1992, p. 3)

It is important to note, however, that the use of the Eighth Amendment has not been restricted to health care. Female inmates, for example, have increasingly relied upon this constitutional protection in establishing class-action lawsuits to address sexual assaults and harassment within prisons (Laderberg, 1998; Wool, 2008).

The life of a person with mental illness who is involved with the criminal justice system must be examined within a continuum rather than a singular event: preinvolvement (events leading up to court involvement), active involvement (serving prison or jail time), and postinvolvement (release back into the community). Roskes, Feldman, Arrington, and Leisher (1999) note that ex-offenders (parolees or released) are grossly misunderstood and not provided with appropriate treatment, thus increasing the likelihood of their rearrest and the start of the vicious cycle all over again. Further, it would be simplistic to think of offenders with mental illness not to be co-morbid, particularly involving substance abuse. Successful treatment, as a result, is challenging and costly for correctional systems.

Finally, alternatives to prisons for offenders with mental illness have been advocated because this population group represents a substantial segment of correctional inmates, and incarceration exacerbates this condition (Schaefer & Stefancic, 2003). These alternatives will play an increasingly important role in the future in any efforts to reduce prison population groups and costs.

It does not take a historian to realize that there is a tremendous coincidence between the closing down of mental institutions with a lack of community services and the reemergence of correctional facilities as the new mental health institutions in this country. An historical perspective on how the mentally ill were incarcerated in prisons in the nineteenth century led to major social changes in treatment of these individuals (Rothman, 1971). It will only be a question of time before this group will be discovered once again just as they were well over 100 years ago.

C. Provision of HIV/AIDS Services

The health seriousness of HIV/AIDS is well acknowledged in this society. However, this disease has brought with it numerous challenges (social, legal, and economic) that have had a profound impact on the nation's prison system (National Commission on Correctional Health Care, 2005a). Braithwaite, Hammett, and Mayberry (1996) warn the nation about how AIDS in prison is part of an epidemic that is being ignored, that will not go away, and may well come back to haunt communities when inmates return from prison. HIV transmission among prisoners is similar to that outside of prisons: unsafe sex, tattooing, and sharing needles. Macher, Kibble, and Wheeler (2006) specifically have documented the transmission of HIV within one correctional facility. Because of the overrepresentation of people of color in prisons, including African Americans, as well as the sentencing for drug-related offenses, HIV and AIDS have a high likelihood of occurrence in prisons and in their communities when prisoners are released (Grinstead et al., 2005).

Schneider (1998) presents a graphic example of how prisoners who are HIV-positive, undiagnosed, or became infected in prison can have deadly consequences in the community upon their release:

> Those who contract AIDS in jail bring it home to their loved ones, as the teenage poet Gil C. Alicea learned the hard way . . . After waiting ten years for his father to return from prison, Alicea was delighted to see his family reunited and his mother expecting a child. His hopes were shattered when he learned that his new sister carried the AIDS virus, as did his mother and his father, all of whom have since died. The story is not uncommon in neighborhoods so saturated with HIV that prison is only one additional risk. (p. 436)

Springer and colleagues (2004, 2008) call for the creation of more effective community-release programs to help ensure that treatments started within prisons are sustained in the community. The importance of early identification, treatment, and care continuity cannot be overly stressed, and this is why prisoner health has to be considered a public health matter by society and not just a prison issue (*New York Times*, 2001b).

The importance of developing an accurate picture of the prevalence of HIV represents an initial, yet critical, step in the development of interventions. Advocates of mandatory testing are increasing in numbers and argue that such testing represents an important step in protecting other non-infected inmates and the general public, and treating inmates who are HIV-positive. Reverend Jesse Jackson has called for mandatory HIV testing of inmates and considers correctional facilities as the epicenter of the AIDS crisis in this country (Positive Population, 2002e). Rev. Jackson views HIV testing as an "opportunity and a privilege" as long as it is not "discriminatorily applied." He goes on to draw an analogy of mandatory HIV testing to mandatory vaccinations in school, thus destigmatizing the act of testing.

The increased effectiveness of early treatment of HIV has increased the attractiveness of early identification and education programs within prisons. Critics of mandatory testing, however, argue that the ability of prisons to maintain confidentiality is one of the major reasons against HIV testing. Loss of privacy, social stigma, and discrimination are powerful factors that cannot be ignored by advocates of mandatory testing (Gostin & Webber, 1998). When guards and other prison personnel accidentally or deliberately violate the rights of HIV-positive inmates, it can have deleterious consequences for the identified inmates. One North Carolina study found that the vast majority (71%) of female inmates were willing to voluntarily undergo HIV testing, negating the need for mandatory testing (Cotten-Oldenburg, Jordon, Martin & Sadowski, 1999).

Despite the visible need and the opportunity to provide information and support around HIV, Hammett, Gaiter, and Crawford (1998) noted:

> in 1994 most state and federal correctional facilities reported using written and/or audiovisual materials on HIV/AIDS, only 48% of 1,207 facilities were providing "instructor-led" HIV education for inmates, and only 7% were offering peer-led programs. (p. 104)

As the numbers of inmates with primary languages other than English enter correctional systems, information must be provided in a form that can be understood.

Although incarceration provides health care personnel with an opportunity to do prevention and early identification and treatment of HIV, there are significant obstacles to accomplishing these goals (Polonsky et al., 1994). Various jurisdictions employ different approaches to prevention and control. Testing policies, integrated or segregated HIV-positive inmates, availability of condoms, bleach or clean needles, high medication costs, fear of HIV by inmates, lack of access to voluntary testing, mistrust, low level of competence on the part of medical staff, and lack of uniform treatment standards all combine to limit access to effective treatment for inmates (Kantor, 2006; *Prison Project*, 2000). Some prisons do not even wish to acknowledge publicly that drug abuse and sexual activity are occurring within their institutions.

A 2002 survey of U.S. prisoners found that 44% of them engage in sexual acts while imprisoned, while 70% of inmates had their first same-sex partner in prison (*Corrections Professional*, 2005e). Cozza and Braithwaite (1999), in their study of preoperative male-to-female transgender inmates, found that they were 5.8 times more likely to have more than one sex partner and 13.7 times more likely to have a main sex partner while in prison than nontransgender inmates. A *New York Times* editorial (2005a) recommended the distribution of condoms in the nation's prisons, since 95% do not do so. In 2006, the National Minority AIDS Council, among other groups, issued a series of recommendations focused on addressing the AIDS epidemic in the African American/Black community. One of those recommendations specifically addressed the incarcerated and the need to distribute condoms (Dunham, 2006). Incarcerated African Americans/Blacks are at high risk for contracting HIV since they represent 40% of those imprisoned but only 13% of the U.S. population. It is estimated that there are 1.1 million people in the country with HIV; African Americans/Blacks constitute 47% of the total and 40% of the 500,000 people who have died from AIDS (Dunham, 2006). Thus, the council recommends making condoms available within prisons and jails, as well as the undertaking of an extensive HIV-prevention educational campaign.

As of 2005, Mississippi and Vermont were the only two states in the country that distributed condoms to inmates (AIDS Policy & Law, 2005a). Jail systems in New York, Philadelphia, Los Angeles, San Francisco, and Washington, D.C., also distribute condoms (AIDS Policy & Law, 2005a; Dunham, 2006). Condom distribution is common in many European prisons; in Canada, some provincial systems even provide bleach for sanitizing of needles in addition to condoms (Malisow, 2006). However, most U.S. correctional systems take the position that Texas takes by refusing to distribute condoms because sex is not allowed in prison (Malisow, 2006).

Reluctance to distribute condoms generally taps into prison administrator fears that forces recognition of sexual activity, particularly in states where such an act is a punishable crime, or fears that condoms can be used to hide drugs and other illegal items that can be swallowed and retrieved at a later time (Kantor, 2006). Fear of public reaction, as in the case of California governor Arnold Schwarzenegger's veto in late 2006, is also a powerful force. The *Los Angeles Times* editorial referred to the governor's veto as "another cynical political maneuver" and a "fundamentally irresponsible choice to make the world more dangerous for inmates and civilians alike" (News-Medical.Net, 2006). The *New York Times*, in a more recent editorial (July 18, 2007), strongly recommended that Gov. Schwarzenegger not veto again a landmark bill passed by the California State Legislature to distribute condoms to inmates requesting them in an effort to reduce the spread of HIV/AIDS. Unfortunately, Gov. Schwarzenegger did veto this once again in 2007.

Ironically, economic forces may be substantial in having correctional systems avoid addressing HIV and AIDS in a comprehensive and effective way. For example, there is a significant disincentive in the case of managed care companies to address this topic. Early identification and treatment of persons who are HIV-positive represents a moral and financial commitment that will limit profits for this industry severely. Identifying inmates who are HIV-positive necessitates provision of care. However, if they are not identified, then health care companies are not liable because they had no knowledge of the condition. In essence, it becomes a catch-22.

Braithwaite, Hammet, and Mayberry (1996) advocate the availability of condoms and educational programs that use other inmates as peer counselors. Stone (1997) notes: "When designing health programs for inmates, one has to consider the messenger as well as the message" (p. 4). Obot and colleagues (1997), in their ethnographic assessment of HIV-risk reduction programs in correctional facilities, stress the efficacy and effectiveness of using peers, in this case fellow inmates, in carrying out education programs. Barriers to effective prevention services within prisons can be as simple as finding time in schedules for prevention education and having available qualified staff to provide the education (Klein et al., 2002).

The high rate of HIV and AIDS in prison necessitates the development of special linkages between prisons and community health services for follow-up with released inmates (Rich et al., 2001; Roberts, Kennedy & Hammett, 2004; The Body, 2001a). Klein and colleagues (2002, 2005), for example, discuss ways to meet capacity building and technical assistance needs of community-based organizations to better meet the needs of returning ex-inmates.

HIV-positive inmates face considerable challenges in seeking necessary treatment (Cusac, 2000). Prisons, by their very structure, mission, operation, and staffing, make the treatment of HIV and AIDS challenging (Nation's Health, 1991). The following of a prescribed treatment regimen is considered one of the key elements for increasing the quality and longevity of life for inmates with HIV because interruptions in treatment can allow drug-resistant viruses to compromise the health of the patient (Frank, 1999). Efforts to individualize treatment are predicated on a willingness and ability of correctional staff to get to better know the inmate with HIV, flexibility in structuring activities to place treatment regime as a priority, and, last but certainly not least, a willingness to destigmatize the inmate with HIV within the prison structure. For those inmates who are HIV-positive and are to be released from prison, the challenge becomes how they can continue their treatment while successfully making a reentry back to their families, community, and society.

The consequences of failure to do so have wide public health ramifications (DeCarlo & Zack, 1996). One study of Latino male inmates in a California state prison found that 51% reported having had sex within the first twelve hours after release, and 11% reported injecting drugs within twenty-four hours after release (Morales, Gomes, & Marin, 1995). Therefore, outreach needs to be done regarding high risk behaviors and safer practices.

D. Provision of End-of-Life Care

The field of death and dying has evolved slowly to recognize the importance of cultural context in the planning of death education and hospice care. Unfortunately, the same cannot be said for death within prisons. The importance of cultural context to better understand and address the needs of inmates can be seen across the life span, and death and dying are not exempted from life-span stages. The "browning" of the nation's prisons has direct implications for hospice and end-of-life care and for the importance of culturally specific and competent programs and services.

Increasing numbers of scholarly debates on the ethics of withholding end-of-life care behind bars are emerging (Cohn, 1999; Mahon, 1999). Mahon (1999), who attributes changes in attitudes to the overcrowding of prisons and the issues that brings to these institutions, notes:

> For those who are concerned with health care at the end of life, it is imperative to understand that the terminally ill dying in U.S. prisons and jails must be given access to the clinical advances available to the general population. With the meteoric increase in the size of the U.S. prison population since the 1970s, prisons have become the largest health care providers in the nation . . . prisons become a critical frontier for acute,

chronic, and end-of-life care, particularly for the poor, urban men and women (p. 21).

Depriving inmates of end-of-life care can be construed as cruel and unusual punishment and a violation of the Eighth Amendment.

The ability of prisons to provide terminally ill inmates with comprehensive end-of-life care is not without a set of challenges (Taylor, 2002). Ratcliff and Cohn (2000) identified seven critical challenges in prisons' providing end-of-life care:

1. Prisons have been constructed and run to promote conformity rather than stressing or valuing individual preference.
2. Overcrowding has worked effectively against treating inmates as individuals.
3. Provision of drugs to address pain generally is frowned upon.
4. Fear of lawsuits resulting from poor provision of health care results in prisons pursuing aggressive treatment even when the inmate does not wish this course of action.
5. Emphasis on security mitigates against communication and service delivery.
6. Effective treatment can be thwarted by overcrowding and inmate classification.
7. Providing a quality hospice service requires prisons to acknowledge their inadequacies and be willing to receive assistance.

Cohn (1999) strongly argues that efforts to provide end-of-life care for prisoners would be fruitless without an examination of the ethical values underlying the correctional system of care in this country:

> The health care needs of the aging and growing population only present a more urgent occasion to discuss barriers to improving care at the end of life. Ethical arguments can be useful in making a case for valuing prisoners as human beings, fulfilling our social contract with them, recognizing the need for just policies, and allowing for social utility. What remains is action on those philosophical arguments. (p. 254)

The introduction of advance care directives is considered an important step in the provision of end-of-life care for dying inmates (Levine, 2005). An advance care directive can be defined as instructions for medical personnel on medical decisions if one is unable to make such decisions because of a condition such as a coma. The introduction of an ethical decision-making process on death and dying would not be easy within a context that often has questionable ethical standards pertaining to health needs of inmates.

SPECIAL POPULATIONS

The increased presence of special population groups in the nation's prison system, such as elders, women, and youth, brings with it a set of challenges in identifying and addressing health care needs for groups other than males within a certain age category (Anno et al., 2004).

A. Older Adults

There is little disputing that American society has undergone rapid and significant changes in the past fifty years, and more changes lay ahead that may be even more dramatic. The American dream of the 1950s of a house with a white picket fence, a job with a decent salary that was guaranteed for life, health, and high quality education for the children is possible only for a select few families of color in this society.

The status and image of elders in this society, too, has undergone radical shifts in the past fifty years. They are expected to spend their "golden years enjoying themselves in health and leisure. However, the image of elders serving hard time and looking forward to death behind bars is not often covered in national discussions of Social Security, prescription drug coverage, or Medicare reform. Nevertheless, this image will become an even greater reality in the twenty-first century in this and other countries around the world (*Arizona Republic,* 2005; Friedberg, 1999; Montgomery, 1997; Murray, 1998; Novak, 1997; Tysver, 1998; Wittmeier, 1999).

Wheeler, Connelly, and Wheeler's (1994) observations regarding Oklahoma are also applicable to other states across the country fifteen years later:

> The aging of the United States population and future crime trends by the elderly will not leave any state's correctional department untouched. As the demands by society for stricter sentencing grow and legislators respond with mandatory sentences, these types of crime and their penalties will ensure that Oklahoma's prison population will age. Older inmates will force a larger quantity and diversity of services on institutions, placing more pressure on already overcrowded institutions and their budgets. Dealing with those issues will be an increasing priority for all corrections departments in years to come (p. 1).

Guber and Petersilia (2006) made an extensive review of approaches for better meeting the needs of California's older adults, but with implications for the rest of the country. The complexity of the challenges of better meeting the needs of older adult inmates while maximizing tax dollars necessitates a multifaceted approach involving sentencing reform, creation of special housing, and the introduction of innovative models. The authors recommend the creation of geriatric units because they increase service delivery efficiency, reduce overall costs (reduced transportation and security costs), and improve safety of inmates. In addition, they recommend sentencing reform as necessary, greater use of early-release options, introduction of prevention (health promotion) programs, and development of new models of service delivery that actively utilize younger inmates in helper roles. This latter recommendation builds upon the pioneering work being accomplished in prison hospice programs.

The increased health care needs of older prisoners not only require specialized settings but also staff with the following competencies (Morton, 1992):

1. greater respect for the inmate/patient
2. greater awareness of the aging process
3. greater understanding of the levels of functioning of an older person
4. recognition of the impact of reduced levels of functioning on a person
5. recognition of the problem medications can cause
6. knowledge of and assessment of what resources are available to treat or improve presenting problems

These staff qualities and competencies highlight the multifaceted roles required to meet the specialized needs of older inmates. In addition, these roles demand that prison systems institute extensive staff training and support; the nature and extent of this support is unprecedented (Guber & Petersilia, 2006). Cianciolo and Zupan (2004) note that, although there is general acknowledgment of the importance of preparing a workforce to effectively address the needs of older adults, the correctional system has made little progress on this subject. There is an unquestioned need to prepare correctional staff for the unique challenges and rewards of meeting the needs of older inmates.

Concern about rising health costs fueled by an increasingly aging inmate population is not new in this country. For example, an early 1990s survey of state correctional programs and older inmates found that 30% of the states cited rising costs as the most pressing need, followed by 26% who cited meeting the special needs of elders with chronic health problems and limited activities of daily living (ADL) functions (Aday, 1994).

Early or compassionate release of elders is a topic that has received increased recognition from humanitarian and cost-savings perspectives. However, like any form of compassionate-release program, there is considerable debate about the virtues of allowing elders to leave before the completion of their sentence. One Arizona official summed up the prevailing view on this subject:

> Officials caution that the cost-saving benefits of releasing aging or ill inmates have to be carefully weighed against public-safety risks and the needs to make sure justice is served . . . releasing them is still not a popular option. States that do allow early releases generally stipulate inmates must be physically incapacitated or suffering from an illness so debilitating that they are incapable of presenting a danger to society. (Villa, 2005, p. 1)

The arguments resting on cost savings, however, have been very persuasive. It has been estimated that if nonviolent inmates over the age of fifty-five were released from state and federal prisons, the savings to correctional systems would be approximately $900 million in the first year alone. If release were to be restricted to those sixty-five or older, the savings in the initial year would be over $175 million (National Center on Institutions & Alternatives, 1998). Not surprisingly, any effort seriously to calculate the economic costs of elder prisoners is difficult. Take the case of Dr. Charles Friedgood, though:

> According to information he supplied, his total bill for medical care in the past few years, including treatment for cancer and heart disease, has been $250,000. Dr. Friedgood was sentenced to 25 years to life in 1977 for murdering his wife. (Butterfield, 1997b, p. E3)

This case, however, also illustrates the dilemma society faces if, by cutting costs to the prison, a prisoner is released who, while medically expensive, has been judged to deserve incarceration. Neeley, Addison, and Craig-Moreland (1999) note that older inmates generally fall into one of four possible categories:

1. first-time offenders
2. chronic offenders
3. recidivists
4. those who have grown old while in prison

Thus, older prisoners, in general, do not fit typical stereotypes of prisoners in this country. For example, 25% have been incarcerated less than one year, and 68% for less than five years (Butterfield, 1997a). Further compounding rational discourse on the subject is that the vast majority (67%) of these inmates has been imprisoned for a violent crime.

Prioritizing who should be incarcerated and who should be released will place elder inmates in a difficult position. Freedom is not without its consequences, particularly for those inmates who have served lengthy prison sentences. Elders may well fear release back into a community that may not be welcoming and may lack health care resources. A former regional director of prisoners comments on the inherent contradiction of maintaining ill and aged inmates in prison (Lang, 1999):

> Some of these people are in their 80s and I had one guy who was 101
> . . . Some continue to be violent, but the majority in my experience are
> not. It doesn't make a lot of sense to me to keep those people confined
> when we need those beds for young violent offenders coming into the
> system. And it doesn't seem to make much sense economically. (p. 2)

These contradictions are ever present on a day-to-day basis within almost all of this nation's correctional facilities (Failing & Sears, 2001).

Greco's (2002) description of the impact of an aging population on health care provision within New York state prisons also can be generalized across the country:

> Prison health care is based on an antiquated sick-call system originally
> conceived to treat common illnesses like flu. It is not designed to serve
> the large number of prisoners who are chronically, acutely, or terminally
> ill. There are signs that the system is overloaded. Triage is performed by
> whatever personnel are available that day, including correctional officers
> who have no medical training (p. 315).

Reentry of older adult inmates will bring its unique share of challenges, however (Lowey, Williams & Abraldes, 2008).

B. Women

Young (2001) found that the availability of services for chronic physical illnesses, disabilities, and mental health care among female inmates was not consistent when compared to their male counterparts. Young (1998), in a study of 129 women inmates, found that women of color use fewer health services when compared to their White, non–Latina counterparts. The increased number of women in correctional systems has raised critical issues related to female inmates receiving basic parity with men regarding health care (Belknap, 2003; Freudenberg, 2002b; Ross & Lawrence, 1998; Young, 1998). Sterk, Theall, and Elifson (2005) argue that the unique needs of women must be taken into account in any design of intervention and prevention programs within and outside of criminal justice systems.

A 1996 national survey of jail inmates found that fewer than 47% of female inmates received a medical examination to determine their health status upon entry, compared to 49% for males (Harlow, 1998). Gynecological examinations, for example, are not conducted routinely during admission or at any other time while incarcerated (Anderson, 2003; National Commission on Correctional Health Care, 2005b). Stoller (2003) argues that prisons represent spaces where women's health gets further compromised by rules, custodial priorities, poor health care management, incompetence, and indifference fueled by sexist attitudes. This perspective applies to women of all ages. However, older adult female inmates face even more challenges in having their health needs met (Reivere & Young, 2004).

The increased number of women in prisons was the central theme of a 2005 national conference in an effort to tailor programs specifically for women rather than adapt male programs to women inmate needs (Lohn, 2005). The Massachusetts Public Health Association (2003) actively advocates for parity with men regarding programs and services:

> Parity . . . does not suggest that female offenders should receive identical programs and services as men, but speaks to the need for access to a similar number of offerings and resources. This parity should include, but not be limited to: access to health services (including regular gynecological exams and screenings), recreation, substance abuse treatment, mental health services, education, and job training (p. 23).

The National Women's Law Center (n.d., p. 1) also raises arguments about women inmates having parity with men: "Because prison health care systems were created for men, routine gynecological care, such as pap smears, breast exams, and mammograms, is extremely rare in prisons. Care, as a result, is frequently only administered once the situation becomes an emergency." In comparison to the more obvious health care needs of women based on physical differences between men and women, there historically has been limited research on the needs of women and what constitutes effective provision of services to women under correctional supervision (Berkman,

1995). This is especially salient when considering the implications for providing services to a diverse prison population with varying cultural backgrounds and differing spoken languages (Day, 2001). As a consequence, the provision of these gender-specific services is out of the ordinary within a correctional context. For example, the staffing of services very often requires women to be hired.

A survey of U.S. women's prisons in the early 1990s had a number of important findings:

1. Less than 50% provided any form of prenatal care.
2. Only 15% offered special diets and nutritional programs for pregnant inmates.
3. Only 15% provided specialized counseling to assist new mothers to find placements for their infants after birth.
4. Only 11% provided postnatal counseling (Wooldredge & Masters, 1993).

Conditions have improved since that survey but still have considerable room for improvement.

A 1999 study found that almost 50% of those pregnant when imprisoned and 80% of those pregnant when incarcerated received prenatal care (Greenfield & Snell, 1999). Poor pregnancy outcome among African American women in the general population (infant mortality and low-birth-weight babies) makes them as inmates a high-risk group (Byrd & Clayton, 2002).

Although data could not be obtained on the number of female inmates who received gynecological examinations at the time of incarceration, as stated earlier, gynecological examinations are not the norm in this country (National Commission on Correctional Health Care, 2005b). According to the American Social Health Association, more than half of all women avoided going to a gynecologist during the year preceding the study (Marsa, 2001). This statistic, however, was far greater for women of color when compared to their White, non-Latina counterparts. Only one in four indicated that they did receive routine gynecological exams during the past year, and an additional 28% said they just do not get annual examinations. Also, the increase in the number of pregnant women entering prisons has been so dramatic that one advocate has recommended that all female inmates receive a pregnancy test upon entering correctional systems (Anno, 1991).

Kyei-Aboagye, Vragovic, and Chong (2000) made a series of recommendations for providing prenatal care on-site, including eliminating the need to bring inmates to outside clinics for the specialized services. External visits are widely considered one of the most expensive features of health care services within prisons, and providing on-site service should result in considerable savings.

Gender-specific treatment strategies are finding greater acceptance within correctional settings and in successful reentry programs (Blitz, Wolff, Pan & Pogorzelski, 2005). Further, the special needs of women prisoners with HIV/AIDS bring an often overlooked dimension to services for this population (Zaitzow & West, 2003). The emergence of hepatitis B and C among incarcerated and reincarcerated women, also increases the importance of gender-targeted interventions within and outside of prisons (Macalino et al., 2005).

C. Youth

The increased number of youth being sent to adult prisons requires research to determine how the health status of these youth has changed as a result of being imprisoned. The age of juvenile inmates requires specialized treatment and personnel who have the requisite competencies to treat them. In other words, staff who are used to and competent in treating adults cannot be expected to be equally adept at meeting the needs of juveniles.

Life without the possibility of parole, as already noted, is very common in most states (Cordes & Reed, 2005). However, it takes on greater meaning when it applies to youth. In 2005, a *New York Times* survey found that there were 2,200 inmates serving a life sentence without parole for crimes committed prior to their eighteenth birthday, of whom 350 were under the age of fifteen (Liptak, 2005c). Glick, Sturgeon, and Venator-Santiago (1998) note that adult correctional systems must be prepared to differentiate the needs of youth from those of adult inmates and to take into account the developmental stage in designing initiatives. The increasing number of youth serving life sentences without parole makes this population group of sufficient importance to warrant special attention to health care needs.

PREVENTING AND CONTAINING COMMUNICABLE DISEASES

Restum (2005) highlights the threat to communities of contracting communicable diseases from returning inmates and substandard follow-up care. Weinbaum, Sabin, and Santibanez (2005), too, raise how best to prevent and contain communicable diseases, bringing a public health perspective to prison health care, including a tremendous potential for minimizing the spread of infectious diseases within the community upon the release of in-mates. Wohl (2005,) sums up quite well the challenges and dilemmas in car-ing for HIV-infected prisoners, but observations are also applicable to other communicable diseases:

> The challenges . . . are myriad and generally include the constraints that accompany working within a system designed primarily to meet secu-rity, rather than medical needs. Budgetary restraints, a patient population that suffers disproportionately from mental and physical co-morbidities and less-than-ready access to subspecialty experts further complicates care of these patients. (p. 1)

Another example is the spread of hepatitis C (HCV), as stated earlier in this book (Munoz-Plaza et al., 2005; Paris, Pradham, Allen & Cassidy, 2005). The morbidity of hepatitis C is high, and there is no national policy for screening or treatment in federal and state correctional systems. Unfortu-nately, the prevalence of hepatitis C virus infection among the incarcerated has not been studied sufficiently (Alexander, 2002; National Commission on Correctional Health Care, 1999). The testing and treatment of this disease will have a far-reaching impact since many of the prisoners will eventually be released and returned to their families and communities (Cox, 2000; Fackelmann, 1999b). In 2000, there were an estimated 585,000 prisoners re-leased from state prisons, or three times the total released in 1980. New York State, for example, released 30,000 inmates in 1999 (Cox, 2000). This wave of people leaving prisons started in 1996, when 500,000 were released, and is expected to continue even though a sizable percentage will remain in prison and become aged in confinement.

Treatment costs of hepatitis C range from approximately $9,000 to $14,000 a year per inmate for injections of interferon, or $12,000 to $16,000 for a combination of interferon and ribauirin, without guarantee of results (Cook, 1999b). In a recent Massachusetts report, the figure for one year of a treatment regimen was estimated to be $25,000 (Massachu-setts Public Health Association, 2003). High costs and the lack of evidence concerning effective treatment have convinced correctional systems to withhold treatment. Liver transplants, in cases where treatment was with-held or ineffective, however, can cost from $250,000 to $300,000. D'An-gelo (2003) strongly recommends that HCV treatment and prevention can-not be artificially separated from addiction treatment and case management upon inmate release. In addition, the psychiatric aspects of treating inmates with HCV only recently have been investigated (Burke, 2001).

Limited treatment options combine with a poor prospect for a vaccine combine to make inmates with HCV a difficult population to manage within prisons (Hammett, Gaiter & Crawford, 1998; Maruschak, 1999). Liver transplants are costly and controversial when involving prisoners. Long waiting lists and an expected jump of 500% in transplants in the general population by the year 2008 increase the likelihood of family members being called upon in increasing numbers to participate in liver transplants (Carmichael, 2002).

The prevention of infectious diseases within prisons is a lot less costly than the treating of diseases, and hepatitis B is a case in point. One estimate of vaccinating 100,000 California prisoners against hepatitis B noted that it would cost $2.6 million. However, treating 30,000 cases of the virus would cost an estimated $330 million (Shapinsky, 1999). The increasing representation of Latinos within the correctional system makes HBV prevention and early intervention a priority and a challenge at the same time because of potential cultural and language barriers.

Although the public threat of tuberculosis (TB) is very real within prisons, correctional systems have failed in their responsibilities to address this disease: "This may be due to lack of funding, to lack of political will, or to public indifference but, most likely, it is a combination of all three of these factors. Let's not forget that TB in any segment of the population endangers every member of society" (Laniado-Laborin, 2001, p. 682). Failure systematically to address the problem of tuberculosis within prisons has placed inmates as well as those entrusted to guard and serve them at higher risk of contracting this disease, not to mention their families and neighbors.

PROMOTION OF HEALTHY LIFESTYLES

The promotion of quality and comprehensive health care for prisoners has great value for society. For example, health promotion and older adults in jails has started to receive greater attention (Kuhlmann & Ruddell, 2005). Loeb, Steffensmeier, and Lawrence (2007) found that there was no significant difference between older adult men who were incarcerated or in the community when examining self-efficacy for health management or health status. There were, however, significant differences in participation in health promotion programs, and this may be the result of lack of availability or awareness of such programs.

Health promotion also benefits prison staff by reducing stress and encouraging them to pursue healthier lifestyles. In addition, limiting the spread of diseases among prisoners benefits their families and communities upon their release. Further, prison presents an excellent opportunity to help prisoners who abuse drugs to change, and such prisoners represent a very high percentage of the prison population. These benefits translate into sizable budget savings for taxpayers and a healthy society (Squires, 1996; World Health Organization, 2000). Interestingly, there is an increasing recognition that correctional systems are serving as the health care nexus for the diagnosis and treatment of various forms of infections, particularly HIV and hepatitis B and C (Kendig et al., 1994).

The introduction of heart-healthy meals and antitobacco programs are but two examples of how some prison systems are attempting to reduce diseases and improve health outcomes and, in the process, also reduce health care costs (Montgomery, 1997; O'Hagan, 2001; Patrick & Marsh, 2001). In 2001, more than 30 states had banned smoking in prison (O'Hagan, 2001), compared to 18 states in 1995 (*Corrections Professional*, 2005b). In 2005, it was estimated that 75% of all U.S. correctional facilities were smoke-free (*Corrections Professional*, 2005a).In 2005, California became the latest state to institute a smoke-free policy in its state prisons (*Christian Science Monitor*, 2005).

One correctional system (Los Angeles County Sheriff's Office) has instituted a ban on tobacco products as a means of reducing pollutants in the air and decreasing the chance of upper respiratory virus infections (Anonymous, 2001b). In 2005, a New York City prisoner sued the New York City Corrections Department, claiming he got cancer from secondhand smoke (Maull, 2005).

However, prison systems attempting to provide healthy meals face considerable challenges, as noted by one menu program developer:

> We try to provide low-fat, healthful items and we make nutritional adjustments for inmates with special needs, such as those with diabetes and AIDS . . . But we have to watch the cost of the meals. (Creating meals that are) healthful, acceptable to inmates and cost effective is very hard to achieve (LaVecchia, 1997, p. 26).

HEALTH STATUS OF SOON-TO-BE-RELEASED INMATES

For inmates fortunate enough to win release from prisons, there are a whole set of challenges that bring with them dilemmas for both prisons and communities (Davis, 2002; Jarrett, Adeyemi & Huggins, 2006; Maeve, 2003; Urban Institute, 2002; Willmott & Olphen, 2005; Wolff, 2005). These challenges are increased further in the case of former inmates of color, however (Cooke, 2005). Watson, Simpson, and Hostick (2004) note: "The health problems in prison largely reflect, but magnify, the problems present in the communities which the prisons serve. There is, therefore, an inevitable interplay in terms of health between prisons and the communities which they serve" (p. 125). Kantor (2006) notes that returning prisoners may place a low priority on health care compared to finding jobs, adequate housing, and reconnecting and rebuilding relationships severed or strained as a result of incarceration. The topic of the returning older inmate, however, has generally escaped discussion in this country, although this population group is becoming increasingly more visible in the United Kingdom (Crawley & Sparks, 2006).

Prisoner reentry into the community will have a disproportionate impact on communities of color since prisoners of color account for 64% of the prison population (Davis, 2002; Patterson & Greifinger, 2002; Willmott & Olphen, 2005). Reentry into the community undoubtedly further will exacerbate the health disparities in urban areas of the country. Poor and inadequate health care in prisons will result in prisoners who entered these systems returning back to their communities in more weakened states (physically and mentally) than when they initially left their respective communities. The comments of Franklin, Fearn, and Franklin (2005), although specifically related to HIV-positive released female inmates, also can apply to other groups:

> While the majority of female inmates are poor and come from financially distressed communities, . . . they are left with few health care options upon release. Consequently, treatment for infectious and communicable diseases becomes the responsibility of an already overburdened public health system (e.g., Medicaid) which bears the brunt of the medical expense (p. 108).

For the most part, federal law prohibits use of federal funds under Medicaid, Medicare, and the Veterans Administration for health care in correctional facilities. This often is identified by advocates as a key financial impediment for providing quality health care in prisons. However, the transition from prison to community is another important factor often cited as a barrier in the provision of continuity of health care to ex-inmates (Bazelon Center for Mental Health Law, n.d.; Centers for Medicare & Medicaid Services, 2008; Justice Center, n.d.).

Once one is imprisoned, federal health care coverage either is terminated or suspended, depending upon the state. Upon their release, ex-inmates face numerous challenges in getting this coverage reinstated (Feldman, 2007, A16): "That gap left many former prisoners with no choice but to forgo medical care, even in cases of serious illness or addiction . . . 'A person who is receiving Medicaid on the day they get arrested is no less in need of Medicaid the day they get out . . . When people come out of jail or come out of prison, the more barriers you put between them and a successful re-entry, the higher a rate of failure they're going to have.'" It is not unusual, for example, to hear of cases where an inmate's Medicaid card is confiscated by prison officials upon incarceration and lost upon release from prison, causing undue delay in an ex-inmate receiving health services (Consensus Project, n.d.). One state that recently realized this is New York. New York State successfully passed legislation in 2007 that suspends, rather than terminates, Medicaid benefits for prisoners while they are incarcerated, thus facilitating reentry into the community without having to wait several months before benefits restarting (Matthews, 2007).

Successful reentry into society from prison is complex (Maruna, 2001). However, there is no disputing the importance of health, both psychological and physical, on the reentry process (Freudenberg, 2002b; Jarrett, Adeyemi, & Huggins, 2006; Leukefeld et al., 2006; Williams, 2007). Ross (2004), in an editorial in the *Medical Journal of Australia*, highlights the exceedingly high death rates of released prisoners, adult and juvenile. Heroin-related deaths accounted for over 50% of these deaths. Similar consequences can no doubt be found in this country.

When the health of inmates is compromised severely by mental illness, HIV, or hepatitis B or C, for example, they have all they can do just to reenter and actively engage in obtaining needed treatment (Wolff, 2005). Lee, Connolly, and Dietz (2005) advocate mandatory discharge medication and follow-up treatment for offenders with mental illnesses that may result in a decrease in recidivism. Wolff (2005), in turn, advocates a social investment strategy for community reintegration of inmates with severe and persistent mental illness as a means of maximizing financial return for taxpayers. Discharge planning and continuity of care can cover a wide dimension, from giving inmates information about possible community resources to actively connecting them with services (Kantor, 2006).

Lincoln and colleagues (2006) identified five key elements regarding health care after incarceration: early detection, effective treatment, education, prevention, and continuity of care. Continuity of care in these situations becomes prominent in their lives (Maeve, 2003). However, continuity of care needs to be conceptualized from two perspectives, each with a particular set of goals that are complementary. These perspectives are from correctional institutions to the community and from the community to the institution. The institutional side needs to have trained staff and a commitment to make the shift for prisoners back into society successful. Identifying and working closely with community-based services with staff and expertise in working with released prisoners accomplishes this. The community side needs trained staff with expertise in addressing ex-inmates' needs and a commitment to advocate for them (Barr, 1999; Richie, Freudenberg & Page, 2001).

There have been a number of major commissioned reports on the topic of inmate health care, as is to be expected when a subject starts to receive national visibility and is no longer considered a local issue (Urban Institute, 2002). The National Commission on Correctional Health Care Report (2003h, p. 60) represents the latest attempt to systematically address the issues associated with inmate health care. The report identified ten policy recommendations, or goals, listed here and seen in various forms throughout this chapter:

---

1. Promote surveillance of selected communicable diseases, chronic diseases, and mental illnesses among inmates in all correctional jurisdictions.
2. Promote the use of nationally accepted evidence-based clinical guidelines for prisons and jails to assure appropriate use of resources for preventing, diagnosing, and treating selected communicable diseases, common chronic diseases, and mental illnesses that are prevalent among inmates.
3. Establish a federally funded national vaccine program for inmates to protect them and the public from selected vaccine-preventable communicable diseases.
4. Develop and maintain a national literature database for correctional health care professionals, including a compendium of policies, standards, guidelines, and peer-reviewed literature.
5. Establish a national advisory panel on ethical decision making by correctional and health authorities to help them address ethical dilemmas encountered in correctional health care.
6. Identify and eliminate barriers to successful implementation of public health policy.
7. Support research in correctional health care to identify and address problems unique to correctional settings.
8. Improve the delivery of inmate health care in correctional systems.
9. Implement primary and secondary disease prevention measures.
10. Provide prerelease planning of health care and related services for all soon-to-be-released inmates.

The recommendations outlined above acknowledge the importance of a multifaceted viewpoint on correctional health care and the important role public health can play in collaborating with public safety. The problems of health care within prisons are not restricted to those who are imprisoned:

> Public policies on crime, poverty, substance abuse, and other socioeconomic issues affect the health status of the incarcerated population.

> Current social policies create a mandate for public health programs and complex clinical services within correctional facilitates. Most prisoners are discharged from the facilities, and their health should be protected for the sake of the larger community, if not to contribute to their rehabilitative potential . . . Correctional health care should be a consideration as our nation makes decisions about health care systems of the future (Thorburn, 1995, p. 564).

The following summary of prisoner health status highlights this observation: 17% of cases of people with AIDS in the United States are people who have been through the correctional system; 35% of all people with tuberculosis have been incarcerated at one point in their lives; 30% of all people with hepatitis C have spent time incarcerated at one point in their lives; and 15% of all people with hepatitis B have spent time incarcerated. The interrelationship between prisons and society must be conceptualized as fluid, particularly in the case of inmates who will be released back into society. Further, health care needs cannot be separated from housing and employment needs (Cooke, 2004; Kushel et al., 2005). There is greater and greater pressure to find ways of facilitating this reentry because of budgetary concerns on the part of state and local governments (Anno, 2002; Richie, Freudenberg & Page, 2001; Willmott & Olphen, 2005). Finally, a Federal Bureau of Prisons study on the skill sets and health care needs of released offenders identified the importance of newly released inmates departing with specific skills and the importance of breaking down external barriers to health care (Gaes & Kendig, 2003).

It no doubt has become clearer to correctional systems across the United States that there is no one best approach to addressing health and long-term care within correctional institutions. The "best" approaches are very much dictated by the circumstances surrounding incarceration. Nevertheless, any successful strategy to address the needs of inmates invariably will involve one or a combination of the strategies identified in this chapter. Each of these strategies, in turn, must be sufficiently flexible to take into account changing prisoner profiles, availability of local resources, and the local political climate that either facilitates or severely hinders consideration of certain strategies such as compassionate release, for example.

The recommendations put forth in this chapter will not be easy to accept by prison systems, elected officials, and the general public alike. Development of collaborative partnerships, regardless of the "problem" being addressed and the interested parties, is never easy to accomplish. Thus, this and the other recommendations put forth in this chapter must be accepted as challenges under the best of circumstances. Nevertheless, the immense costs associated with maintaining prisoners only will continue to increase in the early part of the twenty-first century, not to mention the heavy toll it will take on inmates, their families, and communities.

There is little doubt concerning the immensity of the subject matter and the consequences of continuing to ignore this incarceration crisis for this and future generations. The costs to the nation far exceed the financial savings that often are used to justify changes in policy. The costs only truly can be measured in the social consequences of developing a system that often has little respect or compassion for human beings. For every adult who is incarcerated, a family, neighborhood, and community likely lacks help with its struggle to achieve health and wellbeing.

REFERENCES

Abramsky, S. (2002, July 1). The shame of prison health. *Centerforce News & Landmark Reports*, 1–5.

Abramson, M. F. (1972). The criminalization of mentally disordered behavior: Possible side-effects of a new mental health law. *Hospital & Community Psychiatry, 23,* 101–107.

Ackerman, J. (2008). Trapped: Mental illness in America's prisons: Inside Kentucky's correctional psychiatric treatment unit. *InDepth*, April, 1-4.

Acoca, L. (1998). Defusing the time bomb: Understanding and meeting the growing health care needs of incarcerated women in America. *Crime & Delinquency, 44,* 49–69.

Adams, D. L. & Leath, B. A. (2002). Correctional health care: Implications for public health policy. *Journal of the National Medical Association, 94,* 294–298.

Adams Jr., W. E. (1995). The incarceration of older criminals: Balancing safety, cost, and humanitarian concerns. *NOVA Law Review, 19,* 465–486.

Aday, R. H. (1994). Golden years behind bars: Special programs and facilities for elderly inmates. *Federal Probation, 58,* 47–54.

Aday, R. H. (2003). *Aging prisoners: Crisis in American corrections.* Westport, CT: Praeger Publishers.

Agence France Presse–English. (2005, October 12). Rights groups seek to shame U.S. over child lifers in prisons. Retrieved October 12, 2005, from http://web.lexis-nexis.com/universe/document?_m=c3286b005ae067f

AIDS Alert Archives. (2000, October 1). Prisons, jails often face uphill battle in dealing with HIV-infected inmates. Author, 1–4.

AIDS Counseling Education Program. (1998). *Breaking the walls of silence: AIDS and women in a New York State maximum-security prison.* Woodstock & New York: Overlook Press.

AIDS in Prison Project. (2001). FACTS SHEET: National, New York State, New York City. New York: Author, 1–2.

AIDS Policy & Law. (1997). California is considering early release of dying inmates. Author, 12, 4.

AIDS Policy & Law. (2005a). Condoms. Author, 20, 2.

Albanese, E. (2000). Trends in the region: Utah officials grapple with high cost of ill, elderly prisoners. *Bond Buyer, 224,* 30.

Albert, T. (2002, March 2). *Calif. prison system settles class action suit over care: Prisoners find lawsuit an effective way to change the health care they receive.* Retrieved June 18, 2002, from http://www.ama-assn.org/amednews/2002/03/04/prse0304.htm

Alemagno, S. A. (2001). Women in jail: Is substance abuse treatment enough? *American Journal of Public Health, 91,* 798–800.

Alemagno, S. A., Wilkinson, M. & Levy, I. (2004). Medical education goes to prison: Why? *Academic Medicine, 79,* 123–127.

Alexander, B. (2002, September). Locked-up Latinos get counted out: Language, data gaps miss youth in criminal justice systems, study says. *Youth Today, 11,* 56.

Alexander, E. (2002, Winter/Spring). Hepatitis C emerges as major health threat in U.S. prisons. *National Prison Project Journal,* 1–3.

Alexander, E. (2003). Private prisons and health care: The HMO from hell. In A. Campbell, A. Coyle & R. Neufeld (Eds.). *Capitalist punishment: Prison privatization and human rights* (pp. 64–74). Atlanta: Clarity Press.

Allen, C. E. (2001, March 1). Incarcerated women overlooked. *The Nation's Health,* 1.

Allen, W. & Bell, K. (1998, September 27). Death, neglect, and the bottom line: Push to cut costs poses risks. *St. Louis Post-Dispatch,* pp. 1–2.

Allison, T. L. & Clark, J. H. (2001). Making correctional health care smarter. *Corrections Today, 63,* 64–66, 68–70, 139.

Alpert, B. (2001, April 26). Question persists on prisoner care; answers could cost La. millions per year. *The Times-Picayune* (New Orleans), p. 15.

Altman, L. K. (1999, September 1). Much more AIDS in prisons than in general population. *The New York Times,* p. A14.

Amankwaa, A. A., Amankwaa, L. C. & Ochie, C. O. (1999). Revisiting the debate of voluntary versus mandatory HIV/AIDS testing in prisons. *Journal of Health & Human Services Administration, 22,* 220–236.

Ambers, C. (2006). Graying prisons: States face challenges of an aging inmate population. *State News,* November/December, 8-11.

Ambrosio, T. J. & Schiraldi, V. (1997). *From classrooms to cell blocks: A national perspective.* Washington, DC: Justice Policy Institute.

American Academy of Pediatrics. (2005). Health care for children and adolescents in the juvenile correctional care system. *Pediatrics, 107,* 799–803.

American Civil Liberties Union. (2002). *ACLU statement for the record for the Senate Judiciary Committee Hearings on Prison Rape.* New York:Author.

American Civil Liberties Union (2005). ACLU applauds Supreme Court Decision protecting prisoners from racial discrimination. Retrieved October 9, 2005, from www.aclu.org/court/cfm?ID=17533&c=286

American Civil Liberties Union. (2006). *Abandoned & abused: Orleans Parrish prisoners in the wake of Hurricane Katrina.* Washington, D.C.: Author.

American Civil Liberties Union. (2007). *National Prison Project: 2005-2006 litigation docket*. New York: Author.

American Civil Liberties Union. (2008, June 17). U.N. expert hears problems with immigration and detention medical care. http://blog.aclu.org/category/prisoners-rights/ Accessed 6-18-08

American Diabetes Association. (2005). Diabetes management in correctional institutions. *Diabetes Care, 28*, S53–S60.

American Psychiatric Association. (2000). *Psychiatric services in jails and prisons: A task force report of the American Psychiatric Association*. Washington, DC: Author.

American Public Health Association. (2003a). *Standards for health services in correctional institutions*. Washington, DC: Author.

American Public Health Association. (2003b, April 16). *New manual provides guidelines on prison health care*. Washington, DC: Author.

Amnesty International. (2000). Pregnant and imprisoned in the United States. *Birth, 27*, 266–271.

Anderson, C. (2003, July 28). Prison populations, costs climbing. *Boston Globe*, p. A2.

Anderson, D. C. (1998). *Sensible justice: Alternatives to Prison*. New York: Haworth Press.

Anderson, T. L. (2003). Issues in the availability of health care for women prisoners. In S. F. Sharp & R. Muraskin (Eds.). *The incarcerated woman: Rehabilitative programming in women's prisons* (pp. 49–60). Upper Saddle River, NJ: Prentice Hall.

Anno, B. J. (1991). *Prison health care: Guidelines for the management of an adequate delivery system*. Chicago, IL: National Commission on Correctional Health Care.

Anno, B. J. (1993, February 3). Health care for prisoners: How soon is soon enough? *Journal of the American Medical Association*, 633–634.

Anno, B. J., Faiver, K. L. & Harness, J. K. (1998). Defining appropriate and necessary health care. In K. L. Faiver (Ed.). *Health care management issues in corrections* (pp. 69–92). Lanham, MD: American Corrections Association.

Anno, J. (2001). *Correctional health care: Guidelines for the management of an adequate delivery system* (NIC-017521). Washington, DC: National Institute of Justice.

Anno, J. (2002). Prison health care services. *The public health dimensions of prisoner reentry: Addressing the health needs and risks of returning prisoners and their families* (pp. 5–6). Meeting Summary, National Reentry Roundtable Meeting, The Urban Institute, Los Angeles, December 11–12, 2002. Washington, DC: Author.

Anno, J., Graham, C., Lawrence, J. E., Shansky, R., Bisbee, J. & Blackmore, J. (2004). *Correctional Health Care: Addressing the needs of elderly, chronically ill, and terminally ill inmates*. Washington, DC: National Institute of Corrections.

Anonymous. (1997, September 8). Dying in prison. *The Press Democrat*, p. 1.

Anonymous. (2001a). HIV population continues to increase; affects females 60% more than males. *Corrections Digest, 32*, 1.

Anonymous. (2001b). Smoke-free jails reduce transmission of infectious diseases. *Corrections Digest, 32*, 2–3.

Anzel, D.M. (2000, December). Health care services in California prisons. *Los Ángeles Times*, p. B9.

Aoki, N. (1999, June 28). State prison to be used solely for inmates who need assisted-living care. *Virginian-Pilot and Ledger Star* (Norfolk, Va.), pp. 13–14.

Aoki, N., Dunn, K., Fukui, T., Beck, R., Schull, W. J. & Li, H. K. (2004). Cost-effectiveness analysis of telemedicine to evaluate diabetic retinopathy in a prison population. *Diabetes Care, 27*, 1095–1101.

Applebaum, K. L., Manning, T. D. & Noonan, J. D. (2002). A university-state-corporation partnership for providing correctional mental health services. *Psychiatric Services, 53*, 185–189.

Arrayan, K. (2003). *Bridging the gap between people with disabilities the criminal justice system: A training manual for ND criminal justice personnel.* Minot, ND: Minot State University, North Dakota Center for Persons with Disabilities.

Arax, M. (1994, January 6). State prison releases woman dying of AIDS. *Los Angeles Times*, p. A3.

Arax, M. (1999, October 29). Abuses at women's prisons under renewed scrutiny. *Los Angeles Times*, p. A1.

Arax, M. & Gladstone, M. (1998, October 18). Only California uses deadly force in inmate fights. *Los Angeles Times*, p. A1.

Arizona Republic. (2005, May 9). Aged inmates' care stresses state prison budget. Author, p. 2.

Arndt, S., Turvey, C. L. & Flaum, M. (2002). Older offenders, substance abuse, and treatment. *American Journal of Geriatric Psychiatry, 10*, 733–739.

Associated Press. (2002a, February 4). Inmate's suit asks state to pay for sex change. *The Boston Globe*, p. B2.

Associated Press. (2002b, June 16). In California's county jails, suicides are up sharply. Retrieved August 1, 2002, from http://www.namiscc.org/News/2002/Summer/JailSuicides.htm

Associated Press. (2005, September 19). Wyoming looks to cut cost of prison health care. *Billings Gazette* (Wyoming), p. 1.

Associated Press. (2006a, February 27). 46 inmates have died in Kansas jails and prisons in past 18 months. Retrieved November 13, 2006, from http://web.lexi-exis.com/universe/document?_m=58db700c47c82d874909e65c99d189c

Associated Press. (2006b, February 14). Second inmate in six days dies from possible overdose. Retrieved November 13, 2006, from http://web.lexis-nexis.com/universe/document?_m=65ee769c3485be793c3ad033f176995

Associated Press State & Local Wire. (2005a, May 22). Co-pay fee for inmates has intended result of reducing sick-call visits. Author. Retrieved October 5, 2005, from http://web.lexis.com/universe/document?_m=0a9d6f39052f2e

Associated Press State & Local Wire. (2005b, October 5). Feds begin inquiry into Delaware prison health care. Author. Retrieved October 6, 2005, from http://web.lexis-nexis.com/universe/document?_m=a8882b32184fd3

Associated Press State & Local Wire. (2005c, October 6). Prison officials say they are making progress with private prisons. Author. Retrieved October 11, 2005, from http://web.lexis.com/universe/document?_m=3e532643e152a2

Auerhahn, K. & Leonard, E. D. (2000). Docile bodies? Chemical restraints and the female inmate. *Journal of Criminal Law and Criminology, 90*, 599–619.

Awofeso, N. (2005a). Making prison health care more efficient. *British Medical Journal, 331*, 248–249.

Awofeso, N. (2005b). Prisoner healthcare co-payment policy: A cost-cutting measure that might threaten inmates' health. *Applied Health & Economic Health Policy, 4*, 159–164.

Axinn, J. & Stern, M. J. (2008). *Social welfare: A history of the American response to need* (7th ed.). Boston: Allyn & Bacon.

Baillargeon, J., Kelley, M. F., Leach, C. T., Baillargeon, G. & Pollock, B. H. (2004). Methicillin-Resistant *Staphylococcus aureus* infection in the Texas prison system. *Clinical Infectious Diseases, 38*, e92–e95.

Baker, A. (2005). Palliative and end-of-life care in the serious and persistently mentally ill population. *Journal of the American Psychiatric Nurses Association, 11*, 298–303.

Baker, D. P. (1999, July 2). Older inmates get new home. *The Washington Post*, p. B4.

Baldwin, K. M. & Jones, J. (2000). *Health issues specific to incarcerated women: Information from state maternal and child health programs.* Baltimore, MD: Health Policy Center, Johns Hopkins University School of Public Health.

Ballard, S. R. (2001, July 23). Why AIDS is rising among Black women. *Jet*, 18–19.

Barnes, H. E. (1922). Some leading phases of the evolution of modern penology. *Political Science Quarterly, 37*, 251–280.

Barr, H. (1999). *Prisons and jails: Hospital of last resort.* New York: Correctional Association of New York & the Urban Justice Center.

Barry, E. M. (2000). Women prisoners on the Cutting Edge: Development of the activist women prisoners' rights movement. *Social Justice, 27*, 168–172.

Baskin, D. R., Sommers, I., Tessler, R. & Steadman, H. J. (1989). Role incongruence and gender variation in the provision of prison mental health services. *Journal of Health and Social Behavior, 30*, 305–314.

Baton Rouge Advocate (1998, October 9). State creating prison for ill, elderly inmates. Author, p. 1.

Bauersmith, J. & Gent, R. (2002). The Broward County Jails hospice program: Hospice in the jail. *Journal of Palliative Medicine, 5*, 667–670.

Bauman, V. (2005, May 25). Bill would restrict smoking inside N.C. prisons/ Associated Press State & Local Wire. Retrieved October 5, 2005, from http://web.lexis-nexis.com/universe/document?_m=3734924cb9a6ff

Bauserman, R. L., Ward, M. A., Eldred, L. & Swetz, A. (2001). Increasing voluntary HIV testing by offering oral tests in incarcerated populations. *American Journal of Public Health, 91*, 1226–1229.

Bazelon Center for Mental Health Law. (2008). *Goodman & United States v. Georgia.* www.bazelon.org/issues/disabilityrights/incourt/goodman.htm. Accessed 3-20-08.

Bazelon Center for Mental Health Law. (n.d.). What happens to my medical care while I am in jail or prison? Washington, DC: Author. www.bazelon.org/issues/criminalization/publications/arrested/medicalcare.htm. Accessed 3-25-08.

Beatty, P., Holman, B. & Schiraldi, V. (2000). *Poor prescription: The costs of imprisoning drug offenders in the United States.* Washington, DC: Justice Policy Institute.

Beck, A. J. & Marushack, L. M. (2001). *State and federal corrections information systems: An inventory of data elements and an assessment of reporting capabilities.* Washington, DC: U.S. Department of Justice, Office of Justice Programs, Bureau of Justice Statistics.

Beck, A. J. & Maruschak, L. M. (2004). *Hepatitis testing and treatment in state prisons.* Washington, DC: Department of Justice, Bureau of Justice Statistics Special report.

Beck, J. A. (1999). Compassionate release from New York State prisons: Why are so few getting out? *Journal of Law, Medicine & Ethics, 27,* 216–233.

Becker, G. (2004). Deadly inequality in the health care "safety net": Uninsured ethnic minorities' struggle to live with life-threatening illnesses. *Medical Anthropological Quarterly, 18,* 258–275.

Belenko, S., Langley, S., Crimmins, S. & Chaple, M. (2004). HIV risk behaviors, knowledge, and prevention education among offenders under community supervision: A hidden risk group. *AIDS Education and Prevention, 16,* 367–385.

Belenko, S., Peugh, J., Califano Jr., J. A. & Foster, S. (1999). *Substance abuse and the prison population.* New York: Center for Addictions and Substance Abuse.

Belkin, D. (2005, June 23). Assisted living, in prison: Longer sentences force state to provide new care for aging inmates. *The Boston Globe,* p. 1.

Belknap, J. (2001). *The invisible women: Gender, crime, and justice* (2nd ed.). Belmont, CA: Wadsworth.

Belknap, J. (2003). Responding to the needs of women prisoners. In S. F. Sharp & R. Muraskin (Eds.). *The incarcerated woman: Rehabilitative programming in women's prisons* (pp. 93–106). Upper Saddle River, NJ: Prentice Hall.

Bell, C. (1992, April 28). *Correctional health care: A prescription for a healthier America.* Testimony before the Subcommittee on Labor, Health and Human Services, U.S. House of Representatives, Washington, DC.

Bell, K. & Allen, W. (1998, September 27). Health care workers must be on constant guard. *St. Louis Post-Dispatch,* pp. 1–2.

Bellin, E. Y., Fletcher, D. D. & Safyer, S. M. (1993). Assertion of tuberculosis infection with increased time in or admission to the New York City jail system. *Journal of the American Medical Association, 269,* 2228–2231.

Belluck, P. (2001, April 21). Desperate for prison guards, some states even rob the cradle. *The New York Times,* pp. A1, A10.

Bender, E. (2003, December 5). Suicidal inmates can often be identified. *Psychiatric News* (APA), 44.

Berkman, A. (1995). Prison health: The breaking point. *American Journal of Public Health, 85,* 1616–1618.

Bernstein, K. T., Chow, J. M., Ruiz, J., Schachter, J., Horowtiz, E., Bunnell, R. & Bolan, G. (2006). Chlamydia trachomatis and neisseria gonorrhoeae infections among men and women entering California prisons. *American Journal of Public Health, 96,* 1862–1866.

Berry, F., Spilka., K., & Sarkissian, L. (2008, June 22). Guest opinion: DMR name change long overdue. *The Daily News Tribune*. Retrieved June 22, 2008 from www.dailynewstribune.com/editorials/x1816435948/Guest-opinion-DMR-name-change-long-overdue.

Betteridge, J. G. (2001). Inquest into the death of a prisoner co-infected with HIV and Hepatitis C: How many more will there be? *Canadian HIV/AIDS Policy Law Review, 6*, 65–69.

Beyerlein, T. (1997, April 27). Aging convicts series: Prison grays 1st of 2 parts. *Dayton Daily News*, p. 2–3.

Binswanger, I. A., White, M. C, Perez-Stable, E. J., Goldenson, J. & Tulsky, J. P. (2005). Cancer screening among jail inmates: Frequency, knowledge, and willingness. *American Journal of Public Health, 95*, 1781–1787.

Birnbauer, B. (2001, May 15). After release, though freedom. *The Age* (Australia), 1.

Black, C. (1989, June 12). Aging behind bars: Effects of the graying of America's prisons. *The Boston Globe*, p. 3.

Blankenship, K. M., Smoyer, A. B., Bray, S. J. & Mattocks, K. (2005). Black–white disparities in HIV/AIDS: The role of drug policy and the corrections system. *Journal of Health Care for the Poor & Underserved, 16*, 140–156.

Blint, D. F. (2000, December 9). Inmates learning how to care for those dying in prisons. *The Hartford Courant*, p. 1.

Blint, D. F. (2003, April 12). Suicides in prisons on rise, data show. *The Hartford Courant*, p. 1.

Blitz, C. L., Wolff, N. & Paap, K. (2006). Availability of behavioral health treatment for women in prison. *Psychiatric Services, 57*, 356–360.

Blitz, C. L., Wolff, N., Pan, K. Y. & Pogorzelski, W. (2005). Gender-specific behavioral health and community release patterns among New Jersey prison inmates: Implications for treatment and community reentry. *American Journal of Public Health, 95*, 1741–1746.

Blumberg, M. & Laster, J. D. (1999). The impact of HIV/AIDS on corrections. In K. C. Haas & G. P. Alpert (Eds.). *The dilemmas of corrections: Contemporary readings* (4th ed.). (pp. 574–591). Long Grove, IL: Waveland Press.

Blumstein, A. (2000). Disaggregating the violence trends. In A. Blumstein & J. Wellman (Eds.). *The crime drop in America* (pp. 13–44). New York: Cambridge University Press.

Blumstein, A. (2001). Race and criminal justice. In N. J. Smelser, W. J. Wilson & Faith Mitchell (Eds.). *America becoming: Racial trends and their consequences* Vol. 2 (pp. 21–31). Washington, DC: National Research Council.

Blumstein, A. & Wallman, J. (Eds.). (2000). *The crime drop in America*. New York: Cambridge University Press.

Bock, N. N., Reeves, M., LaMarre, M. & DeVoe, B. (1998). Tuberculosis case detection in a state prison system. *Public Health Reports, 13*, 359–364.

Body, The: AIDS Action. (2001a, May). HIV prevention and care for incarcerated populations. Washington, DC, 1–4.

Body, The: AIDS Action. (2001b, July). Incarcerated populations and HIV/IDS. Washington, DC, 1–3.

Bolger, M. (2005). Dying in prison: Providing palliative care in challenging environments. *International Journal of Palliative Nursing, 11*, 619–620.

Bonner, R. & Rimer, S. (2000, November 14). "It's a cruel thing to do, to put me to sleep": How a death-row inmate with a mental age of six will die on Thursday—unless the state of Texas shows mercy. *The Guardian* (London), p. 18.

Bosworth, M. (2003). Gender, race, and sexuality in prison. In B. H. Zaitzow & J. Thomas (Eds.). *Women in prison: Gender and social control* (pp. 137–153). London: Lynne Rienner Publishers.

Boxer, S. (2001, April 7). When emotion worms its way into law. *The New York Times*, pp. A15, A17.

Boyle, J. P., Honeycutt, A. A., Narayan, K. M., Hoerger, T. J., Geiss, L. S., Chen, H. & Thompson, T. J. (2001, November). Projection of diabetes burden through 2050: Impact of changing demography and disease prevalence in the U.S. *Diabetes Care*, 22–32.

Braithwaite, R., Braithwaite, K. & Poulson, R. (1999). HIV and TB in prison. In *From AIDS to the internet: Correctional realities* (pp. 1–7). Lanham, MD: American Correctional Association.

Braithwaite, R., Hammett, T. M. & Mayberry, R. M. (1996). *Prisons and AIDS: A Public health challenge.* San Francisco: Jossey-Bass.

Braithwaite, R., Treadwell, H. M. & Arriola, K. R. J. (2005). Health disparities and incarcerated women: A population ignored. *American Journal of Public Health, 95*, 1679–1681.

Broader, J. M. (2002, January 19). No hard time for prison budgets. *The New York Times*, p. 5.

Brown, L. B. (1998). The joint effort to supervise and treat elderly offenders: A new solution to a current corrections problem. *Ohio State Law Journal, 59*, 259–302.

Brunswick, M. (2005, January 6). "Meth-mouth" plagues many state prisoners; more incarcerated addicts are in need of urgent dental care. *Star Tribune* (Minneapolis, MN), p. A1.

Buck, J. M., Morrow, K. M., Margolis, A., Eldridge, G., Sosman, J., MacGowan, R., Binson, D., Kacanek, D. & Flanigan, T. P. (2006). Hepatitis B vaccination in prison: The perspectives of formerly incarcerated men. *Journal of Correctional Health Care, 12*, 12–23.

Building Blocks for Youth. (1999). *The problem of overrepresentation of minority youth in the justice system.* Washington, DC: Author.

Building Blocks for Youth. (2000). *About the color of justice.* Washington, DC: Author.

Building Blocks for Youth. (2001). *Fact sheet: Latino youth in the juvenile justice system.* Washington, DC: Author.

Bureau of Indian Affairs. (2008). *Answers to frequently asked questions.* Washington, DC: Author.

Bureau of Justice Statistics. (1999). *Mental illness among U.S. inmates.* Washington, DC: Government Printing Office.

Bureau of Justice Statistics. (2001a). *HIV in prisons and jails, 1999* (NCJ 187456). Washington, DC: Department of Justice.

Bureau of Justice Statistics. (2001b). *Corrections statistics.* Washington, DC: Government Printing Office.

Bureau of Justice Statistics. (2002). *Prisoners in 2001* (NCJ Pub. No. 195-189). Washington, DC: Department of Justice.

Bureau of Justice Statistics. (2004a). *HIV in prisons, 2001.*Washington, DC: Department of Justice.

Bureau of Justice Statistics. (2004b). *Hepatitis testing and treatment in state prisons.* Washington, DC: Department of Justice.

Bureau of Justice Statistics. (2004c). *Prisoners in 2003.* Washington, DC: Department of Justice.

Bureau of Justice Statistics. (2004d). *Probation and parole statistics.* Washington, DC: Department of Justice.

Bureau of Justice Statistics. (2004e). *State prison expenditures,* 2001. Washington, D.C.: U.S. Department of Justice.

Bureau of Justice Statistics. (2005a). *Prison statistics: Summary findings on June 30, 2004.* Washington, DC: Author.

Bureau of Justice Statistics. (2005b). *HIV in prisons, 2003.* Washington, DC: Author.

Bureau of Justice Statistics. (2005c). *Suicide and homicide in state prisons and local jails.* Washington, DC: Author.

Bureau of Justice Statistics. (2005d). *Sexual violence reported by correctional authorities, 2004.* Washington, DC: Author.

Bureau of Justice Statistics. (2005e). *Key crime & justice facts at a glance.* Washington, DC: Author.

Bureau of Justice Statistics. (2005f). *Probation and parole statistics.* Washington, DC: Author.

Bureau of Justice Statistics. (2006). *Mental health problems of prison and jail inmates.* Washington, D.C.: U.S. Department of Justice.

Bureau of Justice Statistics. (2006a). *Prison statistics.* Washington, DC: Author.

Bureau of Justice Statistics. (2006b). *Expenditure and employment statistics.* Washington, DC: Author.

Bureau of Justice Statistics. (2006c). *Jail statistics.* Washington, DC: Author.

Bureau of Justice Statistics. (2008). *Sexual victimization in State and Federal prisons reported by inmates, 2007.* Washington, D.C.: U.S. Department of Justice.

Bureau of Justice Statistics. (2008). HIV in prisons, 2006. Washington, D.C.: U.S. Department of Justice.

Burke, K. W. (2001). Psychiatric aspects of hepatitis C treatment in prison. *Corrections Today, 63,* 75–78.

Burrell, S. & Warboys, L. (2000, July). *Special education and the juvenile justice system.* Washington, D.C.: Office of Juvenile Justice and Delinquency Prevention.

Burton-Rose, D., Pens, D. & Wright, P. (Eds.). (1998). *The celling of America: An inside look at the U.S. prison industry.* Monroe, ME: Common Courage Press.

Butterfield, F. (1997a, January 30). Many Black men barred from voting. *The New York Times*, p. A12.

Butterfield, F. (1997b, July 6). Bursting homes with bars: America's aging violent prisoners. *The New York Times*, p. E3.

Butterfield, F. (2001a, May 31). U.S. crime figures were stable in '00 after 8-year drop. *The New York Times*, pp. A1, A14.

Butterfield, F. (2001b, February 12). California lacks resources for law on drug offenders, officials say. *The New York Times*, p. 16.

Butterfield, F. (2001c, September 2). States ease laws on time in prison. *The New York Times*, pp. 1, 16.

Butterfield, F. (2002a, August 28). Study finds big increase in black men as inmates since 1980. *The New York Times*, p. A12.

Butterfield, F. (2002b, September 23). Some experts fear political influence on crime data agencies. *The New York Times*, p. 23.

Butterfield, F. (2003a, January 28). Infections in newly freed inmates are a rising concern. *The New York Times*, p. A14.

Butterfield, F. (2003b, July 28). Study finds 2.6% increase in U.S. prison population. *The New York Times*, p. A8.

Butterfield, F. (2003c, November 10). With cash tight, states reassess long jail terms. *The New York Times*, pp. A1, A16.

Butterfield, F. (2003d, November 14). Study calls California parole system a $1 billion failure. *The New York Times*, p. A14.

Butterfield, F. (2004a, May 3). With longer sentences, cost of fighting crime is higher. *The New York Times*, p. A15.

Butterfield, F. (2004b, May 4). Repaving the long road out of prison. *The New York Times*, p. A18.

Butterfield, F. (2004c, July 26). U.S. "correctional population" hits new high. *The New York Times*, p. A10.

Butterfield, F. (2004d, November 8). Despite drop in crime, an increase in inmates. *The New York Times*, p. A12.

Butterfield, F. (2004e, May 12). Almost 10% of all prisoners are now serving life terms. *The New York Times*, p. A17.

Byock, I. R. (2002). Dying well in corrections: Why should we care? *Journal of Correctional Health Care, 9*, 2–7.

Byrd, W. M. & Clayton, L. A. (2002). *An American health dilemma: Race, medicine, and health care in the United States 1900–2000.* New York: Routledge.

Byrne, D. (1997, August 24). Imprisoned with AIDS. *Chicago Sun-Times*, p. 1.

Cahal, W. (2002). The birth of a prison hospice program. *Journal of Correctional Health Care, 9*, 125–129.

Caldwell, C., Jarvis, M. & Rosenfield, H. (2001). Issues impacting today's geriatric female offenders. *Corrections Today, 63*, 110, 112–114.

California Prison Health Care Receivership Corporation. (2008). FAQ's. http://www .cprinc.org/faq.htm Accessed 6-27-08

California Study examines TB, HIV, and hepatitis. (1995, December). *Correct Care*, 3.

Cambanis, T. (2002, August 29). Inmate wins treatment ruling: Gender identity disorder cited. *Boston Globe*, p. B5.

Canberra Times (Australia). (2006, October 6). Call to cut hepatitis C in jail. Author, p. 1.

Capital Times. (2006, August 7). Prison population aging fast in state; health costs are soaring. Author, p. A5.

Carmichael, M. (2002, April 22). Risking life to give life. *Newsweek*, 53.

Carroll, L.A. (2001). Geriatrics in the prison system. Retrieved November 12, 2003, from www.ycp.edu/besc/Journal/2001/Article_1.htm

Cassidy, W. (2003, July 1). Hepatitis C infection in prisons. *Centerforce–News & Landmark Reports*, 1–2.

Caulkins, J. P., Rydell, C. P., Schwabe, W. L. & Chiesa, J. (1997). *Mandatory minimum drug sentences: Throwing away the key or the taxpayers' money?* Santa Monica, CA: Rand Corporation.

Cayley, D. (1998). *The expanding prison: The crisis in crime and punishment and the search for alternatives*. Toronto: House of Anasi.

Center for Substance Abuse Treatment. (1997). National treatment improvement evaluation study. Rockville, MD: Author.

Center on Crime, Communities & Culture. (1996, November). *Mental illness in U.S. jails: Diverting the nonviolent, low-level offender*. Research Brief, pp. 1–6.

Centers for Disease Control. (1995). *Controlling TB in correctional institutions 1995*. Atlanta: Author.

Centers for Disease Control. (1996, June 7). Prevention and control of tuberculosis in correctional facilities: Recommendations of the Advisory Council for the Elimination of Tuberculosis. *Morbidity & Mortality Weekly Report, 45* (RR-8), 1–27.

Centers for Disease Control and Prevention. (1998, October 16). Recommendations for prevention and control of hepatitis C virus (HCV) infection and HCV-related chronic disease. *Morbidity & Mortality Weekly Report, 47* (RR-19), 1–39.

Centers for Disease Control and Prevention. (2001a). *Health, United States 2000*. Retrieved March 2, 2002, from http://www.cdc.go/nchs/data/hus/tasles/2000/02hus047.pdf

Centers for Disease Control and Prevention. (2001b). *Providing services to inmates living with HIV*. Atlanta: Author.

Centers for Disease Control & Prevention. (2001c). *Women, injection drug use, and the criminal justice system*. Atlanta: Author.

Centers for Disease Control and Prevention. (2003). Prevention and control of infectious inmates with hepatitis viruses in correction settings. *MMWR, 52* (No. RR-1), 1–30.

Centers for Disease Control and Prevention. (2004). Tuberculosis transmission in multiple correctional facilities—Kansas, 2002–2003. *MMWR, 53* (32), 734–738.

Centers for Disease Control and Prevention. (2006). Prevention and control of tuberculosis in correctional and detention facilities. *MMWR, 55* (RR-9), 1–44.

Centers for Disease Control and Prevention. (2007a). *Traumatic brain injury in prisons and jails: An unrecognized problem.* Atlanta, GA: Author.

Centers for Disease Control and Prevention. (2007b). *Developmental Disabilities.* Retrieved January 29, 2007, from http://www.cdc.gov/ncbddd/dd/ddl.htm

Centers for Medicare & Medicaid Services. (2008). Psychiatric hospitals. Washington, DC: Department of Health & Human Services.

Centre for Evidence Based Mental Health. (2001). *Characteristics of female prisoners who self-harm.* Oxford, UK: Author.

Centre for Infectious Disease Prevention and Control. (2001). *Tuberculosis epi update.* Ottawa: Public Health Agency of Canada.

Chambliss, W. J. (1999). *Power, politics, & crime.* Boulder, CO: Westview Press.

Chaneles, S. (1987). Growing old behind bars. *Psychology Today, 21,* 47, 49, 53.

Charles, B. L. (2000). Telemedicine can lower costs and improve access. *Healthcare Financial Management, 54,* 66–70.

Charuvastra, A., Stein, J., Schwartzappel, B., Spaulding, A., Horowitz, E., Macalino, G. & Rich, J. D. (2001). Hepatitis B vaccination practices in state and federal prisons. *Public Health Reports, 116,* 203–209.

Chaves, F., Dronda, F., Cave, M.D. et al. (1997). A longitudinal study of transmission of tuberculosis in a large prison population. *American Journal of Respiratory & Critical Care Medicine, 155,* 719–725.

Children's Defense Fund. (2007). *America's cradle to prison pipeline.* Washington, D.C.: Author.

Christian Science Monitor. (2005, July 7). Snuffing out tobacco in prisons. Author, p. 8.

Christie, N. (2000). *Crime control as industry: Towards Gulags, Western Style* (3rd ed.). New York: Routledge.

Cianciolo, P. K. & Zupan, L. L. (2004). Developing a training program on issues in aging for correctional workers. *Gerontological & Geriatric Education, 24,* 23–38.

Clark, J. (1991, September/October). Correctional care issues in the nineties—forecast and recommendations. *American Jails,* 18–23.

Clary, M. (1999, September 28). Law enforcement; Florida inmate's death calls guards' practices into question. *Los Angeles Times,* p. A5.

Clear, T. R. (2008). Impact of incarceration on community public safety and public health. In R. Greifinger (Ed.). *Public health behind bars: From prisons to communities* (pp. 13–24). New York: Springer Publishing Co.

Clemmitt, M. (2007, January 5). Prison health care. *CQ Researcher, 17,* 1–24.

Clines, F. X. (2000, August 11). Some inmates must pay for their stay in prison. Kentucky, jail time can now cost as much as $50 a day. *The New York Times,* p. 1.

Clinical Practice Guidelines. (2005). Management of Methicillin-Resistant Staphylucoccus aureus (MRSA) infections. Washington, DC: Federal Bureau of Prisons.

CNN.Com. (2001, July 15). Report: 16 percent of state prison inmates mentally ill. Retrieved January 8, 2002, from http://www.cnn/.com/2001/us/07/15/prisons,mental.health/

Coalition for Federal Sentencing Reform. (1998). Nursing homes behind bars: The elderly in prison. Newsletter, 2, 1–4.

Cobb, K. (1997, October 29). Prison hospice set up for dying lifers: If you're in this Louisiana penitentiary, it's likely you'll die here. Care program eases the way. *The Gazette* (Montreal), p. A22.

Codd, V. (2001). Women and the Prison Industrial Complex. *Off Our Backs: A Women's News Journal, 31,* 8–9.

Cohn, F. (1999). The ethics of end-of-life care for prison inmates. *Journal of Law, Medicine & Ethics, 27,* 252–259.

Colimore, E. (2005a, June 7). More inmates older, straining health expenses. *The Philadelphia Inquirer,* p. 6.

Collica, K. (2002). Levels of knowledge and risk perceptions about HIV/AIDS among female inmates in New York State: Can prison-based HIV programs set the stage for behavior change? *The Prison Journal, 82,* 101–124.

Collins, W. C. & Grant, D. C. (1999). The Prison Litigation Reform Act. In *From AIDS to the internet: Correctional realities* (pp. 149–155). Lanham, MD: American Correctional Association.

Consensus Project. (N.D.). *An explanation of federal Medicaid and Disability Program rules.* Justice Center. http://consensusproject.org/projects/benefits/federal-benefits Accessed 3-25-08

Congressional Judiciary Commiteee Report on H.R. 1349. (2000, September 14). *Federal Prisoner Health Care Copayment of 2000.* Washington, D.C.: Author.

Conklin, T. J., Lincoln, T. & Tuthill, R. W. (2000). Self-reported health and prior health behaviors of newly admitted correction inmates. *American Journal of Public Health, 90,* 1939–1941.

Connolly, K., McDermid, L., Schiraldi, V. & Macallair, D. (1996). *From classrooms to cell blocks: How prison building affects higher education and African American enrollment in California.* San Francisco: Justice Policy Institute.

Conover, T. (2000). *Newjack: Guarding Sing Sing.* New York: Random House.

Cook, J. R. (2001). *Asphalt justice: A critique of the criminal justice system in America.* Westport, CT: Praeger Publishers.

Cook, R. (1999a, October 12). Prison hepatitis soaring; authorities expect a six-fold increase by June; treatment of disease is costly and uncertain. *The Atlanta Journal and Constitution,* p. C1.

Cook, R. (1999b, September 3). Jail ailments help drive up state's costs. *The Atlanta Journal and Constitution,* p. E1.

Cooke, C. L. (2004). Joblessness and homelessness as precursors of health problems in formerly incarcerated African American men. *Journal of Nursing Scholarship, 36,* 155–160.

Cooke, C. L. (2005). Going home: Formerly incarcerated African American men return to families and communities. *Journal of Family Nursing, 11,* 388–404.

Cordes, H. J. & Reed, L. (2005, October 8). No mercy for lifers, but is it now time? Life sentence commutations high in 'lifers' 'life means life.' *Omaha World-Herald* (Nebraska), p. A1.

Correctional Association of New York. (2000). *Health care in New York state prisons: A report of findings and recommendations by the prison visiting committee of the Correctional Association of New York.* New York: Author.

Correctional Association of New York. (2004). *Mental health in the House of Corrections.* New York: Author.

Correctional Technology. (2001). *Correctional health care overview.* Retrieved September 19, 2002, from http:www.corrtechnology.com/index_background.htm

Corrections Professional. (2005a, April 29). Corrections medical personnel can impact smoking cessation. Author, 10, p. 1.

Corrections Professional. (2005b, July 22). California prisons enforce new smoking ban. Author, 10, p. 1.

Corrections Professional. (2005c, July 22). Solutions are few. Author, 10, p. 2.

Corrections Professional. (2005d, May 27). Inmate health care baffles experts. Author, 10, p. 1.

Corrections Professional. (2005e, June 24). Battle to prevent AIDS through inmate condom distribution heats up. Author, 10, p. 1.

Corrections Professional. (2005f, July 22). State, county lockups under siege for poor medical care. Lawsuits abound, changes imminent to halt meltdown. Author, 10, p. 3.

Corrections Professional. (2005g, May 13). Medicaid to cover addicts under new bill. Author, 10, p. 1.

Corrections Professional. (2005h, May 13). World TB day brings correction's battle to forefront. Author, 10, p. 2.

Corrections Professional. (2005i, July 22). Telemedicine rebounds as prisons struggle with staffing. Author, 10, p. 4.

Corrections Professional. (2005j, July 22). Telemedicine helps control prison health costs. Author, 10, 4.

Corrections Professional. (2005k, December 9). Prisons, jails make inroads to prevent suicide, homicides: U.S. suicide rates the lowest in 25 years. Author, 11, 1.

Corrections Professional. (2006a, July 21). U.S. prison and jail populations continue to rise. Author, 11, p. 1.

Corrections Professional. (2006b, June 23). National study examines rise in female inmate populations. Author, 11, p. 1.

Corrections Professional. (2006c, May 26). Health care costs on the rise in U.S. prisons. Author, 11, p. 1

Correia, K. M. (2000). Suicide assessment in a prison environment: A proposed protocol. *Criminal Justice and Behavior, 27,* 581–599.

Cortes, D. (2002, Winter). Diabetes is major health problem among Latinos. *The Gaston Institute Report, 3,* 10.

Cotten-Oldenburg, N. U., Jordan, B. K., Martin, S. L. & Sadowski, L. S. (1999). Voluntary HIV testing in prison: Do women inmates at high risk for HIV accept HIV testing? *AIDS Education Prevention, 11*, 28–37.

Council of State Government. (1997). Survey of prison health care outstationing. Washington, DC: Author.

Couturier, L. (2001). Suicide prevention in a large state department of corrections. *Corrections Today, 63*, 90–97.

Couturier, L., Mave, F. & McVey, C. (2005, April). Releasing inmates with mental illness and co-occuring disorders into the community. *Corrections Today, 67*, 82–85.

Covington, S. S. (2000). Helping women to recover: Creating gender-specific treatment for substance-abusing women and girls in community corrections. In M. McMahon (Ed.). *What works—assessment to assistance programs for women in community corrections* (pp. 171–233). Lanham, MD: American Correctional Association.

Cowley, G. (2002, April 22). Hepatitis: The insidious spread of a killer virus. *Newsweek*, 46–53.

Cox, M. (2000, February 4). Prison care substandard/improvements aside, group urges changes. *Newsday*, p. A37.

Coyle, A. (1997). Health care and the prisoner: A human rights perspective. *Journal of Clinical Forensic Medicine, 4*, 181–184.

Cozza, S. T. & Braithwaite, R. L. (1999). Transsexual orientation in HIV risk behaviours in an adult male prison. *International Journal of STD AIDS, 10*, 28–31.

Crary, D. (1999, December 19). High chairs in prison as number of inmate mothers soars, a lucky few get to live with their kids. *Buffalo News* (Buffalo, NY), p. 1.

Crawley, E. (2005). Institutional thoughtlessness in prisons and its impacts on the day-to-day prison lives of elderly men. *Journal of Contemporary Criminal Justice, 21*, 350–363.

Crawley, E. & Sparks, R. (2006). Is there life after imprisonment: How elderly men talk about imprisonment and release. *Criminology & Criminal Justice, 6*, 63–82.

Cropsey, K.L., Wexler, H.K., Melnick, G., Taxman, F.S. & Young, D.W. (2007). Specialized prisons and services: Results from a national survey. *The Prison Journal, 87*, 58–85.

Crowder, C. (2006, May 28). Inmates grow sick and old in a system intent on meting out punishment for a lifetime. Soaring costs distress prisons. Officials seek alternatives as system groans under weight of health care costs. *Birmingham News* (Alabama), p. A1.

Currie, E. (1998). *Crime and punishment in America: Why the solutions to America's most stubborn social crisis has not worked and what will.* New York: Metropolitan Books.

Curry, L. (2001). Tougher sentencing, economic hardships and rising violence. *Corrections Today, 63*, 74–76.

Cusac, A. M. (2000). The judge gave me ten years. He didn't sentence me to death. *The Progressive, 64*, 22–29.

Daane, D. M. (2003). Pregnant prisoners: Health, security, and special needs issues. In S. F. Sharp & R. Muraskin (Eds.). *The incarcerated woman: Rehabilitative programming in women's prisons* (pp. 61–72). Upper Saddle River, NJ: Prentice Hall.

Dabney, D. A. & Vaughn, M. S. (2000). Incompetent jail and prison doctors. *Prison Journal, 80,* 151–182.

Daley, M., Love, C. T., Shepard, D. S., Petersen, C. B., White, K. L. & Hall, F. B. (2004). Cost-effectiveness of Connecticut's in-prison substance abuse treatment. *Journal of Offender Rehabilitation, 39,* 69–92.

Daly, K. & Maher, L. (Eds.). (1998). *Criminology at the crossroads: Feminist readings in crime and justice.* New York: Oxford University Press.

D'Angelo, L. (2003). Hepatitis C: The need for a public health approach to treatment and prevention in the criminal justice population. *Fortune News, 38,* 10–12.

Daniels, A. E. (2006). Preventing suicide in prison: A collaborative responsibility of administrative, custodial, and clinical staff. *Journal of the American Academy of Psychiatry & Law, 34,* 165–175.

Daniels, A. E. & Fleming, J. (2006). Suicides in a state correctional system, 1992–2002: A Review. *Journal of Correctional Health, 12,* 24–35.

Danton, E. R. (2001, February 3). Inmates given role in prison hospice. *The Hartford Courant,* p. B1.

Dardis, L. (2007). Maine Hospice/Corrections Partnership. *Maine Link, 7, 1,* 6–7.

Davis, K. (2000, June). The shocking plight of Black women prisoners. *Ebony,* 18–20.

Davis, L. (2002). Health profile of the prison population. *The public health dimensions of prisoner reentry: Addressing the health needs and risks of returning prisoners and their families.* Meeting Summary, National Reentry Roundtable Meeting, The Urban Institute, Los Angeles, December 11–12, 2002 (pp. 2–4). Washington, DC: Author.

Davis, L.A. (2005). *People with intellectual disabilities in the criminal justice system: Victims and suspects.* Silver Spring, MD: The Arc.

Day, S. (2001). Cruel but not unusual: The punishment of women in U.S. prisons. *Monthly Review* (New York), *53(3),* 42–55.

Dean-Gaitor, H. D. & Fleming, P. L. (1999). Epidemiology of AIDS in incarcerated persons in the United States, 1994–1996. *AIDS, 13,* 2429–2435.

DeCarlo, P. & Zack, B. (1996). *What are inmates' HIV prevention needs?* San Francisco: Center for AIDS Prevention Studies at the University of California, San Francisco.

DeGroot, A. S. (2001). HIV among incarcerated women: An epidemic behind the walls. *Corrections Today, 63,* 77–81, 97.

DeGroot, A. S., Bick, J., Thomas, D. & Stubblefield, F. (2001). HIV clinical trials in correctional settings: Right or retrogression? *AIDS Reader, 11,* 34–40.

Delgado, M. (2000). *Community social work practice within an urban context: The potential of a capacity-enhancement perspective.* New York: Oxford University Press.

Delgado, M. (2001). *Where are all the young men and women of color? Capacity enhancement practice in the criminal justice system.* New York: Columbia University Press.

Delgado, M. (2004). *Death at an early age and the urban scene: The role of memorial murals in helping communities to heal.* Westport, CT: Praeger Press.

Delgado-Vega, D. (2003). LOLA hepatitis C prison project. *Fortune News, 38,* 14–17.

Demars, R. & Walsh, K. (1981). Use of medical services during a 2-month period in the Seattle-King County (Washington) jail. *Public Health Reports, 96,* 452–457.

DePree, J. (2006). Deaf and incarcerated.

Dey, E. A. (2003). Hepatitis C and the American prisoner. *Fortune News, 38,* 8.

Dike, C. C. (2006). Commentary: Coerced community mental health treatment—an added burden on an overstretched system. *Journal of the American Academy of Psychiatry & Law, 34,* 300–302.

Disability Rights Legal Center. (2008). *Systematic disability discrimination Issues in Los Angeles County Jail.* Los Angeles: Author.

Doarn, C. R., Justis, D., Chaudhri, M. S. & Merrell, R. C. (2005). Integration of telemedicine practice into correctional medicine: An evolving standard. *Journal of Correctional Health Care, 11,* 253–270.

Doherty, M. D. (2002). Mentally ill inmates. Retrieved January 12, 2003, from http://www.iejs.com/Corrections/Mentally_Ill_Inmates.htm

Dollar & Sense. (2001). Prison explosion. Author, p. 7.

Domino, M. E., Norton, E. C., Morrissey, J. P. & Thakur, N. (2004). Cost shifting to jails after a change to managed mental health care. *Health Services Research, 39,* 1379–1401.

Donaldson, S. (1993, December 29). The rape crisis behind bars. *The New York Times,* p. 1.

Dondis, J. (2005, March 3). Debate on free transplants for inmates: Should inmates qualify for publicly financed organ transplants? *ABC News.* Retrieved March 17, 2008, from http://abcnews.go/WNT?story?id=130458&page=1

Donnelly, J. (2007, September 3). Inmate health program a model: $7.4m grant fuels Hampden plan. *The Boston Globe,* pp. A1, A12.

Don't let inmates' hepatitis C go untreated. (2000, July 26). Editorial in *Centerforce–News & Landmark Reports,* 1

Dowdy, Z. R. (1997, December 26). AIDS drugs help cut Mass. prison deaths. *The Boston Globe,* p. A1.

Dreiling, G. L. (2003, October 15). Dying to get out. *Riverfront Times* (St. Louis, Missouri), p. 1.

Dressel, P., Porterfield, J. & Barnhill, S. K. (1998). Mothers behind bars. *Corrections Today, 60,* 90–94.

Drinan, R. F. (2000, February 18). Prison system unjust, unworkable. *National Catholic Reporter,* 1.

Drucker, D. M. (2005, May 27). State prisons going smoke free. *San Bernardino Sun* (California), p. 1.

Dubler, N. N. (1998). The collision of confinement and care: End-of-life care in prisons and jails. *Journal of Law, Medicine & Ethics, 26,* 149–156.

Dugger, R. L. (1995). Life and death in prison. In T. J. Flanagan (Ed.). *Long-term imprisonment: Policy, science, and correctional practice* (pp. 171–173). Thousand Oaks, CA: Sage Publications.

Dunhan, W. (2006, November 16). Condoms urged in prisons to curb AIDS in blacks. *Yahoo News*. Retrieved November 27, 2006, from http://news.yahoo.com/com/s/nm/20061116/hl_nm/aids_blacks_dc

Dunlop, B. D., Rothman, M. B. & Entzel, P. (2000a). Introduction. In M. B. Rothman, B. D. Dunlop & P. Entzel (Eds.). *Elders, crime, and the criminal justice system: Myths, perceptions, and reality in the 21st century* (pp. xxix–xxvii). New York: Springer Publishing Co.

Dunlop, B. D., Rothman, M. B. & Entzel, P. (2000b). Epilogue: Policy implications for the 21st century. In M. B. Rothman, B. D. Dunlop & P. Entzel (Eds.). *Elders, crime, and the criminal justice system: Myths, perceptions, and reality in the 21st century* (pp. 331–358). New York: Springer Publishing Co.

Dyer, J. (2000). *The perpetual prisoner machine: How America profits from crime.* Boulder, CO: Westview Press.

Ebony. (2001). 10 biggest killers of Black women. Author, October, 48–50.

Edwards, K. A. (2000). Stigmatizing the stigmatized: A note on the mentally ill prison inmates. *International Journal of Offender Therapy & Comparative Criminology, 44*, 480–489.

Egelko, B. (2001, March 14). Suit claims prisoner health care is inadequate. *The San Francisco Chronicle*, p. A15.

Eliason, M. J., Taylor, J. Y. & Williams, R. (2004). Physical health of women in prison: Relationship to oppression. *Journal of Correctional Health Care, 10*, 175–203.

Elikann, P. T. (1996). *The tough-on-crime myth: real solutions to cut crime.* New York: Insight Books.

Ellis, V. (1997, September 3). Bill would expedite dying inmates' release. *Los Angeles Times*, p. A3.

Elser, C. (1998, August 9). Aging behind bars: Lengthy jail terms have left PA. with costly problem of caring for elderly inmates. *Allentown Morning Call* (PA), p. 1.

Elsner, A. (2004). *Gates of injustice: The crisis in America's prisons.* Upper Saddle River, NJ: Prentice Hall.

Enders, S. R., Paterniti, D. A. & Meyers, F. J. (2005). An approach to develop effective health care decision making for women in prison. *Journal of Palliative Care, 8*, 432–439.

Eskenazi, J. (2003, December 19). Orthodox inmate fights the law to keep kosher—and wins. *Jewish News Weekly of Northern California* (San Francisco), 1–2.

Fackelmann, K. (1999a, October 19). Lack of drugs puts inmates on death row. *USA TODAY*, p. D9.

Fackelmann, K. (1999b, October 19). Hepatitis C behind bars: Deadly liver disease could break out as infected prisoners go home. *USA TODAY*, p. D1.

Fagan, J. (2004). Crime, law, and the community: Dynamics of incarceration in New York City. In M. Tonry (Ed.). *The future of imprisonment* (pp. 27–59). New York: Oxford University Press.

Failing, L. & Sears, R. (2001). Medical treatment and mentally incompetent inmates. *Corrections Today, 63,* 106–110.

Faiver, K. L. (1998a). Special issues of aging. In K. L. Faiver (Ed.). *Health care management issues in corrections* (pp. 123–132). Lanham, MD: American Corrections Association.

Faiver, K. L. (1998b). Special mental health issues. In K. L. Faiver (Ed.). *Health care management issues in corrections* (pp. 143–167). Lanham, MD: American Corrections Association.

Faiver, K. L. (1998c). Preventing contagion. In K. L. Faiver (Ed.). *Health care management issues in corrections* (pp. 83–100). Lanham, MD: American Corrections Association.

Faiver, K. L. (1998d). What is happening in health? In K. L. Faiver (Ed.). *Health care management issues in corrections* (pp. 1–24). Lanham, MD: American Corrections Association.

Faiver, K. L. (1998e). Issues in health professional ethics: Some practical considerations. In K. L. Faiver (Ed.). *Health care management issues in corrections* (pp. 219–254). Lanham, MD: American Correctional Association.

Faiver, K. L. (1998f). Ensuring access to care. In K. L.Faiver (Ed.). *Health care management issues in corrections* (pp. 101–122). Lanham, MD: American Corrections Association.

Falter, R. G. (1999). Selected predictors of health care needs of inmates over age 50. *Journal of Correctional Health Care, 6,* 149–175.

Families to Amend California's 3-Strikes. (2001). *Costs of prisons and jails.* Sacramento, CA: Author.

Family Practice News. (2000, January 1). STDs in incarcerated women. Author, 2.

Farley, J., Vasdev, S., Fischer, B., Haydon, E., Rehm, J. & Farley, T. A. (2005). Feasibility and outcome of HCV treatment in a Canadian federal prison system. *American Journal of Public Health, 95,* 1737–1739.

Fazel, S. & Lubbe, S. (2005). Prevalence and characteristics of mental disorders in jails and prisons. *Current Opinions in Psychiatry, 18,* 550–554.

Fazel, S., Hope, T., O'Donnell, I., Piper, M. & Jacoby, R. (2001). Health of elderly male prisoners: Worse than the general population, worse than younger prisoners. *Age and Aging, 30,* 403–407.

Federal Bureau of Prisons. (2004, May). *Quick facts.* Washington, DC: Author.

Feer, R. A. (1961). Imprisonment for debt in Massachusetts before 1800. *The Mississippi Valley Historical Review, 48,* 252–269.

Fehr, S. C. (2000, July 14). In drug war, treatment is back. *The Christian Science Monitor,* 1–2.

Feldman, C. (2007, July 27). In new state law, a wait-free return to Medicaid rolls after prison. *The New York Times,* p. A16.

Fellner, J. (2006). A corrections quandary: Mental illness and prison rates. *Harvard Civil Rights–Civil Liberties Law Review, 41,* 391–412.

Fields, G. (2007, August 14). On tribal land, tragic arson leads to a life sentence. *Wall Street Journal,* p. A1.

Fierros, E.G. & Conroy, J.W. (2002) Double jeopardy: An exploration of restrictiveness and race in special education. In D.J. Losen & G. Orfield (Ed.). *Racial inequity in special education* (pp.39-70). Cambridge. MA: Harvard Education Press.

Finn, P. (1996). No-frills prisons and jails: A movement in flux. *Federal Probation, 60,* 35–44.

Firestone, D. (2001a, May 23). National briefing South: Alabama: Prison crowding crisis. *The New York Times,* A20.

Firestone, D. (2001b, June 9). U.S. figures show prison population is now stabilizing. *The New York Times,* pp. A1, A10.

Fiscella, K., Franks, P., Doescher, M. P. & Saver, B. G. (2002). Disparities in health care by race, ethnicity, and language among the uninsured: Findings from a national sample. *Medical Care, 40,* 52–59.

Fiscella, K., Pless, N., Meldrum, S. & Fiscella, P. (2004). Alcohol and opiate withdrawal in U.S. jails. *American Journal of Public Health, 94,* 1522–1524.

Fitzgibbons, M. F. & Gunter, T. (2000). Telemedicine and mental health in jails: A new tool for an old problem. *Corrections Today, 62,* 104–109.

Flanagan, N. A. (2004). Transitional health care for offenders being released from United States prisons. *Canadian Journal of Nursing Research, 36,* 38–58.

Flanagan, T. J. (1992). Long-term incarceration: Issues of science, policy and correctional policy. *Correctional Service Canada, 4,* 1–9.

Flanagan, T. J. (Ed.). (1995). *Long-term imprisonment: Policy, science, and correctional practice.* Thousand Oaks, CA: Sage Publications.

Flanagan, T. J. (1996). Reform or punish: Americans' views of the correctional system. In T. J. Flanagan & D. R. Longmire (Eds.). *Americans view crime and justice: A national public opinion survey* (pp. 75–92). Thousand Oaks, CA: Sage Publications.

Florida Corrections Commission. (1999). *Annual report.* Tallahassee: Author.

Flynn, E. E. (2000). Elders as perpetrators. In M. B. Rothman, B. D. Dunlap & P. Entzel (Eds.). *Elders, crime, and the juvenile justice system: Myths, perceptions, and reality in the 21st century* (pp. 43–83). New York: Springer Publishing Co.

Fogel, C. I. (1993). Hard time: The stressful nature of incarceration for women. *Issues in Mental Health Nursing, 14,* 367–377.

Fogel, C. I. & Belya, M. (1999). The lives of incarcerated women: Violence, substance abuse, and at risk for HIV. *Journal of the Association of Nurses in AIDS Care, 10,* 66–74.

Foster, D. (2000, December 16). Fort Lyon Hospital getting new lease on life: U.S. government gift to become state prison for elderly, mentally ill. *Denver Rocky Mountain News,* p. A44.

Fox, J. A. (2000, September 4). Prisons alone are no lockbox for crime. *The Boston Herald,* p. 45.

Fox, R. K., Currie, S. L., Evans, J., Wright, T. L., Tobler, L., Phelps, B., Busch, M. P. & Page-Shafer, K. A. (2005). Hepatitis C virus infection among prisoners in the California state correctional system. *Clinical Infectious Diseases, 41,* 177–186.

Frank, L. (1999). Prisons and public health: Emerging issues in HIV treatment adherence. *Journal of the Association of Nurses in AIDS Care, 10,* 24–32.

Franklin, C. A., Fearn, N. E. & Franklin, T. W. (2005). HIV/AIDS among female prison inmates: A public health concern. *California Journal of Health Promotion, 3,* 99–112.

Freudenberg, N. (2002a). Adverse effects of U.S. jail and prison policies on the health and well-being of women of color. *American Journal of Public Health, 92(12),* 1895–1899.

Freudenberg, N. (2002b). Community health care services. *The public health dimensions of prisoner reentry: Addressing the health needs and risks of returning prisoners and their families* (pp. 7–8). Meeting Summary, National Reentry Roundtable Meeting, The Urban Institute, Los Angeles, December 11–12, 2002. Washington, DC: Author.

Freudenberg, N., Daniels, J., Crum, M., Perkins, T. & Richie, B. E. (2005). Coming home from jail: The social and health consequences of community reentry for women, male adolescents, and their families and communities. *American Journal of Public Health, 95,* 1725–1736.

Friedberg, A. (1999, March 23). Graying of prisoners: Aging criminals pose little threat, cost big bucks, early release advocates say. *The Gazette* (Colorado Springs), p. A1.

Friedman, M. (1998, January 11). Opinion: There's no justice in the war on drugs. *The New York Times,* p. A26.

Friends Committee on Legislation of California. (2001, June 11). Analysis of SB 396: Health care for prisoners.

Fritsch, J. & Rohde, D. (2001a, April 8). Lawyers often fail New York poor. *The New York Times,* pp. 1, 28–29.

Fritsch, J. & Rohde, D. (2001b, April 9). For the poor, a lawyer with 1,600 clients. *The New York Times,* pp. A1, A16.

Fritsch, J. & Rohde, D. (2001c, April 10). On appeals, the poor find little leverage. *The New York Times,* pp. A1, A19.

Fuhrman, M. (2002, September 30). Sick inmates pose risk. *Columbia Daily Tribune* (MO), p. 1.

Fullon, S. (2005, August 6). Faking illness could cost inmates. *Morning Call* (Allentown, PA), p. B7.

Fung, J. (2002, March 3). Transplants for prisoners: Though controversial, the constitution protects right to organ transplants. Retrieved August 1, 2003, from wysinyg://23/http://www.abcnews.go....ransplant_prisoners_FUNG020303.html

Furillo, A. (2005, July 1). Prison health care fix carries big price. *Sacramento Bee,* p. A3.

Gaes, G. & Kendig, N. (2003, January 30–31). *The skill sets and health care needs of released offenders.* Washington, DC: U.S. Department of Health and Human Services Conference.

Gainsborough, J. & Mauer, M. (2000). *Diminishing returns: Crime and incarceration in the 1990s.* Washington, DC: Sentencing Project.

Gaiter, J. L., Potter, R. H. & O'Leary, O. (2006). Disproportionate rates of incarceration contribute to health disparities. *American Journal of Public Health, 96,* 1148–1149.

Gallagher, E. M. (2001). Elders in prison: Health and well-being of older inmates. *International Journal of Law and Psychiatry, 24,* 325–333.

Garcia, M. (2000, September 29). Inmates, staff to get TB tests. *The Kansas City Star,* p. B3.

Gardner, E. (1998). The legal rights of inmates with physical disabilities. Retrieved May 5, 2002, from http://lawlib.slu.edu/plr/141/gardner.htm

Gardner, H. (1985). *Frames of mind: The theory of multiple intelligences.* New York: Basic Books.

Garland, D. (2001). *The culture of control: Crime and social order in contemporary society.* Chicago: University of Chicago Press.

Garrity, T. F., Hiller, M. L., Staton, M., Webster, J. M. & Leukefeld, C. G. (2002). Factors predicting illness and health services use among male Kentucky prisoners with a history of drug abuse. *The Prison Journal, 82,* 295–313.

Gaseau, M. (2001a, February 26). Innovations in substance abuse programming— What is working. Corrections.com. Retrieved December 11, 2002, from http://database.corrections.com/news/results 2.asp?ID=718

Gaseau, M. (2001b, February 12). Managing elderly inmates. Retrieved May 8, 2002, from http://database.corrections.com/news/results2.asp?ID=684

Gaseau, M. (2001c). Spotlight: Correctional health care exposure to infectious disease. *HEPP HIV Education Prison Project, 4,* 1–4.

Gaseau, M. & Caramanis, C. (1999, February 15). Success of inmate fees increases their popularity among prisons and jails. Retrieved November 23, 2002, from http://database.corrections.com/news/results2asp.?ID=106

George, E. (1999). The new prison culture: Making millions from misery. In S. Cook & S. Davies (Eds.). *Harsh punishment: International experiences of women's imprisonment* (pp. 189–210). Boston: Northeastern University Press.

Gibson, K. (2005). U.S.: Developments in the treatment of HIV-positive prisoners in two states. *HIV AIDS Policy Law Review, 10,* 33.

Gilbert, E. (1999). Crime, sex, and justice: African American women in U.S. prisons. In S. Cook & S. Davies (Eds.). *Harsh punishment: International experiences of women's imprisonment* (pp. 230–249). Boston: Northeastern University Press.

Gladstone, M. (2005, January 23). California pays thousands to guard hospitalized inmates. *San Jose Mercury News,* p. 1.

Glaser, J. B. & Greifinger, R. B. (1993, January 15). Correctional health care: A public health opportunity. *Annals of Internal Medicine,* 139–145.

Glick, B., Sturgeon, W. & Venator-Santiago, C. (1998). *No time to play: Youthful offenders in adult correctional systems.* Lanham, MD: American Correctional Association.

Glionna, J. M. (2001, April 21). Guards on death row face escalating dangers. *Los Angeles Times,* p. A1.

Goffman, E. (1961). *Asylum: Essays on the social situation of mental patients and other inmates.* New York: Anchor Books.

Goldkuhle, U. (1999). Professional education for correctional nurses. A community-based partnership model. *Journal of Psychosocial Nursing & Mental Health Services, 37,* 38–44.

Goldstein, E. H., Hradecky, G., Vilke, G. M. & Chan, T. C. (2006). Impact of a standardized protocol to address Staphylococcus aureus skin infections at a large, urban county jail system. *Journal of Correctional Health Care, 12,* 181–188.

Golembeski, C. & Fullilove, R. (2005). Criminal (in) justice in the city and its associated health consequences. *American Journal of Public Health, 95,* 1701–1706.

Goodnough, A. (2006, November 16). Officials clash over mentally ill in Florida jails. *The New York Times,* pp. A1, A20.

Gordon, R. E. (2000). *The funhouse mirror: Reflections on prison.* Pullman, WA: Washington State University Prison.

Gostin, L. O. (1995). The resurgent tuberculosis epidemic in the era of AIDS. *Maryland Law Review, 64,* 1–13.

Gostin, L. O. & Webber, D. W. (1998). HIV infection and AIDS in the public health and health care systems: The role of law and litigation. *Journal of the American Medical Association, 279,* 1108–1113.

Goulet, J. L., Balacos, K., Altice, F. L., Thompson, A. S., Khoshnood, K. & Selwyn, P. A. (1998). Association between mental illness and HIV risk among incarcerated women. *Paper presented at the 12th World AIDS Conference.* Geneva, Switzerland.

Government Accounting Office. (2000, June 14). *Federal prisons: Responses to questions related to continuing high costs for an increasing inmate population.* (G-G-D-00-160R). Washington, DC: Author.

Greco, R. (2002). Brief: Older prisoners. In *Project 2015: The future of aging in New York State* (pp. 315–316). New York: Office of Aging, New York State.

Greene, J. (2003). Bailing out private jails. In T. Herival & P. Wright (Eds.). *Prison nation: The warehousing of America's poor* (pp. 138–147). New York: Routledge.

Greenfield, L. A. & Snell, T. L. (1999). *Women offenders: Bureau of Justice Statistics: Special report.* Washington, DC: U.S. Department of Justice.

Greifinger, R. (2005). Commentary: Health status in U.S. and Russian prisons: More in common, less in contrast. *Journal of Public Health Policy, 26,* 60–68.

Greifinger, R. (Ed.). (2008). *Public health behind bars: From prisons to communities.* New York: Springer Publishing Co.

Griffin, R. (1998, October 24). Black women and breast cancer. *America,* 5–6.

Griffith, R.W. (2001, May 18). Hospice round the world. *HealthandAge.Com* http://www.healthandage.com/html/min/gentle_endings/web/hospice/_usa.htm Accessed 7-3-08

Grinstead, O. A., Faigeles, B., Comfort, M., Seal, D., Nealey-Moore, J., Belcher, L. & Morrow, K. (2005). HIV/STD, and hepatitis risk to primary female partners of men being released from prison. *Women Health, 41,* 63–80.

Grodeck, B. (1999, March). The invisible epidemic. *Men's Fitness*, 2–4.

Gubler, T. & Petersilia, J. (2006). *Elderly prisoners are literally dying for reform*. Palo Alto: California Sentencing & Corrections Policy Series, Stanford Criminal Justice Center Working Papers.

Gustafson, A. (2007, July 8). Prison suicides linked to isolation. *Statesmen Journal* (Denver), p.1.

Gutjrie, P. (2000, November 28). The many faces of addiction; with new initiatives and insights, a problem that exacts a heavy toll on lives and society comes into clearer focus. *The Atlanta Journal and Constitution*, p. C1.

Haberman, E. L. (2001, August 1). Mission seemingly impossible: Community placement of chronic care inmates. *Corrections Today, 63*, 115–118.

Hackett, T. (2000, August 27). A dead end for inmates. *New York Daily News*, p. 12.

Hader, S., Smith, D., Moore, J. & Holmberg, S. (2001). HIV infection in women in the United States: Status at the millennium. *Journal of the American Medical Association, 285*, 1186–1192.

Haggerty, M. F. (2000). Incarcerated populations & HIV. *Community Research Initiatives on AIDS, 9*, 1–5.

Hall, B. & Gabor, P. (2004). Peer suicide prevention in a prison. *Crisis, 25*, 19–26.

Hall, C. (2006, September 25). Jails, prisons test to prevent outbreak of tuberculosis. *The Blade* (Toledo, Ohio), p. 1.

Hallinan, J. T. (2001). *Going up the river: Travels in a prison nation*. New York: Random House.

Hammett, T. (2002). Linkages between prison and community health services. *The public health dimensions of prisoner reentry: Addressing the health needs and risks of returning prisoners and their families*. Meeting Summary, National Reentry Roundtable Meeting, The Urban Institute, Los Angeles, December 11–12, 2002 (pp. 12–14.). Washington, DC: Author.

Hammett, T. M., Gaiter, J. L., & Crawford, C. (1998). Reaching seriously at-risk populations: Health interventions in criminal justice settings. *Health Education & Behavior, 25(1)*, 99–120.

Hammett, T. M., Harmon, P. & Rhodes, W. (2003). The burden of infectious disease among inmates and releasees from correctional facilities. In *The health status of soon-to-be-released inmates: A report to Congress* Vol. 2 (pp. 13–37). Chicago: National Commission on Correctional Health Care.

Hansell, J. B. (1998). Is HIV extraordinary? *Michigan Law Review, 96*, 1095–1117.

Hanser, R. D. (2002). Inmate suicide in prisons: An analysis of legal liability under 42 USC Section 1983. *The Prison Journal, 82*, 459–477.

Harcourt, B. F. (2007, January 15). The mentally ill, behind bars. *The New York Times*, p. A19.

Harden, J. & Hill, M. (1998). (Eds.). *Breaking the rules: Women in prison and feminist therapy*. New York: Haworth Press.

Harding, T. W. (2000). *Do prisons need special health policies and programmes?* Geneva, Switzerland: University Institute of Legal Medicine.

Harlow, C. (1998). *Profile of jail inmates 1996.* Washington, DC: Bureau of Justice Statistics, U.S. Department of Justice.

Harlow, C. (2003). *Education and corrections populations.* Washington, DC: Bureau of Justice Statistics, U.S. Department of Justice.

Harrington, S. P. M. (1999, May 5). New bedlam: Jails—not psychiatric hospitals—now care for the indigent mentally ill. *The Humanist,* 1–4.

Harris, O. & Miller, M. R. (Eds.). (2003). *Impacts of incarceration on the African American family.* Somerset, NJ: Transaction Publishers.

Harrison, J. (2005, September 19). New Maine court under way; system seeks to reduce incarceration of people with mental illness. *Bangor Daily News* (ME), p. B1.

Harry, B., Klinger, J.K., Sturges, K.M. & Moore, R.F. (2002) Of rocks and soft places: Using qualitative methods to investigate disproportionality. In D.J. Losen & G. Orfield (Ed.). *Racial inequity in special education* (pp.71-92). Cambridge. MA: Harvard Education Press

Hartwell, S. W. (2004). Comparison of offenders with mental illness only and offenders with dual diagnoses. *Psychiatric Services, 55,* 145–150.

Hassan, S. & Gordon, R.M. (2003). Developmental disability, crime, and *Criminal justice: A literature review.* British Columbia, Canada: Criminology Research Centre, Simon Fraser University.

Hayden, C. H., Mangura, I., Patterson, G. E., Passannante, M. B. & Reichman, L. B. (2005). Tuberculin testing and treatment of latent TB infection among long-term jail inmates. *Journal of Correctional Health Care, 11,* 99–117.

Hayes, L. M. (1999). Suicide in adult correctional facilities: Key ingredients to prevention and overcoming the obstacles. *Journal of Law, Medicine & Ethics, 27,* 260–268.

Health & Medicine Weekly. (2003, February 24). Public Health: Poor health of prison inmates a problem. Author, 39.

Healthcare Info Tech Business Report Archives. (1999, May 28). Telemedicine could mean big savings for prison healthcare. Author, 1.

Hegstrom, E. (2001, April 7). INS workers exposed to tuberculosis at jail. *The Houston Chronicle,* p. 31.

Heines, V. (2005). SPEAKING OUT to improve the health of inmates. *American Journal of Public Health, 95,* 1685–1688.

Heinlein, G. (2003, September 24). Aging inmates drive up state health costs. *DetroitNews.Com,* pp. 1–2.

Hellard, M. E. & Aitken, C. K. (2004). HIV in prison: What are the risks and what can be done? *Sex Health, 1,* 107–113.

Henderson, D., Schaeffer, J. & Brown, L. (1998). Gender-appropriate mental health services for incarcerated women: *Issues and challenges. Family and Community Health, 21,* 42–53.

Hengesh, D. J. (1996). Closing the loop: A continuum of care for community corrections. In *Community corrections* (pp. 1–4). Lanham, MD: American Correctional Association.

Hensley, C. & Tewsbury, R. (2005). Wardens' perceptions of prison sex. *The Prison Journal, 85*, 186–197.

Hernandez, G. (2005, December 6). Can gay inmates be protected? *Advocate*, 38.

Hicks, N. (2005, July 3). State prison population gets grayer. *Lincoln Journal Star* (Nebraska), p. C1.

Hill, M. (2005, June 9). Watchdog group says mentally ill underserved. *Associated Press State & Local Wire*. Retrieved October 15, 2005, from http://0-web.lexi-nexis .com.library.simmons.edu/universe/document?_m=1bda007cda2dd2

Hill, M. (2007, June 3). New York prison creates dementia unit: Needs of older inmates treated. *The Boston Globe*, p.A16. Human Rights Watch. (2001).

Hirsch, A. (1992). *The rise of the penitentiary: Prisons and punishment in early America.* New Haven, CT: Yale University Press.

Ho, T. (2003). Complex issues about mentally retarded defendants. In A.J. McKee (Ed.). International Encyclopedia of Justice Studies. http://www.iejs.com/Mental_ Health/mentally_retarded_defendants.htm Accessed 6-25-08

Hoge, S. K. (2008). Providing transition and outpatient services to the mentally ill released from correctional institutions. In R. Greifinger (Ed.). *Public health behind bars: From prisons to communities* (pp. 461–477). New York: Springer Publishing Co.

Holden, K. (2001). Chronic and disability conditions: The economic costs to individuals and society. *The Public Policy and Aging Report, 11*, 3–10.

Holman, B. (1999, July 25). *Old men behind bars. Op-ed by Barry Holman.* Washington, DC: National Center on Institutions and Alternatives.

Holman, J. R. (1997, April). Prison care: Our penitentiaries are turning into nursing homes. Can we afford it? *Modern Maturity*, 30–36.

Hornblum, A. M. (1998). *Acres of skin: Human experiments at Holmesburg Prison.* New York: Routledge.

Hornung, C. A., Anno, B. J., Greifinger, R. B. & Gadre, S. (2003a). Health care for soon-to-be-released inmates: A survey of state prison systems. In *The health status of soon-to-be-released inmates: A report to Congress* Vol. 2 (pp. 1–11). Chicago: National Commission on Correctional Health Care.

Hornung, C. A., Anno, B. J., Greifinger, R. B. & Gadre, S. (2003b). A projection model of the prevalence of selected chronic diseases in the inmate population. In *The health status of soon-to-be-released inmates: A report to Congress* Vol. 2 (pp. 39–56). Chicago: National Commission on Correctional Health Care.

Hoskins, I. A. (2004). A guest editorial: Women's health care in correctional facilities: A lost colony. *Obstetrical and Gynecological Survey, 59(4)*, 234–236.

Hospice Management Advisor Archives. (1999, February 1). Growing prison population will need hospice care. Author, 3–7.

Hospice Management Advisor Archives. (2000, August 1). A new lesson in dying: Prison hospice program gives inmates sense of dignity. Author, 1–4.

Hot Topics in Health Care. (2000). *A new lesson in dying: Prison hospice program gives inmates sense of dignity.* Retrieved February 2, 2001, from http://www.ahcpub .com/ahc_root_html/hot/archieve/hma082000.html

Houston Chronicle. (2001, March 24). Awareness; mustn't overlook TB as a contemporary threat. Author, p. 38.

Houston Voice. (2005, May 5). Transgendered man says he was raped in Brazoria County Jail. Author, p. 2.

Howell, E. (2002). Review of evaluation literature on health outcomes. *The public health dimensions of prisoner reentry: Addressing the health needs and risks of returning prisoners and their families* (pp. 17–18). Meeting Summary, National Reentry Roundtable Meeting, The Urban Institute, Los Angeles, December 11–12, 2002. Washington, DC: Author.

Hoxie, N. J., Chen, M. H., Prieve, A., Haase, B., Pfister, J. & Vergeront, J. M. (1998). HIV seroprevalence among male prison inmates in the Wisconsin correctional system. *Wisconsin Medical Journal, 97,* 28–31.

Hudson, P. L., Schofield, P., Kelly, B., Hudson, R., Street, A., O'Connor, M., Kristjanson, L. J., Ashby, M. & Aranda, S. (2006). Responding to desire to die statements from patients with advanced disease: Recommendations for health professionals. *Palliative Medicine, 20,* 703–710.

Hudson, R. B. (2000). Aging and criminal justice: Images and institutions. *The Public Policy and Aging Report, 10,* 2–3.

Hughes, G. D. (1996). Community corrections: The major agenda item for the nineties. In *Community Corrections* (pp. 5–8). Lanham, MD: American Correctional Association.

Hughes, Z. (2000, March). Why so many Black women are overweight—and what they can do about it. *Ebony,* 15–17.

Huling, Y. & Mauer, M. (2000, March 30). Locked up in the census count: How our nation's burgeoning prison population is reversing rural population loss. *Chicago Tribune,* p. 1.

Human Rights Watch. (2001). *No escape: Male rape in prisons.* New York: Author.

Human Rights Watch. (2003). *Ill equipped: U.S. prisons and offenders with mental illness.* New York: Author.

Hurley, L. (2005, May 10). Baltimore judge calls for investigation into prison health care. *The Daily Record* (Baltimore), p. 1.

Hurst, J. & Morain, D. (1994, October 17). A system strains at its bars: The state prison population is exploding. *Los Angeles Times,* p. A1.

Hutton, M. D., Cauthen, G. M. & Bloch, A. B. (1993). Results of a 29-state survey of tuberculosis in nursing homes and correctional facilities. *Public Health Reports, 108,* 305–314.

IDU/HIV Prevention. (2001a, August). Women, injection drug use, and the criminal justice system. Author, 1–2.

IDU/HIV Prevention. (2001b, August). Working with the criminal justice system. Author, 1–2.

IDU/HIV Prevention. (2001c, August). Helping inmates return to the community. Author, 1–3.

IDU/HIV Prevention. (2002a, September). Vaccines to prevent hepatitis A and hepatitis B. Author, 1–4.

IDU/HIV Prevention. (2002b, September). Medical management of chronic hepatitis B and chronic hepatitis C. Author, 1–4.

Iguchi, M. Y., London, J. A., Forge, N. G., Hickman, L., Fain, T. & Riehman, K. (2002). Elements of well-being affected by criminalizing the drug user. *Public Health Reports, 117*, Supplement 1, S146–S150.

Institute of Medicine. (2006). *Ethical considerations for research involving prisoners.* Washington, DC: National Academy.

Isaacs, E. & Hammer-Tomizuka, Z. (2001, February 27). Prison hepatitis crisis a public time bomb. *The Arizona Republic*, p. B7.

Jackson Sr., J. L. (2001, July 10). *Liberty and justice for some: Mass incarceration comes at a moral cost to every American.* Retrieved January 10, 2001, from wysiwyg://469// http://www.mojones.com/prisons/liberty.html

Jacobi, J. V. (2005). Prison health, public health: Obligations and opportunities. *American Journal of Law & Medicine, 31*, 447–478.

Jacobs, J. B. (2004). Prison reform amid the ruins of prisoners' rights. In M. Tonry (Ed.). *The future of imprisonment* (pp. 179–196). New York: Oxford University Press.

Jacobson, M. (2005). How to reduce crime and end mass incarceration. New York: New York University Press.

Jarrett, N. C., Adeyemi, S. A. & Huggins, T. (2006). Bridging the gap: Health care to newly released men. *Journal of Health Care for the Poor and Underserved, 17*, 70–80.

Johnson, B., Golub, A. & Dunlap, E. (2000). The rise and decline of hard drugs, drug markets, and violence in inner-city New York. In A. Blumstein & J. Wallman (Eds.). *The crime drop in America* (pp. 164–206). New York: Cambridge University Press.

Johnson, J. (2002, June 22). Jail suicides reach record pace in state. *Los Angeles Times*, p. 1.

Johnson, K. (2006, December 28). Inmate suicides linked to solitary: Calif., Texas seek to reverse trend. *USA Today*, p. 1.

Jones, D. W. et al. (2002). Risk factors for coronary heart disease in Americans. *Archives of Internal Medicine, 162*, 2565–2571.

Jones, G., Connelly, M. & Wagner, K. (2001). *Aging offenders and the criminal justice system.* Maryland: State Commission on Criminal Sentencing Policy.

Jones, R. P. (2001, April 25). Deficit in prison health care covered. *Milwaukee Journal Sentinel*, p. B2.

Jones, T. F., Craig, A. S., Valway, S. E., Woodley, C. L. & Schaffner, W. (1999). Transmission of tuberculosis in a jail. *Annals of Internal Medicine, 131*, 557–563.

Jonsson, P. (2003, September 5). As prisoners age, should they go free? *The Christian Science Monitor*, 1.

Jordan, P. D. (1969). The close and stinking jail. *Pacific Northwest Quarterly, 60*, 1–9.

Jorden, J. (2002, March 20). *Inmate to go to death without limb.* AP Online. Retrieved February 4, 2002, from wysiwyg://515/http//library.Northe...412F6dkxwCDWg GWgtWWUAHHBBE@cbx=0

Josefson, D. (1999, January 2). Prisoner wants to donate his second kidney. *British Medical Journal*, 2.

Justice Center. (n.d.). *An explanation of Federal Medicaid and Disability program rules.* Washington, DC: State Council of Governments. Retrieved March 25, 2008, from http://consensusproject.org/projects/benefits/federalbenefits

Justis, D. & Lyckholm, L. (n.d.). *Palliative care over telemedicine to correctional facilities.* Richmond: Virginia Commonwealth University.

KK Kahn, A.J., et al. (2005). Ongoing transmission of hepatitis B virus infection among inmates at a state correctional facility. *American Journal of Public Health*, 95, 1793-1799.

Kahn, S. (2000). Fire in the belly: A model program stresses community involvement. AIDS Info in NYC. Retrieved February 9, 2005, from http://www.aids infonyc.org/hivplus/issue6/report/model.html

Kantor, E. (2006, April). HIV transmission and prevention in prisons. *HIV InSite.* Retrieved November 12, 2006, from http://hininsite.ucsf.edu/InSite?page=kb-07-04-13

Kaplan, D. W., Feinstein, R. A., Fisher, M. M. & Klein, J. (2001). Health care for children and adolescents in the juvenile correctional care system. *Pediatrics, 107,* 799–803.

Kaplan, S. (1999, July 12). Terminally ill prisoners rarely freed under early parole laws. Stateline.org. Retrieved November 13, 2006, from http://www.stateline.org/live/ViewPage.action?siteNodeld=136&Languageeld=1&contentl

Karmen, A. (2000). *New York murder mystery: The true story behind the crime crash of the 1990s.* New York: New York University Press.

Kates, E., Ransford, P. & Cardozo, C. (2005). *Women in prison in Massachusetts: Maintaining family connections.* Boston: Center for Women in Politics and Public Policy, McCormack Graduate School of Policy Studies, University of Massachusetts.

Katz, I. (2001, January 30). Behind bars: Grey area: many of the 1,000 elderly convicts in British prisons are so infirm that they pose little or no threat to society. *The Guardian* (London), p. 2.

Kauffman, K. (2001). Mothers in prison. *Corrections Today, 63,* 62–65.

Kay, S. L. (1991). *The constitutional dimensions of an inmate's right to health care.* Chicago: National Commission on Correctional Health Care.

Keeper's Voice. (1997). Geriatric prisons more like nursing homes for infirmed, *18,* 1–2.

Kelly, M. S. (2003). The state-of-the-art in substance abuse programs for women in prison. In S. F. Sharp & R. Muraskin (Eds.). *The incarcerated woman: Rehabilitative programming in women's prisons* (pp. 119–148). Upper Saddle River, NJ: Prentice Hall.

Kendig, N. (1998). Tuberculosis control in prisons. *International Journal of Tuberculosis & Lung Disease, 2,* S57–S63.

Kendig, N., Stough, T., Austin, P., Kummer, L., Swetz, A. & Vlahov, D. (1994). Profile of HIV seropositive inmates diagnosed in Maryland's state correctional system. *Public Health Reports, 109,* 756–760.

Kerbs, J. J. (1999). *The correctional continuum of care for elders: Prisons versus community-based alternatives*. Ann Arbor: University of Michigan.

Kerbs, J. J. (2000a). The older prisoner: Social, psychological, and medical considerations. In M. B. Rothman, B. D. Dunlop & P. Entzel (Eds.). *Elders, crime, and the criminal justice system: Myth, perceptions, and reality in the 21st century* (pp. 207–228). New York: Springer Publishing Co.

Kerbs, J. J. (2000b). Arguments and strategies for the selective decarceration of older prisoners. In M. B. Rothman, B. D. Dunlop & P. Entzel (Eds.). *Elders, crime, and the criminal justice system: Myth, perceptions, and reality in the 21st century* (pp. 229–250). New York: Springer Publishing Co.

Kerle, K. E. (1998). *American jails: Looking to the future*. Boston: Butterworth-Heinemann.

Kilborn, P. T. (2001, August 1). Rural towns turn to prisons to reignite their economies. *The New York Times*, pp. A1, A11.

Kim, S. (2003). Incarcerated women in life context. *Women's Studies International Forum, 26*, 95–100.

Kind, R. S. & Mauer, M. (2001). *Aging behind bars: "Three strikes" seven years later*. Washington, DC: Sentencing Project.

Klein, S. J., Cruz, H., O'Connell, D. A., Scully, M. A. & Birkhead, G. S. (2005). A public health approach to "prevention with positives": The New York State HIV/AIDS service delivery system. *Journal of Public Health Management & Practice, 11*, 7–17.

Klein, S. J., Gieryic, S. M., O'Connell, D. A., Hall, J. Y. & Klopf, L. (2002). Availability of HIV prevention services within New York State correctional facilities during 1999–2000; Results of a survey. *The Prison Journal, 82*, 69–85.

Klein, S. J., O'Connell, D. A., Devore, B. S., Wright, L. N. & Birkhead, G. S. (2002). Building an HIV continuum for inmates: New York State's criminal justice initiative. *AIDS Education & Prevention, 14*, 114–123.

Knepper, P. (1993). Thomas Jefferson, criminal code reform, and the founding of the Kentucky Penitentiary at Frankfort. *The Register of the Kentucky Historical Society, 91*, 129–149.

Kobrin, S. (2005, June 26). Dying on our dime: California's prisons are teeming with older inmates who run up staggering medical costs. Latimes.com. Retrieved December 8, 2006, from http://www.latimes.com/features/printedition/magazine/la-tm-oldcons26jun26,03612948.s

Kolker, C. (2000, January 15). Prison hospices offer a haven of mercy. *Los Angeles Times*, p. A1.

Kolodner, M. (2006, July 19). Private prisons expect a boom: Immigration enforcement to benefit detention companies. *The New York Times*, pp. C1, C2.

Krane, J. (1999a, April 15). Death and mourning inside the walls: Funerals become a growing part of prison life. *APB News.Com*, pp. 1–3. Retrieved December 1, 2006 from http://www.apb-news.com/index.php?option=com_content&task-blocategory&id=18eIt

Krane, J. (1999b, April 13). Full health coverage for hard criminals: New laws require first-rate prison elder care. *APB News.Com*, 1–4.

Krane, J. (1999c, April 12). Demographic revolution rocks U.S. prisons. *APB News.Com*, 1–3.

Krane, J. (1999d, April 13). America's oldest prisoners: At least 13 are in their 90s. *APB News.Com*, 1–2.

Krane, J. (1999e, April 12). Should elderly convicts be kept in prison? Some say it's not worth the cost; others call it due justice. *APB News.Com*, 1–4.

Krane, J. (1999f, April 12). The graying of America's prisons: An emerging crisis. Retrieved March 9, 2003, from http://www.angelfire.com/la/kayless/prison.html

Kraut, J. R., Haddix, A. C., Carande-Kulis & Greifinger, R. B. (2003). Cost-effectiveness of routine screening for sexually transmitted diseases among inmates in United States prisons and jails. In *The health status of soon-to-be-released inmates: A report to Congress* Vol. 2 (pp. 81–108). Chicago: National Commission on Correctional Health Care.

Kraut-Becher, J. R., Gift, T. L., Haddix, A. C., Irwin, K. L. & Greifinger, R. B. (2004). Cost-effectiveness of universal screening for Chlamydia and gonorrhea in U.S. jails. *Journal of Urban Health, 81*, 453–471.

Krienert, J. L., Henderson, M. L. & Vandiver, D. M. (2003). Inmates with physical disorders: Establishing a knowledge base. *The Southwest Journal of Criminal Justice, 1*, 13–23.

Kruttschnitt, C. & Gartner, R. (2003). Women's imprisonment. *Crime and Justice, 30*, 1–81.

Kuhlmann, R. & Ruddell, R. (2005). Elderly jail inmates: Problems, prevalence and public health. *California Journal of Health Promotion, 3*, 49–60.

Kupers, T. (1996). *The mental health crisis behind bars and what we must do about it.* San Francisco: Jossey-Bass.

Kupers, T. (2000). Beware of easy answers for the mental health crisis behind bars. *Fortune News, 34*, 8–10.

Kurta, D. L., Mrvos, R. & Krenzelok, E. P. (2006). Poison center utilization by correctional facilities. *Journal of Correctional Health Care, 12*, 54–57.

Kushel, M. B., Hahn, J. A., Evans, J. L., Bangsberg, D. R. & Moss, A. R. (2005). Revolving doors: Imprisonment among the homeless and marginally housed population. *American Journal of Public Health, 95*, 1747–1752.

Kyei-Aboagye, K., Vragovic, O. & Chong, D. (2000). Birth outcomes in incarcerated, high-risk pregnant women. *Journal of Reproductive Medicine, 45*, 190–194.

Laderberg, A. (1998). The "dirty little secret": Why class actions have emerged as the only viable option for women inmates attempting to satisfy the subjective prong of the Eighth Amendment suits for custodial sexual abuse. *William and Mary Law Review, 40*, 323–357.

Lafer, G. & Confessore, N. (1999, September 1). Captive labor: America's prisoners as corporate workforce. *American Prospect*, 66–70.

Laidler, J. (2001, April 22). Inmates get long-distance medical exams. *The Boston Globe*, p. 1.

Lamberti, J. S., Weisman, R. & Faden, D. I. (2004). Forensic assertive community treatment: Preventing incarceration of adults with severe mental illness. *Psychiatric Services, 55,* 1285–1293.

Lang, J. (1999). Aging prison population poses new problems: Aging inmates turning jails into nursing homes. *The Patriot Ledger* (Quincy, MA), pp. 1–2.

Langan, N. P. & Pelissier, B. M. (2001). Gender differences among prisoners in drug treatment. *Journal of Substance Abuse, 13,* 291–301.

Langan, P. A. & Levin. D. J. (2002). *Bureau of Justice Statistics Special Report: Recidivism of prisoners released in 1994.* Washington, DC: U.S. Department of Justice.

Laniado-Laborin, R. (2001, March 1). Tuberculosis in correctional facilities. *Chest, 119,* 681–684.

Larivee, J. L. (1996). Leadership in community corrections. In *Community corrections* (pp. 9–19). Lanham, MD: American Correctional Association.

Laufer, F. N., Arriola, K. R., Dawson-Rose, C. S., Kumaravelu, K. & Rapposelli, K. K. (2002). From jail to community: Innovative strategies to enhance continuity of HIV/AIDS care. *The Prison Journal, 82,* 84–100.

LaVecchia, G. (1997). Feeding a graying prison population. *Food Management, 32,* 26–30.

LeBlanc, A. N. (2003, January 12). Prison is a member of their family. *The New York Times Magazine*, pp. 28–35, 50, 54, 59.

LeDuff, C. (2004, May 23). A jail tour in Los Angeles offers a peek into 5 killings behind bars. *The New York Times*, p. 14.

Lee, C. C., Connolly, P. M. & Dietz, E. O. (2005). Forensic nurses' views regarding medications for inmates. *Journal of Psychosocial Nursing & Mental Health Services, 43,* 32–39.

Lee, F. R. (1994a, September 8). On a Harlem block, hope is swallowed by decay. *The New York Times*, pp. A1, B8.

Lee, F. R. (1994b, September 9). Harlem family battles weight of the past. *The New York Times*, pp. A1, B4.

Lee, F. R. (1994c, September 10). A drug dealer's rapid rise and ugly fall. *The New York Times*, pp. 1, 22.

Lehrer, E. (2001). Hell behind bars: The crime that dare not speak its name. *National Review, 53,* p. 2.

Leukefeld, C. G., Hiller, M. L., Webster, J. M., Tindall, M. S., Martin, S. S., Duvall, J., Tolbert, V. E. & Garrity, T. F. (2006). A prospective examination of high-cost health services utilization among drug using prisoners reentering the community. *Journal of Behavioral Health Services Research, 33,* 73–85.

Levine, S. (2002, August 5). Criminal care at a high price. *U.S. News & World Report,* 104–105.

Levine, S. F. (2005). Improving end-of-life care of prisoners. *Journal of Correctional Health Care, 11,* 317–331.

Levitt, S. D. & Venkatesh, S. A. (1998). *An economic analysis of a drug-selling gang's finances.* Cambridge, MA: National Bureau of Economic Research.

Lewin, T. (2001, April 15). Little sympathy or remedy for inmates who are raped. *The New York Times,* pp. 1, 17.

Lewis, D. O., Pincus, J. H., Shanok, S. S. & Glaser, G. H. (1982). Psychomotor epilepsy and violence in a group of incarcerated adolescent boys. *American Journal of Psychiatry, 139,* 882–887.

Lguchi, M. Y. (2005). How criminal system racial disparities may translate into health disparities. *Journal of Health Care for the Poor and Underserved, 16,* 48–56.

Liebling, A. (2000). Prison suicide and prisoner coping. *Crime and Justice, 26,* 283–360.

Light, J. (2000). Look for that Prison Label. *The Progressive, 64,* 21–24.

Lin, J. T. & Mathews, F. (2005). Cancer pain management in prisons: A survey of primary care practitioners and inmates. *Journal of Pain & Symptom Management, 29,* 466–473.

Lincoln, T., Kennedy, S., Tuthill, R., Roberts, C., Conklin, T. J. & Hammett, T. M. (2006). Facilitators and barriers to continuing healthcare after jail: A community-integrated program. *Journal of Ambulatory Care Management, 29,* 2–16.

Lincoln, T., Miles, J. R. & Scheibel, S. (2008). Community health and public health considerations. In R. Greifinger (Ed.). *Public health behind bars: From prisons to communities* (pp. 508–534). New York: Springer Publishing Co.

Lindeman, M. (2000). Out of sight. Out of mind. The transinstitution of the mentally ill. *Fortune News, 34,* 12.

Lindenauer, M. R. & Harness, J. K. (1981). Care as part of the cure—a historical overview of correctional health care. *Journal of Prisons, 1,* 56–66.

Linder, J. F., Enders, S. R., Craig, E., Richardson, J. & Meyers, F. J. (2002). Hospice care for the incarcerated in the United States: An introduction. *Journal of Palliative Medicine, 5,* 549–552.

Linder, J. F., Knauf, K., Enders, S. R. & Meyers, F. J. (2002). Prison hospice and pastoral care services in California. *Journal of Palliative Medicine, 5,* 903–908.

Linder, J. F. & Meyers, F. J. (2007). Palliative care for prison inmates: "Don't let me die in prison." *Journal of the American Medical Association, 298,* 894–901.

Lindt, P. (2005, June 21). There has been an increase in the prison population throughout the USA of TB, HIV, and MRSA. *Lancaster Intelligence Journal* (PA), 1.

Liptak, A. (2003a, February 11). Court allows making inmate sane enough for execution. *The New York Times,* pp. A1, A25.

Liptak, A. (2003b, October 26). Alabama prison at center of suit over AIDS policy. *The New York Times,* p. 13.

Liptak, A. (2005a, September 25). Inmate was considered "property" of gang, witness tells jury in prison rape lawsuit. *The New York Times,* p. 11.

Liptak, A. (2005b, October 2). To more inmates, life term means dying behind bars. *The New York Times,* pp. A1, A18.

Liptak, A. (2005c, October 3). Locked away forever after crimes as teenagers. *The New York Times,* pp, A1, A12.

Liptak, A. (2005d, October 5). Serving life, with no chance of redemption. *The New York Times*, pp. A1, A13.

Lipton, E. (2001, January 11). 22 years later, unsanitary jail conditions still exist, judge finds. *The New York Times*, p. B3.

LIS Inc. (2003). *Corrections agency collaborations with public health.* Longmont, CO: U.S. Department of Justice, National Institute of Corrections, Information center.

Loeb, S. J., Staffensmeier, D. & Lawrence, F. (2007). Comparing incarcerated and community-dwelling older men's health. *Western Journal of Nursing Research, 20,* 20.

Lohn, M. (2005, October 12). As more women go to prison, institutions struggle to adapt. *Associated Press State & Local Wire.* Retrieved October 12, 2005, from http://web.lexis.com/universe/document?_m=dafb8ece3d12f84

Los Angeles Times. (2000, December 30). Health care services in California prisons. Author, p. B9.

Losen, J. & Orfield, G. (2002). Introduction: Racial inequity in special education. In D.J. Losen & G. Orfield (Ed.). *Racial inequity in special education* (pp. xv–xxxvii). Cambridge. MA: Harvard Education Press.

Los Angeles Times. (2001a, January 15). Treatment with teeth. Author, p. 6.

Louisiana State University Law Center. (2000). *Liability for prison and post-release health care—Lugo v. Senkowski, 114 F, Supp, 2nd 111* (N.D.N.Y. Sep. 25, 2000). Baton Rouge: LSU Law Center.

Lowenstein, T. K. (2001, January 1). Collateral damage. *American Prospect,* 1–5.

Ludlow, R. (2005a, February 5). Prison health care rife with problems, medical team says. *Columbus Dispatch* (OH), p. B4.

Ludlow, R. (2005b). Prisons to get 21 extra doctors; state settles inmate lawsuit that alleged poor health care. *Columbus Dispatch* (OH), p. E1.

Lundstrom, S. (1994). Dying to get out: A study on the necessity, importance, and effectiveness of prison early release programs for elderly inmates suffering from HIV disease and other terminal-centered illnesses. *Brigham Young University Journal of Public Law, 9,* 155–188.

Lurigio, A. J. (2000). Persons with serious mental illness in the criminal justice system: Background, prevalence, and principles of care. *Criminal Justice Policy Review, 11,* 312–328.

Lyerla, R. (2003). What is the value of immunizing prison inmates against hepatitis B? In *The health status of soon-to-be-released inmates: A report to Congress* Vol. 2 (pp. 135–139). Chicago: National Commission on Correctional Health Care.

Macalino, G. E., Vlahov, D., Dickerson, B. P., Schwartzapfel, B. & Rich, J. D. (2005). Community incidence of hepatitis B and C among reincarcerated women. *Clinical Infectious Diseases, 41,* 998–1002.

Macalino, G. E., Vlahov, D., Sanford-Colby, S., Patel, S., Sabin, K., Salas, C. & Rich, J. D. (2004). Prevalence and incidence of HIV, hepatitis B virus, and hepatitis C virus infections among males in Rhode Island prisons. *American Journal of Public Health, 94,* 11218–12223.

Macallair, D. & Schriradi, V. (2000, June 23). If your job depends on it, throwing non-violent drug users in jail makes sense. *San Jose Mercury News*, pp. 1–2.

MacGowan, R., Eldridge, G., Sosman, J. M., Khan, R., Flanigan, T., Zack, B., Margolis, A., Askew, J., Fiztgerald, C. & Project Start Study Group. (2006). HIV counseling and testing of young men in prison. *Journal of Correctional Health Care, 12*, 203–213.

Macher, A., Kibble, D. & Wheeler, D. (2006). HIV transmission in correctional facility. *Emerging Infectious Diseases, 12*, 669–671.

Macher, A., Kibble, D., Bryant, K, Cody, A., Pilcher, T. & Jahn, D. (2005). Educating correctional health care providers and inmates about drug-drug interactions: HIV-medications and illicit drugs. *California Journal of Health Promotion, 3*, 139–143.

MacIntyre, C. R., Kendig, N., Kummer, L., Birago, S., Graham, N. M. & Plant, A. J. (1999). Unrecognized transmission of tuberculosis in prisons. *European Journal of Epidemiology, 15*, 705–709.

Mackenzie, D. L. (2000). *Sentencing and corrections in the 21st century: Setting the stage for the future.* Washington, DC: National Institute of Justice, Office of Justice Program, U.S. Department of Justice.

MacNeil, J. R., Lobato, M. N. & Moore, M. (2005). An unanswered health disparity: Tuberculosis among correctional inmates, 1993–2003. *American Journal of Public Health, 95*, 1800–1805.

Maddow, R. (2000, January). Big business. Private HMOs tap a new niche: Prisons. *HIV Plus*, 11–13.

Maeve, M. K. (2003). Nursing care partnerships with women leaving jail: Effects on health and crime. *Journal of Psychosocial Nursing, 41(9)*, 30–40.

Magee, C. G., Hult, J. R., Turalba, R. & McMillan, S. (2005). Preventive care for women in prison: A qualitative community health assessment of the Papanicolaou Test and follow-up treatment at a California state women's prison. *American Journal of Public Health, 95*, 1712–1717.

Mahon, N. B. (1999). Introduction. Death and dying behind bars—cross-cutting themes and policy imperatives. *Journal of Law, Medicine & Ethics, 27*, 215–215.

Mahon, W. (1996). New York inmates' HIV risk behaviors: The implications for prevention policy and programs. *American Journal of Public Health, 86*, 1211–1215.

Maker, J. (2000). *KELN Bibliography: The quality of care of elderly inmates in prison.* Manhattan: University of Kansas.

Males, M. & Macallair, D. (2000). *The color of justice: An analysis of juvenile court transfers in California.* Washington, DC: Building Blocks for Youth.

Malisow, C. (2006, September 21). Penal violations; Texas prisons say they can't allow condoms because they don't allow sex. *Houston Press* (TX), p. 1.

Malveaux, J. (2001). Prisons, justice and education. *Black Issues in Higher Education, 18*, 32–34.

Mapes, J. (2005, April 29). Prisons are a growth industry in Oregon. *The Oregonian*, p. 1.

Mara, C. M. (2004). Chronic illness, disability, and long-term care in the prison setting. In P. R. Katz, M. D. Mezey, & M. B. Kapp (Eds.). *Vulnerable populations in the long term care continuum* (pp. 39–56). New York: Springer Publishing Co.

Marable, M. (1999). Race-ing justice: The Prison-Industrial Complex. *African American Male Research, 4*, 1–3.

Marable, M. (2000, November 1). Education works, prisons don't, Harlem teach-in. ZNET Commentary. Retrieved October 10, 2006, from http://www.zmag.org/ZSustainers/ZDaily/2000-11/01marable.htm

Marcalino, G. F., Dhawan, D. & Rich, J. D. (2005). A missed opportunity: Hepatitis C screening in prisoners. *American Journal of Public Health, 95*, 1739–1740.

Marcus-Mendoza, S. T. & Wright, M. A. (2003). Treating the woman prisoner: The impact of a history of violence. In S. F. Sharp & R. Muraskin (Eds.). *The incarcerated woman: Rehabilitative programming in women's prisons* (pp. 107–117). Upper Saddle River, NJ: Prentice Hall.

Mare, C. M. (2004). Chronic illness, disability, and long-term care in the prison setting. In P. R. Katz, M. D. Mesey & M. B. Kapp (Eds.). *Vulnerable populations in the long term care continuum* (pp. 39–56). New York: Springer Press.

Marks, A. (1999, May 5). More states turn to treatment in drug war. *The Christian Science Monitor, 2.*

Marley, P. (2005, February 18). Critics question savings in privatization plan. *The Milwaukee Journal Sentinel,* p. 1.

Maroney, M. K. (2005). Caring and custody: Two faces of the same reality. *Journal of Correctional Health Care, 11*, 157–169.

Marquart, J. W., Merianos, D. E. & Doucet, G. (2000). The health-related concerns of older prisoners: Implications for policy. *Aging and Society, 20*, 79–96.

Marquart, J. W., Merianos, D. E., Herbert, J. L. & Carroll, L. (1997). Health conditions at prisons: A review of research and emerging areas of inquiry. *Prison Journal, 77*, 184–208.

Marsa, L. (2001, May 15). Many lack gynecological care. *Los Angeles Times,* p. 1.

Marshall, J. D. L, Fordyce, M. W. & Rich, J. D. (2008). Screening for public purpose: Promoting an evidence-based approach to screening of inmates to improve public health. In R. Greifinger (Ed.). *Public health behind bars: From prisons to communities* (pp. 249–264). New York: Springer Publishing Co.

Marshall, T., Simpson, S. & Stevens, A. (2000). *Toolkit for health assessment in prison.* England: HM Prison Service NHS Executive.

Martin, K. (2001, April 2). Diagnosing public health's role in jails. Retrieved March 16, 2001, from http://database.corrections.com/news/results2asp?ID=821

Martin, M. (2003, February 26). State warned on elderly inmate crisis. *San Francisco Chronicle,* p. 1.

Martin, S. L., Rieger, R. H., Kupper, L. L., Meyer, R. E. & Qaqish, B. F. (1997). The effect of incarceration during pregnancy on birth outcomes. *Public Health Reports 112*, 340–346.

Maruna, S. (2001). *Making good: How ex-convicts reform and rebuild their lives.* Washington, DC: American Psychological Association.

Maruschak, L. M. (1999). *HIV in Prisons 1997.* Bureau of Justice Statistics Bulletin. Washington, DC: Bureau of Justice Statistics. Retrieved June 12, 2007, from www.ojp.usdoj.gov/bjs/pub/pdf/hivp97.pdf

Maruschak, L. M. (2004). HIV in prisons, 2001. Bureau of Justice Statistics Bulletin, U.S. Department of Justice, Office of Justice Programs.

Maruschak, L.M. (2008). *Medical problems of prisoners, 2004.* Washington, D.C.: Bureau of Justice Statistics.

Maruschak, L. M. & Beck, A. J. (2001). *Medical problems of inmates, 1997* (Special Report). Washington, DC: Bureau of Justice Statistics.

Massachusetts Developmental Disabilities Council. (2007). *What Is a Developmental Disability?* Retrieved January 29, 2007, from http://www.mass.gov/mddc/about/mission.htm

Massachusetts Public Health Association (2003). *Correctional health: The missing key to improving the public's health and safety.* Boston: Author.

Mathew, P., Elting, L., Cooksley, C., Owen, S. & Lin, J. (2005). Cancer in an incarcerated population. *Cancer, 104,* 2197–2204.

Maue, F. R. (2001). An overview of correctional mental health issues. *Corrections Today, 63,* 8–9.

Mauer, M. (1999a). *Race to incarcerate: The sentencing project.* New York: Free Press.

Mauer, M. (1999b). *The crisis of the young African American male and the criminal justice system.* Washington, DC: Sentencing Project.

Mauer, M. (2000). *Race to incarcerate.* New York: Free Press.

Maull, F. (2005). *The prison hospice movement.* The Journal of Science and Healing, 1, 477–479.

Maull, F. W. (1998). Issues in prison hospice: Toward a model for the delivery of hospice care in a correctional setting. *Hospice Journal, 13,* 57–82.

Maull, S. (2005, April 21). Former inmate says he got cancer from second-hand smoke in NYC jail. *Associated Press State & Local Wire.* Retrieved October 15, 2005, from http://0-web.lexis-nexis.com.library.simmons.edu/universe/document?_m=e40ec309633e6b

Mauro, T. (1999a, January 10). Disability act applies to prisons. *USA Today,* p. 1.

Mauro, T. (1999b, January 20). Disability act applies to prisons. *USA Today,* p. 1.

McCaffrey, B. R. (2000, June 6). In-prison drug programs should be expanded/treatment for chronic abuse costs less than incarceration. *The San Francisco Chronicle,* p. 1.

McCarthy, B. (1985). Mentally ill and mentally retarded offenders in corrections. *Source book on the mentally disordered prisoner.* Washington, DC: U.S. Department of Justice, National Institute of Corrections.

McClain, P. J., Sheehan, B. F. & Butler, L. L. (1998). Substantive rights retained by prisoners. *Georgetown Law Journal, 86,* 1953–2003.

McClellan, D. S. (2002). Coming to the aid of women in U.S. prisons. *Monthly Review, 54(2),* 33–44.

McCormack, L. (2003, July 1). Aging inmates, growing costs. *Tennessean.Com.* pp. 1–6.

McCormick, P. T. (2000). Just punishment and America's prison experiment. *Theological Studies, 61,* 508–524.

McDonald, D. C. (1995). *Managing prison health care and costs* (NCJ-152768). Washington, DC: Department of Justice.

McGrath, J. (2002). Raising the "civilized minimum" of pain amelioration for prisoners to avoid cruel and unusual punishment. *Rutgers Law Review, 54,* 649–684.

McGuire, M. D. (2005). The impact of prison rape on public health. *California Journal of Health promotion, 3,* 72–83.

McKeown, B. (2000, April 16). What to do about aging cons. *The Gazette* (Colorado Springs), p. 1.

McKinley, J. (2007, December 30). Infection hits a California prison hard, and experts ask why. *The New York Times,* p. 10.

McKneally, M. F. & Sade, R. M. (2003). The prisoner dilemma: Should convicted felons have the same access to heart transplantation as ordinary citizens? Opposing views. *The Journal of Thoracic and Cardiovascular Surgery, 125,* 451–453.

McMahon, M. (2000). Assisting female offenders: Art or science?—Chairperson's commentary. In M. McMahon (Ed.). *What works—Assessment to assistance: Programs for women in community corrections* (pp. 279–328). Lanham, MD: American Correctional Association.

McMahon, P. (2003, August 11). Aging inmates present prison crisis. *USA Today,* p. 1.

McQueen, M. P. (1992, January 25). City told to isolate ill inmates. *Newsday,* p. 11.

McTighe, L. (2004, October 29). Prison health care: Activist campaign targets hepatitis, HIV care for prisoners, and continuity of care after release. *AIDS Treatment News,* p. 7.

Medical World News. (1971). Medicine behind bars: Hostility, horror and the Hippocratic Oath. Author, 23, 26–29, 31, 34–35.

Mellow, J. (2008). Written health informational needs for reentry. In R. Greifinger (Ed.). *Public health behind bars: From prisons to communities* (pp. 265–279). New York: Springer Publishing Co.

Mental Health Weekly. (2001a, July 23). Federal report: 16 percent of state prisoners have mental illness. Author, 2.

Mental Health Weekly. (2001b, March 19). Treatment gap exists for HIV-positive women. Author, 2.

Merbitz, C., Jain, S., Good, G. L. & Jain, A. (1995). Reported head injury and disciplinary rule infraction in prison. *Journal of Offender Rehabilitation, 22,* 11–19.

Merianos, D. E., Marquart, J. W., Damphousse, K. & Hebert, J. L. (1997). From the outside in: Using public health data to make inferences about older inmates. *Crime & Delinquency, 43,* 298–313.

Mertz, K. J., Schwebke, J. R., Gaydos, C., Beidinger, H. A., Tulloch, S. D. & Levine, W. C. (2002). *Sexually Transmitted Diseases, 29*, 271–276.

Metzner, J. & Dvoskin, J. (2006). An overview of correctional psychiatry. *Psychiatric Clinical North America, 29*, 761–772.

Meystre, S. (2005). The current state of telemonitoring: A comment on the literature. *Telemedicine J. E. Health, 11*, 63–69.

Miles, S.H. (2004). Abu Ghraib: Its legacy for military medicine. (Health and Human Rights). *The Lancet, 364*, 725.

Miller, K. R. (2004). Linguistic diversity in a deaf population: Implications for due process. *Journal of Deaf Studies & Deaf Education, 9*, 112–119.

Miller, K. R. (2001). Access to sign language interpreters in the criminal justice system. *American Annals of the Deaf, 146*, 328–330.

Miller, S. K. (2006). Jail health assessment practices: An analysis of national trends as compared to National Commission on Correctional Health Care recommendations. *Journal of Correctional Health Care, 12*, 104–117.

Mitchell, C. S., Gershon, R. R., Lears, M. K., Vlahov, D., Felknor, S., Lubeleczyk, R. A., Sherman, M. F. & Comstock, G. W. (2005). Risk of tuberculosis in correctional healthcare workers. *Journal of Occupational & Environmental Medicine, 47*, 580–586.

Monahan, J. (2004). The future of violence risk management. In M. Tonry (Ed.). *The future of imprisonment* (pp. 237–263). New York: Oxford University Press.

Montgomery, S. (1997, April 28). Prisons urge older inmates to think of health. *Dayton Daily News*, pp. 3–4.

Moore, S. (2007, August 27). Using muscle to improve health care for prisoners: Court appointee works alone in California. *The New York Times*, p. A12.

Morales, T., Gomez, C. A. & Marin, B. V. (1995). *Freedom and HIV prevention: Challenges facing Latino males leaving prisons*. Presented at the 103rd American Psychological Association Convention, New York.

Moran, G. (2001, March 5). Freedom elusive for dying prisoner; State is called slow to aid terminally ill. *The San Diego Union-Tribune*, p. A1.

Morash, M., Haarr, R. N., & Rucker, L. (1994). A comparison of programming for women and men in U.S. prisons in the 1980s. *Crime & Delinquency, 40(2)*, 197–221.

Morbidity and Mortality Weekly Report. (1999). High prevalence of chlamydial and gonoccal infection in women entering jails and juvenile detention centers. Vol. 48, 793–797.

Morgan, K. (1989). Convict runaways in Maryland, 1745–1775. *Journal of American Studies, 23*, 253–268.

Morrell, R. F. & Merbitz, C. (1998). Traumatic brain injury in prisoners. *Journal of Offender Rehabilitation, 27*, 1–8.

Morris, R. B. (1950). The course of peonage in a slave state. *Political Science Quarterly, 65*, 238–263.

Morton, J. B. (1992). *Administrative overview of the elderly inmates*. Washington, DC: National Institute of Corrections.

Mosely, K. & Tewsbury, R. (2006). Prevalence and predictors of HIV risk behaviors among male prison inmates. *Journal of Correctional Health Care, 12,* 132–144.

Moskowitz, E. (2006, June 22). Prison costs burst budget: Lawmakers grouse about the funding. *Concord Monitor* (New Hampshire), p. 1.

Mozes, A. (2000, November 17). Mentally ill patients at risk for HIV, TB, and Hepatitis. *Reuters Health Information Services,* p. 1.

Mueller, J. (1996). Locking up tuberculosis. *Corrections Today, 58,* 100–101.

Mullen, C. A. (1997). *Imprisoned selves: An inquiry into prisons and academe.* Washington, DC: University Press of America.

Munoz-Plaza, C. E., Strauss, S. M., Astone, J. M., Des Jarlais, D. C. & Hagan, H. (2005). Hepatitis C service delivery in prisons: Peer education from the "guys in blue." *Journal of Correctional Health Care, 11,* 347–368.

Murphy, C. (2001, April 30). Crime and punishment. *Fortune Magazine,* 131–135.

Murphy, D. S. (2005). Health care in the Federal Bureau of Prisons: Fact or faction. *California Journal of Public Health, 3,* 23–37.

Murray, F. J. (1998, June 16). Court requires state prisons to obey disabilities law. *The Washington Times,* p. 2.

Myers, J, Zack, B., Kramer, K., Gardner, M., Rucobo, G. & Costa-Taylor, S. (2005). Get connected: An HIV prevention case management program for men and women leaving California prisons. *American Journal of Public Health, 95,* 1682–1684.

Nadal, A. B. & Travis, T. M. (1997). New York inmate health care needs pose treatment, design challenges. *Corrections Today, 56,* 126–130.

Narevic, E., Garrity, T. F., Schoenberg, N. E., Hiller, M. L., Webster, J. M., Leukefeld, C. G. & Staton, T. M. (2006). Factors predicting unmet health services needs among incarcerated substance abusers. *Substance Use & Misuse, 41,* 1077–1094.

National Adult Literacy and Learning Disabilities Center. (1996). From the director . . . *Linkages, 3,* 1–2.

National Alliance for the Mentally Ill. (2001). *Dual diagnosis: Mental illness and substance abuse.* Arlington, VA: Author.

National Cancer Institute. (2004). *Human papillomavirus and cancer: Questions and answers.* Bethesda, MD: Author.

National Center on Education, Disability and Juvenile Justice. (1999). *Special education in correctional facilities.* College Park, MD: Author.

National Center on Education, Disability and Juvenile Justice. (2005). *Summary of class-action litigation involving special education claims in juvenile and adult correctional facilities.* College Park, MD: Author.

National Center on Institutions and Alternatives. (1998). *Executive summary on elders and prisons.* Washington, DC: Author.

National Commission on Correctional Health Care. (1992). *Mental health in correctional settings.* Chicago: Author.

National Commission on Correctional Health Care. (1993a). *Health care funding for incarcerated youth.* Chicago: Author.

National Commission on Correctional Health Care. (1993b). *Third party re-imbursement for correctional health care.* Chicago: Author.

National Commission on Correctional Health Care. (1994a). *Administrative management of HIV in corrections.* Chicago: Author.

National Commission on Correctional Health Care. (1994b). *Correctional health care and the prevention of violence.* Chicago: Author.

National Commission on Correctional Health Care. (1994c). *Women's health care in correctional settings.* Chicago: Author.

National Commission on Correctional Health Care. (1995). *Continuity of care.* Chicago: Author.

National Commission on Correctional Health Care. (1997a). *Use of telemedicine technology in correctional facilities.* Chicago: Author.

National Commission on Correctional Health Care. (1997b). *Management of hepatitis B virus in correctional facilities.* Chicago: Author.

National Commission on Correctional Health Care. (1998). *Health services to adolescents in adult correctional facilities.* Chicago: Author.

National Commission on Correctional Health Care. (1999). *The management of hepatitis C in correctional institutions.* Chicago: Author.

National Commission on Correctional Health Care. (2001). *New hope for juveniles with mental illness.* Chicago: Author.

National Commission on Correctional Health Care. (2003a). Executive Summary. In *The health status of soon-to-be-released inmates: A report to Congress* (pp. ix–xxii). Chicago: Author.

National Commission on Correctional Health Care. (2003b). Introduction. In *The health status of soon-to-be-released inmates: A report to Congress* (pp. 1–8). Chicago: Author.

National Commission on Correctional Health Care. (2003c). History of the project. In *The health status of soon-to-be-released inmates: A report to Congress* (pp. 9–13). Chicago: Author.

National Commission on Correctional Health Care. (2003d). Prevalence of communicable disease, chronic disease, and mental illness among the inmate population. In *The health status of soon-to-be-released inmates: A report to Congress* (pp. 15–28). Chicago: Author.

National Commission on Correctional Health Care. (2003e). Improving correctional health care: A unique opportunity to protect public health. In *The health status of soon-to-be-released inmates: A report to Congress* (pp. 29–34). Chicago: Author.

National Commission on Correctional Health Care. (2003f). Cost-effectiveness of prevention, screening, and treatment of disease among inmates. In *The health status of soon-to-be-released inmates: A report to Congress* (pp. 35–48). Chicago: Author.

National Commission on Correctional Health Care. (2003g). Barriers to prevention, screening, and treatment—and overcoming them. In *The health status of soon-to-be-released inmates: A report to Congress* (pp. 49–58). Chicago: Author.

National Commission on Correctional Health Care. (2003h). Policy recommendations. In *The health status of soon-to-be-released inmates: A report to Congress* (pp. 59–69). Chicago: Author.

National Commission on Correctional Health Care (2005a). Position Statement: Administrative management of HIV in correctional institutions (Update). *Journal of Correctional Health Care, 11,* 369–375.

National Commission on Correctional Health Care (2005b). Position Statement: Women's health care in correctional settings (Update). *Journal of Correctional Health Care, 11,* 381–389.

National Drug Control Policy. (2000). *Strategy Report.* Washington, DC: Author.

National Institute of Corrections. (2003). Characteristics of women in the criminal justice system. *Guiding Principles and Gender Responsive Strategies.* Retrieved April 9, 2003, from www.nicic.org/pubs/2003/018017.pdf

National Institute of Justice. (1999). *Telemedicine can reduce correctional health care costs: An evaluation of a prison telemedicine network.* Washington, DC: U.S. Department of Justice.

National Women's Law Center. (n.d.) *Women in prison.* Retrieved January 11, 2005, from www.unix.oit.umass.edu

Nation's Health. (1991). AIDS care in prisons very poor, says national commission. Author, 21, p. 1.

Native American Advisory Group. (2003). *Report of the Ad Hoc Advisory Group on Native American Sentencing Issues.* Washington, DC: Author.

Neeley, C. L., Addison, L. & Craig-Moreland, D. (1999). Addressing the needs of elderly offenders. In *From Aids to the internet: Correctional realities* (pp. 49–54). Lanham, MD: American Correctional Association.

Nelson, S. B., Friedman, H. B. & Gaydos, C. A. (2005). Should female federal inmates be screened for chlamydial and gonococcal infections? *Journal of Correctional Health Care, 11,* 137–155.

Ness, C. (2001, March 21). Census shows jump for people living in jails, nursing homes. *The San Francisco Chronicle,* p. A6.

Newsday. (2002, January 26). Inmate given a new heart. Author, p. A20.

News-Medical.Net. (2004, April 23). Hepatitis B vaccination for inmates. Retrieved November 14, 2006, from http://www.news-medical.net/?id=780

News-Medical.Net. (2006, October 5). Schwarzenegger's veto of prison condom distribution bill politically motivated. Retrieved November 15, 2006, from http://www.news-medical.net/?id=20404

New York City Department of Corrections. (1997). Report on the New York City Department of Corrections. New York: Author.

New York Law Journal. (2005, April 29). Decision of interest; New York County Supreme Court; former inmate alleging medical malpractice can also calm civil rights violation. Author, p. 22.

New York State Developmental Disabilities Planning Council. (2005). *Who we are . . . What we do.* Retrieved January 29, 2007, from http://www.ddpc.state.ny.us/pages

New York Times. (1999, May 29). Hepatitis C found rife among inmates. Author, p. A16.

New York Times. (2001a, February 18). A softer way to fight drug abuse. Author, p. 12.

New York Times. (2001b, May 21). AIDS in prison. Author, p. 1.

New York Times. (2005a, April 29). A simple way to fight HIV and AIDS. Author, p. A26.

New York Times. (2005b, July 22). Editorial: Fighting AIDS behind bars. Author, p. A20.

New York Times. (2005c, July 1). Receiver ordered for prison health system. Author, p. A11.

New York Times. (2005d, October 12). Sexual slavery in prison. Author, p. 22.

New York Times. (2007, July 18). Fights AIDS behind bars. Author, p. A18.

New York Times. (2008, March 10). Prison nation [editorial]. Author, p. A20.

Nichols, M., Bench, L.L., Morlok, E. & Liston, K. (2003). Analysis of mentally retarded and lower-functioning offender correctional programs. *Corrections Today,* 65, 119-121.

Niebuhr, G. (2001, April 12). Promise and pitfalls in taking religion to prison. *The New York Times,* p. A22.

Nieves, E. (2000, March 6). The 2000 campaign: The initiative. *The New York Times,* p. A1.

Nieves, E. (2002, July 12). Released from jail, despite his pleas, 92-year-old is later found dead. *The New York Times,* p. A12.

Norland, S., Sowell, R. E. & DiChiara, A. (2003). Assumptions of coercive treatment: A critical review. *Criminal Justice Policy Review, 14,* 505–521.

Novak, T, (1997, November 2). Aging prisoners put a strain on system. *Chicago Sun-Times,* p. 4.

Obot, E. G., Braithwaite, R. L., Mayberry, R., Gunn, E. L., Harris, B., Harrison, A., Morris, R., Murdaugh, H. & Cozza, S. (1997). Ethnographic assessment of HIV risk reduction programs in correctional facilities. *Journal of Health Education, 28,* 1–10.

O'Connor, L. (2003, May 11). Jail, prison official guard health care dollars. *Jackson Citizen Patriot* (MI), pp. 1–2.

O'Connor, M. F. (2004). Finding boundaries inside prison walls: Case study of a terminally ill inmate. *Death Studies, 28,* 63–76.

Ogden, A. (2001, March). Do prison inmates have a right to vegetarian meals? *Vegetarian Journal,* pp. 1–2.

O'Hagan, M. (2001, April 15). Md. prisons brace for ban on cigarettes; health concerns spark prohibition at lockups. *The Washington Post,* p. C1.

Okie, S. (1998, October 12). U.S. WP: Inmates with kidney disease call transplant policy. *The Washington Post,* p. A01.

O'Morain, P. (2000, July 27). Hepatitis C report more common in prisons than HIV. *The Irish Times* (Dublin, Ireland), p. 3.

Okie, S. (2005). Glimpses of Guantanamo- Medical ethics and the war on terror. *The New England Journal of Medicine, 353,* 2529-2534.

Onishi, N. (2007, November 3). As Japan ages, prisons adapt to going gray. *The New York Times,* pp. A1, A9.

Onorato, M. (2001). HIV infection among incarcerated women. *HEPP: HIV & Hepatitis Prison Project, 4,* 1–9.

Ornduff, J. S. (1996). Releasing the elderly inmate: A solution to prison overcrowding. *Elder Law Journal, 4,* 173–200.

Ort, R. S. (1999). Mental illness as a chronic condition. In *From AIDS to the internet: Correctional realities* (pp. 25–36). Lanham, MD: American Correctional Association.

Ortiz, M. M. (2000). Managing special populations. *Corrections Today, 62,* 64–68.

Ostreicher, L. (2003, January). When prisoners come home. *GothamGazette.Com,* pp. 1–5. Retrieved March 13, 2008, from http://www.gothamgazette.com/article/socialservices/20030117/15/187

Owen, B. (1999). Women and imprisonment in the United States: The gendered consequences of the U.S. imprisonment binge. In S. Cook & S. Davies (Eds.). *Harsh punishment: International experiences of women's imprisonment* (pp. 81–98). Boston: Northeastern University Press.

Ozgen, H. & Ozcan, Y. A. (2002). A national study of efficiency for dialysis centers: An examination of market competition and facility characteristics for production of multiple dialysis outputs. *Health Services Research, 37,* 711–732.

Palevitz, B. A. (2001, March 19). AIDS in women. *The Scientist, 6.*

Pankratz, H. (1998, February 21). "Lifer" says state has duty to help him die. *The Denver Post,* p. B4.

Parece, M. S., Herrera, G. A., Voigt, R. F., Middlekauff, S. L., & Irwin, K. L. (1999). STD testing policies and practices in U.S. city and county jails. *Sexually Transmitted Diseases,* 431–437.

Parenti, C. (1999). *Lockdown America: Police and prisons in the age of crisis.* New York: Verso Press.

Paris, J., Pradham, M. M., Allen, S. & Cassidy, W. M. (2005). Cost of hepatitis C treatment in the correctional setting. *Journal of Correctional Health Care, 11,* 199–212.

Parker, F. R. & Paine, C. J. (1999). Informed consent and the refusal of medical treatment in the correctional setting. *Journal of Law, Medicine & Ethics, 27,* 240–251.

Pasko, L. (2002). Villain or victim: Regional variation and ethnic disparity in federal drug offense sentencing. *Criminal Justice Policy Review, 13,* 307–328.

Patrick, S. & Marsh, R. (2001). Current tobacco policies in U.S. adult male prisons. *The Social Science Journal, 37,* 27–34.

Patterson, R. & Greifinger, B. (2002). *The public health dimensions of prisoner reentry: Addressing the health needs and risks of returning prisoners and their families* (pp. 15–16). Meeting Summary, National Reentry Roundtable Meeting, The Urban Institute, Los Angeles, December 11–12, 2002. Washington, DC: Author.

Patterson, R. F. & Greifiner, R. B. (2008). Treatment of mental illness in correctional settings. In R. Greifinger (Ed.). *Public health behind bars: From prisons to communities* (pp. 347–367). New York: Springer Publishing Co.

Pavello, de L. (1999). *Current reproductive health and HIV prevention issues for incarcerated women.* Paper presented at the 1999 National HIV Prevention Conference. Atlanta, Georgia. August 30–September 1, 1999.

Paz, R. S. (2008). Accommodating disabilities in jails and prisons. In R. Greifinger (Ed.). *Public health behind bars: From prisons to communities* (pp. 42–55). New York: Springer Publishing Co.

Pediatrics. (2000). Imprisonment. Author, July, 2.

Pelissier, B., Wallace, S., O'Neil, J. A., Gaes, G. G., Camp, S., Rhodes, W. & Saylor, W. (2001). Federal prison residential drug treatment reduces substance abuse and arrests after release. *American Journal of Drug and Alcohol Abuse, 27*, 315–337.

Pendleton, R. (2000, June 24). Work camp for older inmates opens longer terms mean more aging prisoners. *The Florida Times-Union* (Jacksonville), p. 2.

Perez, A. (2005). States wrangle with corrections budgets: Criminal justice budgets challenge states as costs and inmate populations increase. *State Legislatures, 31*, 19–20.

Perez, J. H. (1997). AIDS behind bars: We should all care. *Body Positive, 10*, 1–6.

Peters, R. H. & Bekman, N. M. (2008). Treatment and reentry approaches for offenders with co-occurring disorders. In R. Greifinger (Ed.). *Public health behind bars: From prisons to communities* (pp. 368–384). New York: Springer Publishing Co.

Peters, R. H., Strozier, A. L., Murrin, M. R. & Kearns, W. D. (1998). Treatment of substance-abusing jail inmates: Examination of gender differences. *Journal of Substance Abuse Treatment, 14*, 339–349.

Petersilia, J. (1997). Justice for all? Offenders with mental retardation and the California correctional system. *The Prison Journal, 77(4)*, 358–380.

Petersilia, J. (2000a, November). When prisoners return to the community: Political, economic, and social consequences. (NCJ Pub. No.184253). *Sentencing & Corrections issues for the 21st century*, 9. Washington, DC: National Institute of Justice.

Petersilia, J. (2000b). *Doing justice? Criminal offenders with developmental disabilities.* Berkely: California Policy Research Center Brief, *12*, 1–5.

Petersilia, J. (2003). *When prisoners come home: Parole and prisoner reentry.* New York: Oxford University Press.

Pew Center on the States. (2008). *One in 100: Behind bars in America 2008.* Washington, DC: Pew Charitable Trusts.

Pfankuch, T. B. (1999, February 9). Prison AIDS costly inmate treatment hits $19 million. *The Florida Times-Union* (Jacksonville), p. 1.

Pfeiffer, M. B. (2003, November 15). Inmates' health care is in crisis, panel told: Hepatitis C called prison epidemic. *Poughkeepsie Journal* (NY), p. 1.

Pfeiffer, M. B. (2005a, April 1). Prison health care is killing inmates. *The Times Union* (Albany, NY), p. A9.

Pfeiffer, M. B. (2005b, April 4). Prison "health care" is killing people who are incarcerated. *The Times Union* (Albany, NY), p. A7.

Pfeiffer, S. (2002, August). *One strike against the elderly: Growing old in prison.* Retrieved July 3, 2003, from http://journalism.medill.northwestern.edu/docket/01-1127aging.html

Pisu, M., Meltzer, M. I. & Lyeria, R. (2002). Cost-effectiveness of hepatitis B vaccination of prison inmates. *Vaccine, 13*, 312–321.

Pitchford, R. (2005, June 26). Inmates growing old in Louisiana prisons; health care becoming big challenge for system. *The Advocate* (Baton Rouge, LA), pp. 1–B, S.

Plain Dealer. (1997, June 11), A cure for medical con games. Author, p. B10.

Pollak, O. (1941). The criminality of old age. *Journal of Criminal Psychopathology, 3*, 213–235.

Polonsky, S., Kerr, S., Harris, B., Gaiter, J., Fictner, R. R. & Kennedy, M. G. (1994). HIV prevention in prisons and jails: Obstacles and opportunities. *Public Health Reports, 109*, 615–625.

Porterfield, E. (1999, July 27). New facility more nursing home than jail. *Seattle Post-Intelligencer*, pp. 2–3.

Positive Populations. (2002). Civil rights leader endorses mandatory HIV testing of inmates. Author, 3, (2), 8–9.

Positive Populations. (2003). Treatment advocate raises level of awareness, concerns about HIV/HCV co-infections. Author, 4, (4), 8–10, 11.

Potter, J. (1991, July/August). Future trends in intake and discharge. *American Jails*, pp. 5, 34–36.

Potter, R. H. (2002). Guest editor comments: Corrections, health care, and public health. *The Prison Journal, 82*, 5–7.

Powell, M. (2006, November 25). In NYC, fewer inmates and less crime. *The Boston Globe*, p. A11.

Preston, J. (2008, March 28). 304,000 inmates eligible for deportation, official say. *The New York Times*, p. A15.

Preston, P. (2003). Should there be separate justice systems for special needs populations? Results from the Penn State public opinion poll. *Criminal Justice Policy Review, 14*, 322–338.

Price, C. A. (2006). *Aging inmate population study.* Charlotte: North Carolina Department of Correction Division of Prisons.

Primm, A. B., Osher, F. C. & Gomez, M. B. (2005). Race and ethnicity, mental health services and cultural competence in the criminal justice system: Are we ready to change? *Community Mental Health Journal, 41*, 557–569.

Prison Issues. (2004). Prison issues. Retrieved August 8, 2005, from http://faculty.news.edu/toconnor/111/111lect3htm

Prison Project. (2000, January). Special Report: Prisons—in the big house. 1–2.

Prison Reform Trust. (1997). *The effects of American sentencing policy changes on the courts, prisons and crime.* London: Author.

Public Health & Corrections. (2002, July). Health status of inmates: Congress calls for the facts, 1–4.

Public Health & Corrections. (2003, March). HIV prevention community planning groups and correctional institutions: A collaboration for all. Author, 1–6.

Pugh, T. (1998, September 5). More states may institute mandatory HIV testing in prisons. *The Miami Herald*, p. 1.

Purdy, M. (1997, May 26). As AIDS increases behind bars, costs dim promise of new drugs. *The New York Times*, p. 1.

Purvis, B. (2006, August 7). Cheaper prison options sought: As number of older prisoners rises, so do costs for care. *The Milwaukee Journal Sentinel* (WI), p. 1.

Quinn, M.M., Rutherford, R.B. & Leone, P.E. (2001). *Students with disabilities in correctional facilities.* Arlington, VA: The Educational Resources Information Center.

Raimer, B. G. & Stobo, J. D. (2004). Health care delivery in the Texas prison system: The role of academic medicine. *Journal of the American Medical Association, 292,* 485–489.

RAND Corporation. (1997). Criminal justice policies toward the mentally retarded are unjust and waste money. *Rand Research Brief*, 1–3.

RAND Corporation. (2003). Prisoner reentry: What are the public health challenges? *Rand Research Brief*, 1–2.

Ratcliff, M. (2000). Dying inside the walls. *Innovations in End-of-Life Care, 2,* 1–5.

Ratcliff, M. & Cohn, F. (2000, February). Hospice with GRACE: Reforming care for terminally ill inmates. *Corrections Today, 62,* 64–67.

Ratcliff, M. & Craig, E. (2004). The GRACE Project: Guiding end-of-life care in corrections 1998–2001. *Journal of Palliative Medicine, 7,* 373–379.

Rathbone, C. (2005). *A world apart: Women, prison, and life behind bars.* New York: Random House.

Rau, J. (2007, December 28). Prison healthcare costs outpace Calif. inmate population. *The Boston Globe*, p. A21.

Ray, N., Harmon, T. & Trojnor, L. (1991). *Inmates with developmental disabilities in New York State correctional facilities.* New York: New York State Commission on the Quality of Care for the Mentally Disabled.

Reams, P. (1998). *American Correctional Health Services Administration Code of Ethics.* Alpharetta, GA: American Correctional Health Services Administration.

Reams, P., Smith, M. N., Fletcher, J. & Spencer, E. (1998, April). Making a case for bioethics in corrections. *Corrections Today*, 112–178.

Reams, P., Smith, M. N., Fletcher, J. & Spencer, E. (1999). Making a case for bioethics in corrections. In *From AIDS to the internet: Correctional realities* (pp. 55–66). Lanham, MD: American Correctional Association.

Redlich, A. D., Steadman, H. J., Robbins, P. C. & Swanson, J. W. (2006). Use of the criminal justice system to leverage mental health treatment: Effects on treatment adherence and satisfaction. *Journal of the American Academy of Psychiatry & Law, 34,* 292–299.

Reich, K. (2002, March 12). Suit calls prison haircutting unsanitary; lawsuit: activists claim that use of unsterilized instruments has exposed thousands of inmates to HIV and hepatitis. *Los Angeles Times*, Part 2, 7.

Reiman, J. (1996) . . . *and the poor get prison: Economic bias in American criminal justice.* Boston: Allyn & Bacon.

Restum, Z. G. (2005). Public health implications of substandard correctional health care. *American Journal of Public Health, 95,* 1689–1691.

Reuell, P. (2005, August 14). Mental illness rampant inside women's prison. *The Boston Herald,* p. 6.

Reuters. (2003, April 18). Drugs may aid fight against hepatitis C. *Boston Globe,* p. A2.

Reuters Health Service. (2002, February 15). Many prison inmates worldwide found mentally ill. Author, p. 1.

Reviere, R. & Young, V. D. (2004). Aging behind bars: Health care for older female inmates. *Journal of Women & Aging, 16,* 55–69.

Reynolds, M., Mezey, G., Chapman, M., Wheeler, M., Drummond, C. & Baldacchino, A. (2005). Co-morbid post-traumatic stress disorder in a substance misusing clinical population. *Drug & Alcohol Dependence, 77,* 251–258.

Rhodes, W., Johnston, P., McMullen, Q. & Hozik, L. (2000). *Unintended consequences of sentencing policy: The creation of long-term healthcare obligations.* Cambridge, MA: ABT Associates.

Rich, J. D., Holmes, L., Salas, C., Macalino, G., Davis, D., Ryczek, J. & Flannigan, T. (2001). Successful linkage of medical care and community services for HIV-positive offenders being released from prison. *Journal of Urban Health, 78,* 279–289.

Rich, J. et al. (2001). Successful linkage of medical care and community services for HIV-positive offenders being released from prisons. *Journal of Urban Health, 78,* 279–288.

Richie, B. E., Freudenberg, N. & Page, J. (2001). Reintegrating women leaving jail into urban communities: A description of a model program. *Journal of Urban Health, 78,* 290–303.

Rideau, W. & Wikberg, R. (1992). *Life sentences: Rage and survival behind bars.* New York: Times Books.

Ridzon, R. (2003). Taking control of tuberculosis in corrections. *HIV Education Prison Project, 6,* 1–5.

Rikard, R.V. & Rosenberg, E. (2007). Aging inmates: A convergence of trends in the American criminal justice system. *Journal of Correctional Health Care, 13,* 150–162.

Robbins, I. P. (1999). Managed health care in prisons as cruel and unusual punishment. *Journal of Criminal Law and Criminology, 90,* 195–220.

Roberts, C., Kennedy, S., & Hammett, T. M. (2004). Linkages between in-prison and community-based health services. *Journal of Correctional Health Care, 10,* 333–368.

Roberts, C. A., Lobato, M. N., Bazerman, L. B., Kling, R., Reichard, A. A. & Hammett, T. H. (2006). Tuberculosis prevention and control in large jails: A challenge for tuberculosis elimination. *American Journal of Preventive Medicine, 30,* 125–130.

Robertson, J. E. (2003). Rape among incarcerated men: Sex, coercion and STDs. *AIDS Patient Care and STDs, 8,* 423–430.

Rohde, D. (2001a, February 2). After long climb, prison population falls in New York. *The New York Times*, p. A1.

Rohde, D. (2001b, August 6). A health danger from a needle becomes a scourge behind bars. *The New York Times*, pp. A1, A14.

Rohde, D. (2001c, August 9). Soaring rates of hepatitis C pose dilemma in U.S. prisons. *The New York Times*, p. A1.

Rosenberg, E. (2002). Aging inmates and applied gerontology. *Southern Gerontology, 16,* 3.

Rosenblatt, E. (Ed.). (1996). *Criminal injustice: Confronting the prison crisis.* Boston: South End Press.

Rosenfield, A. H. (1992). Enabling the disabled: Issues to consider in meeting handicapped offenders' needs. *Corrections Today, 54,* 110–114.

Rosenfield, H. A. (1993). Older inmates where do we go from here? *Journal of Prison & Jail Health, 12,* 51–58.

Roskes, E., Feldman, R., Arrington, S. & Leisher, M. (1999). A model program for the treatment of mentally ill offenders in the community. *Community Mental Health Journal, 35,* 461–472.

Ross, P. H. & Lawrence, J. E. (1998). Healthcare for women offenders. *Corrections Today, 60,* 122–129.

Ross, S. (2004). The hidden tragedy of offender deaths. *The Medical Journal of Australia, 181,* 469–470.

Rothman, D. J. (1971). *The discovery of the asylum: Social order and disorder in the new republic.* Boston: Little Brown & Co.

Rothman, M. B. & Dunlop, B. D. (2000). Elders and the criminal justice system: A policy perspective. *The Public Policy and Aging Report, 1,* 10–12.

Ruffins, P. (2002). Fighting to be heard: Black criminologists seek proper context to explain racism's influence on Black crime. *Black Issues in Higher Education, 18,* 20–24.

Russell, M. (1994). Too little, too late, too slow: Compassionate release of terminally ill prisoners—Is the cure worse than the disease? *Widener Journal of Public Law, 3,* 811–854.

Russell, M. & Stewart, J. (2001). Disablement, prison, and historical segregation. *Monthly Review, 53,* 61–75.

Russell, S. (2000, September 12). No record of lab tests for 650 state inmates: Earlier exams for AIDS, other diseases were faked. *The San Francisco Chronicle*, p. A1.

Rydell, C. P. & Everingham, S. S. (1994). *Controlling cocaine: Supply versus demand programs.* Santa Monica, CA: RAND Corporation.

Sacramento Bee. (2005, June 20). Controls would hold down costs of California prison health care. Author, p. A23.

Salcido, R., Chen, L., Whitley, R. & D'Amico, T. (2003). *Seroprevalence of hepatitis B and C markers among inmates entering the Nevada State Correctional System.* Presentation at the National Hepatitis Coordinators' Conference, San Antonio, Texas, January 27, 2003.

Salive, M. E., Vlahov, D. & Brewer, T. F. (1990). Co-infection with tuberculosis and HIV-1 in male inmates. *Public Health Reports, 105,* 307–310.

San Diego Union-Tribune. (2001, April 10). The big fix; implementing drug treatment faces hurdles. Author, p. B8.

San Francisco Chronicle. (2001, March 15). Improve prison health facilities. Author, p. A26.

San Francisco Chronicle. (2000, June 6). In-prison drug programs should be expanded. Author, p. 23.

Sarapata, M., Herrmann, D., Johnson, T. & Aycock, R. (1998). The role of head injury in cognitive functioning, emotional adjustment and criminal behavior. *Brain Injury, 12,* 821–842.

Satel, S. (2003, November 1). Out of the asylum, into the cell [letter to the editor]. *The New York Times OP-ED,* p. A29.

Satter, G. (2001). *Rates and causes of death among prisoners and offenders under community supervision.* London: Great Britain Home Office Research Development and Statistical Directorate.

Schaefer, N. J. & Stefancic, A. (2003). Alternate to prison programs for the mentally ill offender. *Journal of Offender Rehabilitation, 38,* 41–55.

Scheffenacker, E.B. (2007). Who pays for hospice care? *AlaskaUSA* http://hfo.cuna .org/10014)article/1167/html Accessed 7-3-08

Scheffey, T. B. (2005). Mental health staff personally liable. *Civil and Family, 7,* 17.

Schindler, J. (1999, November 11). Model prison hospice eases pain at Angola. *The Times-Picayune,* p. F1.

Schlosser, E. (1998). The prison-industrial complex. *The Atlantic Monthly, 282,* 51–52, 54–58, 62–66, 68–70, 72–77.

Schneider, C. L. (1998). Racism, drug policy, and AIDS. *Political Science Quarterly, 113,* 427–446.

Schreiber, C. (1999, July 19). Behind bars: Aging prison population challenges correctional health systems. *Nurse Week,* 1–2.

SeniorJournal. Com (2006, January 11). Prisons not safe for vulnerable senior citizens. Retrieved November 27, 2006, from http://www.seniorjournal.com/NEWS/ Aging/6-03-12-PrisonsNotSafe.htm

Sentementes, G. S. (2005, June 2). State costs for inmates' health care could rise 60%. *The Baltimore Sun,* p. A1.

Sentencing Project. (2001). *Slowing of prison growth likely linked to both crime and criminal justice policy.* Washington, DC: Author.

Sentencing Project. (2002a). *Fact sheet: Women in prison.* Washington, DC: Author.

Sentencing Project. (2002b). *Hispanic prisoners in the United States.* Washington, DC: Author.

Sentencing Project. (2004). *The federal prison population: A statistical analysis.* Washington, DC: Author.

Sentencing Project. (2005a). *Life sentences: Denying welfare benefits to women convicted of drug offenses* (State Modifications Updated January 2005). Washington, DC: Author.

Sentencing Project. (2005b). *New incarceration figures: Growth in population continues.* Washington, DC: Author.

Sered, S. S. & Fernandopulle, R. (2005). *Uninsured in America: Life & death in the land of opportunity.* Berkeley: University of California Press.

Severance, T. A. (2004). Concerns and coping strategies of women inmates concerning release: "It's going to take somebody in my corner." *Journal of Offender Rehabilitation, 38,* 73–97.

Seward, S. & Wallace, B. (1994, October 5). Inmates suffer despite calls for reform. *The San Francisco Chronicle,* p. A1.

Seyfer, J. (2000, July 27). Study says incarceration for drug offenders has increased at startling rate. *San Francisco Gate News,* p. 1.

Seymour, C. & Hairston, F. (Eds.). (2001). *Children with parents in prison: Child welfare policy, program, and practice issues.* Somerset, NJ: Transaction Publications.

Shafer, M. S., Arthur, B. & Franczak, M. J. (2004). An analysis of post-booking jail diversion programming for persons with co-occurring disorders. *Behavioral Science Law, 22,* 771–785.

Shah, A. (2006). An audit of a specialist old age psychiatry liaison service to a medium and a high secure forensic psychiatry unit. *Medical Science & Law, 46,* 99–104.

Shapinsky, D. (1999, November 13). *Is prison health care ailing: Critics say poor care creates public health threat.* Retrieved November 19, 2001, from http://www.freepublic .com/forum/a382dce721335. htm

Shea, S. (2006). Health delivery system changes required when integrating telemedicine into existing treatment flows of information and patients. *Telemedicine & Telecare, 12,* 585–590.

Sheeler, J. (2001, March 25). Veterans at Ft. Lyon make way for prison. Aging heroes to die or scatter within year. *The Denver Post,* p. B1.

Shellenbarger, P. (2006, November 17). Dying ex-con: Prison's health care system failed. *The Grand Rapids Press* (MI), p. 1.

Shimkus. J. (2002, Spring). Prison hospice comforts the dying, touches the living. *CorrectCare,* 1–3.

Shinkman, R. (2000, June 19). Healthcare behind bars. *Modern Healthcare,* 2–5.

Shuster, B. (2001, November 30). Sheriff approves handout of condoms to gay inmates. *Los Angles Times,* p. A38.

SIECUS Report. (1997). *The hidden epidemic: Confronting sexually transmitted diseases.* Washington, DC: Author.

Sigurdson, C. (2000). The Mad and The Bad and The Abandoned: The mentally ill in prisons and jails. *Corrections Today, 62,* 70–78.

Sinatra, S. T. (2000, December). Heart sense for women. *Healthy & Natural Journal,* 12–14.

Singer, M. I., Bussey, J., Song, L. Y. & Lunghofer, L. (1995). The psychosocial issues of women serving time in jail. *Social Work,* 40, 103–113.

Sit-DuVall, M. (2000, November 5). M.D. TV; Start-up's teleconferencing lets doctors treat from afar. *The Houston Chronicle,* p. 1.

Sizemore, B. (2000, March 7). Elderly and blacks bear the brunt of age: The cost of housing older inmates goes up. *The Virginian-Pilot and The Ledger-Star* (Norfolk, Va.), p. 1.

Skogan, W. G. (1990). *Disorder and decline: Crime and the spiral of decay in American neighborhoods*. Berkeley: University of California Press.

Skolnick, A. A. (1998a, October 28). Prison deaths spotlight how boards handle impaired, disciplined physicians. *JAMA Medical News & Perspectives, 16*, 1–9.

Skolnick, A. A. (1998b). Correctional and community health care collaborations. *Journal of the American Medical Association, 279*, 98–99.

Slevin, P. (2001, February 18). Prison firms seek inmates and profits; management woes, loss of business noted. *The Washington Post*, p. A3.

Slevin, P. (2006, June 8). US prison study faults system and the public. *The Washington Post*, p. A4.

Slipy, S. Marie. (1995). Telemedicine and interconnection services reduce costs at several facilities. *Health Management Technology*, 52–54.

Sluder, R. D. & Sapp, A. D. (1994). Peering into the crystal bowl to examine the future. *American Jails, 58*, 3–10.

Smart, G. (2005, August 14). Ladies days in jail. *Sunday News* (Lancaster, PA), p. 1.

Smith, B. & Dailard, C. (1994). Female prisoners and AIDS: On the margins of public health and social justice. *AIDS & Public Policy Journal, 9*, 78–85.

Smith, B. V. (1993, Spring). *Special needs of women in the criminal justice system*. Rockville, MD: Center for Substance Abuse Treatment Communiqué, pp. 31–33.

Snyder, B. (2000, June 28). Mental illness high in state jails. *The Tennessean*, p. 1.

Social Justice. (2000). Overview: Critical resistance to the prison-industrial complex. Author, 27, 1–3.

Solove, D. J. (1996). Faith profaned: The Religious Restoration Act and religion in the prisons. *Yale Law Journal, 106*, 0044–0094.

Sowell, R. L., Phillips, K. D., Seals, B. F., Julious, C. H., Rush, C. & Spruill, L. K. (2001). Social service and case management needs of HIV-infected persons upon release from prison/jail. *Lippincotts Case Management, 6*, 157–168.

Spaulding, A., Stephenson, B., Macalino, G., Ruby, W., Clarke, J. G. & Flannigan, T. P. (2002). Human immunodeficiency virus in correctional facilities: A review. *Clinical Infectious Diseases, 35*, 305–312.

Spaulding, A., Weinbaum, C. M., Lau, D. T., Sterling, R., Seeff, L. B., Margolis, H. S. & Hoofnagle, J. H. (2006). A framework for management of hepatitis C in prisons. *Annals of Internal Medicine, 144*, 762–769.

Springer, S. A. & Altice, F. L. (2008). Improving the care for HIV-infected prisoners: An integrated prison-release health model. In R. Greifinger (Ed.). *Public health behind bars: From prisons to communities* (pp. 13–24). New York: Springer Publishing Co.

Springer, S. A., Pesanti, E., Hodges, J., Macura, T., Doros, G. & Altice, F. L. (2004). Effectiveness of antiretroviral therapy among HIV-infected prisoners: Reincarceration and the lack of sustained benefit after release to the community. *Clinical Infectious Diseases, 38*, 1754–1760.

Squires, N. (1996). Promoting health in prisons: Requires more than a change in who purchases health services for prisoners. *British Medical Journal, 313*, 1161.

Stack, B. W. (2000, July 18). Released mentally ill addicts to get help. *Post-Gazette* (Pittsburgh, Pa), p. 1.

Stahl, E. & West, M. (2001). Growing population of mentally ill offenders redefines correctional facility design. *Corrections Today, 63*, 72–74.

Stana, R. M. (2000). *Federal prisons: Curbing health care costs for an increasing inmate population.* Washington, DC: General Accounting Office.

Starr, B. (1999, September 15). Not only is our society aging, our prisoners are aging as well—and it is costing a fortune. *San Diego Union Tribune*, p. 1.

Stashenko, J. (1999, January 11). Measure would make room in prisons. *Times Union* (Albany, NY), p. 5.

Stead, W. W. (1978). Undetected tuberculosis in prison: Source of infection for community at large. *Journal of the American Medical Association, 240*, 2544–2547.

Stein, A. (2004, April 30). *Prison stocks: A secure pick?* Retrieved September 18, 2005, from http://money.cnn.com/2004/04/30/news/midcaps/prison_companies/index.htm

Steiner, E. (2003). Early release for seriously ill and elderly prisoners: Should French practices be followed? *Probation Journal, 50*, 267–276.

Stephan, J.J. (1999). *State prison expenditures, 1996.* Washington, D.C.: Department of Justice.

Sterk, C. E., Theall, K. & Elifson, K. W. (2005). African American female drug users and HIV risk reduction challenges with criminal involvement. *Journal of Health Care for the Poor and Underserved, 16*, 89–107.

Sternberg, S. (1999, September 1). AIDS, HIV infection higher in prison. *USA TODAY*, p. 1A.

Sterngold, J. (2002, January 31). Inmate's transplant prompts questions of costs and ethics. *The New York Times*, p. A16.

Sterngold, J. (2005, July 1). U.S. seizes state prison health care. Judge cites preventable deaths of inmates, "depravity" of system. *San Francisco Chronicle*, p. A1.

Sterngold, J. & Martin, M. (2005, July 3). California's prisons in crisis. *The San Francisco Chronicle*, p. A1.

Stevenson, B. (2001, November 15). THE BIG ISSUE: Who says crime doesn't pay? *The Evening Mail* (Birmingham, England), p. 12.

Stockett, L. & Fields, H. F. (1999). *Issue brief: Prevention and treatment of HIV, STDS & TB in correctional settings.* Washington, DC: American Psychological Association.

Stockman, F. (2001, April 22). Two jails, two approaches to inmate management. *Boston Globe*, pp. B1, B4.

Stolberg, S. G. (2001, April 1). Behind bars, new effort to care for the dying. *The New York Times*, p. A1.

Stoller, N. (2003). Space, place and movement as aspects of health care in three women's prisons. *Social Science & Medicine, 56*, 2263–2275.

Stone, A. (1997, Spring). An epidemic ignored. *Public Health*, 1–5.

Stone, C. (1999, April). Race, crime, and the administration of justice: A summary of the available facts. *National Institute of Justice Journal, 26–32*.

Stone, T. H. (1997). Therapeutic implications of incarceration for persons with severe mental disorders: Searching for rational health policy. *American Journal of Criminal Law, 24*, 283–325.

Stone, T. T., Kaiser, R. M. & Mantese, A. (2006). Health care quality in prisons: A comprehensive matrix for evaluation. *Journal of Correctional Health Care, 12*, 89–103.

Strupp, H. & Willmott, D. (2005). *Dignity denied: The price of imprisoning older women in California*. San Francisco: Legal Services for Prisoners with Children.

Substance Abuse and Mental Health Services Administration. (2000). Substance abuse treatment in adult and juvenile correctional facilities. Rockville, MD: Author.

Sullivan, L. (2005, August 10). "Meth Mouth" strains prison health-care budgets. *National Public Radio*. Retrieved October 6, 2005, from http://www.npr.org/templates/story/story.php?storyId=4793417

Talbert, M. (2002). *State correctional education programs: State policy update*. Washington, D.C.: National Institute for Literacy.

Talvi, S. J. A. (2001). Hepatitis C: A silent epidemic strikes U.S. prisons. Retrieved December 3, 2002, from http://www.lipmagazine.org/articles/feattalvi_109_p.htm

Talvi, S. J. A. (2003). Hepatitis C. In T. Herivel & P. Wright (Eds.). *Prison nation: The warehousing of America's poor* (pp. 181–186). New York: Routledge.

Tanner, R. (2002, May 9). Disparities seen in safety at U.S. jails: Experts say more oversight needed. *The Boston Globe*, p. A5.

Tarbuck, A. (2001). Editorial: Health of elderly prisoners. *Age and Ageing, 30*, 369–370.

Taylor, C. S. (1997). *Growing up behind bars: Confinement, youth development, and crime*. East Lansing: Michigan State University.

Taylor, P. A. (2002). Grief and hospice care for the correctional community: Training, nurturing, and mentoring staff. *Journal of Correctional Health Care, 9*, 169–174.

Taylor, Z. & Nguyen, C. (2003). Cost-effectiveness of preventing tuberculosis in prison populations. In *The health status of soon-to-be-released inmates: A report to Congress* Vol. 2 (pp. 109–124). Chicago: National Commission on Correctional Health Care.

Texas Department of Criminal Justice. (2000). Mentally Retarded Offender Program. Austin, TX: Author.

Templer, D. I., Kasiraj, J., Trent, N. H., Trent, A., Hughey, B., Keller, W. J., Orling, R. A. & Thomas-Dobson, S. (1992). Exploration of head injury without medical attention. *Perceptual and Motor Skills, 75*, 195–202.

Theis, S. (1996, April 30). Prison death may involve race, gangs. *The Cincinnati Enquirer*, p. 1.

Thigpen, M. L. & Hunter, S. M. (1998). *Hospice and palliative care in prisons*. Longmont, CO: U.S. Department of Justice, National Institute of Corrections, Information Center.

Thomas, J. (2003). Conclusion: Moving forward. In B. H. Zaitzow & J. Thomas (Eds.). *Women in prison: Gender and social control* (pp. 205–213). London: Lynne Rienner Publishers.

Thompson, D. (2006, August 10). Aging inmates costing taxpayers more. *The Associated Press State & Local Wire*. Retrieved November 22, 2006, from http://web,lexisnexis.com/universe/document?_m=f1822757f84e9befb45f315d326f1a32

Thompson, D. (2004, June 2). Prison system's spiraling health care costs examined. *The San Diego Union-Tribune*, p. 1.

Thorburn, K. M. (1993). *Correctional health care issues for substance abusing offenders.* Rockville, MD: Center for Substance Abuse Treatment.

Thorburn, K. M. (1995). Health care in correctional facilities. *The Western Journal of Medicine, 163,* 560–566.

Thorburn, K. M. (1998, October 19). Is it getting worse behind bars? *St Louis Post-Dispatch,* p. 1.

Thorburn, K. M. (1999). Research letters: Injury monitoring in US prison systems. *Journal of the American Medical Association, 282,* 1–2.

Tierney, J. (2005, July 19). Punishing pain. *The New York Times,* p. 21.

Tilman, T. (2000). Hospice in prison: The Louisiana State Penitentiary hospice program. *Innovations in End-of-Life Care, 2,* 813–814.

Tomlinson, D. M. & Schechter, C. B. (2003). Cost-effectiveness analysis of annual screening and intensive treatment for hypertension and diabetes mellitus among prisoners in the United States. In *The health status of soon-to-be-released inmates: A report to Congress* Vol. 2 (pp. 141–156). Chicago: National Commission on Correctional Health Care.

Tonry, M. (1995). *Malign neglect: Race, crime, and punishment in America.* New York: Oxford University Press.

Tonry, M. (2004). Has the prison a future? In M. Tonry (Ed.). *The future of imprisonment* (pp. 3–24). New York: Oxford University Press.

Tonry, M. & Petersilia, J. (2000). *Prisons research at the beginning of the 21st century.* Washington, DC: National Institute of Justice.

Torok, L. (1999). The faith . . . in prison (religion in prisons). *America,* 1–4.

Torrey, E. Fuller. (1997). *Out of the shadows: Confronting America's mental health crisis.* New York: John Wiley & Sons.

Torrey, E. F., Stiber, J., Ezekiel, J., Wolfe, S. M., Sharfstein, J., Noble, J. H. & Flynn, L. M. (1993). Criminalizing the seriously mentally ill: The abuse of jails as mental hospitals. *Innovations & Research, 2,* 11–14.

Truzzi, D. (2005, October 9). Prison suicides defy precautions. *Hartford Courant* (CT), p. 1.

Tucker, W., Olfson, M., Simring, S., Goodman, W. & Bienenfeld, S. (2006). A pilot survey of inmate preferences for on-site, visiting consultant, and telemedicine psychiatric services. *CNS Spectrums, 11,* 783–787.

Tuhus, M. (2001, April 22). Seeking a way out of crowded prisons. *The New York Times (Connecticut Weekly),* p. 3.

Tulsky, J. P., White, M. C., Dawson, C., Hoynes, T. M., Goldenson, J. & Schecter, G. (1998). Screening for tuberculosis in jail and clinic follow-up after release. *American Journal of Public Health, 88,* 223–236.

Turvey, A. S. & Flaum, M. (2002). Older offenders, substance abuse, and treatment. *American Journal of Geriatric Psychiatry, 10,* 733–739.

Twedt, S. (2005, August 8). Addicts get treatment—behind bars. *Pittsburgh Post-Gazette* (PA), p. A1.

Twersky-Glasner, A. & Sheridan, M.J. (2005). Vocational, educational and psychological assessments of deaf inmates. *Justice Policy Journal, 2,* 1-26.

Twiddy, D. (2005, October 15). U.S. Supreme Court stays order requiring abortion. *Associated Press State & Local Wire.* Retrieved October 15, 2005, from http://0-web.lexis.com.library.simmons.edu/universe/document?_m=839315b36a7bef

Tysver, R. (1998, October 6). Too old to do time? Aging prisoners cost a lot more. *Omaha World-Herald,* p. 12.

Unknown Author. (2002, June 9). California struggling with growing numbers of elderly prisoners. Retrieved April 4, 2003, from http://www.globalaging.org/elders rights/us/Caprisons.htm

Urban Institute. (2002). *The public health dimensions of prisoner reentry: Addressing the health needs and risks of returning prisoners and their families.* Meeting Summary, National Reentry Roundtable Meeting, Los Angeles, December 11–12, 2002. Washington, DC: Author.

Urban Strategies Council. (2008). Important legislation and court cases related to incarcerated people. http://64.233.169.104/search?q=cache:8gmosuSNuHMJ: www.urbanstrate gies.org/docume.. Accessed 6-27-08

U.S. Department of Health & Human Services. (2001). *Healthy people 2000.* Washington, D.C.: Author.

U.S. Administration on Developmental Disabilities. (2007). *What Is Developmental Disability?* Retrieved January 29, 2007, from http://www.acf.dhhs.gov/programs/ add/Factsheet.html

U.S. Department of Health & Human Services. (2005). *Healthy people 2010 midcourse review.* Washington, DC: Author.

U.S. Department of Justice. (1997). *Prison medical care: Special needs population and cost control. Special issues in corrections.* Longmont, CO: U.S. Department of Corrections Information Center.

U.S. Department of Justice. (1998). *Hospice and palliative care in prisons: Special issues in corrections.* Longmont, CO: National Institute of Corrections Information Center.

U.S. Department of Justice. (2001). *Provision of mental health care in prisons: Special issues in corrections.* Longmont, CO: National Institute of Corrections Information Center.

U.S. Newswire. (2005, October 12). Thousands of children in U.S. sentenced to life without parole. Author. Retrieved October, 12, 2005, from http://web.lexis .com/universe/document?_m=4e84780d08334b

U.S. Newswire. (2006, November 20). HIV-positive state, federal prisons decreased for fifth consecutive year; more than one-third of jail inmates reported medical problem in national survey. Author. Retrieved November 27, 2006, from http://web.lexisnexis.com/universe/document?_m=272bb09d2697e8027ef611b7b23a5a

U.S. Renal Data System. (2002). National Institute of Diabetes and Digestive and Kidney Disease. Bethesda, MD: National Institute of Health.

Van Wormer, K. S. & Bartollas, C. (2000). *Women and the criminal justice system.* Boston: Allyn & Bacon.

Varghese, B. & Peterman, T. A. (2001). Cost-effectiveness of HIV counseling and testing in U.S. Prisons. In *The health status of soon-to-be-released inmates: A report to Congress* Vol. 2 (pp. 125–133). Chicago: National Commission on Correctional Health Care.

Varghese, S. & Fields, H. F. (1999). *The link between substance abuse and infectious disease in correctional settings.* Washington, DC: American Psychological Association.

Vernon, M. (1995). New rights for inmates with hearing loss. *Corrections Today, 57,* 140.

Vernon, M. & Miller, K. (2005). Obstacles faced by deaf people in the criminal justice system. *American Annals of the Deaf, 150,* 283–291.

Veysey, B. M. & Bichler-Robertson, G. (2003a). Providing psychiatric services in correctional settings. In *The health status of soon-to-be-released inmates: A report to Congress* Vol. 2 (pp. 157–165). Chicago: National Commission on Correctional Health Care.

Veysey, B. M. & Bichler-Robertson, G. (2003b). Prevalence estimates of psychiatric disorders in correctional settings. In *The health status of soon-to-be-released inmates: A report to Congress* Vol. 2 (pp. 57–80). Chicago: National Commission on Correctional Health Care.

Villa, J. (2005, June 11). Aged inmates' care puts stress on state. *The Arizona Republic* (Phoenix), p. 1.

Vlahov, D., Nelson, K. E., Quinn, T. C. & Kendig, N. (1993). Prevalence and incidence of hepatitis C virus infection among male prison inmates in Maryland. *European Journal of Epidemiology, 9,* 566–569.

VOA News. (2006, June 29). Immigrants in U.S. justice system: Low numbers, high image. Retrieved August 10, 2007, from http://www.voanews.com/english/archieve/2006-06-29-voa44.cfm?renderforprint=

Wacquant, L. (2002, Spring). Four strategies to curb carceral costs of managing imprisonment in the United States. *Studies in Political Economy, 19,* 19–30.

Walker, N. (1995). The unintended effects of long-term imprisonment. In T. J. Flanagan (Ed.). *Long-term imprisonment: Policy, science, and correctional practice* (pp. 95–105). Thousand Oaks, CA: Sage Publications.

Walker, S., Spohn, C. & DeLeone, M. (2000). *Race, ethnicity and crime in America: The color of justice* (2nd ed.). Belmont, CA: Wadsworth.

Wallace, B. & Sward, S. (1994a, October 3). Health care adequate, official asserts. *The San Francisco Chronicle,* p. A7.

Wallace, B. & Sward, S. (1994b, October 4). Suicidal inmates often ignored—until too late. *The San Francisco Chronicle*, p. A1.

Wall Street Journal. (2007, August). *On tribal land, tragic arson leads to life Sentence.* Author, p. 1A.

Walsh, D. (1996, May 26). Mother of murderer disabled in failed prison suicide wins suit. *Los Angeles Daily News*, p. 8.

Ward, M. (2005a, January 26). Daily cost for felons down, but fears loom; more inmates could mean 2-year budget increase of $200 million. *Austin American-Statesman* (TX), p. B1.

Ward, M. (2005b, October 8). Prison sex case hinges on credibility; officials say there's no proof of ex-con's claims he was raped. *Austin American-Statesman* (TX), p. A1.

Ward, M. & Bishop, B. (2001, December 16). "Deadly inadequacies" plague inmate wards. *Austin Statesman* (TX), pp. 1–4.

Warren, J. (2002, June 9). The graying of prisons. *Los Angeles Times*, pp. 1–2.

Washington Policy Center. (2003). *Prison health care: Healing a sick system through private competition.* Seattle, WA: Author.

Washington Post. (2005, February 28). How to reduce racial disparity in prisons. Author, p. A 16.

Washington University School of Law. 92008). Civil Rights Litigation Clearinghouse. http://clearinghouse.wustl.edu/detail.php?id=572 Accessed 6-27-08

Waterson, K. (1996). *Women in prison: Inside the concrete womb* (2nd ed.). Boston, MA: Northeastern University Press.

Watson, R., Stimpson, A. & Hostick, T. (2002). *Health care and change management in the context of prisons: Part 1 rapid review of the literature in two parts.* England: University of Hull.

Watson, R., Stimpson, A. & Hostick, T. (2004). Prison health care: A review of the literature. *International Journal of Nursing Studies, 41*, 119–128.

Weed, W. S. (2001, July 10). Incubating disease: Prisons are rife with infectious illnesses and threaten to spread them to the public. *Mother Jones*, pp. 2–4.

Wees, G. (1995). Violence on the rise in U.S. prisons. *Corrections Compendium, 20*, 9–27.

Weinbaum, C. M., Sabin, K. M. & Santibanez, S. S. (2005). Hepatitis B, hepatitis C, and HIV in correctional populations: A review of epidemiology and prevention. *AIDS, 19*, S41–S45.

Weiner, J. & Anno, B. J. (1992, July 1). The crisis in correctional health care: The impact of the National Drug Control Strategy on correctional health services. *Annals of Internal Medicine*, 71–77.

Weissenstein, M. (2005, July 13). City jails ceasing policy of coercing gynecological exams. *Associated Press State & Local Wire.* Retrieved October 15, 2005, from http://0-web.lexis-nexis.com.library.simmons.edu/universe.edu/universe/document?_m=4e1c82bb54 15a7

Welsh, W. N. & Zajac, G. (2004). A census of prison-based drug treatment programs: Implications for programming, policy, and evaluation. *Crime & Delinquency, 50*, 108–133.

Welsh-Huggins, A. (2005, July 30). Prisons increase patrols, rec time in face of inmate suicides. *Associated Press State & Local Wire*. Retrieved October 15, 2005, from http://0-web.lexis-nexis.com.library.simmons.edu/universe/document?_m= 3d22f097105e7d

Wexler, H. K. (2003). The promise of prison-based treatment for dually diagnosed inmates. *Journal of Substance Abuse Treatment, 25*, 223–231.

Wheeler, M., Connelly, M. & Wheeler, B. (1994). *The aging of prison populations: Directions for Oklahoma*. Oklahoma: Office of Criminal Justice.

Wilcock, K., Hammett, T. M. & Parent, D. G. (1995). *Controlling tuberculosis in community corrections*. Washington, DC: National Institute of Justice.

Wilkinson, R. A. & Unwin, T. (1999). Intolerance in prison: A recipe for disaster. *Corrections Today, 61*, 98–101.

Williams, B. (2001, February 24). Fostering compassion inside prison walls. *The Hartford Courant* (CT), p. A13.

Williams, B. & Abraldes, R. (2008). Growing older: Challenges of prison and reentry for the aging population. In R. Greifinger (Ed.). *Public health behind bars: From prisons to communities* (pp. 56–72). New York: Springer Publishing Co.

Williams, B. A., Lindquist, K., Sudore, R. L., Strupp, H. M., Willmott, D. J. & Walter, L. C. (2006). Being old and doing time: Functional impairment and adverse experiences of geriatric female prisoners. *Journal of the American Geriatric Society, 54*, 702–707.

Williams, L. & Schulte-Day, S. (2006). Pregnant in prison—The incarcerated woman's experience: A preliminary descriptive study. *Journal of Correctional Health Care, 12*, 78–88.

Williams, N.H. (2007). *Prison health and the health of the public: Ties that bind*. Atlanta, Georgia: National Center for Primary Health Care, Morehouse School of Medicine.

Williams, R. D. (1998, October). Breast cancer detection among women prisoners in the Southern United States. *Family and Community Health*, 21–30.

Williams, R. R. (2001, May 15). Once there's death, there's no more hope. *The Baltimore Sun*, p. 9A.

Willmott, D. & Olphen, J. V. (2005). Challenging the health impacts of incarceration: the role for community health workers. *Californian Journal of Health Promotion, 3*, 38–48.

Wimsatt, W. U. (2000). *No more prisons*. New York: Soft Skull Press.

Winter, M. M. (2003). County jail suicides in a Midwestern state: Moving beyond the use of profiles. *The Prison Journal, 83*, 130–148.

Winton, R. (2008, May 29). *Disabled allege poor care in jails*. Los Angeles Times, p.B-1.

Wittmeier, C. (1999, August 16). What to do with aging prisoners? *Alberta Report* (Canada), p. 21.

Wohl, D. A. (2005, November/December). Dilemmas in the care of the HIV-infected incarcerated individual. *Infectious Diseases in Corrections Report*, 1–9.

Wolfe, M. I., Xu, F., Patel, P., O'Cain, M., Schillinger, J. A., St. Louis, M. E. & Finelli, L. (2001). An outbreak of syphilis in Alabama prisons: Correctional health policy and communicable disease control. *American Journal of Public Health, 91*, 1220–1225.

Wolff, N. (1998). Interactions between mental health and law enforcement systems: Problems and prospects for cooperation. *Journal of Health Politics, Policy and Law, 23*, 133–154.

Wolff, N. (2002). Role of families and social networks in improving health outcomes. *The public health dimensions of prisoner reentry: Addressing the health needs and risks of returning prisoners and their families* (pp. 12–14). Meeting Summary, National Reentry Roundtable Meeting, Los Angeles, December 11–12, 2002. Washington, DC: Author.

Wolff, N. (2005). Community reintegration of prisoners with mental illness: A social investment perspective. *International Journal of Law & Psychiatry, 28*, 43–58.

Wolff, N. & Veysey, B. (2001). *Correctional health care in New Jersey jails.* Brunswick, NJ: Institute for Health, Health Care Policy and Aging Research, Rutgers University.

Women's Prison Association. (2003a). *WPA Focus on women & justice: Barriers to reentry.* New York: Author.

Women's Prison Association. (2003b). *The population of women in prison increases rapidly.* New York: Author.

Wood, B. (1987). Prisons, workhouses, and the control of slave labour in low country Georgia, 1763–1815. *Slavery & Abolition, 8*, 247–271.

Woodward, R. P. (2008). Electronic health records systems and continuity of care. In R. Greifinger (Ed.). *Public health behind bars: From prisons to communities* (pp. 493–507). New York: Springer Publishing Co.

Wool, J. (2008). Litigating for better medical care. In R. Greifinger (Ed.). *Public health behind bars: From prisons to communities* (pp. 25–41). New York: Springer Publishing Co.

Wooldredge, J. D. & Masters, K. (1993). Confronting problems faced by pregnant inmates in state prison. *Crime & Delinquency, 39*, 195–203.

World Disease Weekly. (2006a, May 16). Prison health; MRSA outbreak among prison inmates associated with low personal hygiene. Author, p. 2025.

World Disease Weekly. (2006b, October 10). Avian influenza; prisons are unprepared for flu pandemic. Author, p. 160.

Wright, K.N. & Bronstein, L. (2007). Organizational analysis of prison hospice. *The Prison Journal, 87*, 391–407.

Yalamanchili, K., Badu, S. & Sukhija, R. (2005). Diabetes ketoacidosis in correctional health care. *Journal of Correctional Health Care, 11*, 289–294.

Yampolskaya, S. & Winston, N. (2003). Hospice care in prison: General principles and outcomes. *American Journal of Hospice and Palliative Medicine, 20*, 290–296.

Yates, J. & Gillespie, W. (2000). The elderly and prison policy. *Journal of Aging & Social Policy, 11*, 167–175.

Yorston, G. A. & Taylor, P. J. (2006). Commentary: Older offenders—No place to go? *Journal of the American Academy of Psychiatry & Law, 34*, 333–337.

Young, D. S. (1997). *Health status and service use among incarcerated women.* Doctoral Dissertation, University of Washington. (UMI Microfilm No. 9736404) Ann Arbor, MI: Uni. Microfilms.

Young, D. S. (1998). Ethnicity and health service use in a woman's prison. *Journal of Multicultural Social Work, 7,* 69–93.

Young, V. (2001). Meeting the health care needs of new women inmates: A national survey of prison practices. *Journal of Offender Rehabilitation, 34,* 31–48.

Zack, B., Flanigan, T. & DeCarlo, P. (2000). What is the role of prisons in HIV, Hepatitis, STD and TB prevention? *Centerforce (Brown University) Fact Sheet* #13ER.

Zaitzow, B. H. (2001). Whose problem is it anyway? Women prisoners and HIV/AIDS. *International Journal of Offender Therapy and Comparative Criminology, 45,* 673–690.

Zaitzow, B. H. & Thomas, J. (2003). "Doing gender" in a women's prison. In B. H. Zaitzow & J. Thomas (Eds.). *Women in prison: Gender and social control* (pp. 21–38). London: Lynne Rienner Publishers.

Zaitzow, B. H. & West, A. D. (2003). Doing time in the shadow of death: Women Prisoners and HIV/AIDS. In S. F. Sharp & R. Muraskin (Eds.). *The incarcerated woman: Rehabilitative programming in women's prisons* (pp. 73–90). Upper Saddle River, NJ: Prentice Hall.

Zielbauer, P. V. (2003a, November 9). Courts' drug treatment system is found to help offenders steer clear of crime. *The New York Times,* p. 28.

Zielbauer, P. V. (2003b, September 28). The American agenda for fighting crime: More prison time . . . and less. *The New York Times,* p. 25.

Zielbauer, P. V. (2004, January 16). City detains its low-level inmates in jail at high expense. *The New York Times,* p. A17.

Zielbauer, P. V. (2005a, February 27). As health care in jails goes private, 10 days can be a death sentence. *The New York Times,* pp. 1, 26–28.

Zielbauer, P. V. (2005b, February 28). Missed signals in New York jails open way to a season of suicides. *The New York Times,* pp. A1, A18–A19.

Zielbauer, P. V. (2005c, March 1). A spotty record of health care at juvenile sites in New York. *The New York Times,* pp. A1, A20.

Zielbauer, P. V. (2005d, August 1). A company's troubled answer for inmates with H.I.V. *The New York Times,* pp. A1, A11.

Zielbauer, P. V. (2005e, June 10). Inmates' medical care failing in evaluation by health department. *The New York Times,* p. A21.

Zielbauer, P. V. (2005f, June 10). Medical care at Rikers fails in evaluation. *The New York Times,* p. B1.

Zielbauer, Paul von. (2005 December 30). New York prepares to close jail unit for gays. *The New York Times,* p. A23.

Zimmermann, N., Wald, F. S. & Thompson, A. S. (2002). The needs and resources for hospice care in the Connecticut prison system: A feasibility study. *Illness, Care & Loss, 10,* 204–232.

Zimring, F. E. & Hawkins, G. (1991). *The scale of imprisonment*. Chicago: University of Chicago Press.

Zimring, F. R. & Hawkins, G. (2004). Democracy and the limits of punishment: A preface to prisoners' rights. In M. Tonry (Ed.). *The future of imprisonment* (pp. 157–178). New York: Oxford University Press.

Zinkernagel, C., Taffe, P., Rickenbach, M., Amiet, R., Ledergerber, B., Volkart, A-C, Rauchfleisch, V., Kiss, A., Werder, V., Vernazza, P., Battegay, M. & Swiss HIV Cohort Study. (2001). Importance of mental health assessment in HIV-infected outpatients. *Journal of Acquired Immune Deficiency Syndromes, 28*, 240–249.

Zweig, J. M., Naser, R. L., Blackmore, J. & Schaffer, M. (2006). *Addressing sexual violence in prisons: A national snapshot of approaches and highlights of innovative strategies*. Washington, DC: Urban institute Justice Policy Center.

INDEX